THE
OXFORD LIBRARY OF
ENGLISH
POETRY

THE
OXFORD LIBRARY OF
ENGLISH
POETRY

Chosen and Edited by
JOHN WAIN

VOLUME II

Sackville to Keats

GUILD PUBLISHING LONDON

This edition published 1986 by
Book Club Associates
by arrangement with Oxford University Press

Introduction and selection © John Wain 1986

Printed in Great Britain
by Richard Clay (The Chaucer Press) Ltd.
Bungay, Suffolk

CONTENTS

CONTENTS

vi

CONTENTS

vii

CONTENTS

CONTENTS

CONTENTS

CONTENTS

CONTENTS

CONTENTS

CHARLES SACKVILLE, EARL OF DORSET
1638–1706

Song

Written at Sea, in the First Dutch War (1665), *the night before an Engagement*

To all you ladies now at land
    We men at sea indite;
But first would have you understand
    How hard it is to write:
The Muses now, and Neptune too,
We must implore to write to you—
      With a fa, la, la, la, la.

For though the Muses should prove kind,
    And fill our empty brain,
Yet if rough Neptune rouse the wind
    To wave the azure main,
Our paper, pen, and ink, and we,
Roll up and down our ships at sea—
      With a fa, la, la, la, la.

Then if we write not by each post,
    Think not we are unkind;
Nor yet conclude our ships are lost
    By Dutchmen or by wind:
Our tears we'll send a speedier way,
The tide shall bring them twice a day—
      With a fa, la, la, la, la.

The King with wonder and surprise
    Will swear the seas grow bold,
Because the tides will higher rise
    Than e'er they did of old:
But let him know it is our tears
Bring floods of grief to Whitehall stairs—
      With a fa, la, la, la, la.

Should foggy Opdam chance to know
   Our sad and dismal story,
The Dutch would scorn so weak a foe,
   And quit their fort at Goree:
For what resistance can they find
From men who've left their hearts behind?—
     With a fa, la, la, la, la.

Let wind and weather do its worst,
   Be you to us but kind;
Let Dutchmen vapour, Spaniards curse,
   No sorrow we shall find:
'Tis then no matter how things go,
Or who's our friend, or who's our foe—
     With a fa, la, la, la, la.

To pass our tedious hours away
   We throw a merry main,
Or else at serious ombre play;
   But why should we in vain
Each other's ruin thus pursue?
We were undone when we left you—
     With a fa, la, la, la, la.

But now our fears tempestuous grow
   And cast our hopes away;
Whilst you, regardless of our woe,
   Sit careless at a play:
Perhaps permit some happier man
To kiss your hand, or flirt your fan—
     With a fa, la, la, la, la.

When any mournful tune you hear,
   That dies in every note
As if it sigh'd with each man's care
   For being so remote,
Think then how often love we've made
To you, when all those tunes were play'd—
     With a fa, la, la, la, la.

In justice you cannot refuse
   To think of our distress,
When we for hopes of honour lose
   Our certain happiness:

All those designs are but to prove
Ourselves more worthy of your love—
  With a fa, la, la, la, la.

And now we've told you all our loves,
  And likewise all our fears,
In hopes this declaration moves
  Some pity for our tears:
Let's hear of no inconstancy—
We have too much of that at sea—
  With a fa, la, la, la, la.

SIR CHARLES SEDLEY

1639–1701

Love Still has Something of the Sea

LOVE still has something of the sea
  From whence his mother rose;
No time his slaves from doubt can free,
  Nor give their thoughts repose.

They are becalmed in clearest days,
  And in rough weather tossed;
They wither under cold delays,
  Or are in tempests lost.

One while they seem to touch the port:
  Then straight into the main,
Some angry wind in cruel sport
  Their vessel drives again.

At first disdain and pride they fear,
  Which, if they chance to 'scape,
Rivals and falsehood soon appear
  In a more dreadful shape.

By such degrees to joy they come,
  And are so long withstood,
So slowly they receive the sum,
  It hardly does them good.

3

'Tis cruel to prolong a pain,
   And to defer a joy,
Believe me, gentle Celemene,
   Offends the wingèd boy.

An hundred thousand oaths your fears
   Perhaps would not remove,
And if I gazed a thousand years
   I could no deeper love.

APHRA BEHN

1640–1689

Song

LOVE in fantastic triumph sate
   Whilst bleeding hearts around him flowed,
For whom fresh pains he did create
   And strange tyrannic power he showed:
From thy bright eyes he took his fires,
   Which round about in sport he hurled;
But 'twas from mine he took desires
   Enough t' undo the amorous world.

From me he took his sighs and tears,
   From thee his pride and cruelty;
From me his languishments and fears,
   And every killing dart from thee.
Thus thou and I the god have armed
   And set him up a deity;
But my poor heart alone is harmed,
   Whilst thine the victor is, and free!

Song

How strongly does my passion flow;
Divided equally 'twixt two?
Damon had ne'er subdued my heart,
Had not Alexis took his part;
Nor could Alexis powerful prove,
Without my Damon's aid, to gain my love.

When my Alexis present is,
Then I for Damon sigh and mourn;
But when Alexis I do miss,
Damon gains nothing but my scorn.
But if it chance they both are by,
For both alike I languish, sigh, and die.

Curse then, thou mighty wingèd god,
This restless fever in my blood;
One golden-pointed dart take back:
But which, O Cupid, wilt thou take?
If Damon's, all my hopes are crost;
Or that of my Alexis, I am lost.

JOHN WILMOT, EARL OF ROCHESTER
1647–1680

The Bowl

VULCAN, contrive me such a cup
  As Nestor used of old;
Show all thy skill to trim it up,
  Damask it round with gold.

Make it so large that, filled with sack
  Up to the swelling brim,
Vast toasts on the delicious lake
  Like ships at sea may swim.

Engrave not battle on his cheek:
  With war I've nought to do.
I'm none of those that took Maestrich,
  Nor Yarmouth leaguer knew.

Let it no name of planets tell,
  Fixed stars or constellations,
For I am no Sir Sidrophel,
  Nor none of his relations.

But carve thereon a spreading vine,
   Then add two lovely boys;
Their limbs in amorous folds entwine,
   The type of future joys.

Cupid and Bacchus my saints are;
   May drink and love still reign!
With wine I wash away my care
   And then to love again.

Upon Nothing

NOTHING! thou elder brother even to Shade:
Thou hadst a being ere the world was made,
And well fixed, art alone of ending not afraid.

Ere Time and Place were, Time and Place were not,
When primitive Nothing Something straight begot;
Then all proceeded from the great united What.

Something, the general attribute of all,
Severed from thee, its sole original,
Into thy boundless self must undistinguished fall;

Yet Something did thy mighty power command,
And from thy fruitful Emptiness' hand
Snatched men, beasts, birds, fire, water, air, and land.

Matter, the wicked'st offspring of thy race,
By Form assisted, flew from thy embrace,
And rebel Light obscured thy reverend dusky face.

With Form and Matter, Time and Place did join;
Body, thy foe, with these did leagues combine
To spoil thy peaceful realm, and ruin all thy line;

But turncoat Time assists the foe in vain,
And bribed by thee, destroys their short-lived reign,
And to thy hungry womb drives back thy slaves again.

Though mysteries are barred from laic eyes,
And the divine alone with warrant pries
Into thy bosom, where the truth in private lies,

Yet this of thee the wise may truly say:
Thou from the virtuous nothing dost delay,
And to be part of thee the wicked wisely pray.

Great Negative, how vainly would the wise
Inquire, define, distinguish, teach, devise,
Didst thou not stand to point their blind philosophies!

Is or Is Not, the two great ends of Fate,
And True or False, the subject of debate,
That perfect or destroy the vast designs of state—

When they have racked the politican's breast,
Within thy bosom most securely rest,
And when reduced to thee, are least unsafe and best.

But Nothing, why does Something still permit
That sacred monarchs should in council sit
With persons highly thought at best for nothing fit,

While weighty Something modestly abstains
From princes' coffers, and from statesmen's brains,
And Nothing there like stately Nothing reigns?

Nothing! who dwells with fools in grave disguise,
For whom they revered shapes and forms devise,
Lawn sleeves and furs and gowns, when they like thee look wise:

French truth, Dutch prowess, British policy,
Hibernian learning, Scotch civility,
Spaniards' dispatch, Danes wit are mainly seen in thee;

The great man's gratitude to his best friend,
Kings' promises, whores' vows—towards thee they bend,
Flow swiftly into thee, and in thee ever end.

Against Constancy

TELL me no more of constancy,
The frivolous pretense
Of cold age, narrow jealousy,
Disease, and want of sense.

UPON NOTHING: Lawn sleeves] part of a bishop's regalia

Let duller fools, on whom kind chance
   Some easy heart has thrown,
Despairing higher to advance,
   Be kind to one alone.

Old men and weak, whose idle flame
   Their own defects discovers,
Since changing can but spread their shame,
   Ought to be constant lovers.

But we, whose hearts do justly swell
   With no vainglorious pride,
Who know how we in love excel,
   Long to be often tried.

Then bring my bath, and strew my bed,
   As each kind night returns;
I'll change a mistress till I'm dead—
   And fate change me to worms.

The Mistress

AN age in her embraces passed
   Would seem a winter's day,
Where life and light with envious haste
   Are torn and snatched away.

But oh, how slowly minutes roll
   When absent from her eyes,
That feed my love, which is my soul:
   It languishes and dies.

For then no more a soul, but shade,
   It mournfully does move
And haunts my breast, by absence made
   The living tomb of love.

You wiser men, despise me not
   Whose lovesick fancy raves
On shades of souls, and heaven knows what:
   Short ages live in graves.

Whene'er those wounding eyes, so full
   Of sweetness, you did see,
Had you not been profoundly dull,
   You had gone mad like me.

Nor censure us, you who perceive
   My best beloved and me
Sigh and lament, complain and grieve:
   You think we disagree.

Alas! 'tis sacred jealousy,
   Love raised to an extreme:
The only proof 'twixt her and me
   We love, and do not dream.

Fantastic fancies fondly move
   And in frail joys believe,
Taking false pleasure for true love;
   But pain can ne'er deceive.

Kind jealous doubts, tormenting fears,
   And anxious cares, when past,
Prove our hearts' treasure fixed and dear,
   And make us blest at last.

Impromptu on Charles II

GOD bless our good and gracious King,
   Whose promise none relies on;
Who never said a foolish thing,
   Nor ever did a wise one.

A Song of a Young Lady to Her Ancient Lover

ANCIENT person, for whom I
All the flattering youth defy,
Long be it ere thou grow old,
Aching, shaking, crazy, cold;
   But still continue as thou art,
   Ancient person of my heart.

On thy withered lips and dry,
Which like barren furrows lie,
Brooding kisses I will pour
Shall thy youthful [heat] restore
(Such kind showers in autumn fall,
And a second spring recall);
    Nor from thee will ever part,
    Ancient person of my heart.

Thy nobler part, which but to name
In our sex would be counted shame,
By age's frozen grasp possessed,
From [his] ice shall be released,
And soothed by my reviving hand,
In former warmth and vigor stand.
All a lover's wish can reach
For thy joy my love shall teach,
And for thy pleasure shall improve
All that art can add to love.
    Yet still I love thee without art,
    Ancient person of my heart.

ANNE, COUNTESS OF WINCHILSEA

?1660–1720

A Nocturnal Reverie

IN such a night, when every louder wind
Is to its distant cavern safe confined;
And only gentle zephyr fans his wings,
And lonely Philomel, still waking, sings;
Or from some tree, famed for the owl's delight,
She, holloaing clear, directs the wanderers right:
In such a night, when passing clouds give place,
Or thinly veil the heaven's mysterious face;
When in some river, overhung with green,
The waving moon and trembling leaves are seen;
When freshened grass now bears itself upright,
And makes cool banks to pleasing rest invite,
Whence springs the woodbind, and the bramble-rose,
And where the sleepy cowslip sheltered grows;

Whilst now a paler hue the foxglove takes,
Yet chequers still with red the dusky brakes:
When scattered glow-worms, but in twilight fine,
Show trivial beauties watch their hour to shine;
Whilst Salisbury stands the test of every light,
In perfect charms and perfect virtue bright.
When odours, which declined repelling day,
Thro' temperate air uninterrupted stray;
When darkened groves their softest shadows wear
And falling waters we distinctly hear;
When through the gloom more venerable shows
Some ancient fabric, awful in repose,
While sunburnt hills their swarthy looks conceal,
And swelling haycocks thicken up the vale:
When the loosed horse now, as his pasture leads,
Comes slowly grazing through the adjoining meads.
Whose stealing pace, and lengthened shade we fear,
Till torn-up forage in his teeth we hear:
When nibbling sheep at large pursue their food,
And unmolested kine re-chew the cud;
When curlews cry beneath the village walls,
And to her straggling brood the partridge calls;
Their short-lived jubilee the creatures keep,
Which but endures, while tyrant man does sleep:
When a sedate content the spirit feels,
And no fierce light disturbs, whilst it reveals;
But silent musings urge the mind to seek
Something, too high for syllables to speak;
Till the free soul to a composedness charmed,
Finding the elements of rage disarmed,
O'er all below a solemn quiet grown,
Joys in the inferior world, and thinks it like her own:
In such a night let me abroad remain,
Till morning breaks, and all's confused again;
Our cares, our toils, our clamours are renewed,
Our pleasures, seldom reached, again pursued.

MATTHEW PRIOR

1664–1721

A Better Answer

DEAR Chloe, how blubbered is that pretty face!
  Thy cheek all on fire, and thy hair all uncurled:
Prithee quit this caprice; and, as old Falstaff says,
  Let us e'en talk a little like folks of this world.

How canst thou presume, thou hadst leave to destroy
  The beauties which Venus but lent to thy keeping?
Those looks were designed to inspire love and joy:
  More ordinary eyes may serve people for weeping.

To be vexed at a trifle or two that I writ,
  Your judgement at once, and my passion, you wrong:
You take that, for fact, which will scarce be found wit;
  Ods life! must one swear to the truth of a song?

What I speak, my fair Chloe, and what I write, shows
  The difference there is betwixt nature and art:
I court others in verse—but I love thee in prose;
  And they have my whimsies—but thou has my heart.

The god of us verse-men, you known, child, the sun,
  How after his journeys he sets up his rest:
If at morning o'er earth 'tis his fancy to run;
  At night he declines on his Thetis's breast.

So when I am wearied with wandering all day,
  To thee, my delight, in the evening I come:
No matter what beauties I saw in my way,
  They were but my visits, but thou art my home.

Then finish, dear Chloe, this pastoral war;
  And let us like Horace and Lydia agree;
For thou art a girl as much brighter than her,
  As he was a poet sublimer than me.

JONATHAN SWIFT

1667–1745

Stella's Birthday 1720

ALL travellers at first incline
Where'er they see the fairest sign;
And, if they find the chambers neat,
And like the liquor and the meat,
Will call again, and recommend
The Angel Inn to every friend.
What though the painting grows decayed,
The house will never lose its trade:
Nay, though the treacherous tapster, Thomas,
Hangs a new angel two doors from us,
As fine as dauber's hands can make it,
In hopes that strangers may mistake it,
We think it both a shame and sin
To quit the true old Angel Inn.

  Now this is Stella's case in fact;
An angel's face, a little cracked;
(Could poets, or could painters fix
How angels look at thirty-six:)
This drew us in at first to find
In such a form an angel's mind;
And every virtue now supplies
The fainting rays of Stella's eyes.
See at her levee crowding swains,
Whom Stella freely entertains
With breeding, humour, wit, and sense,
And puts them but to small expense;
Their mind so plentifully fills,
And makes such reasonable bills,
So little gets for what she gives,
We really wonder how she lives!
And had her stock been less, no doubt
She must have long ago run out.

  Then who can think we'll quit the place,
When Doll hangs out a newer face;
Or stop and light at Chloe's Head,
With scraps and leavings to be fed?

Then, Chloe, still go on to prate
Of thirty-six, and thirty-eight;
Pursue your trade of scandal-picking,
Your hints, that Stella is no chicken;
Your innuendoes, when you tell us
That Stella loves to talk with fellows:
And let me warn you to believe
A truth, for which your soul should grieve;
That should you live to see the day
When Stella's locks must all be grey,
When age must print a furrowed trace
On every feature of her face;
That you, and all your senseless tribe,
Could art, or time, or nature bribe
To make you look like beauty's queen,
And hold for ever at fifteen;
No bloom of youth can ever blind
The cracks and wrinkles of your mind;
All men of sense will pass your door,
And crowd to Stella's at four score.

On the Death of Dean Swift

THE time is not remote when I
Must by the course of nature die;
When, I foresee, my special friends
Will try to find their private ends:
And tho' 'tis hardly understood
Which way my death can do them good,
Yet thus methinks I hear 'em speak:
'See how the Dean begins to break!
Poor gentleman, he droops apace!
You plainly find it in his face.
That old vertigo in his head
Will never leave him till he's dead.
Besides, his memory decays:
He recollects not what he says;
He cannot call his friends to mind,
Forgets the place where last he din'd;
Plies you with stories o'er and o'er;
He told them fifty times before.
How does he fancy we can sit
To hear his out-of-fashion wit?

But he takes up with younger folks,
Who for his wine will bear his jokes.
Faith! he must make his stories shorter,
Or change his comrades once a quarter:
In half the time he talks them round,
There must another set be found.

    'For poetry he's past his prime;
He takes an hour to find a rhyme;
His fire is out, his wit decay'd,
His Fancy sunk, his Muse a jade.
I'd have him throw away his pen;—
But there's no talking to some men . . .

    Behold the fatal day arrive!
'How is the Dean?'—'He's just alive.'
Now the departing pray'r is read:
'He hardly breathes.'—'The Dean is dead.'

    Before the passing bell begun,
The news thro' half the town is run.
'O, may we all for death prepare!
What has he left? And who's his heir?'
'I know no more than what the news is;
'Tis all bequeath'd to public uses'—
'To public use! a perfect whim!
What had the public done for him?
Mere envy, avarice, and pride:
He gave it all—but first the died.
And had the Dean, in all the nation,
No worthy friend, no poor relation?
So ready to do strangers good,
Forgetting his own flesh and blood!'

    Now Grub Street wits are all employ'd;
With elegies the town is cloy'd:
Some paragraph in ev'ry paper
To curse the Dean or bless the Drapier.

    The doctors, tender of their fame,
Wisely on me lay all the blame:
'We must confess his case was nice;
But he wou'd never take advice.
Had he been rul'd, for aught appears,
He might have liv'd these twenty years;
For when we open'd him we found
That all his vital parts were sound.

    From Dublin soon to London spread,
'Tis told at Court, 'The Dean is dead.'

Kind Lady Suffolk, in the spleen,
Runs laughing up to tell the Queen.
The Queen, so gracious, mild, and good,
Cries 'Is he gone! 'Tis time he shou'd.
He's dead, you say; why, let him rot.
I'm glad the medals were forgot.
I promis'd him, I own, but when?
I only was a princess then;
But now, as consort of a king,
You know, 'tis quite a diff'rent thing' ...

   'Perhaps I may allow the Dean
Had too much satire in his vein,
And seem'd determin'd not to starve it,
Because no age cou'd more deserve it.
Yet malice never was his aim;
He lash'd the vice, but spar'd the name;
No individual cou'd resent
Where thousands equally were meant.
His satire points at no defect
But what all mortals may correct;
For he abhorr'd that senseless tribe
Who call it humour when they gibe.
He spar'd a hump or crooked nose,
Whose owners set up not for beaux.
True, genuine dullness mov'd his pity,
Unless it offer'd to be witty.
Those who their ignorance confest
He ne'er offended with a jest;
But laugh'd to hear an idiot quote
A verse from Horace, learn'd by rote.
Vice, if it e'er can be abash'd,
Must be or ridicul'd or lash'd.
If you resent it, who's to blame?
He neither knew you nor your name.
Shou'd vice expect t'escape rebuke
Because its owner is a duke?

   'He knew a hundred pleasant stories,
With all the turns of Whigs and Tories:
Was cheerful to his dying day;
And friends wou'd let him have his way.

   'He gave the little wealth he had
To build a house for fools and mad;
And show'd by one satiric touch,
No nation wanted it so much.

That kingdom he hath left his debtor,
I wish it soon may have a better.'
And since you dread no further lashes,
Methinks you may forgive his ashes.

A Description of the Morning

Now hardly here and there a hackney coach
Appearing, show'd the ruddy morn's approach.
Now Betty from her master's bed had flown,
And softly stole to discompose her own;
The slip-shod 'prentice from his master's door
Had par'd the dirt, and sprinkl'd round the floor.
Now Moll had whirl'd her mop with dext'rous airs,
Prepar'd to scrub the entry and the stairs.
The youth with broomy stumps began to trace
The kennel's edge, where wheels had worn the place.
The small-coal man was heard with cadence deep,
Till drown'd in shriller notes of chimney-sweep:
Duns at his Lordship's gate began to meet;
And brick-dust Moll had scream'd thro' half the street.
The turnkey now his flock returning sees,
Duly let out a-nights to steal for fees:
The watchful bailiffs take their silent stands,
And schoolboys lag with satchels in their hands.

A Description of a City Shower

Careful observers may foretell the hour,
By sure prognostics, when to dread a show'r.
While rain depends, the pensive cat gives o'er
Her frolics, and pursues her tail no more.
Returning home at night, you'll find the sink
Strike your offended sense with double stink.
If you be wise, then go not far to dine:
You'll spend in coach hire more than save in wine.
A coming show'r your shooting corns presage,
Old aches throb, your hollow tooth will rage;
Saunt'ring in coffee-house is Dullman seen;
He damns the climate, and complains of spleen.
Meanwhile the South, rising with dabbled wings,
A sable cloud athwart the welkin flings,

That swill'd more liquor than it cou'd contain,
And, like a drunkard, gives it up again.
Brisk Susan whips her linen from the rope,
While the first drizzling show'r is borne aslope;
Such is that sprinkling which some careless quean
Flirts on you from her mop, not quite so clean;
You fly, invoke the gods; then turning stop
To rail; she, singing, still whirls on her mop.
Nor yet the dust had shunn'd th' unequal strife,
But, aided by the wind, fought still for life,
And wafted with its foe by violent gust,
'Twas doubtful which was rain and which was dust.
Ah, where must needy poet seek for aid,
When dust and rain at once his coat invade?
Sole coats! where dust, cemented by the rain,
Erects the nap, and leaves a cloudy stain!
Now in contiguous drops the flood comes down,
Threat'ning with deluge this devoted town.
To shops in crowds the draggl'd females flie,
Pretend to cheapen goods, but nothing buy.
The Templar spruce, while ev'ry spout's abroach,
Stays till 'tis fair, yet seems to call a coach.
The tuck'd-up sempstress walks with hasty strides,
While streams run down her oil'd umbrella's sides.
Here various kinds, by various fortunes led,
Commence acquaintance underneath a shed.
Triumphant Tories and desponding Whigs
Forget their feuds, and join to save their wigs.
Box'd in a chair the beau impatient sits,
While spouts run clatt'ring o'er the roof by fits,
And ever and anon with frightful din
The leather sounds; he trembles from within.
So when Troy chairmen bore the wooden steed,
Pregnant with Greeks impatient to be freed,
(Those bully Greeks who, as the moderns do,
Instead of paying chairmen, ran them thro',)
Laocoon struck the outside with his spear,
And each imprison'd hero quak'd for fear.
  Now from all parts the swelling kennels flow,
And bear their trophies with them as they go:
Filth of all hues and odour, seem to tell
What street, they sail'd from, by their sight and smell.
They, as each torrent drives with rapid force,
From Smithfield to St. Pulchre's shape their course,

And in huge confluence join'd at Snowhill ridge,
Fall from the Conduit prone to Holborn Bridge.
Sweeping from butchers' stalls, dung, guts and blood,
Drown'd puppies, stinking sprats, all drench'd in mud,
Dead cats and turnip tops come tumbling down the flood.

WILLIAM CONGREVE

1670–1729

from *The Mourning Bride*

Music

MUSIC has charms to soothe a savage breast,
To soften rocks, or bend a knotted oak.
I've read that things inanimate have moved,
And, as with living souls, have been informed,
By magic numbers and persuasive sound.
What then am I? Am I more senseless grown
Than trees, or flint? O force of constant woe!
'Tis not in harmony to calm my griefs. ...
Why do I live to say you are no more?
Why are all these things thus—Is it of force?
Is there necessity I must be miserable?
Is it of moment to the peace of Heaven
That I should be afflicted thus?—If not,
Why is it thus contrived? Why are things laid
By some unseen hand, so, as of sure consequence
They must to me bring curses, grief of heart,
The last distress of life, and sure despair?

The Aisle of a Temple

'TIS dreadful!
How reverend is the face of this tall pile,
Whose ancient pillars rear their marble heads,
To bear aloft its arched and pond'rous roof,
By its own weight made steadfast and immoveable,
Looking tranquillity! It strikes an awe
And terror on my aching sight: the tombs

And monumental caves of Death look cold,
And shoot a chillness to my trembling heart.
Give me thy hand, and let me hear thy voice;
Nay, quickly speak to me, and let me hear
Thy voice—my own affrights me with its echoes.

AMBROSE PHILIPS (Namby Pamby)

1671–1749

Wit and Wisdom

IN search of wisdom, far from wit I fly;
Wit is a harlot beauteous to the eye,
In whose bewitching arms our early time
We waste, and vigour of our youthful prime.
But when reflection comes with riper years,
And manhood with a thoughtful brow appears;
We cast the mistress off to take a wife,
And, wed to wisdom, lead a happy life.

To Miss Margaret Pulteney

DIMPLY damsel, sweetly smiling,
All caressing, none beguiling,
Bud of beauty, fairly blowing,
Every charm to nature owing,
This and that new thing admiring,
Much of this and that enquiring,
Knowledge by degrees attaining,
Day by day some virtue gaining,
Ten years hence, when I leave chiming,
Beardless poets, fondly rhyming
(Fescu'd now, perhaps, in spelling),
On thy riper beauties dwelling,
Shall accuse each killing feature
Of the cruel, charming creature,
Whom I knew complying, willing,
Tender, and averse to killing.

JOSEPH ADDISON
1672–1719

Hymn

Thanksgiving after Travel

How are Thy servants blest, O Lord!
   How sure is their defence!
Eternal wisdom is their guide,
   Their help Omnipotence.

In foreign realms, and lands remote,
   Supported by Thy care,
Through burning climes I passed unhurt,
   And breathed in tainted air.

Thy mercy sweetened every soil,
   Made every region please;
The hoary Alpine hills it warmed,
   And smoothed the Tyrrhene seas.

Think, O my soul, devoutly think,
   How, with affrighted eyes,
Thou saw'st the wide-extended deep
   In all its horrors rise!

Confusion dwelt in every face,
   And fear in every heart;
When waves on waves, and gulfs on gulfs,
   O'ercame the pilot's art.

Yet then from all my griefs, O Lord,
   Thy mercy set me free;
Whilst, in the confidence of prayer,
   My soul took hold on Thee.

For though in dreadful whirls we hung
   High on the broken wave,
I knew Thou wert not slow to hear,
   Nor impotent to save.

The storm was laid, the winds retired,
  Obedient to Thy will;
The sea that roared at Thy command,
  At Thy command was still.

In midst of dangers, fears, and death,
  Thy goodness I'll adore;
And praise Thee for Thy mercies past,
  And humbly hope for more.

My life, if Thou preserv'st my life,
  Thy sacrifice shall be;
And death, if death must be my doom,
  Shall join my soul to Thee.

ISAAC WATTS

1674–1748

Hymn

WHEN I survey the wondrous Cross
On which the Prince of glory died,
My richest gain I count but loss,
And pour contempt on all my pride.

Forbid it, Lord, that I should boast
Save in the Cross of Christ my God;
All the vain things that charm me most,
I sacrifice them to His Blood.

See from His Head, His Hands, His Feet,
Sorrow and love flow mingling down;
Did e'er such love and sorrow meet,
Or thorns compose so rich a crown!

Were the whole realm of nature mine,
That were an offering far too small;
Love so amazing, so Divine,
Demands my soul, my life, my all.

To Christ, Who won for sinners grace
By bitter grief and anguish sore,
Be praise from all the ransom'd race
For ever and for evermore.

ISAAC WATTS

Against Idleness and Mischief

How doth the little busy Bee
    Improve each shining Hour,
And gather Honey all the Day
    From ev'ry op'ning Flow'r!

How skilfully she builds her Cell!
    How neat she spreads the Wax!
And labours hard to store it well
    With the sweet Food she makes.

In Works of Labour or of Skill
    I would be busy too:
For *Satan* finds some Mischief still
    For idle Hands to do.

In Books, or Work, or healthful Play,
    Let my first Years be past,
That I may give for every Day
    Some good Account at last.

JOHN PHILIPS

1676–1709

from *Cyder*

Apple-Culture

When swelling buds their od'rous foliage shed,
And gently harden into fruit, the wise
Spare not the little offsprings, if they grow
Redundant; but the thronging clusters thin
By kind avulsion; else, the starv'ling brood,
Void of sufficient sustenance will yield
A slender Autumn; which the niggard soul
Too late shall weep, and curse his thrify hand
That would not timely ease the pond'rous boughs.

It much conduces all the cares to know
Of gard'ning, how to scare nocturnal thieves,
And how the little race of birds that hop
From spray to spray, scooping the costliest fruit
Insatiate, undisturb'd. Priapus' form
Avails but little; rather guard each row
With the false terrors of a breathless kite.
This done, the tim'rous flock with swiftest wing
Scud through the air; their fancy represents
His mortal talons, and his rav'nous beak
Destructive; glad to shun his hostile gripe,
They quit their thefts, and unfrequent the fields.

Besides, the filthy swine will oft invade
Thy firm inclosure, and with delving snout
The rooted forest undermine; forthwith
Alloo thy furious mastiff, bid him vex
The noxious herd, and print upon their ears
A sad memorial of their past offence.

The flagrant Procyon will not fail to bring
Large shoals of slow, house-bearing snails, that creep
O'er the ripe fruitage, paring slimy tracts
In the sleek rinds, and unprest Cyder drink.
No art averts this pest; on thee it lies,
With morning and with ev'ning hand to rid
The preying reptiles; nor, if wise, wilt thou
Decline this labour, which itself rewards
With pleasing gain, whilst the warm limbec draws
Salubrious water from the nocent brood.

Myriads of wasps now also clustering hang,
And drain a spurious honey from thy groves,
Their winter food; tho' oft repuls'd, again
They rally, undismay'd: but fraud with ease
Ensnares the noisome swarms; let ev'ry bough
Bear frequent vials, pregnant with the dregs
Of moyle, or mum, or treacle's viscous juice;
They, by th' alluring odour drawn, in haste
Fly to the dulcet cates, and crowding sip
Their palatable bane; joyful thou'lt see

The clammy surface all o'erstrewn with tribes
Of greedy insects, that with fruitless toil
Flap filmy pennons oft, to extricate
Their feet, in liquid shackles bound, till death
Bereave them of their worthless souls: such doom
Waits luxury, and lawless love of gain.

THOMAS PARNELL

1679–1718

from *A Night Piece on Death*

How deep yon azure dyes the sky!
Where orbs of gold unnumber'd lie,
While thro' their ranks in silver pride
The nether crescent seems to glide.
The slumb'ring breeze forgets to breathe,
The lake is smooth and clear beneath,
Where once again the spangled show
Descends to meet our eyes below.
The grounds which on the right aspire,
In dimness from the view retire:
The left presents a place of graves,
Whose wall the silent water laves.
That steeple guides thy doubtful sight
Among the livid gleams of night.
There pass with melancholy state,
By all the solemn heaps of fate,
And think, as softly-sad you tread
Above the venerable dead,
'Time was, like thee they life possessed
And time shall be, that thou shalt rest.'
Those graves, with bending osier bound,
That nameless heave the crumbled ground,
Quick to the glancing thought disclose
Where toil and poverty repose.
The flat smooth stones that bear a name,
The chisel's slender help to fame,
(Which ere our set of friends decay
Their frequent steps may wear away)
A middle race of mortals own,

Men, half ambitious, all unknown.
The marble tombs that rise on high,
Whose dead in vaulted arches lie,
Whose pillars swell with sculptur'd stones,
Arms, angels, epitaphs, and bones,
These (all the poor remains of state),
Adorn the rich, or praise the great;
Who while on earth in fame they live,
Are senseless of the fame they give.

Ha! While I gaze, pale Cynthia fades,
The bursting earth unveils the shades!
All slow, and wan, and wrapped with shrouds,
They rise in visionary crowds,
And all with sober accent cry,
'Think, mortal, what it is to die.'

Song

WHEN thy beauty appears
    In its graces and airs
All bright as an angel new dropped from the sky,
At distance I gaze and am awed by my fears:
    So strangely you dazzle my eye!

But when without art
    Your kind thoughts you impart,
When your love runs in blushes through every vein;
When it darts from your eyes, when it pants in your heart,
    Then I know you're a woman again.

There's a passion and pride
    In our sex (she replied),
And thus, might I gratify both, I would do:
Still an angel appear to each lover beside,
    But still be a woman to you.

EDWARD YOUNG

1683–1765

from *Night Thoughts*

Introduction

TIRED Nature's sweet restorer, balmy sleep!
He, like the world, his ready visit pays,
Where fortune smiles; the wretched he forsakes:
Swift on his downy pinion flies from woe,
And lights on lids unsullied with a tear!

   From short, (as usual) and disturbed repose,
I wake: how happy they who wake no more!
Yet that were vain, if dreams infest the grave.
I wake, emerging from a sea of dreams
Tumultuous; where my wrecked, desponding thought
From wave to wave of fancied misery,
At random drove, her helm of reason lost;
Though now restored, 'tis only change of pain,
A bitter change; severer for severe:
The day too short for my distress! and night
Even in the zenith of her dark domain,
Is sunshine, to the colour of my fate.

   Night, sable goddess! from her ebon throne,
In rayless majesty, now stretches forth
Her leaden sceptre o'er a slumbering world:
Silence, how dead! and darkness, how profound!
Nor eye, nor listening ear an object finds;
Creation sleeps. 'Tis, as the general pulse
Of life stood still, and Nature made a pause;
An awful pause! prophetic of her end.

   Silence, and darkness! solemn sisters! twins
From ancient night, who nurse the tender thought
To reason; and on reason built resolve,
(That column of true majesty in man!)
Assist me: I will thank you in the grave;
The grave, your kingdom: there this frame shall fall
A victim sacred to your dreary shrine:
But what are ye? Thou, who didst put to flight
Primaeval silence, when the morning stars
Exulting, shouted, o'er the rising ball;

O thou! whose word from solid darkness struck
That spark; the sun, strike wisdom from my soul;
My soul, which flies to thee, her trust, her treasure;
As misers to their gold, while others rest.

Through this opaque of nature, and of woe,
This double night, transmit one pitying ray,
To lighten and to cheer: O teach my mind,
(A mind that fain would wander from its woe,)
Lead it through various scenes of life and death,
And from each scene, the noblest truths inspire:
Nor less inspire my conduct, than my song;
Teach my best reason, reason; my best will
Teach rectitude; and fix my firm resolve
Wisdom to wed, and pay her long arrear.
Nor let the vial of thy vengeance poured
On this devoted head, be poured in vain.

The bell strikes one: we take no note of time,
But from its loss. To give it then a tongue
Is wise in man. As if an angel spoke,
I feel the solemn sound. If heard aright,
It is the knell of my departed hours:
Where are they? With the years beyond the flood:
It is the signal that demands dispatch;
How much is to be done! my hopes and fears
Start up alarmed, and o'er life's narrow verge
Look down—on what? a fathomless abyss;
A dread Eternity! how surely mine!
And can Eternity belong to me,
Poor pensioner on the mercies of an hour?

How poor, how rich, how abject, how august,
How complicate, how wonderful is man!
How passing wonder He, who made him such!
Who centred in our make such strange extremes!
From different natures, marvellously mixed,
Connexion exquisite of distant worlds!
Distinguished link in being's endless chain!
Midway from nothing to the Deity!
A beam ethereal sullied, and absorbed!
Though sullied, and dishonoured, still divine!
Dim miniature of greatness absolute!
An heir of glory! a frail child of dust!
Helpless immortal! insect infinite!
A worm! A god! I tremble at myself,
And in myself am lost! At home a stranger,

Thought wanders up and down, surprised, amazed,
And wondering at her own: how reason reels!
O what a miracle to man is man,
Triumphantly distressed! what joy, what dread!
Alternately transported, and alarmed!
What can preserve my life? or what destroy?
An angel's arm can't snatch me from the grave;
Legions of angels can't confine me there.
    'Tis past conjecture; all things rise in proof:
While o'er my limbs sleep's soft dominion spread:
What, though my soul fantastic measures trod,
O'er fairy fields; or mourned along the gloom
Of pathless woods; or down the craggy steep
Hurled headlong, swam with pain the mantled pool;
Or scaled the cliff; or danced on hollow winds,
With antic shapes, wild natives of the brain?
Her ceaseless flight, though devious, speaks her nature
Of subtler essence than the trodden clod;
Active, aerial, towering, unconfined,
Unfettered with her gross companion's fall:
Even silent night proclaims my soul immortal:
Even silent night proclaims eternal day:
For human weal, Heaven husbands all events,
Dull sleep instructs, nor sport vain dreams in vain.
    Why then their loss deplore, that are not lost?
Why wanders wretched thought their tombs around
In infidel distress? are angels there?
Slumbers, raked up in dust, ethereal fire?
They live! they greatly live a life on earth
Unkindled, unconceived; and from an eye
Of tenderness, let heavenly pity fall
On me, more justly numbered with the dead:
This is the desert, this the solitude;
How populous, how vital, is the grave!
This is creation's melancholy vault,
The vale funereal, the sad cypress gloom;
The land of apparitions, empty shades:
All, all on earth is shadow, all beyond
Is substance; the reverse is folly's creed;
How solid all, where change shall be no more!

THOMAS TICKELL

1686–1740

To the Earl of Warwick, on the Death of Mr. Addison

IF, dumb too long, the drooping Muse hath stayed,
And left her debt to Addison unpaid,
Blame not her silence, Warwick, but bemoan,
And judge, oh judge, my bosom by your own.
What mourner ever felt poetic fires!
Slow comes the verse, that real woe inspires:
Grief unaffected suits but ill with art,
Or flowing numbers with a bleeding heart.

   Can I forget the dismal night, that gave
My soul's best part for ever to the grave!
How silent did his old companions tread,
By midnight lamps, the mansions of the dead,
Through breathing statues, then unheeded things,
Through rows of warriors, and through walks of kings!
What awe did the slow solemn knell inspire;
The pealing organ, and the pausing choir;
The duties by the lawn-robed prelate paid;
And the last words, that dust to dust conveyed!
While speechless o'er thy closing grave we bend,
Accept these tears, thou dear departed friend,
Oh gone for ever, take this long adieu;
And sleep in peace, next thy loved Montague!

   To strew fresh laurels let the task be mine,
A frequent pilgrim, at thy sacred shrine;
Mine with true sighs thy absence to bemoan,
And grave with faithful epitaphs thy stone.
If e'er from me thy loved memorial part,
May shame afflict this alienated heart;
Of thee forgetful if I form a song,
My lyre be broken, and untuned my tongue,
My grief be doubled, from thy image free,
And mirth a torment unchastised by thee.

   Oft let me range the gloomy isles alone
(Sad luxury! to vulgar minds unknown)
Along the walls where speaking marbles show
What worthies form the hallowed mould below:
Proud names, who once the reins of empire held;

In arms who triumphed; or in arts excelled;
Chiefs, graced with scars, and prodigal of blood;
Stern patriots, who for sacred freedom stood;
Just men, by whom impartial laws were given;
And saints, who taught, and led, the way to heaven
Ne'er to these chambers, where the mighty rest,
Since their foundation, came a nobler guest,
Nor e'er was to the bower of bliss conveyed
A fairer spirit, or more welcome shade.

In what new region, to the just assigned,
What new employments please th' unbodied mind?
A wingèd Virtue through th' ethereal sky,
From world to world unwearied does he fly?
Or curious trace the long laborious maze
Of heaven's decrees where wondering angels gaze?
Does he delight to hear bold seraphs tell
How Michael battled, and the dragon fell?
Or, mixed with milder cherubim, to glow
In hymns of love, not ill essayed below?
Or dost thou warn poor mortals left behind,
A task well suited to thy gentle mind?
Oh, if sometimes thy spotless form descend,
To me thy aid, thou guardian Genius, lend!
When rage misguides me, or when fear alarms,
When pain distresses, or when pleasure charms,
In silent whisperings purer thoughts impart,
And turn from ill a fray and feeble heart;
Lead through the paths thy virtue trod before,
Till bliss shall join, nor death can part us more.

That awful form (which, so the heavens decree,
Must still be loved and still deplored by me)
In nightly visions seldom fails to rise,
Or, roused by fancy, meets my waking eyes.
If business calls, or crowded courts inivte,
Th' unblemished statesman seems to strike my sight;
If in the stage I seek to soothe my care,
I meet his soul, which breathes in Cato there;
If pensive to the rural shades I rove,
His shape o'ertakes me in the lonely grove:
'Twas there of Just and Good he reasoned strong,
Cleared some great truth, or raised some serious song;
There patient showed us the wise course to steer,
A candid censor, and a friend severe;
There taught us how to live; and (oh! too high

The price for knowledge) taught us how to die.
　　Thou hill, whose brow the antique structures grace,
Reared by bold chiefs of Warwick's noble race,
Why, once so loved, whene'er the bower appears,
O'er my dim eyeballs glance the sudden tears!
How sweet were once thy prospects fresh and fair,
Thy sloping walks, and unpolluted air!
How sweet the glooms beneath thy agèd trees,
Thy noontide shadow, and thy evening breeze!
His image thy forsaken bowers restore;
Thy walks and airy prospects charm no more,
No more the summer in the glooms allayed,
Thy evening breezes, and thy noon-day shade.
　　From other ills, however fortune frowned,
Some refuge in the muse's art I found:
Reluctant now I touch the trembling string,
Bereft of him, who taught me how to sing,
And these sad accents, murmured o'er his urn,
Betray that absence, they attempt to mourn.
Oh! must I then (now fresh my bosom bleeds,
And Craggs in death to Addison succeeds)
The verse, begun to one lost friend, prolong,
And weep a second in th' unfinished song!
　　These works divine, which on his death-bed laid
To thee, O Craggs, th' expiring sage conveyed,
Great, but ill-omened monument of fame,
Nor he survived to give, nor thou to claim.
Swift after him thy social spirit flies,
And close to his, how soon! thy coffin lies.
Blest pair! whose union future bards shall tell
In future tongues: each other's boast! farewell.
Farewell! whom joined in fame, in friendship tried,
No chance could sever, nor the grave divide.

ALLAN RAMSAY

1686–1758

The Lass of Patie's Mill

THE lass of Patie's mill,
   Sae bonny, blithe, and gay,
In spite of all my skill,
   She stole my heart away.
When tedding out the hay,
   Bareheaded on the green,
Love 'midst her locks did play,
   And wantoned in her een.

Her arms white, round, and smooth;
   Breasts rising in their dawn;
To age it would give youth,
   To press them with his hand.
Through all my spirits ran
   An ecstacy of bliss,
When I such sweetness fan'
   Wrapt in a balmy kiss.

Without the help of art,
   Like flowers which grace the wild,
Her sweets she did impart,
   Whene'er she spoke or smiled:
Her looks they were so mild,
   Free from affected pride,
She me to love beguiled;—
   I wished her for my bride.

Oh! had I all the wealth
   Hopetoun's high mountains fill,
Insured long life and health,
   And pleasure at my will;
I'd promise, and fulfil,
   That none but bonnie she,
The lass of Patie's mill,
   Should share the same with me.

An Thou Were My Ain Thing

AN thou were my ain thing,
I would love thee, I would love thee;
An thou were my ain thing
   How dearly I would love thee.

Like bees that suck the morning dew,
Frae flowers of sweetest scent and hue,
Sae wad I dwell upon thy mow
   And gar the gods envý me.

Sae lang 's I had the use of light
I'd on thy beauties feast my sight,
Syne in saft whispers through the night
   I'd tell how much I loved thee.

How fair and ruddy is my Jean!
She moves a goddess o'er the green.
Were I a king thou should be queen—
   Nane but myself aboon thee.

I'd grasp thee to this breast of mine,
Whilst thou like ivy on the vine
Around my stronger limbs should twine,
   Formed handy to defend thee.

Time's on the wing and will not stay,
In shining youth let's make our hay;
Since love admits of no delay,
   O let na scorn undo thee.

While love does at this altar stand
Hae, here's my heart, gie me thy hand,
And with ilk smile thou shalt command
   The will of him who loves thee.

An thou were my ain thing,
I would love thee; I would love thee;
An thou were my ain thing,
   How dearly I would love thee.

mow] mouth

34

JOHN GAY

1685-1732

Fable XXI
The Rat-catcher and Cats

THE rats by night such mischief did,
Betty was every morning chid:
They undermined whole sides of bacon,
Her cheese was sapped, her tarts were taken,
Her pasties, fenced with thickest paste,
Were all demolished and laid waste.
She cursed the cat for want of duty,
Who left her foes a constant booty.

An engineer, of noted skill,
Engaged to stop the growing ill.

From room to room he now surveys
Their haunts, their works, their secret ways,
Finds where they 'scape an ambuscade,
And whence the nightly sally's made.

An envious cat, from place to place,
Unseen, attends his silent pace,
She saw that, if his trade went on.
The purring race must be undone,
So, secretly removes his baits,
And every strategem defeats.

Again he sets the poisoned toils,
And puss again the labour foils.

What foe (to frustrate my designs)
My schemes thus nightly countermines?
Incensed, he cries: this very hour
The wretch shall bleed beneath my power.

So said. A ponderous trap he brought,
And in the fact poor puss was caught.

Smuggler, says he, thou shalt be made
A victim to our loss of trade.

The captive cat with piteous mews
For pardon, life and freedom sues.
A sister of the science spare,
One int'rest is our common care.

What insolence! the man replied,
Shall cats with us the game divide?

35

Were all your interloping band
Extinguished, or expelled the land,
We rat-catchers might raise our fees,
Sole guardians of a nation's cheese!
    A cat, who saw the lifted knife,
Thus spoke, and saved her sister's life.
    In every age and clime we see,
Two of a trade can ne'er agree,
Each hates his neighbour for encroaching;
Squire stigmatizes squire for poaching;
Beauties with beauties are in arms,
And scandal pelts each other's charms;
Kings too their neighbour kings dethrone,
In hope to make the world their own
But let us limit our desires,
Not war like beauties, kings and squires,
For though we both one prey pursue,
There's a game enough for us and you.

Mr. Pope's Welcome from Greece

Upon his having finished his translation of Homer's 'Iliad'

LONG hast thou, friend! been absent from thy soil,
    Like patient Ithacus at siege of Troy;
I have been witness of thy six years' toil,
    Thy daily labours, and thy night's annoy,
Lost to thy native land, with great turmoil,
    On the wide sea, oft threat'ning to destroy:
Methinks with thee I've trod Sigæan ground,
And heard the shores of Hellespont resound.

Did I not see thee when thou first sett'st sail
    To seek adventures fair in Homer's land?
Did I not see thy sinking spirits fail,
    And wish thy bark had never left the strand?
Ev'n in mid ocean often didst thou quail,
    And oft lift up thy holy eye and hand,
Praying the Virgin dear, and saintly choir,
Back to the port to bring thy bark entire.

Cheer up, my friend, thy dangers now are o'er;
　　Methinks—nay, sure the rising coasts appear;
Hark how the guns salute from either shore,
　　As thy trim vessel cuts the Thames so fair:
Shouts answ'ring shouts, from Kent and Essex roar,
　　And bells break loud thro' every gust of air:
Bonfires do blaze, and bones and cleavers ring,
As at the coming of some mighty king.

Now pass we Gravesend with a friendly wind,
　　And Tilbury's white fort, and long Blackwall;
Greenwich, where dwells the friend of human kind,
　　More visited than or her park or hall,
Withers the good, and (with him ever join'd)
　　Facetious Disney, greet thee first of all:
I see his chimney smoke, and hear him say,
Duke! that's the room for Pope, and that for Gay.

Come in, my friends, here shall ye dine and lie,
　　And here shall breakfast, and here dine again;
And sup, and breakfast on, (if ye comply)
　　For I have still some dozens of champagne:
His voice still lessens as the ship sails by;
　　He waves his hand to bring us back in vain;
For now I see, I see proud London's spires;
Greenwich is lost, and Deptford dock retires.

Oh, what a concourse swarms on yonder key!
　　The sky re-echoes with new shouts of joy:
By all this show, I ween, 'tis Lord May'r's day,
　　I hear the voice of trumpet and hautboy.—
No, now I see them near—oh, these are they
　　Who come in crowds to welcome thee from Troy.
Hail to the bard whom long as lost we mourn'd,
From siege, from battle, and from storm return'd!

Of goodly Dames, and courteous Knights, I view
　　The silken petticoat and broider'd vest,
Yea peers and mighty Dukes with ribands blue
　　(True blue fair emblem of unstained breast.)
Others I see as noble and more true,
　　By no court badge distinguish'd from the rest.
First see I Methwen of sincerest mind
As Arthur grave, yet soft as woman kind.

What lady's that to whom he gently bends?
  Who knows not her? ah! those are Wortley's eyes.
How art thou honour'd number'd with her friends?
  For she distinguishes the good and wise.
The sweet tongu'd Murray near her side attends.
  Now to my heart the glance of Howard flies.
Now Harvey fair of face I mark full well,
With thee youth's youngest daughter, sweet Lepell.

I see two lovely sisters hand in hand,
  The fair hair'd Martha and Teresa brown,
Madge Bellenden the tallest of the land
  And smiling Mary soft and fair as down.
Yonder I see the cheerful Duchess stand
  For friendship, zeal and blithsome humour known.
Whence that loud shout in such a hearty strain?
Why, all the Hamiltons are in her train.

See next the decent Scudamore advance,
  With Winchelsea still meditating song.
With her Miss Howe came there by chance,
  Nor knows with whom or why she comes along.
Far off from these see Santlow fam'd for dance,
  And frolic Bicknell and her sister young,
With other names by me not to be nam'd,
Much lov'd in private, not in public fam'd.

But now behold the female band retire,
  And the shrill music of their voice is still'd:
Methinks I see famed Buckingham admire
  That in Troy's ruin thou had'st not been kill'd,
Sheffield who knows to strike the living lyre
  With hand judicious like thy Homer skill'd.
Bathurst impetuous hastens to the coast
Whom you and I strive who shall love the most.

See generous Burlington, with goodly Bruce,
  (But Bruce comes wafted in a soft sedan)
Dan Prior next, belov'd by every muse,
  And friendly Congreve, unreproachful man!
(Oxford by Cunningham hath sent excuse)
  See hearty Watkins comes with cup and can;
And Lewis, who has never friend forsaken;
And Laughton whisp'ring asks—Is Troy town taken?

Earl Warwick comes, of free and honest mind;
    Bold, gen'rous Craggs, whose heart was ne'er disguis'd:
Ah why, sweet St. John, cannot I thee find?
    St. John for ev'ry social virtue priz'd. —
Alas! to foreign climates he's confin'd,
    Or else to see thee here I well surmiz'd:
Thou too, my Swift, dost breathe Boeotian air;
When wilt thou bring back wit and humour here?

Harcourt I see for eloquence renown'd,
    The mouth of justice, oracle of law!
Another Simon is beside him found,
    Another Simon, like as straw to straw.
How Lansdowne smiles, with lasting laurel crown'd!
    What mitred prelate there commands our awe?
See Rochester approving nods his head,
And ranks one modern with the mighty dead.

Carlton and Chandos thy arrival grace;
    Hanmer, whose eloquence th' unbiass'd sways;
Harley, whose goodness opens in his face,
    And shews his heart the seat where virtue stays.
Ned Blount advances next, with busy pace,
    In haste, but saunt'ring, hearty in his ways:
I see the friendly Carylls come by dozens,
Their wives, their uncles, daughters, sons, and cousins.

Arbuthnot there I see, in physic's art,
    As Galen learn'd, or famed Hippocrate;
Whose company drives sorrow from the heart,
    As all disease his medicines dissipate:
Kneller amid the triumph bears his part,
    Who could (were mankind lost) a new create:
What can th' extent of his vast soul confine?
A painter, critic, engineer, divine!

Thee Jervas hails, robust and debonair,
    Now have we conquer'd Homer, friends, he cries:
Dartneuf, grave joker, joyous Ford is there,
    And wond'ring Maine, so fat with laughing eyes:
(Gay, Maine, and Cheney, boon companions dear,
    Gay fat, Maine fatter, Cheney huge of size)
Yea Dennis, Gildon, (hearing thou has riches)
And honest, hatless Cromwell, with red breeches.

O Wanley, whence com'st thou with shorten'd hair,
  And visage from thy shelves with dust besprent?
'Forsooth (quoth he) from placing Homer there,
  For ancients to compyle is myne entente:
Of ancients only hath Lord Harley care;
  But hither me hath my meeke lady sent:—
In manuscript of Greeke rede we thilke same,
But book yprint best plesyth myn gude dame.'

Yonder I see, among th' expecting crowd,
  Evans with laugh jocose, and tragic Young;
High-buskin'd Booth, grave Mawbert, wand'ring Frowd,
  And Titcomb's belly waddles slow along.
See Digby faints at Southern talking loud,
  Yea Steele and Tickell mingle in the throng;
Tickell whose skiff (in partnership they say)
Set forth for Greece, but founder'd in the way.

Lo the two Doncastles in Berkshire known!
  Lo Bickford, Fortescue, of Devon land!
Lo Tooker, Eccleshall, Sykes, Rawlinson:
  See hearty Morley takes thee by the hand.
Ayrs, Grahame, Buckridge joy thy voyage done,
  But who can count the leaves, the stars, the sand.
Lo Stonor, Fenton, Caldwell, Ward, and Broome,
Lo thousands more, but I want rhyme and room.

How lov'd! how honour'd thou! yet be not vain;
  And sure thou art not, for I hear thee say,
All this, my friends, I owe to Homer's strain,
  On whose strong pinions I exalt my lay.
What from contending cities did he gain;
  And what rewards his grateful country pay?
None, none were paid—why then all this for me?
These honours, Homer, had been just to thee.

40

ALEXANDER POPE
1688–1744

from *An Essay on Criticism*

I

'TIS hard to say, if greater want of skill
Appear in writing or in judging ill;
But, of the two, less dangerous is the offence
To tire our patience, than mislead our sense.
Some few in that, but numbers err in this,
Ten censure wrong for one who writes amiss;
A fool might once himself alone expose,
Now one in verse makes many more in prose.
  'Tis with our judgments as our watches, none
Go just alike, yet each believes his own.
In poets as true genius is but rare,
True taste as seldom is the critic' share,
Both must alike from Heaven derive their light,
These born to judge, as well as those to write.
Let such teach others who themselves excel,
And censure freely who have written well.
Authors are partial to their wit, 'tis true,
But are not critics to their judgment too?
  Yet, if we look more closely, we shall find
Most have the seeds of judgment in their mind:
Nature affords at least a glimmering light;
The lines, though touch'd but faintly, are drawn right.
But as the slightest sketch, if justly traced,
Is by ill colouring but the more disgraced,
So by false learning is good sense defaced;
Some are bewilder'd in the maze of schools,
And some made coxcombs Nature meant but fools.
In search of wit these lose their common sense,
And then turn critics in their own defence:
Each burns alike, who can, or cannot write,
Or with a rival's, or an eunuch's spite.
All fools have still an itching to deride,
And fain would be upon the laughing side.
If Mævius scribble in Apollo's spite,
There are who judge still worse than he can write.

Some have at first for wits, than poets pass'd,
Turn'd critics next, and proved plain fools at last.
Some neither can for wits nor critics pass,
As heavy mules are neither horse nor ass.
Those half-learn'd witlings, numerous in our isle,
As half-form'd insects on the banks of Nile;
Unfinish'd things, one knows not what to call,
Their generation's so equivocal:
To tell them would a hundred tongues require,
Or one vain wit's, that might a hundred tire.

But you who seek to give and merit fame,
And justly bear a critic's noble name,
Be sure yourself and your own reach to know,
How far your genius, taste, and learning go;
Launch not beyond your depth, but be discreet,
And mark that point where sense and dulness meet.

Nature to all things fix'd the limits fit,
And wisely curb'd proud man's pretending wit.
As on the land while here the ocean gains,
In other parts it leaves wide sandy plains;
Thus in the soul while memory prevails,
The solid power of understanding fails;
Where beams of warm imagination play,
The memory's soft figures melt away.
One science only will one genius fit:
So vast is art, so narrow human wit:
Not only bounded to peculiar arts,
But oft in those confined to single parts.
Like kings we lose the conquests gain'd before,
By vain ambition still to make them more:
Each might his servile province well command,
Would all but stoop to what they understand.

First follow Nature, and your judgment frame
By her just standard, which is still the same:
Unerring Nature, still divinely bright,
One clear, unchanged, and universal light,
Life, force, and beauty, must to all impart,
At once the source, and end, and test of Art.
Art from that fund each just supply provides;
Works without show, and without pomp presides:
In some fair body thus th' informing soul
With spirits feeds, with vigour fills the whole,
Each motion guides, and every nerve sustains;
Itself unseen, but in th' effects remains.

Some, to whom Heaven in wit has been profuse,
Want as much more to turn it to its use;
For wit and judgment often are at strife,
Though meant each other's aid, like man and wife.
'Tis more to guide, than spur the Muse's steed;
Restrain his fury, than provoke his speed:
The winged courser, like a generous horse,
Shows most true mettle when you check his course.

   Those rules of old discover'd, not devised,
Are Nature still, but Nature methodised:
Nature, like liberty, is but restrain'd
By the same laws which first herself ordain'd.

   Hear how learn'd Greece her useful rules indites,
When to repress, and when indulge our flights:
High on Parnassus' top her sons she show'd,
And pointed out those arduous paths they trod;
Held from afar, aloft, the immortal prize,
And urged the rest by equal steps to rise.
Just precepts thus from great examples given,
She drew from them what they derive from Heaven.
The generous critic fann'd the poet's fire,
And taught the world with reason to admire.
Then criticism the Muse's handmaid proved,
To dress her charms, and make her more beloved:
But following wits from that intention stray'd,
Who could not win the mistress, woo'd the maid;
Against the poets their own arms they turn'd,
Sure to hate most the men from whom they learn'd.
So modern 'pothecaries, taught the art
By doctor's bills to play the doctor's part,
Bold in the practice of mistaken rules,
Prescribe, apply, and call their masters fools.
Some on the leaves of ancient authors prey,
Nor time nor moths e'er spoil'd so much as they:
Some drily plain, without invention's aid,
Write dull receipts how poems may be made.
These leave the sense, their learning to display,
And those explain the meaning quite away.

   You then whose judgment the right course would steer,
Know well each Ancient's proper character:
His fable, subject, scope in every page;
Religion, country, genius of his age:
Without all these at once before your eyes,
Cavil you may, but never criticise.

Be Homer's works your study and delight,
Read them by day, and meditate by night;
Thence form your judgment, thence your maxims bring,
And trace the Muses upward to their spring.
Still with itself compared, his text peruse;
And let your comment be the Mantuan Muse.

When first young Maro in his boundless mind
A work to outlast immortal Rome design'd,
Perhaps he seem'd above the critic's law,
And but from Nature's fountains scorn'd to draw:
But when to examine every part he came,
Nature and Homer were, he found, the same.
Convinced, amazed, he checks the bold design;
And rules as strict his labour'd work confine,
As if the Stagyrite o'erlook'd each line.
Learn hence for ancient rules a just esteem;
To copy Nature is to copy them.

Some beauties yet no precepts can declare,
For there's a happiness as well as care.
Music resembles poetry, in each
Are nameless graces which no methods teach,
And which a master-hand alone can reach.
If, where the rules not far enough extend,
(Since rules were made but to promote their end)
Some lucky licence answer to the full
The intent proposed, that licence is a rule.
Thus Pegasus, a nearer way to take,
May boldly deviate from the common track.
Great wits sometimes may gloriously offend,
And rise to faults true critics dare not mend;
From vulgar bounds with brave disorder part,
And snatch a grace beyond the reach of art,
Which, without passing through the judgment, gains
The heart, and all its end at once attains.

*   *   *

II

Of all the causes which conspire to blind
Man's erring judgment, and misguide the mind,
What the weak head with strongest bias rules,
Is PRIDE, the never-failing vice of fools.
Whatever Nature has in worth denied,
She gives in large recruits of needless pride;

For as in bodies, thus in souls we find
What wants in blood and spirits, swell'd with wind:
Pride, where wit fails, steps in to our defence,
And fills up all the mighty void of sense.
If once right reason drives that cloud away,
Truth breaks upon us with resistless day.
Trust not yourself; but your defects to know,
Make use of every friend—and every foe.
A little learning is a dangerous thing;
Drink deep, or taste not the Pierian spring:
There shallow draughts intoxicate the brain,
And drinking largely sobers us again.
Fired at first sight with what the Muse imparts,
In fearless youth we tempt the height of arts,
While from the bounded level of our mind,
Short views we take, nor see the lengths behind;
But more advanced, behold with strange surprise
New distant scenes of endless science rise!
So pleased at first the towering Alps we try,
Mount o'er the vales, and seem to tread the sky,
The eternal snows appear already passed,
And the first clouds and mountains seem the last:
But, those attain'd, we tremble to survey
The growing labours of the lengthen'd way,
The increasing prospect tires our wandering eyes,
Hills peep o'er hills, and Alps on Alps arise!
   A perfect judge will read each work of wit
With the same spirit that its author writ:
Survey the WHOLE, nor seeks slight faults to find
Where Nature moves, and rapture warms the mind,
Nor lose, for that malignant dull delight,
The generous pleasure to be charm'd with wit.
But in such lays as neither ebb nor flow,
Correctly cold, and regularly low,
That shunning faults, one quiet tenor keep;
We cannot blame indeed—but we may sleep.
In wit, as Nature, what affects our hearts
Is not th' exactness of peculiar parts;
'Tis not a lip, or eye, we beauty call,
But the joint force and full result of all.
Thus when we view some well-proportion'd dome,
(The world's just wonder, and ev'n thine, O Rome!)
No single parts unequally surprise,
All comes united to th' admiring eyes;

No monstrous height, or breadth or length appear;
The whole at once is bold and regular.
    Whoever thinks a faultless piece to see,
Thinks what ne'er was, nor is, nor e'er shall be,
In every work regard the writer's end,
Since none can compass more than they intend;
And if the means be just, the conduct true,
Applause, in spite of trivial faults, is due.
As men of breeding, sometimes men of wit,
To avoid great errors, must the less commit:
Neglect the rules each verbal critic lays,
For not to know some trifles, is a praise.
Most critics, fond of some subservient art,
Still make the whole depend upon a part:
They talk of principles, but notions prize,
And all to one loved folly sacrifice.

*   *   *

    Some to Conceit alone their taste confine,
And glittering thoughts struck out at every line;
Pleased with a work where nothing's just or fit;
One glaring chaos and wild heap of wit.
Poets, like painters, thus, unskill'd to trace
The naked Nature and the living grace,
With gold and jewels cover every part,
And hide with ornaments their want of art.
True wit is Nature to advantage dress'd;
What oft was thought, but ne'er so well express'd;
Something, whose truth convinced at sight we find,
That gives us back the image of our mind.
As shades more sweetly recommend the light,
So modest plainness sets off sprightly wit.
For works may have more wit than does 'em good,
As bodies perish through excess of blood.
    Others for Language all their care express,
And value books, as women men, for dress:
Their praise is still,—The style is excellent;
The sense, they humbly take upon content.
Words are like leaves; and where they most abound,
Much fruit of sense beneath is rarely found.
False eloquence, like the prismatic glass,
Its gaudy colours spreads on every place;
The face of Nature we no more survey,
All glares alike, without distinction gay:

But true expression, like th' unchanging sun,
Clears and improves whate'er it shines upon,
It gilds all objects, but it alters none.
Expression is the dress of thought, and still
Appears more decent, as more suitable;
A vile conceit in pompous words express'd
Is like a clown in regal purple dress'd:
For different styles with different subjects sort,
As several garbs, with country, town, and court.
Some by old words to fame have made pretence,
Ancients in phrase, mere moderns in their sense;
Such labour'd nothings, in so strange a style,
Amaze the unlearn'd, and make the learned smile.
Unlucky as Fungoso in the play,
These sparks with awkward vanity display
What the fine gentleman wore yesterday;
And but so mimic ancient wits at best,
As apes our grandsires, in their doublets dress'd.
In words, as fashions, the same rule will hold;
Alike fantastic, if too new, or old:
Be not the first by whom the new are tried,
Nor yet the last to lay the old aside.
   But most by numbers judge a poet's song:
And smooth or rough, with them, is right or wrong:
In the bright muse, though thousand charms conspire,
Her voice is all these tuneful fools admire;
Who haunt Parnassus but to please their ear,
Not mend their minds; as some to church repair,
Not for the doctrine, but the music there.
These equal syllables alone require,
Though oft the ear the open vowels tire;
While expletives their feeble aid do join;
And ten low words oft creep in one dull line:
While they ring round the same unvaried chimes,
With sure returns of still expected rhymes;
Where'er you find 'the cooling western breeze,'
In the next line, it 'whispers through the trees':
If crystal streams 'with pleasing murmurs creep':
The reader's threaten'd (not in vain) with 'sleep.'
Then, at the last and only couplet fraught
With some unmeaning thing they call a thought,
A needless Alexandrine ends the song,
That, like a wounded snake, drags its slow length along.
Leave such to tune their own dull rhymes, and know

What's roundly smooth, or languishingly slow;
And praise the easy vigour of a line,
Where Denham's strength, and Waller's sweetness join.
True ease in writing comes from art, not chance,
As those move easiest who have learn'd to dance.
'Tis not enough no harshness gives offence,
The sound must seem an echo to the sense:
Soft is the strain when Zephyr gently blows,
And the smooth stream in smoother numbers flows;
But when loud billows lash the sounding shore,
The hoarse, rough verse should like the torrent roar.
When Ajax strives some rock's vast weight to throw,
The line too labours, and the words move slow:
Not so, when swift Camilla scours the plain,
Flies o'er the unbending corn, and skims along the main.
Hear how Timotheus' varied lays surprise,
And bid alternate passions fall and rise!
While, at each change, the son of Libyan Jove
Now burns with glory, and then melts with love;
Now his fierce eyes with sparkling fury glow,
Now sighs steal out, and tears begin to flow:
Persians and Greeks like turns of Nature found,
And the world's victor stood subdued by sound!
The power of music all our hearts allow,
And what Timotheus was, is DRYDEN now.

Avoid extremes; and shun the fault of such,
Who still are pleased too little or too much.
At every trifle scorn to take offence,
That always shows great pride, or little sense;
Those heads, as stomachs, are not sure the best,
Which nauseate all, and nothing can digest.
Yet let not each gay turn thy rapture move;
For fools admire, but men of sense approve:
As things seem large which we through mists descry,
Dulness is ever apt to magnify.

*   *   *

But where's the man who counsel can bestow,
Still pleased to teach, and yet not proud to know?
Unbiass'd, or by favour, or by spite;
Not dully prepossess'd, nor blindly right;
Though learn'd, well-bred; and though well-bred, sincere;
Modestly bold, and humanly severe:

Who to a friend his faults can freely show,
And gladly praise the merit of a foe?
Bless'd with a taste exact, yet unconfined;
A knowledge both of books and human kind;
Generous converse; a soul exempt from pride;
And love to praise, with reason on his side?

    Such once were critics; such the happy few,
Athens and Rome in better ages knew.
The mighty Stagyrite first left the shore,
Spread all his sails, and durst the deeps explore;
He steer'd securely, and discover'd far,
Led by the light of the Mæonian star.
Poets, a race long unconfined, and free,
Still fond and proud of savage liberty,
Received his laws; and stood convinced 'twas fit,
Who conquer'd Nature, should preside o'er Wit.

    Horace still charms with graceful negligence,
And without method talks us into sense,
Will, like a friend, familiarly convey
The truest notions in the easiest way.
He, who supreme in judgment, as in wit,
Might boldly censure, as he boldly writ,
Yet judged with coolness, though he sung with fire;
His precepts teach but what his works inspire.
Our critics take a contrary extreme,
They judge with fury, but they write with phlegm:
Nor suffers Horace more in wrong translations
By wits, than critics in as wrong quotations.

    See Dionysius Homer's thoughts refine,
And call new beauties forth from every line!

    Fancy and art in gay Petronius please,
The scholar's learning with the courtier's ease.

    In grave Quintilian's copious work, we find
The justest rules and clearest method join'd:
Thus useful arms in magazines we place,
All ranged in order, and disposed with grace,
But less to please the eye, than arm the hand,
Still fit for use, and ready at command.

    Thee, bold Longinus! all the Nine inspire,
And bless their critic with a poet's fire.
An ardent judge, who, zealous in his trust,
With warmth gives sentence, yet is always just:
Whose own example strengthens all his laws:
And is himself that great sublime he draws.

Thus long succeeding critics justly reign'd,
Licence repress'd, and useful laws ordain'd.
Learning and Rome alike in empire grew;
And arts still follow'd where her eagles flew;
From the same foes, at last, both felt their doom,
And the same age saw Learning fall, and Rome.
With Tyranny, then Superstition join'd,
As that the body, this enslaved the mind;
Much was believed, but little understood,
And to be dull was construed to be good;
A second deluge learning thus o'errun,
And the monks finish'd what the Goths begun.
    At length Erasmus, that great injured name,
(The glory of the priesthood, and the shame!)
Stemm'd the wild torrent of a barbarous age,
And drove those holy Vandals off the stage.
    But see! each Muse, in Leo's golden days,
Starts from her trance, and trims her wither'd bays;
Rome's ancient Genius, o'er its ruins spread,
Shakes off the dust, and rears his reverend head.
Then Sculpture and her sister-arts revive;
Stones leaped to form, and rocks began to live;
With sweeter notes each rising temple rung;
A Raphael painted, and a Vida sung.
Immortal Vida: on whose honour'd brow
The poet's bays and critic's ivy grow:
Cremona now shall ever boast thy name,
As next in place to Mantua, next in fame!
    But soon by impious arms from Latium chased,
Their ancient bounds the banish'd Muses pass'd;
Thence Arts o'er all the northern world advance,
But critic-learning flourish'd most in France;
The rules a nation, born to serve, obeys;
And Boileau still in right of Horace sways.
But we, brave Britons, foreign laws despised,
And kept unconquer'd, and uncivilised;
Fierce for the liberties of wit and bold,
We still defied the Romans, as of old.
Yet some there were, among the sounder few
Of those who less presumed, and better knew,
Who durst assert the juster ancient cause,
And here restored Wit's fundamental laws.
Such was the Muse, whose rules and practice tell,
'Nature's chief Masterpiece is writing well,'

Such was Roscommon, not more learn'd than good,
With manners generous as his noble blood;
To him the wit of Greece and Rome was known,
And every author's merit, but his own.
Such late was Walsh—the Muse's judge and friend,
Who justly knew to blame or to commend:
To failings mild, but zealous for desert;
The clearest head, and the sincerest heart.
This humble praise, lamented shade! receive,
This praise at least a grateful Muse may give:
The Muse, whose early voice you taught to sing,
Prescribed her heights, and pruned her tender wing,
(Her guide now lost) no more attempts to rise,
But in low numbers short excursions tries:
Content, if hence the unlearn'd their wants may view,
The learn'd reflect on what before they knew;
Careless of censure, nor too fond of fame;
Still pleased to praise, yet not afraid to blame;
Averse alike to flatter, or offend;
Not free from faults, not yet too vain to mend.

from *Windsor Forest*

To the Right Honourable George Lord Lansdowne

Non injussa cano: Te nostræ, Vare, myricæ,
Te Nemus omne canet; nec Phœbo gratior ulla est,
Quam sibi quæ Vari præscripsit pagina nomen.—VIRG.

[My pastoral Muse her humble tribute brings;
And yet not wholly uninspir'd she sings:
For all who read, and reading, not disdain
These rural poems, and their lowly strain,
The name of Varus oft inscribed shall see
In every grove and every vocal tree,
And all the sylvan reign shall sing of thee:
Thy name, to Phœbus and the Muses known,
Shall in the front of every page be shown;
For he who sings thy praise secures his own.—DRYDEN.]

THY forest, Windsor! and thy green retreats,
At once the Monarch's and the Muse's seats,
Invite my lays. Be present, sylvan maids!
Unlock your springs, and open all your shades.
GRANVILLE commands; your aid, O Muses, bring!
What Muse for GRANVILLE can refuse to sing?

The groves of Eden, vanish'd now so long,
Live in description, and look green in song:
These, were my breast inspired with equal flame,
Like them in beauty, should be like in fame.
Here hills and vales, the woodland and the plain,
Here earth and water seem to strive again;
Not chaos-like together crush'd and bruised,
But, as the world harmoniously confused:
Where order in variety we see,
And where, though all things differ, all agree.
Here waving groves a chequer'd scene display,
And part admit, and part exclude the day;
As some coy nymph her lover's warm address
Not quite indulges, nor can quite repress.
There, interspersed in lawns and opening glades,
Thin trees arise that shun each other's shades.
Here in full light the russet plains extend:
There, wrapt in clouds the bluish hills ascend.
Even the wild heath displays her purple dyes,
And 'midst the desert, fruitful fields arise,
That crown'd with tufted trees and springing corn,
Like verdant isles the sable waste adorn.
Let India boast her plants, nor envy we
The weeping amber, or the balmy tree,
While by our oaks the precious loads are borne,
And realms commanded which those trees adorn.
Not proud Olympus yields a nobler sight,
Though gods assembled grace his towering height,
Than what more humble mountains offer here,
Where, in their blessings, all those gods appear.
See Pan with flocks, with fruits Pomona crown'd,
Here blushing Flora paints th' enamell'd ground,
Here Ceres' gifts in waving prospect stand,
And nodding tempt the joyful reaper's hand;
Rich Industry sits smiling on the plains,
And peace and plenty tell, a STUART reigns.
  Not thus the land appear'd in ages past,
A dreary desert, and a gloomy waste,
To savage beasts and savage laws a prey,
And kings more furious and severe than they;
Who claim'd the skies, dispeopled air and floods,
The lonely lords of empty wilds and woods:
Cities laid waste, they storm'd the dens and caves
(For wiser brutes were backward to be slaves).

What could be free, when lawless beasts obey'd,
And even the elements a tyrant sway'd?
In vain kind seasons swell'd the teeming grain,
Soft showers distill'd and suns grew warm in vain;
The swain with tears his frustrate labour yields,
And famish'd dies amidst his ripen'd fields.
What wonder then, a beast or subject slain
Were equal crimes in a despotic reign?
Both doom'd alike for sportive tyrants bled,
But while the subject starv'd, the beast was fed.
Proud Nimrod first the bloody chase began,
A mighty hunter, and his prey was man;
Our haughty Norman boasts that barbarous name,
And makes his trembling slaves the royal game.
The fields are ravish'd from th' industrious swains,
From men their cities, and from gods their fanes:
The levell'd towns with weeds lie cover'd o'er;
The hollow winds through naked temples roar;
Round broken columns clasping ivy twined;
O'er heaps of ruin stalk'd the stately hind;
The fox obscene to gaping tombs retires,
And savage howlings fill the sacred quires.
Awed by his Nobles, by his Commons cursed,
Th' oppressor ruled tyrannic where he durst,
Stretch'd o'er the poor and Church his iron rod,
And served alike his vassals and his God.
Whom even the Saxon spared, and bloody Dane,
The wanton victims of his sport remain.
But see, the man who spacious regions gave
A waste for beasts, himself denied a grave!
Stretch'd on the lawn his second hope survey,
At once the chaser, and at once the prey:
Lo Rufus, tugging at the deadly dart,
Bleeds in the forest like a wounded hart.
Succeeding monarchs heard the subjects' cries,
Nor saw displeased the peaceful cottage rise.
Then gathering flocks on unknown mountains fed,
O'er sandy wilds were yellow harvests spread.
The forests wonder'd at th' unusual grain,
And sacred transport touch'd the conscious swain.
Fair Liberty, Britannia's goddess, rears
Her cheerful head, and leads the golden years.

* * *

Here too, 'tis sung, of old Diana stray'd,
And Cynthus' top forsook for Windsor shade!
Here was she seen o'er airy wastes to rove,
Seek the clear spring, or haunt the pathless grove;
Here arm'd with silver bows, in early dawn,
Her buskin'd virgins traced the dewy lawn.
  Above the rest a rural nymph was famed,
Thy offspring, Thames! the fair Lodona named:
(Lodona's fate, in long oblivion cast,
The Muse shall sing, and what she sings shall last.)
Scarce could the goddess from her nymph be known,
But by the crescent, and the golden zone.
She scorn'd the praise of beauty, and the care;
A belt her waist, a fillet binds her hair;
A painted quiver on her shoulder sounds,
And with her dart the flying deer she wounds.
It chanced, as eager of the chase, the maid
Beyond the forest's verdant limits stray'd,
Pan saw and loved, and, burning with desire,
Pursued her flight, her flight increased his fire.
Not half so swift the trembling doves can fly,
When the fierce eagle cleaves the liquid sky;
Not half so swiftly the fierce eagle moves,
When through the clouds he drives the trembling doves;
As from the god she flew with furious pace,
Or as the god, more furious, urged the chase.
Now fainting, sinking, pale, the nymph appears;
Now close behind, his sounding steps she hears;
And now his shadow reach'd her as she run,
His shadow lengthen'd by the setting sun;
And now his shorter breath, with sultry air,
Pants on her neck, and fans her parting hair.
In vain on Father Thames she calls for aid,
Nor could Diana help her injured maid.
Faint, breathless, thus she pray'd, nor pray'd in vain:
'Ah, Cynthia! ah—though banish'd from thy train,
Let me, O let me, to the shades repair,
My native shades—there weep, and murmur there.'
She said, and melting as in tears she lay,
In a soft silver stream dissolved away.
The silver stream her virgin coldness keeps,
For ever murmurs, and for ever weeps;
Still bears the name the hapless virgin bore,
And bathes the forest where she ranged before.

In her chaste current oft the goddess laves,
And with celestial tears augments the waves.
Oft in her glass the musing shepherd spies
The headlong mountains and the downward skies,
The watery landskip of the pendant woods,
And absent trees that tremble in the floods;
In the clear azure gleam the flocks are seen,
And floating forests paint the waves with green,
Through the fair scene roll slow the ling'ring streams,
Then foaming pour along, and rush into the Thames.
　　Thou, too, great father of the British floods!
With joyful pride survey'st our lofty woods;
Where towering oaks their growing honours rear
And future navies on thy shores appear.
Not Neptune's self from all her streams receives
A wealthier tribute, than to thine he gives.
No seas so rich, so gay no banks appear.
No lake so gentle, and no spring so clear.
Nor Po so swells the fabling poet's lays,
While led along the skies his current strays,
As thine, which visits Windsor's famed abodes,
To grace the mansion of our earthly gods:
Nor all his stars above a lustre show,
Like the bright beauties on thy banks below;
Where Jove, subdued by mortal passion still,
Might change Olympus for a nobler hill.

from *The Rape of the Lock*

CANTO I

AND now, unveil'd, the toilet stands display'd,
Each silver vase in mystic order laid.
First, robed in white, the nymph intent adores,
With head uncover'd, the cosmetic powers.
A heavn'nly image in the glass appears,
To that she bends, to that her eye she rears;
Th' inferior priestess, at her altar's side,
Trembling, begins the sacred rites of pride.
Unnumber'd treasures ope at once, and here
The various offerings of the world appear;
From each she nicely culls with curious toil,
And decks the goddess with the glitt'ring spoil.

This casket India's glowing gems unlocks,
And all Arabia breathes from yonder box.
The tortoise here and elephant unite,
Transform'd to combs, the speckled and the white.
Here files of pins extend their shining rows,
Puffs, powders, patches, Bibles, billet-doux.
Now awful beauty puts on all its arms;
The fair each moment rises in her charms,
Repairs her smiles, awakens every grace,
And calls forth all the wonders of her face:
Sees by degrees a purer blush arise,
And keener lightnings quicken in her eyes.
The busy sylphs surround their darling care,
These set the head, and those divide the hair,
Some fold the sleeve, while others plait the gown;
And Betty's praised for labours not her own.

CANTO II

NOT with more glories, in th' ethereal plain,
The sun first rises o'er the purpled main,
Than, issuing forth, the rival of his beams
Launch'd on the bosom of the silver Thames.
Fair nymphs and well-dress'd youths around her shone,
But every eye was fix'd on her alone.
On her white breast a sparkling cross she wore,
Which Jews might kiss, and infidels adore.
Her lively looks a sprightly mind disclose,
Quick as her eyes, and as unfix'd as those:
Favours to none, to all she smiles extends;
Oft she rejects, but never once offends.
Bright as the sun, her eyes the gazers strike,
And, like the sun, they shine on all alike.
Yet graceful ease, and sweetness void of pride,
Might hide her faults, if belles had faults to hide:
If to her share some female errors fall,
Look on her face, and you'll forget them all.

This nymph, to the destruction of mankind,
Nourish'd two locks, which graceful hung behind
In equal curls, and well conspired to deck
With shining ringlets the smooth ivory neck.
Love in these labyrinths his slaves detains,
And mighty hearts are held in slender chains.
With hairy springes we the birds betray,
Slight lines of hair surprise the finny prey,

Fair tresses man's imperial race insnare,
And beauty draws us with a single hair.
 Th' adventurous baron the bright locks admired;
He saw, he wish'd, and to the prize aspired.
Resolved to win, he meditates the way,
By force to ravish, or by fraud betray;
For when success a lover's toils attends,
Few ask, if fraud or force attain'd his ends.
 For this, ere Phœbus rose, he had implored
Propitious Heaven, and every power adored:
But chiefly Love—to Love an altar built,
Of twelve vast French romances, neatly gilt.
There lay three garters, half a pair of gloves;
And all the trophies of his former loves:
With tender billet-doux he lights the pyre,
And breathes three amorous sighs to raise the fire.
Then prostrate falls, and begs with ardent eyes
Soon to obtain, and long possess the prize:
The powers gave ear, and granted half his prayer,
The rest, the winds dispersed in empty air.
 But now secure the painted vessel glides,
The sun-beams trembling on the floating tides;
While melting music steals upon the sky,
And soften'd sounds along the waters die;
Smooth flow the waves, the zephyrs gently play,
Belinda smiled, and all the world was gay.
All but the sylph—with careful thoughts oppress'd,
Th' impending woe sat heavy on his breast.
He summons straight his denizens of air;
The lucid squadrons round the sails repair:
Soft o'er the shrouds aërial whispers breathe,
That seem'd but zephyrs to the train beneath.
Some to the sun their insect-wings unfold,
Waft on the breeze, or sink in clouds of gold;
Transparent forms, too fine for mortal sight,
Their fluid bodies half dissolved in light.
Loose to the wind their airy garments flew,
Thin glittering textures of the filmy dew,
Dipp'd in the richest tincture of the skies,
Where light disports in ever-mingling dyes;
While ev'ry beam new transient colours flings,
Colours that change whene'er they wave their wings.
Amid the circle on the gilded mast,
Superior by the head, was Ariel placed;

His purple pinions op'ning to the sun,
He raised his azure wand, and thus begun:
   'Ye sylphs and sylphids to your chief give ear;
Fays, fairies, genii, elves, and dæmons, hear:
Ye know the spheres, and various tasks assign'd
By laws eternal to the aërial kind.
Some in the fields of purest ether play,
And bask and whiten in the blaze of day.
Some guide the course of wand'ring orbs on high,
Or roll the planets through the boundless sky.
Some less refined beneath the moon's pale light
Pursue the stars that shoot athwart the night,
Or suck the mists in grosser air below,
Or dip their pinions in the painted bow,
Or brew fierce tempests on the wintry main,
Or o'er the glebe distil the kindly rain.
Others on earth o'er human race preside,
Watch all their ways, and all their actions guide:
Of these the chief the care of nations own,
And guard with arms divine the British throne.
   'Our humbler province is to tend the fair,
Not a less pleasing, though less glorious care;
To save the powder from too rude a gale,
Nor let the imprison'd essences exhale;
To draw fresh colours from the vernal flowers;
To steal the rainbows, ere they drop in showers,
A brighter wash; to curl their waving hairs,
Assist their blushes and inspire their airs;
Nay, oft, in dreams, invention we bestow,
To change a flounce, or add a furbelow.
   'This day, black omens threat the brightest fair
That e'er deserved a watchful spirit's care;
Some dire disaster, or by force, or flight;
But what, or where, the Fates have wrapp'd in night.
Whether the nymph shall break Diana's law,
Or some frail china-jar receive a flaw;
Or stain her honour or her new brocade;
Forget her prayers, or miss a masquerade;
Or lose her heart, or necklace, at a ball;
Or whether Heaven has doom'd that Shock must fall.
Haste, then, ye spirits! to your charge repair:
The flutt'ring fan be Zephyretta's care;
The drops to thee, Brillante, we consign;
And, Momentilla, let the watch be thine;

Do thou, Crispissa, tend her fav'rite lock;
Ariel himself shall be the guard of Shock.

　'To fifty chosen sylphs, of special note,
We trust th' important charge, the petticoat:
Oft have we known that seven-fold fence to fail,
Though stiff with hoops, and arm'd with ribs of whale;
Form a strong line about the silver bound,
And guard the wide circumference around.

　'Whatever spirit, careless of his charge,
His post neglects, or leaves the fair at large,
Shall feel sharp vengeance soon o'ertake his sins,
Be stopp'd in vials, or transfix'd with pins;
Or plunged in lakes of bitter washes lie,
Or wedged whole ages in a bodkin's eye:
Gums and pomatums shall his flight restrain,
While clogg'd he beats his silken wings in vain:
Or alum styptics with contracting power
Shrink his thin essence like a rivell'd flower:
Or, as Ixion fix'd, the wretch shall feel
The giddy motion of the whirling wheel,
In fumes of burning chocolate shall glow,
And tremble at the sea that froths below!'

　He spoke; the spirits from the sails descend;
Some, orb in orb, around the nymph extend;
Some thrid the mazy ringlets of her hair;
Some hang upon the pendants of her ear:
With beating hearts the dire event they wait,
Anxious and trembling for the birth of Fate.

*　　*　　*

CANTO III

But when to mischief mortals bend their will,
How soon they find fit instruments of ill!
Just then, Clarissa drew with tempting grace
A two-edged weapon from her shining case:
So ladies, in romance, assist their knight,
Present the spear, and arm him for the fight.
He takes the gift with reverence and extends
The little engine on his fingers' ends;
This just behind Belinda's neck he spread,
As o'er the fragrant steams she bends her head.
Swift to the lock a thousand sprites repair,
A thousand wings, by turns, blow back the hair;

And thrice they twitch'd the diamond in her ear;
Thrice she look'd back, and thrice the foe drew near.
Just in that instant, anxious Ariel sought
The close recesses of the virgin's thought:
As on the nosegay in her breast reclin'd,
He watch'd th' ideas rising in her mind,
Sudden he view'd, in spite of all her art,
An earthly lover lurking at her heart.
Amazed, confused, he found his power expired,
Resign'd to fate, and with a sigh retired.
The peer now spreads the glitt'ring forfex wide,
T' inclose the lock; now joins it, to divide.
Ev'n then, before the fatal engine closed,
A wretched sylph too fondly interposed;
Fate urged the shears, and cut the sylph in twain,
(But airy substance soon unites again)
The meeting points the sacred hair dissever
From the fair head, for ever, and for ever!

*   *   *

CANTO IV

BUT anxious cares the pensive nymph oppress'd,
And secret passions labour'd in her breast.
Not youthful kings in battle seized alive,
Not scornful virgins who their charms survive,
Not ardent lovers robb'd of all their bliss,
Not ancient ladies when refused a kiss,
Not tyrants fierce that unrepenting die,
Not Cynthia when her manteau's pinn'd awry,
E'er felt such rage, resentment, and despair,
As thou, sad virgin! for thy ravish'd hair.

   For, that sad moment, when the sylphs withdrew,
And Ariel weeping from Belinda flew,
Umbriel, a dusky, melancholy sprite,
As ever sullied the fair face of light,
Down to the central earth, his proper scene,
Repair'd to search the gloomy Cave of Spleen.

   Swift on his sooty pinions flits the gnome,
And in a vapour reach'd the dismal dome.
No cheerful breeze this sullen region knows,
The dreaded east is all the wind that blows.
Here in a grotto, shelter'd close from air,
And screen'd in shades from day's detested glare,

She sighs for ever on her pensive bed,
Pain at her side, and Megrim at her head.
Two handmaids wait the throne: alike in place,
But diff'ring far in figure and in face.
Here stood Ill-nature like an ancient maid,
Her wrinkled form in black and white array'd;
With store of prayers, for mornings, nights, and noons,
Her hand is fill'd; her bosom with lampoons.

   There Affectation, with sickly mien,
Shows in her cheek the roses of eighteen,
Practised to lisp, and hang the head aside,
Faints into airs, and languishes with pride,
On the rich quilt sinks with becoming woe,
Wrapp'd in a gown, for sickness, and for show.
The fair ones feel such maladies as these,
When each new night-dress gives a new disease.

   A constant vapour o'er the palace flies;
Strange phantoms rising as the mists arise;
Dreadful, as hermits' dreams in haunted shades,
Or bright, as visions of expiring maids.
Now glaring fiends, and snakes on rolling spires,
Pale spectres, gaping tombs, and purple fires:
Now lakes of liquid gold, Elysian scenes,
And crystal domes, and angels in machines.

   Unnumber'd throngs on every side are seen
Of bodies changed to various forms by Spleen.
Here living tea-pots stand, one arm held out,
One bent; the handle this, and that the spout:
A pipkin there, like Homer's tripod walks;
Here sighs a jar, and there a goose-pie talks:
Men prove with child, as powerful fancy works,
And maids turn'd bottles call aloud for corks.

   Safe pass'd the gnome through this fantastic band,
A branch of healing spleen-wort in his hand.
Then thus address'd the power: 'Hail, wayward Queen!
Who rule the sex to fifty from fifteen;
Parent of vapours, and of female wit,
Who give th' hysteric or poetic fit;
On various tempers act by various ways,
Make some take physic, others scribble plays;
Who cause the proud their visits to delay,
And send the godly in a pet to pray;
A nymph there is, that all thy power disdains,
And thousands more in equal mirth maintains.

But oh! if e'er thy gnome could spoil a grace,
Or raise a pimple on a beauteous face,
Like citron waters matrons' cheeks inflame,
Or change complexions at a losing game;
If e'er with airy horns I planted heads,
Or rumpled petticoats, or tumbled beds,
Or caused suspicion when no soul was rude,
Or discomposed the head-dress of a prude,
Or e'er to costive lap-dog gave disease,
Which not the tears of brightest eyes could ease;
Hear me, and touch Belinda with chagrin,
That single act gives half the world the spleen.'
    The Goddess with a discontented air
Seems to reject him, though she grants his prayer.
A wonderous bag with both her hands she binds,
Like that where once Ulysses held the winds;
There she collects the force of female lungs,
Sighs, sobs, and passions, and the war of tongues.
A vial next she fills with fainting fears,
Soft sorrows, melting griefs, and flowing tears.
The gnome rejoicing bears her gifts away,
Spreads his black wings, and slowly mounts to day.
    Sunk in Thalestris' arms the nymph he found,
Her eyes dejected, and her hair unbound.
Full o'er their heads the swelling bag he rent,
And all the furies issued at the vent.
Belinda burns with more than mortal ire,
And fierce Thalestris fans the rising fire;
'O wretched maid!' she spread her hands, and cried,
(While Hampton's echoes, 'Wretched maid!' replied)
'Was it for this you took such constant care
The bodkin, comb, and essence to prepare?
For this your locks in paper durance bound?
For this with torturing irons wreathed around?
For this with fillets strain'd your tender head,
And bravely bore the double loads of lead?
Gods! shall the ravisher display your hair,
While the fops envy and the ladies stare?
Honour forbid! at whose unrivall'd shrine
Ease, pleasure, virtue, all our sex resign.
Methinks already I your tears survey,
Already hear the horrid things they say,
Already see you a degraded toast,
And all your honour in a whisper lost!

How shall I then your helpless fame defend?
'Twill then be infamy to seem your friend!
And shall this prize, th' inestimable prize,
Exposed through crystal to the gazing eyes,
And heighten'd by the diamond's circling rays,
On that rapacious hand for ever blaze?
Sooner shall grass in Hyde Park Circus grow,
And wits take lodgings in the sound of Bow;
Sooner let earth, air, sea, to Chaos fall,
Men, monkeys, lap-dogs, parrots, perish all!'

*   *   *

'Restore the lock!' she cries; and all around
'Restore the lock!' the vaulted roofs rebound.
Not fierce Othello in so loud a strain
Roar'd for the handkerchief that caused his pain.
But see how oft ambitious aims are cross'd,
And chiefs contend till all the prize is lost!
The lock, obtain'd with guilt, and kept with pain,
In every place is sought, but sought in vain:
With such a prize no mortal must be blest,
So Heaven decrees! with Heaven who can contest?
    Some thought it mounted to the lunar sphere,
Since all things lost on earth are treasured there.
There heroes' wits are kept in pond'rous vases,
And beaux' in snuff-boxes and tweezer-cases.
There broken vows, and death-bed alms are found,
And lovers' hearts with ends of riband bound,
The courtier's promises, and sick man's prayers,
The smiles of harlots, and the tears of heirs,
Cages for gnats, and chains to yoke a flea,
Dried butterflies, and tomes of casuistry.
    But trust the Muse—she saw it upward rise,
Though mark'd by none but quick, poetic eyes:
(So Rome's great founder to the heavens withdrew,
To Proculus alone confess'd in view)
A sudden star it shot through liquid air,
And drew behind a radiant trail of hair.
Not Berenice's lock first rose so bright,
The heavens bespangling with dishevell'd light.
The sylphs behold it kindling as it flies,
And pleased pursue its progress through the skies.
    This the beau-monde shall from the Mall survey,
And hail with music its propitious ray.

This the blest lover shall for Venus take,
And send up vows from Rosamonda's lake.
This Partridge soon shall view in cloudless skies,
When next he looks through Galileo's eyes;
And hence th' egregious wizard shall foredoom
The fate of Louis, and the fall of Rome.

Then cease, bright nymph! to mourn thy ravish'd hair,
Which adds new glory to the shining sphere!
Not all the tresses that fair head can boast
Shall draw such envy as the lock you lost.
For, after all the murders of your eye,
When, after millions slain, yourself shall die;
When those fair suns shall set, as set they must,
And all those tresses shall be laid in dust;
This lock, the Muse shall consecrate to fame,
And 'midst the stars inscribe Belinda's name.

from *The Dunciad*

To Dr. Jonathan Swift

Book I

ARGUMENT

The proposition, the invocation, and the inscription. Then the original of the great empire of Dulness, and cause of the continuance thereof. The college of the goddess in the city, with her private academy for poets in particular; the governors of it, and the four cardinal virtues. Then the poem hastes into the midst of things, presenting her on the evening of a Lord Mayor's day, revolving the long succession of her sons, and the glories past and to come. She fixes her eyes on Bays to be the instrument of that great event which is the subject of the poem. He is described pensive among his books, giving up the cause, and apprehending the period of her empire: after debating whether to betake himself to the church, or to gaming, or to party-writing, he raises an altar of proper books, and (making first his solemn prayer and declaration) purposes thereon to sacrifice all his unsuccessful writings. As the pile is kindled, the goddess, beholding the flame from her seat, flies and puts it out by casting upon it the poem of Thulé. She forthwith reveals herself to him, transports him to her temple, unfolds her arts, and initiates him into her mysteries; then announcing the death of Eusden, the Poet Laureate, anoints him, carries him to court, and proclaims him successor.

THE mighty mother, and her son, who brings
The Smithfield muses to the ear of kings,
I sing. Say you, her instruments, the great!
Call'd to this work by Dulness, Jove, and Fate;

You by whose care, in vain decried, and curst,
Still Dunce the second reigns like Dunce the first;
Say, how the goddess bade Britannia sleep,
And pour'd her spirit o'er the land and deep.

    In eldest time, ere mortals writ or read,
Ere Pallas issued from the Thunderer's head,
Dulness o'er all possess'd her ancient right,
Daughter of Chaos and eternal Night:
Fate in their dotage this fair idiot gave,
Gross as her sire, and as her mother grave,
Laborious, heavy, busy, bold, and blind,
She ruled, in native anarchy, the mind.

    Still her old empire to restore she tries,
For, born a goddess, Dulness never dies.

    O thou! whatever title please thine ear,
Dean, Drapier, Bickerstaff, or Gulliver!
Whether thou choose Cervantes' serious air,
Or laugh and shake in Rabelais' easy chair,
Or praise the court, or magnify mankind,
Or thy grieved country's copper chains unbind;
From thy Bœotia though her pow'r retires,
Mourn not, my Swift, at aught our realm acquires.
Here pleased behold her mighty wings outspread
To hatch a new Saturnian age of lead.

    Close to those walls where Folly holds her throne,
And laughs to think Monro would take her down,
Where o'er the gates, by his famed father's hand,
Great Cibber's brazen, brainless brothers stand;
One cell there is, conceal'd from vulgar eye,
The cave of Poverty and Poetry.
Keen, hollow winds howl through the bleak recess,
Emblem of music caused by emptiness.
Hence bards, like Proteus long in vain tied down,
Escape in monsters, and amaze the town.
Hence miscellanies spring, the weekly boast
Of Curll's chaste press, and Lintot's rubric post:
Hence hymning Tyburn's elgiac lines,
Hence journals, medleys, merc'ries, magazines:
Sepulchral lies, our holy walls to grace,
And new-year odes, and all the Grub Street race.

    In clouded majesty here Dulness shone;
Four guardian virtues, round, support her throne:
Fierce champion Fortitude, that knows no fears
Of hisses, blows, or want, or loss of ears:

Calm Temperance, whose blessings those partake
Who hunger and who thirst for scribbling sake:
Prudence, whose glass presents th' approaching jail:
Poetic justice, with her lifted scale,
Where, in nice balance, truth with gold she weighs,
And solid pudding against empty praise.
  Here she beholds the chaos dark and deep,
Where nameless somethings in their causes sleep,
Till Genial Jacob, or a warm third day,
Call forth each mass, a poem, or a play:
How hints, like spawn, scarce quick in embryo lie,
How new-born nonsense first is taught to cry,
Maggots half-form'd in rhyme exactly meet,
And learn to crawl upon poetic feet.
Here one poor word an hundred clenches makes,
And ductile Dulness new meanders takes;
There motley images her fancy strike,
Figures ill-pair'd, and similes unlike.
She sees a mob of metaphors advance,
Pleased with the madness of the mazy dance!
How tragedy and comedy embrace;
How farce and epic get a jumbled race;
How Time himself stands still at her command,
Realms shift their place, and ocean turns to land.
Here gay Description Egypt glads with show'rs,
Or gives to Zembla fruits, to Barca flow'rs;
Glitt'ring with ice here hoary hills are seen,
There painted valleys of eternal green.
In cold December fragrant chaplets blow,
And heavy harvests nod beneath the snow.
  All these, and more, the cloud-compelling queen
Beholds through fogs, that magnify the scene.
She, tinsell'd o'er in robes of varying hues,
With self-applause her wild creation views;
Sees momentary monsters rise and fall,
And with her own fool's-colours gilds them all.
  'Twas on the day, when Thorold rich and grave,
Like Cimon, triumph'd both on land and wave:
(Pomps without guilt, of bloodless swords and maces,
Glad chains, warm furs, broad banners, and broad faces)
Now night descending, the proud scene was o'er,
But lived, in Settle's numbers, one day more.
Now mayors and shrieves all hush'd and satiate lay,
Yet eat, in dreams, the custard of the day;

While pensive poets painful vigils keep,
Sleepless themselves to give their readers sleep.
Much to the mindful queen the feast recalls
What city swans once sung within the walls;
Much she revolves their arts, their ancient praise,
And sure succession down from Heywood's days.
She saw, with joy, the line immortal run,
Each sire impress'd and glaring in his son:
So watchful Bruin forms, with plastic care,
Each growing lump, and brings it to a bear.
She saw old Pryn in restless Daniel shine,
And Eusden eke out Blackmore's endless line;
She saw slow Philips creep like Tate's poor page,
And all the mighty mad in Dennis rage.
　　In each she marks her image full express'd,
But chief in Bays's monster-breeding breast;
Bays, form'd by Nature stage and town to bless,
And act, and be, a coxcomb with success.
Dulness with transport eyes the lively dunce,
Rememb'ring she herself was Pertness once.
Now (shame to Fortune!) an ill run at play
Blank'd his bold visage, and a thin third day:
Swearing and supperless the hero sate,
Blasphemed his gods, the dice, and damn'd his fate.
Then gnaw'd his pen, then dash'd it on the ground,
Sinking from thought to thought, a vast profound!
Plunged for his sense, but found no bottom there,
Yet wrote and founder'd on, in mere despair.
Round him much embryo, much abortion lay,
Much future ode, and abdicated play;
Nonsense precipitate, like running lead,
That slipp'd through cracks and zig-zags of the head;
All that on Folly Frenzy could beget,
Fruits of dull heat, and sooterkins of wit.
Next, o'er his books his eyes began to roll,
In pleasing memory of all he stole,
How here he sipped, how there he plundered snug,
And sucked all o'er, like an industrious bug.
Here lay poor Fletcher's half-eat scenes, and here
The frippery of crucified Molière;
There hapless Shakespeare, yet of Tibbald sore,
Wished he had blotted for himself before.
The rest on outside merit but presume,
Or serve (like other fools) to fill a room;

Such with their shelves as due proportion hold,
Or their fond parents dressed in red and gold;
Or where the pictures for the page atone,
And Quarles is saved by beauties not his own.
Here swells the shelf with Ogilby the great;
There, stamped with arms, Newcastle shines complete:
Here all his suff'ring brotherhood retire,
And 'scape the martyrdom of jakes and fire:
A Gothic library! of Greece and Rome
Well purged, and worthy Settle, Banks, and Broome.
    But, high above, more solid learning shone,
The classics of an age that heard of none;
There Caxton slept, with Wynkyn at his side,
One clasped in wood, and one in strong cow-hide.
There saved by spice, like mummies, many a year,
Dry bodies of divinity appear;
De Lyra there a dreadful front extends,
And here the groaning shelves Philemon bends.
    Of these, twelve volumes, twelve of amplest size,
Redeemed from tapers and defrauded pies,
Inspired he seizes; these are altar raise;
An hecatomb of pure unsullied lays
That altar crowns; a folio common-place
Founds the whole pile, of all his works the base;
Quartos, octavos, shape the less'ning pyre;
A twisted birthday ode completes the spire.
    Then he: 'Great tamer of all human art!
First in my care, and ever at my heart;
Dulness! whose good old cause I yet defend,
With whom my muse began, with whom shall end,
E'er since Sir Fopling's periwig was praise,
To the last honours of the Butt and Bays;
O thou! of bus'ness the directing soul!
To this our head like bias to the bowl,
Which, as more pond'rous, made its aim more true,
Obliquely waddling to the mark in view:
O! ever gracious to perplexed mankind,
Still spread a healing mist before the mind;
And, lest we err by wit's wild dancing light,
Secure us kindly in our native night.
Or, if to wit a coxcomb make pretence,
Guard the sure barrier between that and sense;
Or quite unravel all the reas'ning thread,
And hang some curious cobweb in its stead!

As, forced from wind-guns, lead itself can fly,
And pond'rous slugs cut swiftly through the sky;
As clocks to weight their nimble motion owe,
The wheels above urged by the load below:
Me emptiness and dulness could inspire,
And were my elasticity and fire.
Some demon stole my pen (forgive the offence)
And once betrayed me into common sense:
Else all my prose and verse were much the same;
This prose on stilts, that poetry fall'n lame.
Did on the stage my fops appear confined?
My life gave ampler lessons to mankind.
Did the dead letter unsuccessful prove?
The brisk example never failed to move.
Yet sure had Heav'n decreed to save the state,
Heav'n had decreed these works a longer date.
Could Troy be saved by any single hand,
This grey-goose weapon must have made her stand.
What can I now? my Fletcher cast aside,
Take up the Bible, once my better guide?
Or tread the path by vent'rous heroes trod,
This box my thunder, this right hand my God?
Or chaired at White's amidst the doctors sit,
Teach oaths to gamesters, and to nobles wit?
Or bidst thou rather party to embrace?
(A friend to party thou, and all her race;
'Tis the same rope at different ends they twist;
To dulness Ridpath is as dear as Mist.)
Shall I, like Curtius, desp'rate in my zeal,
O'er head and ears plunge for the commonweal?
Or rob Rome's ancient geese of all their glories,
And cackling save the monarchy of Tories?
Hold—to the minister I more incline;
To serve his cause, O queen! is serving thine.
And see! thy very gazetteers give o'er,
Even Ralph repents, and Henley writes no more.
What then remains? Ourself. Still, still remain
Cibberian forehead, and Cibberian brain.
This brazen brightness, to the squire so dear;
This polished hardness, that reflects the peer:
This arch absurd, that wit and fool delights;
This mess, tossed up of Hockley-hole and White's;
Where dukes and butchers join to wreathe my crown,
At once the bear and fiddle of the town.

'O born in sin, and forth in folly brought!
Works damned, or to be damned! (your father's fault)
Go, purified by flames ascend the sky,
My better and more Christian progeny!
Unstained, untouched, and yet in maiden sheets;
While all your smutty sisters walk the streets.
Ye shall not beg, like gratis-given Bland,
Sent with a pass, and vagrant through the land;
Not sail with Ward, to ape-and-monkey climes,
Where vile Mundungus trucks for viler rhymes:
Not sulphur-tipt, emblaze an ale-house fire;
Not wrap up oranges, to pelt your sire!
O! pass more innocent, in infant state,
To the mild limbo of our father Tate:
Or peaceably forgot, at one be blest
In Shadwell's bosom with eternal rest!
Soon to that mass of nonsense to return,
Where things destroyed are swept to things unborn.'
    With that, a tear (portentous sign of grace!)
Stole from the master of the seven-fold face;
And thrice he lifted high the birthday brand,
And thrice he dropt it from his quiv'ring hand;
Then lights the structure, with averted eyes:
The rolling smokes involve the sacrifice.
The opening clouds disclose each work by turns;
Now flames the Cid, and now Perolla burns;
Great Cæsar roars, and hisses in the fires;
King John in silence modestly expires;
No merit now the dear Nonjuror claims,
Molière's old stubble in a moment flames.
Tears gushed again, as from pale Priam's eyes
When the last blaze sent Ilion to the skies.
    Roused by the light, old Dulness heaved the head,
Then snatched a sheet of Thulé from her bed;
Sudden she flies, and whelms it o'er the pyre;
Down sink the flames, and with a hiss expire.
    Her ample presence fills up all the place;
A veil of fogs dilates her awful face:
Great in her charms! as when on shrieves and may'rs
She looks, and breathes herself into their airs.
She bids him wait her to her sacred dome:
Well pleased he entered, and confessed his home.
So spirits ending their terrestrial race
Ascend, and recognise their native place.

This the great mother dearer held than all
The clubs of Quidnuncs, or her own Guildhall:
Here stood her opium, here she nursed her owls,
And here she planned th' imperial seat of fools.

Here to her chosen all her works she shows;
Prose swelled to verse, verse loit'ring into prose:
How random thoughts now meaning chance to find,
Now leave all memory of sense behind;
How prologues into prefaces decay,
And these to notes are frittered quite away.
How index-learning turns no student pale,
Yet holds the eel of science by the tail:
How, with less reading than makes felons scape,
Less human genius than God gives an ape,
Small thanks to France, and none to Rome or Greece,
A past, vamped, future, old, revived, new piece,
'Twixt Plautus, Fletcher, Shakespeare and Corneille,
Can make a Cibber, Tibbald, or Ozell.

The Goddess then, o'er his annointed head,
With mystic words, the sacred opium shed.
And lo! her bird (a monster of a fowl,
Something betwixt a Heideggre and owl)
Perched on his crown. 'All hail! and hail again,
My son: the promised land expect thy reign.
Know, Eusden thirsts no more for sack or praise;
He sleeps among the dull of ancient days;
Safe, where no critics damn, no duns molest,
Where wretched Withers, Ward, and Gildon rest,
And high-born Howard, more majestic sire,
With 'Fool of Quality' completes the quire.
Thou, Cibber! thou, his laurel shalt support,
Folly, my son, has still a friend at court.
Lift up your gates, ye princes, see him come!
Sound, sound, ye viols; be the cat-call dumb!
Bring, bring the madding bay, the drunken vine;
The creeping, dirty, courtly ivy join.
And thou! his aide-de-camp, lead on my sons,
Light-armed with points, antitheses, and puns.
Let Bawdry, Billingsgate, my daughters dear,
Support his front, and oaths bring up the rear:
And under his, and under Archer's wing,
Gaming and Grub Street skulk behind the king.

'O! when shall rise a monarch all our own,
And I, a nursing-mother, rock the throne;

'Twixt prince and people close the curtain draw,
Shade him from light, and cover him from law;
Fatten the courtier, starve the learned band,
And suckle armies, and dry-nurse the land:
Till senates nod to lullabies divine,
And all be sleep, as at an ode of thine.'
She ceased. Then swells the chapel-royal throat:
'God save King Cibber!' mounts in every note.
Familiar White's, 'God save King Colley!' cries;
'God save King Colley!' Drury Lane replies:
To Needham's quick the voice triumphal rode,
But pious Needham dropt the name of God:
Back to the Devil the last echoes roll,
And 'Coll!' each butcher roars at Hockley Hole.
So when Jove's block descended from on high
(As sings thy great forefather Ogilby)
Loud thunder to its bottom shook the bog,
And the hoarse nation croaked, 'God save King Log!'

Book II

ARGUMENT

The king being proclaimed, the solemnity is graced with public games and sports of various kinds; not instituted by the hero, as by Æneas in Virgil, but for greater honour by the goddess in person (in like manner as the games Pythia, Isthmia, etc., were anciently said to be ordained by the gods, and as Thetis herself appearing, according to Homer, *Odyss.* xxiv., proposed the prizes in honour of her son Achilles). Hither flock the poets and critics, attended, as is but just, with their patrons and booksellers. The goddess is first pleased, for her disport, to propose games to the booksellers, and setteth up the phantom of a poet, which they contend to overtake. The races described, with their divers accidents. Next, the game for a poetess. Then follow the exercises for the poets, of tickling, vociferating, diving: The first holds forth the arts and practices of dedicators, the second of disputants and fustian poets, the third of profound, dark, and dirty party-writers. Lastly, for the critics, the goddess proposes (with great propriety) an exercise, not of their parts, but their patience, in hearing the works of two voluminous authors, one in verse and the other in prose, deliberately read without sleeping. The various effects of which, with the several degrees and manners of their operation, are here set forth; till the whole number, not of critics only, but of spectators, actors, and all present, fall asleep; which naturally and necessarily ends the games.

This labour passed, by Bridewell all descend,
(As morning pray'r and flagellation end)
To where Fleet-ditch with disemboguing streams
Rolls the large tribute of dead dogs to Thames,
The king of dykes! than whom no sluice of mud
With deeper sable blots the silver flood.
'Here strip, my children! here at once leap in,
Here prove who best can dash through thick and thin,
And who the most in love of dirt excel,
Or dark dexterity of groping well.
Who flings most filth, and wide pollutes around
The stream, be his the weekly journals bound;
A pig of lead to him who dives the best;
A peck of coals a-piece shall glad the rest.'
  In naked majesty Oldmixon stands,
And Milo-like surveys his arms and hands;
Then, sighing, thus, 'And am I now three-score?
Ah why, ye gods, should two and two make four?'
He said, and climbed a stranded lighter's height,
Shot to the black abyss, and plunged downright.
The senior's judgment all the crowd admire,
Who but to sink the deeper, rose the higher.
  Next Smedley dived, slow circles dimpled o'er
The quaking mud, that closed, and oped no more.
All look, all sigh, and call on Smedley lost;
'Smedley' in vain resounds through all the coast.
  Then essayed; scarce vanished out of sight,
He buoys up instant, and returns to light:
He bears no token of the sabler streams,
And mounts far off among the swans of Thames.
  True to the bottom see Concanen creep,
A cold, long-winded native of the deep;
If perseverance gain the diver's prize,
Not everlasting Blackmore this denies;
No noise, no stir, no motion canst thou make,
Th' unconscious stream sleep o'er thee like a lake.
  Next plunged a feeble, but a desp'rate pack,
With each a sickly brother at his back:
Sons of a day! just buoyant on the flood,
Then numbered with the puppies in the mud.
Ask ye their names? I could as soon disclose
The names of these blind puppies as of those.
Fast by, like Niobe, (her children gone)
Sits mother Osborne, stupefied to stone!

And monumental brass this record bears,
'These are,—ah no! these were, the gazetteers!'
  Not so bold Arnall; with a weight of skull,
Furious he dives, precipitately dull.
Whirlpools and storms his circling arm invest.
With all the might of gravitation blest.
No crab more active in the dirty dance,
Downward to climb, and backward to advance.
He brings up half the bottom on his head,
And loudly claims the journals and the lead.
  The plunging prelate, and his pond'rous grace,
With holy envy gave one layman place.
When lo! a burst of thunder shook the flood;
Slow rose a form, in majesty of mud;
Shaking the horrors of his sable brows,
And each ferocious feature grim with ooze.
Greater he looks, and more than mortal stares;
Then thus the wonders of the deep declares.
  First he relates, how sinking to the chin,
Smit with his mien the mud-nymphs sucked him in:
How young Lutetia, softer than the down,
Nigrina black, and Merdamante brown,
Vied for his love in jetty bowers below,
As Hylas fair was ravished long ago.
Then sung, how shown him by the nut-brown maids
A branch of Styx here rises from the shades,
That tinctured as it runs with Lethe's streams,
And wafting vapours from the land of dreams,
(As under seas Alpheus' secret sluice
Bears Pisa's off'rings to his Arethuse)
Pours into Thames: and hence the mingled wave
Intoxicates the pert, and lulls the grave:
Here brisker vapours o'er the temple creep,
There, all from Paul's to Aldgate drink and sleep.
  Thence to the banks where rev'rend bards repose,
They led him soft; each rev'rend bard arose;
And Milbourn chief, deputed by the rest,
Gave him the cassock, surcingle, and vest.
'Receive' (he said) 'these robes which once were mine,
Dulness is sacred in a sound divine.'
  'Proceed, great days! till learning fly the shore,
Till birch shall blush with noble blood no more,
Till Thames see Eton's sons for ever play,
Till Westminster's whole year be holiday,

Till Isis' elders reel, their pupils' sport,
And Alma Mater lie dissolved in port!'
  'Enough! enough!' the raptured monarch cries;
And through the iv'ry gate the vision flies.

Epistle to Dr. Arbuthnot

Neque sermonibus vulgi dederis te, nec in præmiis humanis spem posueris rerum tuarum; suis te oportet illecebris ipsa virtus trahat ad verum decus. Quid de te alii loquantur, ipsi videant, sed loquentur tamen.—CICERO.

[And do not yield yourself up to the speeches of the vulgar, nor in your affairs place hope in human rewards: virtue ought to draw you to true glory by its own allurements. Why should others speak of you? Let them study themselves—yet they will speak.]

ADVERTISEMENT

This paper is a sort of bill of complaint, begun many years since, and drawn up by snatches, as the several occasions offered. I had no thoughts of publishing it, till it pleased some persons of rank and fortune (the authors of *Verses to the Imitator of Horace*, and of an *Epistle to a Doctor of Divinity from a Nobleman at Hampton Court*) to attack, in a very extraordinary manner, not only my writings (of which, being public, the public is judge), but my person, morals, and family, whereof, to those who know me not, a truer information may be requisite. Being divided between the necessity to say something of myself and my own laziness to undertake so awkward a task, I thought it the shortest way to put the last hand to this Epistle. If it have anything pleasing, it will be that by which I am most desirous to please, the truth and the sentiment; and if anything offensive, it will be only to those I am least sorry to offend, the vicious or the ungenerous.

Many will know their own pictures in it, there being not a circumstance but what is true; but I have for the most part spared their names, and they may escape being laughed at if they please.

I would have some of them know it was owing to the request of the learned and candid friend to whom it is inscribed that I make not as free use of theirs as they have done of mine. However, I shall have this advantage and honour on my side, that whereas, by their proceeding, any abuse may be directed at any man, no injury can possibly be done by mine, since a nameless character can never be found out but by its truth and likeness.

    P. SHUT, shut the door, good John! fatigued, I said;
    Tie up the knocker, say I'm sick, I'm dead.
    The Dog-star rages! nay 'tis past a doubt,
    All Bedlam, or Parnassus, is let out:
    Fire in each eye, and papers in each hand,
    They rave, recite, and madden round the land.

What walls can guard me, or what shades can hide?
They pierce my thickets, through my grot they glide,
By land, by water, they renew the charge,
They stop the chariot, and they board the barge.
No place is sacred, not the church is free,
Ev'n Sunday shines no Sabbath-day to me:
Then from the Mint walks forth the man of rhyme,
Happy! to catch me, just at dinner-time.

Is there a parson, much bemused in beer,
A maudlin poetess, a rhyming peer,
A clerk, foredoom'd his father's soul to cross,
Who pens a stanza, when he should engross?
Is there, who, lock'd from ink and paper, scrawls
With desperate charcoal round his darken'd walls?
All fly to Twit'nam, and in humble strain
Apply to me, to keep them made or vain.
Arthur, whose giddy son neglects the laws,
Imputes to me and my damn'd works the cause:
Poor Cornus sees his frantic wife elope,
And curses wit, and poetry, and Pope.

Friend to my life! (which did not you prolong,
The world had wanted many an idle song)
What drop or nostrum can this plague remove?
Or which must end me, a fool's wrath or love?
A dire dilemma! either way I'm sped,
If foes, they write, if friends, they read me dead.
Seized and tied down to judge, how wretched I!
Who can't be silent, and who will not lie:
To laugh, were want of goodness and of grace,
And to be grave, exceeds all power of face.
I sit with sad civility, I read
With honest anguish, and an aching head;
And drop at last, but in unwilling ears,
This saving counsel,—'Keep your piece nine years.'

'Nine years!' cries he, who, high in Drury Lane,
Lull'd by soft zephyrs through the broken pane,
Rhymes ere he wakes, and prints before Term ends,
Obliged by hunger, and request of friends:
'The piece, you think, is incorrect? why take it,
I'm all submission; what you'd have it, make it.'

Three things another's modest wishes bound,
My friendship, and a prologue, and ten pound.

Pitholeon sends to me: 'You know his grace,
I want a patron; ask him for a place.'

Pitholeon libell'd me—'But here's a letter
Informs you, Sir, 'twas when he knew no better.
Dare you refuse him? Curll invites to dine,
He'll write a journal, or he'll turn divine.'
Bless me! a packet. ''Tis a strange sues,
A virgin tragedy, an orphan Muse.'
If I dislike it, 'Furies, death and rage!'
If I approve, 'Commend it to the stage.'
There (thank my stars) my whole commission ends,
The players and I are, luckily, no friends;
Fired that the house reject him, ''Sdeath! I'll print it,
And shame the fools—Your interest, Sir, with Lintot.'
Lintot, dull rogue! will think your price too much:
'Not, Sir, if you revise it, and retouch.'
All my demurs but double his attacks:
And last he whispers, 'Do; and we go snacks.'
Glad of a quarrel, straight I clap the door:
Sir, let me see your works and you no more.

'Tis sung, when Midas' ears began to spring
(Midas, a sacred person and a king),
His very minister who spied them first
(Some say his queen) was forced to speak or burst:
And is not mine, my friend, a sorer case,
When every coxcomb perks them in my face!

    A. Good friend, forbear! you deal in dangerous things,
I'd never name queens, ministers, or kings:
Keep close to ears, and those let asses prick,
'Tis nothing——*P*. Nothing? if they bite and kick?
Out with it, DUNCIAD! let the secret pass,
That secret to each fool, that he's an ass:
The truth once told (and wherefore should we lie?)
The Queen of Midas slept, and so may I.

    You think this cruel? Take it for a rule,
No creature smarts so little as a fool.
Let peals of laughter, Codrus! round thee break,
Thou unconcerned canst hear the mighty crack:
Pit, box, and gallery in convulsions hurl'd,
Thou stand'st unshook amidst a bursting world.
Who shames a scribbler? break one cobweb through,
He spins the slight, self-pleasing thread anew:
Destroy his fib or sophistry, in vain,
The creature's at his dirty work again,
Throned in the centre of his thin designs,
Proud of a vast extent of flimsy lines!

Whom have I hurt? has poet yet, or peer,
Lost the arch'd eyebrow, or Parnassian sneer?
And has not Colley still his lord, and whore?
His butchers Henley, his Freemasons Moore?
Does not one table Bavius still admit?
Still to one bishop Philips seem a wit?
Still Sappho——*A.* Hold! for God's sake—you'll offend:
No names—be calm—learn prudence of a friend.
I too could write, and I am twice as tall;
But foes like these——*P.* One flatterer's worse than all.
Of all mad creatures, if the learn'd are right,
It is the slaver kills, and not the bite.
A fool quite angry is quite innocent:
Alas! 'tis ten times worse when they repent.

  One dedicates in high heroic prose,
And ridicules beyond a hundred foes:
One from all Grub Street will my fame defend,
And, more abusive, calls himself my friend.
This prints my letters, that expects a bribe,
And others roar aloud, 'Subscribe, subscribe!'

  There are, who to my person pay their court:
I cough like Horace, and, though lean, am short.
Ammon's great son one shoulder had too high—
Such Ovid's nose,—and, 'Sir! you have an eye.'
Go on, obliging creatures, make me see
All that disgraced my betters met in me.
Say, for my comfort, languishing in bed,
'Just so immortal Maro held his head';
And, when I die, be sure you let me know
Great Homer died three thousand years ago.
Why did I write? what sin to me unknown
Dipp'd me in ink, my parents', or my own?
As yet a child, nor yet a fool to fame,
I lisp'd in numbers, for the numbers came.
I left no calling for this idle trade,
No duty broke, no father disobey'd:
The Muse but served to ease some friend, not wife,
To help me through this long disease, my life;
To second, ARBUTHNOT! thy art and care,
And teach the being you preserved to bear.

  But why then publish? Granville the polite,
And knowing Walsh, would tell me I could write;
Well-natured Garth inflamed with early praise,
And Congreve loved, and Swift endured my lays;

The courtly Talbot, Somers, Sheffield read,
Even mitred Rochester would nod the head,
And St. John's self (great Dryden's friend before)
With open arms received one poet more.
Happy my studies, when by these approved!
Happier their author, when by these beloved!
From these the world will judge of men and books,
Not from the Burnets, Oldmixons, and Cookes.

Soft were my numbers; who could take offence
While pure description held the place of sense?
Like gentle Fanny's was my flowery theme,
A painted mistress, or a purling stream.
Yet then did Gildon draw his venal quill;
I wish'd the man a dinner, and sate still.
Yet then did Dennis rave in furious fret;
I never answer'd—I was not in debt.
If want provoked, or madness made them print,
I waged no war with Bedlam or the Mint.

Did some more sober critic come abroad—
If wrong, I smiled; if right, I kiss'd the rod.
Pains, reading, study, are their just pretence,
And all they want is spirit, taste, and sense.
Commas and points they set exactly right,
And 'twere a sin to rob them of their mite;
Yet ne'er one sprig of laurel graced these ribalds,
From slashing Bentley down to piddling Tibbalds:
Each wight, who reads not, and but scans and spells,
Each word-catcher, that lives on syllables,
Even such small critics, some regard may claim,
Preserved in Milton's or in Shakespeare's name.
Pretty! in amber to observe the forms
Of hairs, or straws, or dirt, or grubs, or worms!
The things, we know, are neither rich nor rare,
But wonder how the devil they got there.

Were others angry—I excused them too;
Well might they rage, I gave them but their due.
A man's true merit 'tis not hard to find;
But each man's secret standard in his mind,
That casting-weight pride adds to emptiness,
This, who can gratify, for who can guess?
The bard whom pilfer'd Pastorals renown,
Who turns a Persian tale for half-a-crown,
Just writes to make his barrenness appear,
And strains from hard-bound brains, eight lines a-year;

He, who still wanting, though he lives on theft,
Steals much, spends little, yet has nothing left:
And he, who now to sense, now nonsense leaning,
Means not, but blunders round about a meaning:
And he, whose fustians' so sublimely bad,
It is not poetry, but prose run mad:
All these, my modest satire bade translate,
And own'd that nine such poets made a Tate.
How did they fume, and stamp, and roar, and chafe!
And swear, not Addison himself was safe.

Peace to all such! but were there one whose fires
True genius kindles, and fair fame inspires;
Blest with each talent, and each art to please,
And born to write, converse, and live with ease;
Should such a man, too fond to rule alone,
Bear, like the Turk, no brother near the throne,
View him with scornful, yet with jealous eyes,
And hate for arts that caused himself to rise;
Damn with faint praise, assent with civil leer,
And, without sneering, teach the rest to sneer;
Willing to wound, and yet afraid to strike,
Just hint a fault, and hesitate dislike;
Alike reserved to blame, or to commend,
A timorous foe, and a suspicious friend;
Dreading e'en fools, by flatterers besieged,
And so obliging, that he ne'er obliged;
Like Cato, give his little senate laws,
And sit attentive to his own applause;
While wits and Templars every sentence raise,
And wonder with a foolish face of praise—
Who but must laugh, if such a man there be?
Who would not weep, if Atticus were he?

What though my name stood rubric on the walls,
Or plaster'd posts, with claps, in capitals?
Or smoking forth, a hundred hawkers load,
On wings of winds came flying all abroad?
I sought no homage from the race that write;
I kept, like Asian monarchs, from their sight:
Poems I heeded (now be rhym'd so long)
No more than thou, great George! a birthday song.
I ne'er with wits or witlings pass'd my days,
To spread about the itch of verse and praise;
Nor like a puppy, daggled through the town,
To fetch and carry, sing-song up and down;

Nor at rehearsals sweat, and mouth'd, and cried,
With handkerchief and orange at my side;
But sick of fops, and poetry, and prate,
To Bufo left the whole Castalian state.
  Proud as Apollo on his forked hill,
Sate full-blown Bufo, puff'd by every quill;
Fed with soft dedication all day long,
Horace and he went hand in hand in song.
His library (where busts of poets dead
And a true Pindar stood without a head)
Received of wits an undistinguish'd race,
Who first his judgment asked, and then a place:
Much they extoll'd his pictures, much his seat,
And flatter'd every day, and some days eat:
Till grown more frugal in his riper days,
He paid some bards with port, and some with praise,
To some a dry rehearsal was assign'd,
And others (harder still) he paid in kind.
Dryden alone (what wonder?) came not nigh,
Dryden alone escaped this judging eye:
But still the great have kindness in reserve,
He help'd to bury whom he help'd to starve.
  May some choice patron bless each grey goose quill!
May every Bavius have his Bufo still!
So when a statesman wants a day's defence,
Or Envy holds a whole week's war with Sense,
Or simple pride for flattery makes demands,
May dunce by dunce be whistled off my hands!
Bless'd be the great! for those they take away,
And those they left me—for they left me GAY;
Left me to see neglected Genius bloom,
Neglected die, and tell it on his tomb:
Of all thy blameless life the sole return
My verse, and QUEENSBERRY weeping o'er thy urn!
  Oh let me live my own, and die so too!
(To live and die is all I have to do:)
Maintain a poet's dignity and ease,
And see what friends, and read what books I please:
Above a patron, though I condescend
Sometimes to call a minister my friend.
I was not born for courts or great affairs:
I pay my debts, believe, and say my prayers;
Can sleep without a poem in my head,
Nor know if Dennis be alive or dead.

Why am I ask'd what next shall see the light?
Heavens! was I born for nothing but to write?
Has life no joys for me? or (to be grave)
Have I no friend to serve, no soul to save?
'I found him close with Swift—Indeed? no doubt
(Cries prating Balbus) something will come out.'
'Tis all in vain, deny it as I will:
'No, such a genius never can lie still';
And then for mine obligingly mistakes
The first lampoon Sir Will or Bubo makes.
Poor guiltless I! and can I choose but smile,
When every coxcomb knows me by my style?

Cursed be the verse, how well soe'er it flow,
That tends to make one worthy man my foe,
Give Virtue scandal, Innocence a fear,
Or from the soft-eyed virgin steal a tear!
But he who hurts a harmless neighbour's peace,
Insults fall'n worth, or beauty in distress,
Who loves a lie, lame slander helps about,
Who writes a libel, or who copies out;
That fop, whose pride affects a patron's name,
Yet absent, wounds an author's honest fame;
Who can your merit selfishly approve,
And show the sense of it without the love;
Who has the vanity to call you friend,
Yet wants the honour, injured, to defend;
Who tells whate'er you think, whate'er you say,
And if he lie not, must at least betray;
Who to the dean and silver bell can swear,
And sees at Canons what was never there;
Who reads, but with a lust to misapply,
Makes satire a lampoon, and fiction lie;
A lash like mine no honest man shall dread,
But all such babbling blockheads in his stead.

Let Sporus tremble——*A.* What? that thing of silk,
Sporus, that mere white curd of ass's milk?
Satire or sense, alas! can Sporus feel,
Who breaks a butterfly upon a wheel?

P. Yet let me flap this bug with gilded wings,
This painted child of dirt, that stinks and stings;
Whose buzz the witty and the fair annoys,
Yet wit ne'er tastes, and beauty ne'er enjoys:
So well-bred spaniels civilly delight
In mumbling of the game they dare not bite.

Eternal smiles his emptiness betray,
As shallow streams run dimpling all the way,
Whether in florid impotence he speaks,
And, as the prompter breathes, the puppet squeaks;
Or at the ear of Eve, familiar toad!
Half froth, half venom, spits himself abroad,
In puns, or politics, or tales, or lies,
Or spite, or smut, or rhymes, or blasphemies.
His wit all see-saw, between that and this,
Now high, now low, now master up, now miss,
And he himself one vile antithesis.
Amphibious thing! that acting either part,
The trifling head, or the corrupted heart;
Fop at the toilet, flatterer at the board,
Now trips a lady, and now struts a lord.
Eve's tempter thus the Rabbins have express'd,
A cherub's face, a reptile all the rest.
Beauty that shocks you, parts that none will trust,
Wit that can creep, and pride that licks the dust.

   Not Fortune's worshipper, nor Fashion's fool,
Not Lucre's madman, nor Ambition's tool,
Not proud, nor servile; be one poet's praise,
That, if he pleased, he pleased by manly ways:
That flattery, even to kings, he held a shame,
And thought a lie in verse or prose the same;
That not in Fancy's maze he wander'd long,
But stoop'd to Truth, and moralised his song:
That not for Fame, but Virtue's better end,
He stood the furious foe, the timid friend,
The damning critic, half-approving wit,
The coxcomb hit, or fearing to be hit;
Laughed at the loss of friends he never had,
The dull, the proud, the wicked, and the mad;
The distant threats of vengeance on his head,
The blow unfelt, the tear he never shed;
The tale revived, the lie so oft o'erthrown,
Th' imputed trash, and dulness not his own;
The morals blacken'd when the writings 'scape,
The libell'd person, and the pictured shape;
Abuse, on all he loved, or loved him, spread,
A friend in exile, or a father dead;
The whisper, that to greatness still too near,
Perhaps yet vibrates on his sovereign's ear—
Welcome for thee, fair Virtue! all the past:

For thee, fair Virtue! welcome even the last!
    A. But why insult the poor, affront the great?
    P. A knave's a knave, to me, in every state;
Alike my scorn, if he succeed or fail,
Sporus at court, or Japhet in a jail,
A hireling scribbler, or a hireling peer,
Knight of the post corrupt, or of the shire;
If on a pillory, or near a throne,
He gain his prince's ear, or lose his own.
    Yet soft by nature, more a dupe than wit,
Sappho can tell you how this man was bit:
This dreaded satirist Dennis will confess
Foe to his pride, but friend to his distress:
So humble, he has knocked at Tibbald's door,
Has drunk with Cibber, nay has rhymed for Moore.
Full ten years slander'd, did he once reply?
Three thousand suns went down on Welsted's lie;
To please a mistress one aspersed his life;
He lash'd him not, but let her be his wife:
Let Budgell charge low Grub Street on his quill,
And write whate'er he pleased, except his will;
Let the two Curlls of town and court abuse
His father, mother, body, soul, and Muse.
Yet why? that father held it for a rule,
It was a sin to call our neighbour fool:
That harmless mother thought no wife a whore:
Hear this, and spare his family, James Moore!
Unspotted names, and memorable long!
If there be force in virtue, or in song.
    Of gentle blood (part shed in honour's cause,
While yet in Britain honour had applause)
Each parent sprung—*A.* What fortune, pray?—*P.* Their own,
And better got, than Bestia's from the throne.
Born to no pride, inheriting no strife,
Nor marrying discord in a noble wife,
Stranger to civil and religious rage,
The good man walk'd innoxious through his age.
No courts he saw, no suits would ever try,
Nor dared an oath, nor hazarded a lie.
Unlearn'd, he knew no schoolman's subtle art,
No language, but the language of the heart.
By nature honest, by experience wise,
Healthy by temperance, and by exercise,
His life, though long, to sickness pass'd unknown,

His death was instant, and without a groan.
O grant me thus to live, and thus to die!
Who sprung from kings shall know less joy than I.
   O friend! may each domestic bliss be thine!
Be no unpleasing melancholy mine:
Me, let the tender office long engage,
To rock the cradle of reposing age,
With lenient arts extend a mother' breath,
Make languour smile, and smooth the bed of death.
Explore the thought, explain the asking eye,
And keep awhile one parent from the sky!
On cares like these if length of days attend,
May Heaven, to bless those days, preserve my friend,
Preserve him social, cheerful, and serene,
And just as rich as when he served a queen.
   A. Whether that blessing be denied or given,
Thus far was right, the rest belongs to Heaven.

JOHN BYROM

1692–1763

The Nimmers

Two foot-companions once in deep discourse—
'Tom,' says the one, 'Let's go and steal a horse.'
'Steal!' says the other, in a huge surprise,
'He that says I'm a thief, I say he lies.'
'Well, well,' replied his friend, 'No such affront;
I did but ask ye: if you won't, you won't.'
So they jogged on, till, in another strain,
The querist moved to honest Tom again.
'Suppose,' says he; 'for supposition's sake—
'Tis but a supposition that I make!—
Suppose that we should filch a horse, I say?'
'Filch? filch?' quoth Tom, demurring by the way;
'That's not so bad as downright theft, I own;
But—yet—methinks—'twere better let alone.
It soundeth something pitiful, and low;
Shall we go filch a horse, you say? why, no;
I'll filch no filching; and I'll tell no lie;
Honesty's the best policy, say I!'

Struck with such vast integrity quite dumb,
His comrade paused; at last, says he, 'Come, come!
Thou art an honest fellow, I agree—
Honest and poor; alas! that should not be,
And dry into the bargain, and no drink!
Shall we go nim a horse, Tom?—What dost think?'

How clear are things when liquor's in the case!
Tom answers quick, with casuistic grace:
'Nim? Yes, yes, yes, let's nim with all my heart;
I see no harm in nimming, for my part.
Hard is the case, now I look sharp into 't,
That honesty should trudge i' th' dirt afoot;
So many empty horses round about,
That honesty should wear its bottoms out!
Besides, shall honesty be choked with thirst?
Were it my Lord Mayor's horse, I'd nim it first!
And, by the by, my lad, no scrubby tit!
There is the best that ever wore a bit
Not far from hence.' 'I take ye,' quoth his friend,
'Is not yon stable, Tom, our journey's end?'
    Good wits will jump; both meant the very steed,
The top o' th' country, both for shape and speed.
So to 't they went, and with a halter round
His feathered neck, they nimmed him off the ground.
    And now, good people, we should next relate
Of these adventurers the luckless fate.
Poor Tom!—but here the sequel is to seek,
Not being yet translated from the Greek.
Some say, that Tom would honestly have peached,
But by his blabbing friend was over-reached;
Others insist upon 't that both the elves
Were, in like manner, halter-nimmed themselves.

It matters not:—the Moral is the thing,
For which our purpose, neighbours, was to sing.
If it should hit some few amongst the throng,
Let 'em not lay the fault upon the song!
Fair warning, all: He that has got a cap
Now put it on, or else beware a rap!
'Tis but a short one, it is true, but yet
Has a long reach with it, *videlicet*:
'Twixt right and wrong, how many gentle trimmers
Will neither steal nor filch, but will be plaguy nimmers.

Desiderium

My spirit longeth for Thee,
  Within my troubled breast;
Although I be unworthy
  Of so divine a Guest.

Of so divine a Guest,
  Unworthy though I be;
Yet has my heart no rest,
  Unless it come from Thee.

Unless it come from Thee,
  In vain I look around;
In all that I can see,
  No rest is to be found.

No rest is to be found,
  But in Thy blessèd love;
O! let my wish be crowned,
  And send it from above!

HENRY CAREY

?1693–1743

Sally in Our Alley

Of all the girls that are so smart
  There's none like pretty Sally;
She is the darling of my heart,
  And she lives in our alley.
There is no lady in the land
  Is half so sweet as Sally;
She is the darling of my heart,
  And she lives in our alley.

Her father he makes cabbage-nets,
  And through the streets does cry 'em;
Her mother she sells laces long
  To such as please to buy 'em:

But sure such folks could ne'er beget
 So sweet a girl as Sally!
She is the darling of my heart,
 And she lives in our alley.

When she is by, I leave my work,
 I love her so sincerely;
My master comes like any Turk,
 And bangs me most severely:
But let him bang his bellyful,
 I'll bear it all for Sally;
She is the darling of my heart,
 And she lives in our alley.

Of all the days that's in the week
 I dearly love but one day—
And that's the day that comes betwixt
 A Saturday and Monday;
For then I'm dressed all in my best
 To walk abroad with Sally;
She is the darling of my heart,
 And she lives in our alley.

My master carries me to church,
 And often am I blamèd
Because I leave him in the lurch
 As soon as text is namèd;
I leave the church in sermon-time
 And slink away to Sally;
She is the darling of my heart,
 And she lives in our alley.

When Christmas comes about again,
 O, then I shall have money;
I'll hoard it up, and box it all,
 I'll give it to my honey:
I would it were ten thousand pound,
 I'd give it all to Sally;
She is the darling of my heart,
 And she lives in our alley.

My master and the neighbours all
  Make game of me and Sally,
And, but for her, I'd better be
  A slave and row a galley;
But when my seven long years are out,
  O, then I'll marry Sally;
Oh, then we'll wed, and then we'll bed—
  But not in our alley!

MATTHEW GREEN

1696–1737

from *The Spleen*

WHEN by its magic lantern Spleen
With frightful figures spread life's scene,
And threat'ning prospects urg'd my fears,
A stranger to the luck of heirs;
Reason, some quiet to restore,
Show'd part was substance, shadow more;
With Spleen's dead weight tho' heavy grown
In life's rough tide I sunk not down,
But swam, 'till Fortune threw a rope,
Buoyant on bladders fill'd with hope.

I always choose the plainest food
To mend viscidity of blood.
Hail! water-gruel, healing pow'r,
Of easy access to the poor;
Thy help love's confessors implore,
And doctors secretly adore;
To thee I fly, by thee dilute—
Through veins my blood does quicker shoot,
And by swift currents throws off clean
Prolific particles of Spleen.

I never sick by drinking grow,
Nor keep myself a cup too low,
And seldom Chloe's lodgings haunt,
Thirsty of spirits which I want.

Hunting I reckon very good
To brace the nerves, and stir the blood:
But after no field-honours itch,
Achiev'd by leaping hedge and ditch.
While Spleen lies soft relax'd in bed,
Or o'er coal-fire inclines the head,
Hygeia's sons with hound and horn,
And jovial cry, awake the morn.
These see her from the dusky plight,
Smear'd by th' embraces of the night,
With roral wash redeem her face,
And prove herself of Titan's race,
And, mounting in loose robes the skies,
Shed light and fragrance as she flies.
Then horse and hound fierce joy display,
Exulting at the hark-away,
And in pursuit o'er tainted ground
From lungs robust field-notes resound.
Then, as St. George the dragon slew,
Spleen pierced, trod down, and dying view;
While all their spirits are on wing;
And woods, and hills, and valleys ring ...

In rainy days keep double guard,
Or Spleen will surely be too hard;
Which, like those fish by sailors met,
Fly highest while their wings are wet.
In such dull weather, so unfit
To enterprise a work of wit,
When clouds one yard of azure sky,
That's fit for simile, deny,
I dress my face with studious looks,
And shorten tedious hours with books.
But if dull fogs invade the head,
That mem'ry minds not what is read,
I sit in window dry as ark,
And on the drowning world remark;
Or at some coffee house I stray
For news, the manna of the day,
And from the hipp'd discourses gather
That politics go by the weather!
Then seek good-humour'd tavern chums,
And play at cards, but for small sums;
Or with the merry fellows quaff,
And laugh aloud with them that laugh;

Or drink a joco-serious cup
With souls who've took their freedom up,
And let my mind, beguil'd by talk,
In Epicurus' garden walk,
Who thought it Heav'n to be serene;
Pain, hell and purgatory, Spleen ...
   Me never did ambition seize,
Strange fever most inflam'd by ease!
The active lunacy of pride,
That courts jilt Fortune for a bride,
This par'dise tree, so fair and high,
I view with no aspiring eye:
Like aspen shake the restless leaves,
And Sodom-fruit our pains deceives,
Whence frequent falls give no surprise
But fits of Spleen call'd growing wise.
Greatness in glittering forms display'd
Affects weak eyes much us'd to shade,
And by its falsely envied scene
Gives self-debasing fits of Spleen.
We shou'd be pleas'd that things are so,
Who do for nothing see the show,
And, middle-siz'd, can pass between
Life's hubbub safe, because unseen;
And midst the glare of greatness trace
A watery sunshine in the face,
And pleasures fled to, to redress
The sad fatigue of idleness.
   Contentment, parent of delight,
So much a stranger to our sight,
Say, goddess, in what happy place
Mortals behold thy blooming face;
Thy gracious auspices impart,
And for thy temple, choose my heart.
They, whom thou deignest to inspire,
Thy science learn, to bound desire;
By happy alchemy of mind
They turn to pleasure all they find;
They both disdain in outward mien
The grave and solemn garb of Spleen,
And meretricious arts of dress,
To feign a joy, and hide distress;
Unmov'd when the rude tempest blows,
Without an opiate they repose;

And cover'd by your shield, defy
The whizzing shafts that round them fly;
Nor, meddling with the gods' affairs,
Concern themselves with distant cares;
But place their bliss in mental rest,
And feast upon the good possess'd.

WILLIAM OLDYS

1696–1761

On a Fly Drinking Out of His Cup

BUSY, curious, thirsty fly!
Drink with me and drink as I:
Freely welcome to my cup,
Couldst thou sip and sip it up:
Make the most of life you may,
Life is short and wears away.

Both alike are mine and thine
Hastening quick to their decline:
Thine's a summer, mine's no more,
Though repeated to threescore.
Threescore summers, when they're gone,
Will appear as short as one!

JOHN DYER

?1698–1758

Grongar Hill

SILENT Nymph, with curious eye!
Who the purple ev'ning lie
On the mountain's lonely van,
Beyond the noise of busy man,
Painting fair the form of things,
While the yellow linnet sings;

Or the tuneful nightingale
Charms the forest with her tale;
Come with all thy various hues,
Come, and aid thy sister Muse;
Now while Phœbus riding high
Gives lustre to the land and sky!
Grongar Hill invites my song,
Draw the landskip bright and strong;
Grongar, in whose mossy cells
Sweetly musing Quiet dwells:
Grongar, in whose silent shade
For the modest Muses made,
So oft I have, the even still,
At the fountain of a rill,
Sate upon a flow'ry bed,
With my hands beneath my head;
And stray'd my eyes o'er Towy's flood,
Over mead and over wood,
From house to house, from hill to hill,
Till Contemplation had her fill.

    About her chequer'd sides I wind,
And leave his brooks and meads behind,
And groves and grottos where I lay,
And vistas shooting beams of day:
Wider and wider spreads the vale,
As circles on a smooth canal:
The mountains round, unhappy fate,
Sooner or later, of all height!
Withdraw their summits from the skies,
And lessen as the others rise:
Still the prospect wider spreads,
Adds a thousand woods and meads,
Still it widens, widens still,
And sinks the newly risen hill.

    Now I gain the mountain's brow,
What a landskip lies below!
No clouds, no vapours intervene,
But the gay, the open scene
Does the face of Nature show,
In the hues of Heav'n's bow!
And swelling to embrace the light,
Spreads around beyond the sight.

    Old castles on the cliffs arise,
Proudly tow'ring in the skies!

Rushing from the woods, the spires
Seem from hence ascending fires!
Half his beams Apollo sheds
On the yellow mountain heads!
Gilds the fleeces of the flocks;
And glitters on the broken rocks!
  Below me trees unnumber'd rise,
Beautiful in various dyes:
The gloomy pine, the poplar blue,
The yellow beech, the sable yew,
The slender fir that taper grows,
The sturdy oak, with broad-spread boughs.
And beyond the purple grove,
Haunt of Phyllis, queen of love!
Gaudy as the op'ning dawn,
Lies a long and level lawn,
On which a dark hill, steep and high,
Holds and charms the wand'ring eye!
Deep are his feet in Towy's flood,
His sides are cloth'd with waving wood,
And ancient towers crown his brow,
That cast an awful look below;
Whose ragged walls the ivy creeps,
And with her arms from falling keeps.
So both a safety from the wind
On mutual dependence find.
  'Tis now the raven's bleak abode;
'Tis now th' apartment of the toad;
And there the fox securely feeds,
And there the pois'nous adder breeds,
Conceal'd in ruins, moss and weeds:
While ever and anon there falls
Huge heaps of hoary, moulder'd walls.
Yet time has seen, that lifts the low,
And level lays the lofty brow,
Has seen this broken pile complete,
Big with the vanity of state:
But transient is the smile of Fate!
A little rule, a little sway,
A sunbeam in a winter's day,
Is all the proud and mighty have
Between the cradle and the grave.
  And see the rivers how they run,
Thro' woods and meads, in shade and sun,

Sometimes swift and sometimes slow,
Wave succeeding wave they go
A various journey to the deep,
Like human life to endless sleep!
Thus is nature's vesture wrought
To instruct our wand'ring thought;
Thus she dresses green and gay,
To disperse our cares away.

Ever changing, ever new,
When will the landskip tire the view!
The fountain's fall, the river's flow,
The woody valleys, warm and low;
The windy summit, wild and high,
Roughly rushing on the sky!
The pleasant seat, the ruin'd tow'r,
The naked rock, the shady bow'r;
The town and village, dome and farm,
Each give each a double charm,
As pearls upon an Ethiop's arm.

See on the mountain's southern side,
Where the prospect opens wide,
Where the evening gilds the tide,
How close and small the hedges lie!
What streaks of meadows cross the eye!
A step, methinks, may pass the stream,
So little distant dangers seem;
So we mistake the future's face,
Ey'd through hope's deluding glass;
As yon summits soft and fair,
Clad in colours of the air,
Which, to those who journey near,
Barren, brown, and rough appear.
Still we tread, tir'd, the same coarse way,
The present's still a cloudy day.

Oh, may I with myself agree,
And never covet what I see:
Content me with an humble shade
My passions tam'd, my wishes laid;
For while our wishes wildly roll,
We banish quiet from the soul:
'Tis thus the busy beat the air;
And misers gather wealth and care.

Now, ev'n now my joy runs high,
As on the mountain turf I lie;

While the wanton Zephyr sings
And in the vale perfumes his wings;
While the waters murmur deep,
While the shepherd charms his sheep;
While the birds unbounded fly,
And with music fill the sky.
Now, ev'n now my joys run high.

    Be full, ye courts, be great who will;
Search for Peace with all your skill:
Open wide the lofty door,
Seek her on the marble floor,
In vain ye search, she is not there,
In vain ye search the domes of care!
Grass and flowers Quiet treads,
On the meads and mountain heads,
Along with Pleasure close ally'd,
Ever by each other's side:
And often, by the murm'ring rill,
Hears the thrush while all is still,
Within the groves of Grongar Hill.

ROBERT BLAIR

1699–1746

from *The Grave*

Peace the End of the Good Man

           SURE the last end
Of the good man is peace! How calm his exit!
Night-dews fall not more gently to the ground,
Nor weary worn-out winds expire so soft.
Behold him! in the evening tide of life,
A life well spent, whose early care it was
His riper years should not upbraid his green:
By unperceived degrees he wears away;
Yet, like the sun, seems larger at his setting!
High in his faith and hopes, look how he reaches
After the prize in view! and, like a bird
That's hampered, struggles hard to get away!
Whilst the glad gates of sight are wide expanded
To let new glories in, the first fair fruits
Of the fast-coming harvest.

All impelled onward alike

On this side, and on that, men see their friends
Drop off, like leaves in autumn; yet launch out
Into fantastic schemes, which the long livers,
In the world's hale and undegenerate days,
Could scarce have leisure for! Fools that we are!
Never to think of death, and of ourselves
At the same time! As if to learn to die
Were no concern of ours. Oh! more than sottish!
For creatures of a day, in gamesome mood
To frolic on Eternity's dread brink,
Unapprehensive; when for aught we know
The very first swol'n surge shall sweep us in.
Think we, or think we not, time hurries on
With a resistless unremitting stream,
Yet treads more soft than e'er did midnight thief,
That slides his hand under the miser's pillow,
And carries off his prize. What is this world?
What but a spacious burial-field unwalled,
Strewed with death's spoils, the spoils of animals
Savage and tame, and full of dead men's bones?
The very turf on which we tread, once lived:
And we that live must lend our carcases
To cover our own offspring; in their turns
They too must cover theirs. 'Tis here all meet!
The shivering Icelander, and sunburnt Moor;
Men of all climes who never met before,
And of all creeds, the Jew, the Turk, and Christian.
Here the proud prince, and favourite yet prouder,
His sovereign's keeper, and the people's scourge,
Are huddled out of sight. Here lie abashed
The great negotiators of the earth,
And celebrated masters of the balance,
Deep read in stratagems, and wiles of courts:
Now vain their treaty-skill! Death scorns to treat.
Here the o'erloaded slave flings down his burthen
From his galled shoulders; and when the cruel tyrant,
With all his guards and tools of power about him,
Is mediating new unheard of hardships,
Mocks his short arm, and quick as thought escapes
When tyrants vex not, and the weary rest.

The Grave-yard on a Stormy Night

SEE yonder hallow'd fane, the pious work
Of names once fam'd, now dubious or forgot,
And buried midst the wreck of things which were:
There lie interr'd the more illustrious dead.
The wind is up: hark how it howls! Methinks
Till now I never heard a sound so dreary.
Doors creak, and windows clap, and night's foul bird,
Rook'd in the spire, screams loud! The gloomy aisles,
Black-plaister'd, and hung round with shreds of 'scutcheons
And tatter'd coats of arms, send back the sound,
Laden with heavier airs, from the low vaults,
The mansions of the dead! Rous'd from their slumbers,
In grim array the grizly spectres rise,
Grin horrible, and obstinately sullen
Pass and repass, hush'd as the foot of night!
Again the screech owl shrieks—ungracious sound!
I'll hear no more; it makes one's blood run chill.

   Quite round the pile, a row of rev'rend elms,
Co-eval near with that, all ragged show,
Long lash'd by the rude winds; some rift half down
Their branchless trunks, others so thin atop
That scarce two crows cou'd lodge in the same tree.
Strange things, the neighbours say, have happen'd here.
Wild shrieks have issu'd from the hollow tombs;
Dead men have come again, and walk'd about;
And the great bell has toll'd unrung, untouch'd!
Such tales their cheer, at wake or gossiping,
When it draws near the witching time of night.

   Oft in the lone churchyard at night I've seen,
By glimpse of moon-shine, chequ'ring through the trees,
The schoolboy, with his satchel in his hand,
Whistling aloud to bear his courage up,
And lightly tripping o'er the long, flat stones,
(With nettles skirted, and with moss o'ergrown)
That tell in homely phrase who lie below.
Sudden he starts! and hears, or thinks he hears,
The sound of something purring at his heels.
Full fast he flies, and dares not look behind him,
Till, out of breath, he overtakes his fellows;
Who gather round, and wonder at the tale

Of horrid apparition, tall and ghastly,
That walks at dead of night, or takes his stand
O'er some new-open'd grave; and, strange to tell,
Evanishes at crowing of the cock!

JAMES THOMSON

1700–1748

from *The Seasons*

FLUSHED by the spirit of the genial year,
Now from the virgin's cheek a fresher bloom
Shoots less and less the live carnation round;
Her lips blush deeper sweets; she breathes of youth;
The shining moisture swells into her eyes
In brighter flow; her wishing bosom heaves
With palpitations wild; kind tumults seize
Her veins, and all her yielding soul is love.
From the keen gaze her lover turns away,
Full of the dear ecstatic power, and sick
With sighing languishment. Ah then, ye fair!
Be greatly cautious of your sliding hearts:
Dare not the infectious sigh; the pleading look,
Downcast and low, in meek submission dressed,
But full of guile. Let not the fervent tongue,
Prompt to deceive with adulation smooth,
Gain on your purposed will. Nor in the bower
Where woodbines flaunt and roses shed a couch,
While evening draws her crimson curtains round,
Trust your soft minutes with betraying man.
    And let the aspiring youth beware of love,
Of the smooth glance beware; for 'tis too late,
When on his heart the torrent-softness pours.
Then wisdom prostrate lies, and fading fame
Dissolves in air away; while the fond soul,
Wrapt in gay visions of unreal bliss,
Still paints the illusive form, the kindling grace,
The enticing smile, the modest-seeming eye,
Beneath whose beauteous beams, belying Heaven,
Lurk searchless cunning, cruelty, and death:
And still, false-warbling in his cheated ear,

Her siren voice enchanting draws him on
To guileful shores and meads of fatal joy.
   Even present, in the very lap of love
Inglorious laid—while music flows around,
Perfumes, and oils, and wine, and wanton hours—
Amid the roses fierce repentance rears
Her snaky crest: a quick-returning pang
Shoots through the conscious heart, where honour still
And great design, against the oppressive load
Of luxury, by fits, impatient heave.
   But absent, what fantastic woes, aroused,
Rage in each thought, by restless musing fed,
Chill the warm cheek, and blast the bloom of life!
Neglected fortune flies; and, sliding swift,
Prone into ruin fall his scorned affairs.
'Tis nought but gloom around: the darkened sun
Loses his light. The rosy-bosomed Spring
To weeping fancy pines; and yon bright arch,
Contracted, bends into a dusky vault.
All Nature fades extinct; and she alone
Heard, felt, and seen, possesses every thought,
Fills every sense, and pants in every vein.
Books are but formal dulness, tedious friends;
And sad amid the social band he sits,
Lonely and unattentive. From the tongue
The unfinish'd period falls: while, borne away
On swelling thought, his wafted spirit flies
To the vain bosom of his distant fair;
And leaves the semblance of a lover, fixed
In melancholy site, with head declined,
And love-dejected eyes.

                    *   *   *

   'Tis done! Dread Winter spreads his latest glooms,
And reigns tremendous o'er the conquered year.
How dead the vegetable kingdom lies!
How dumb the tuneful! Horror wide extends
His desolate domain. Behold, fond man!
See here thy pictured life; pass some few years,
Thy flowering Spring, thy Summer's ardent strength,
Thy sober Autumn fading into age,
And pale concluding Winter comes at last
And shuts the scene. Ah! whither now are fled
Those dreams of greatness? those unsolid hopes

Of happiness? those longings after fame?
Those restless cares? those busy bustling days?
Those gay-spent festive nights? those veering thoughts,
Lost between good and ill, that shared thy life?
All now are vanished! Virtue sole survives—
Immortal, never-failing friend of man,
His guide to happiness on high. And see!
'Tis come, the glorious morn! the second birth
Of heaven and earth! awakening nature hears
The new-creating word, and starts to life
In every heightened form, from pain and death
For ever free. The great eternal scheme,
Involving all, and in a perfect whole
Uniting, as the prospect wider spreads,
To reason's eye refined clears up apace.
Ye vainly wise! ye blind presumptuous! now,
Confounded in the dust, adore that Power
And Wisdom—oft arraigned: see now the cause
Why unassuming worth in secret lived
And died neglected: why the good man's share
In life was gall and bitterness of soul:
Why the lone widow and her orphans pined
In starving solitude; while luxury
In palaces lay straining her low thought
To form unreal wants: why heaven-born truth
And moderation fair wore the red marks
Of superstition's scourge; why licensed pain,
That cruel spoiler, that embosomed foe,
Embittered all our bliss. Ye good distressed!
Ye noble few! who here unbending stand
Beneath life's pressure, yet bear up a while,
And what your bounded view, which only saw
A little part, deemed evil is no more:
The storms of wintry time will quickly pass,
And one unbounded Spring encircle all.

DAVID MALLET

1705–1765

William and Margaret

'Twas at the silent solemn hour,
　When night and morning meet;
In glided Margaret's grimly ghost,
　And stood at William's feet.

Her face was like an April morn,
　Clad in a wintry cloud;
And clay-cold was her lily hand
　That held her sable shroud.

So shall the fairest face appear,
　When youth and years are flown:
Such is the robe that kings must wear,
　When death has reft their crown.

Her bloom was like the springing flower,
　That sips the silver dew;
The rose was budded in her cheek,
　Just opening to the view.

But love had, like the canker-worm,
　Consumed her early prime;
The rose grew pale, and left her cheek;
　She died before her time.

'Awake!' she cried, 'thy true love calls,
　Come from her midnight grave:
Now let thy pity hear the maid,
　Thy love refused to save.

'This is the dark and dreary hour
　When injured ghosts complain;
When yawning graves give up their dead
　To haunt the faithless swain.

'Bethink thee, William, of the fault,
  Thy pledge and broken oath:
And give me back my maiden vow,
  And give me back my troth.

'Why did you promise love to me,
  And not that promise keep?
Why did you swear mine eyes were bright,
  Yet leave those eyes to weep?

'How could you say my face was fair,
  And yet that face forsake?
How could you win my virgin heart,
  Yet leave that heart to break?

'Why did you say, my lip was sweet,
  And made the scarlet pale?
And why did I, young, witless maid!
  Believe the flattering tale?

'That face, alas! no more is fair;
  Those lips no longer red:
Dark are my eyes, now closed in death,
  And every charm is fled.

'The hungry worm my sister is;
  This winding-sheet I wear:
And cold and weary lasts our night,
  Till that last morn appear.

'But hark!—the cock has warned me hence;
  A long and late adieu!
Come, see, false man, how low she lies,
  Who died for love of you.'

The lark sung loud; the morning smiled,
  With beams of rosy red:
Pale William quaked in every limb,
  And raving left his bed.

He hied him to the fatal place
  Where Margaret's body lay;
And stretched him on the grass-green turf,
  That wrapped her breathless clay.

And thrice he called on Margaret's name,
    And thrice he wept full sore;
Then laid his cheek to her cold grave,
    And word spake never more.

CHARLES WESLEY

1707–1788

Wrestling Jacob

COME, O Thou Traveller unknown,
    Whom still I hold, but cannot see,
My Company before is gone,
    And I am left alone with Thee,
With Thee all Night I mean to stay,
And wrestle till the Break of Day.

I need not tell Thee who I am,
    My Misery, or Sin declare,
Thyself hast call'd me by my Name,
    Look on thy Hands, and read it there,
But who, I ask Thee, who art Thou,
Tell me thy Name, and tell me now?

In vain Thou strugglest to get free,
    I never will unloose my Hold:
Art Thou the Man that died for me?
    The Secret of thy Love unfold;
Wrestling I will not let Thee go,
Till I thy Name, thy Nature know.

Wilt Thou not yet to me reveal
    Thy new, unutterable Name?
Tell me, I still beseech Thee, tell,
    To know it Now resolv'd I am;
Wrestling I will not let Thee go,
Till I thy Name, thy Nature know.

'Tis all in vain to hold thy Tongue,
   Or touch the Hollow of my Thigh:
Though every Sinew be unstrung,
   Out of my Arms Thou shalt not fly;
Wrestling I will not let Thee go,
Till I thy Name, thy Nature know.

What tho' my shrinking Flesh complain,
   And murmur to contend so long,
I rise superior to my Pain,
   When I am weak then I am strong,
And when my All of Strength shall fail,
I shall with the GOD-man prevail.

My Strength is gone, my Nature dies,
   I sink beneath thy weighty Hand,
Faint to revive, and fall to rise;
   I fall, and yet by Faith I stand,
I stand, and will not let Thee go,
Till I thy Name, thy Nature know.

Yield to me Now——for I am weak;
   But confident in Self-despair:
Speak to my Heart, in Blessings speak,
   Be conquer'd by my Instant Prayer,
Speak, or Thou never hence shalt move,
And tell me, if thy Name is LOVE.

'Tis Love, 'tis Love! Thou diedst for Me,
   I hear thy Whisper in my Heart.
The Morning breaks, the Shadows flee:
   Pure UNIVERSAL LOVE Thou art,
To me, to All thy Bowels move,
Thy Nature, and thy Name is LOVE.

My Prayer hath Power with GOD; the Grace
   Unspeakable I now receive,
Thro' Faith I see Thee Face to Face,
   I see Thee Face to Face, and live:
In vain I have not wept, and strove,
Thy Nature, and thy Name is LOVE.

I know Thee, Saviour, who Thou art,
  JESUS the feeble Sinner's Friend;
Nor wilt Thou with the Night depart,
  But stay, and love me to the End;
Thy Mercies never shall remove,
Thy Nature, and thy Name is LOVE.

The Sun of Righteousness on Me
  Hath rose with Healing in his Wings,
Wither'd my Nature's Strength; from Thee
  My Soul its Life and Succour brings,
My Help is all laid up above;
Thy Nature, and thy Name is LOVE.

Contented now upon my Thigh
  I halt, till Life's short Journey end;
All Helplessness, all Weakness I,
  On Thee alone for Strength depend,
Nor have I Power, from Thee, to move;
Thy Nature, and thy Name is LOVE.

Lame as I am, I take the Prey,
  Hell, Earth, and Sin with Ease o'ercome;
I leap for Joy, pursue my Way,
  And as a bounding Hart fly home,
Thro' all Eternity to prove
Thy Nature, and thy Name is LOVE.

SAMUEL JOHNSON

1709–1784

from *London*

BY numbers here from shame or censure free,
All crimes are safe, but hated poverty.
This, only this, the rigid law pursues,
This, only this, provokes the snarling muse.
The sober trader at a tatter'd cloak,
Wakes from his dream, and labours for a joke;
With brisker air the silken courtiers gaze,
And turn the varied taunt a thousand ways.

Of all the griefs that harrass the distress'd,
Sure the most bitter is a scornful jest;
Fate never wounds more deep the gen'rous heart,
Than when a blockhead's insult points the dart.

   Has heaven reserv'd, in pity to the poor,
No pathless waste, or undiscover'd shore;
No secret island in the boundless main?
No peaceful desert yet unclaim'd by SPAIN?
Quick let us rise, the happy seats explore,
And bear oppression's insolence no more.
This mournful truth is ev'ry where confess'd,
SLOW RISES WORTH, BY POVERTY DEPRESS'D:
But here more slow, where all are slaves to gold,
Where looks are merchandise, and smiles are sold;
Where won by bribes, by flatteries implor'd,
The groom retails the favours of his lord.

   But hark! th' affrighted crowd's tumultuous cries
Roll thro' the streets, and thunder to the skies;
Rais'd from some pleasing dream of wealth and pow'r,
Some pompous palace, or some blissful bower,
Aghast you start, and scarce with aching sight
Sustain th' approaching fire's tremendous light;
Swift from pursuing horrors take your way,
And leave your little ALL to flames a prey;
Then thro' the world a wretched vagrant roam,
For where can starving merit find a home?
In vain your mournful narrative disclose,
While all neglect, and most insult your woes.

   Should heaven's just bolts Orgilio's wealth confound,
And spread his flaming palace on the ground,
Swift o'er the land the dismal rumour flies,
And public mournings pacify the skies;
And laureat tribe in servile verse relate,
How virtue wars with persecuting fate;
With well-feign'd gratitude the pension'd band
Refund the plunder of the beggar'd land.
See! while he builds, the gaudy vassals come,
And crowd with sudden wealth the rising dome;
The price of boroughs and of souls restore,
And raise his treasures higher than before.
Now bless'd with all the baubles of the great,
The polish'd marble, and the shining plate,
Orgilio sees the golden pile aspire,
And hopes from angry heav'n another fire.

Could'st thou resign the park and play content,
For the fair banks of Severn or of Trent;
There might'st thou find some elegant retreat,
Some hireling senator's deserted seat;
And stretch thy prospects o'er the smiling land,
For less than rent the dungeons of the Strand;
There prune thy walks, support thy drooping flow'rs,
Direct thy rivulets, and twine thy bow'rs;
And, while thy grounds a cheap repast afford,
Despise the dainties of a venal lord:
There ev'ry bush with nature's musick rings,
There ev'ry breeze bears health upon its wings;
On all thy hours security shall smile,
And bless thine evening walk and morning toil.

Prepare for death, if here at night you roam,
And sign your will before you sup from home.
Some fiery fop, with new commission vain,
Who sleeps on brambles till he kills his man;
Some frolic drunkard, reeling from a feast,
Provokes a broil, and stabs you for a jest.
Yet ev'n these heroes, mischievously gay,
Lords of the street, and terrors of the way;
Flush'd as they are with folly, youth and wine,
Their prudent insults to the poor confine;
Afar they mark the flambeau's bright approach,
And shun the shining train, and golden coach.

In vain, these dangers past, your doors you close,
And hope the balmy blessings of repose:
Cruel with guilt, and daring with despair,
The midnight murd'rer bursts the faithless bar;
Invades the sacred hour of silent rest,
And leaves, unseen, a dagger in your breast.

The Vanity of Human Wishes

The Tenth Satire of Juvenal Imitated

LET observation with extensive view,
Survey mankind, from China to Peru;
Remark each anxious toil, each eager strife,
And watch the busy scenes of crowded life;
Then say how hope and fear, desire and hate,
O'erspread with snares the clouded maze of fate,

Where wav'ring man, betray'd by vent'rous pride,
To tread the dreary paths without a guide,
As treach'rous phantoms in the mist delude,
Shuns fancied ills, or chases airy good;
How rarely reason guides the stubborn choice.
Rules the bold hand, or prompts the suppliant voice;
How nations sink, by darling schemes oppress'd,
When vengeance listens to the fool's request.
Fate wings with ev'ry wish th' afflictive dart,
Each gift of nature, and each grace of art,
With fatal heat impetuous courage glows,
With fatal sweetness elocution flows,
Impeachment stops the speaker's pow'rful breath,
And restless fire precipitates on death.

But scarce observ'd, the knowing and the bold
Fall in the gen'ral massacre of gold;
Wide-wasting pest! that rages unconfin'd,
And crouds with crimes the records of mankind;
For gold his sword the hireling ruffian draws,
For gold the hireling judge distorts the laws;
Wealth heap'd on wealth, nor truth nor safety buys,
The dangers gather as the treasures rise.

Let hist'ry tell where rival kings command,
And dubious title shakes the madded land,
When statutes glean the refuse of the sword,
How much more safe the vassal than the lord;
Low skulks the hind beneath the rage of pow'r,
And leaves the wealthy traitor in the Tow'r,
Untouch'd his cottage, and his slumbers sound,
Tho' confiscation's vulturs hover round.

The needy traveller, serene and gay,
Walks the wild heath, and sings his toil away.
Does envy seize thee? crush th' upbraiding joy,
Increase his riches and his peace destroy;
Now fears in dire vicissitude invade,
The rustling brake alarms, and quiv'ring shade,
Nor light nor darkness bring his pain relief,
One shews the plunder, and one hides the thief.

Yet still one gen'ral cry the skies assails,
And gain and grandeur load the tainted gales;
Few know the toiling statesman's fear or care,
Th' insidious rival and the gaping heir.

Once more, Democritus, arise on earth,
With cheerful wisdom and instructive mirth,

SAMUEL JOHNSON

See motley life in modern trappings dress'd,
And feed with varied fools th' eternal jest:
Thou who couldst laugh where want enchain'd caprice,
Toil crush'd conceit, and man was of a piece;
Where wealth unlov'd without a mourner died
And scarce a sycophant was fed by pride;
Where ne'er was known the form of mock debate,
Or seen a new-made mayor's unwieldy state;
Where change of fav'rites made no change of laws,
And senates heard before they judg'd a cause;
How wouldst thou shake at Britain's modish tribe,
Dart the quick taunt, and edge the piercing gibe?
Attentive truth and nature to descry,
And pierce each scene with philosophic eye.
To thee were solemn toys or empty show,
The robes of pleasure and the veils of woe:
All aid the farce, and all thy mirth maintain,
Whose joys are causeless, or whose griefs are vain.

Such was the scorn that fill'd the sage's mind,
Renew'd at ev'ry glance on humankind;
How just that scorn ere yet thy voice declare,
Search every state, and canvass ev'ry pray'r.

Unnumber'd suppliants crowd Preferment's gate,
Athirst for wealth, and burning to be great;
Delusive Fortune hears th' incessant call,
They mount, they shine, evaporate, and fall.
On ev'ry stage the foes of peace attend,
Hate dogs their flight, and insult mocks their end.
Love ends with hope, the sinking statesman's door
Pours in the morning worshiper no more;
For growing names the weekly scribbler lies,
To growing wealth the dedicator flies,
From every room descends the painted face,
That hung the bright Palladium of the place,
And smok'd in kitchens, or in auctions sold,
To better features yields the frame of gold;
For now no more we trace in ev'ry line
Heroic worth, benevolence divine:
The form distorted justifies the fall,
And detestation rids th' indignant wall.

But will not Britain hear the last appeal,
Sign her foes doom, or guard her fav'rites zeal?
Through Freedom's sons no more remonstrance rings,
Degrading nobles and controuling kings;

Our supple tribes repress their patriot throats,
And ask no questions but the price of votes;
With weekly libels and septennial ale,
Their wish is full to riot and to rail.

   In full-blown dignity, see Wolsey stand,
Law in his voice, and fortune in his hand:
To him the church, the realm, their pow'rs consign,
Thro' him the rays of regal bounty shine,
Turn'd by his nod the stream of honour flows,
His smile alone security bestows:
Still to new heights his restless wishes tow'r,
Claim leads to claim, and pow'r advances pow'r;
Till conquest unresisted ceas'd to please,
And rights submitted, left him none to seize.
At length his sov'reign frowns—the train of state
Mark the keen glance, and watch the sign to hate.
Where-e'er he turns he meets a stranger's eye,
His suppliants scorn him, and his followers fly;
At once is lost the pride of aweful state,
The golden canopy, the glitt'ring plate,
The regal palace, the luxurious board,
The liv'ried army, and the menial lord.
With age, with cares, with maladies oppress'd,
He seeks the refuge of monastic rest.
Grief aids disease, remember'd folly stings,
And his last sighs reproach the faith of kings.

   Speak thou, those thoughts at humble peace repine,
Shall Wolsey's wealth, with Wolsey's end be thine?
Or liv'st thou now, with safer pride content,
The wisest justice on the banks of Trent?
For why did Wolsey near the steeps of fate,
On weak foundations raise th' enormous weight?
Why but to sink beneath misfortune's blow,
With louder ruin to the gulfs below?

   What gave great Villiers to th' assassin's knife,
And fixed disease on Harley's closing life?
What murder'd Wentworth, and what exil'd Hyde,
By kings protected, and to kings ally'd?
What but their wish indulg'd in courts to shine,
And pow'r too great to keep, or to resign?

   When first the college rolls receive his name,
The young enthusiast quits his ease for fame;
Through all his veins the fever of renown
Burns from the strong contagion of the gown;

O'er Bodley's dome his future labours spread,
And Bacon's mansion trembles o'er his head.
Are these thy views? proceed, illustrious youth,
And virtue guard thee to the throne of Truth!
Yet should thy soul indulge the gen'rous heat,
Till captive Science yields her last retreat;
Should Reason guide thee with her brightest ray,
And pour on misty Doubt resistless day;
Should no false Kindness lure to loose delight,
Nor Praise relax, nor Difficulty fright;
Should tempting Novelty thy cell refrain,
And Sloth effuse her opiate fumes in vain;
Should Beauty blunt on fops her fatal dart,
Nor claim the triumph of a letter'd heart;
Should no Disease thy torpid veins invade,
Nor Melancholy's phantoms haunt thy shade;
Yet hope not life from grief or danger free,
Nor think the doom of man revers'd for thee:
Deign on the passing world to turn thine eyes,
And pause awhile from letters, to be wise;
There mark what ills the scholar's life assail,
Toil, envy, want, the patron, and the jail.
See nations slowly wise, and meanly just,
To buried merit raise the tardy bust.
If dreams yet flatter, once again attend,
Hear Lydiat's life, and Galileo's end.

    Nor deem, when learning her last prize bestows,
The glitt'ring eminence exempt from foes;
See when the vulgar 'scape, despis'd or aw'd,
Rebellion's vengeful talons seize on Laud.
From meaner minds, tho' smaller fines content,
The plunder'd palace or sequester'd rent;
Mark'd out by dangerous parts he meets the shock,
And fatal Learning leads him to the block:
Around his tomb let Art and Genius weep,
But hear his death, ye blockheads, hear and sleep.

    The festal blazes, the triumphal show,
The ravish'd standard, and the captive foe,
The senate's thanks, the gazette's pompous tale,
With force resistless o'er the brave prevail.
Such bribes the rapid Greek o'er Asia whirl'd,
For such the steady Romans shook the world;
For such in distant lands the Britons shine,
And stain with blood the Danube or the Rhine;

This pow'r has praise, that virtue scarce can warm,
Till fame supplies the universal charm.
Yet Reason frowns on War's unequal game,
Where wasted nations raise a single name,
And mortgag'd states their grandsires wreaths regret,
From age to age in everlasting debt;
Wreaths which at last the dear-bought right convey
To rust on medals, or on stones decay.

On what foundation stands the warrior's pride,
How just his hopes let Swedish Charles decide;
A frame of adamant, a soul of fire,
No dangers fright him, and no labours tire;
O'er love, o'er fear, extends his wide domain,
Unconquer'd lord of pleasure and of pain;
No joys to him pacific scepters yield,
War sounds the trump, he rushes to the field;
Behold surrounding kings their power combine,
And one capitulate, and one resign;
Peace courts his hand, but spreads her charms in vain;
'Think nothing gain'd, he cries, till nought remain,
'On Moscow's walls till Gothic standards fly,
'And all be mine beneath the polar sky.'
The march begins in military state,
And nations on his eye suspended wait;
Stern Famine guards the solitary coast,
And Winter barricades the realms of Frost;
He comes, not want and cold his course delay;—
Hide, blushing Glory, hide Pultowa's day:
The vanquish'd hero leaves his broken bands,
And shows his miseries in distant lands;
Condemn'd a needy supplicant to wait,
While ladies interpose, and slaves debate.
But did not Chance at length her error mend?
Did no subverted empire mark his end?
Did rival monarchs give the fatal wound?
Or hostile millions press him to the ground?
His fall was destin'd to a barren strand,
A petty fortress, and a dubious hand;
He left the name, at which the world grew pale,
To point a moral, or adorn a tale.

All times their scenes of pompous woes afford,
From Persia's tyrant to Bavaria's lord.
In gay hostility, and barb'rous pride,
With half mankind embattled at his side,

Great Xerxes comes to seize the certain prey,
And starves exhausted regions in his way;
Attendant Flattery counts his myriads o'er,
Till counted myriads sooth his pride no more;
Fresh praise is try'd till madness fires his mind,
The waves he lashes, and enchains the wind;
New pow'rs are claim'd, new pow'rs are still bestow'd,
Till rude resistance lops the spreading god;
The daring Greeks deride the martial show,
And heap their valleys with the gaudy foe;
Th' insulted sea with humbler thoughts he gains,
A single skiff to speed his flight remains;
Th' incumber'd oar scarce leaves the dreaded coast
Through purple billows and a floating host.
  The bold Bavarian, in a luckless hour,
Tries the dread summits of Cesarean pow'r,
With unexpected legions bursts away,
And sees defenceless realms receive his sway;
Short sway! fair Austria spreads her mournful charms,
The queen, the beauty, sets the world in arms;
From hill to hill the beacons rousing blaze
Spreads wide the hope of plunder and of praise;
The fierce Croatian, and the wild Hussar,
And all the sons of ravage crowd the war;
The baffled prince in honour's flatt'ring bloom
Of hasty greatness finds the fatal doom,
His foes derision, and his subjects blame,
And steals to death from anguish and from shame.
  Enlarge my life with multitude of days,
In health, in sickness, thus the suppliant prays;
Hides from himself his state, and shuns to know,
That life protracted is protracted woe.
Time hovers o'er, impatient to destroy,
And shuts up all the passages of joy:
In vain their gifts the bounteous seasons pour,
The fruit autumnal, and the vernal flow'r,
With listless eyes the dotard views the store,
He views, and wonders that they please no more;
Now pall the tasteless meats, and joyless wines,
And Luxury with sighs her slave resigns.
Approach, ye minstrels, try the soothing strain,
Diffuse the tuneful lenitives of pain:
No sounds alas would touch th' impervious ear,
Though dancing mountains witness'd Orpheus near;

Nor lute nor lyre his feeble pow'rs attend,
Nor sweeter music of a virtuous friend,
But everlasting dictates crowd his tongue,
Perversely grave, or positively wrong.
The still returning tale, and ling'ring jest,
Perplex the fawning niece and pamper'd guest,
While growing hopes scarce awe the gath'ring sneer,
And scarce a legacy can bribe to hear;
The watchful guests still hint the last offence,
The daughter's petulance, the son's expense,
Improve his heady rage with treach'rous skill,
And mould his passions till they make his will.

Unnumber'd maladies his joints invade,
Lay seige to life and press the dire blockade;
But unextinguish'd Avarice still remains,
And dreaded losses aggravate his pains;
He turns, with anxious heart and crippled hands,
His bonds of debt, and mortgages of lands;
Or views his coffers with suspicious eyes,
Unlocks his gold, and counts it till he dies.

But grant, the virtues of a temp'rate prime
Bless with an age exempt from scorn or crime;
An age that melts with unperceiv'd decay,
And glides in modest Innocence away;
Whose peaceful day Benevolence endears,
Whose night congratulating Conscience cheers;
The gen'ral fav'rite as the gen'ral friend:
Such age there is, and who shall wish its end?

Yet ev'n on this her load Misfortune flings,
To press the weary minutes flagging wings:
New sorrow rises as the day returns,
A sister sickens, or a daughter mourns.
Now kindred Merit fills the sable bier,
Now lacerated Friendship claims a tear.
Year chases year, decay pursues decay,
Still drops some joy from with'ring life away;
New forms arise, and diff'rent views engage,
Superfluous lags the vet'ran on the stage,
Till pitying Nature signs the last release,
And bids afflicted worth retire to peace.

But few there are whom hours like these await,
Who set unclouded in the gulfs of fate.
From Lydia's monarch should the search descend,
By Solon caution'd to regard his end,

In life's last scene what prodigies surprise,
Fears of the brave, and follies of the wise?
From Marlb'rough's eyes the streams of dotage flow,
And Swift expires a driveller and a show.

   The teeming mother, anxious for her race,
Begs for each birth the fortune of a face:
Yet Vane could tell what ills from beauty spring;
And Sedley curs'd the form that pleas'd a king.
Ye nymphs of rosy lips and radiant eyes,
Whom Pleasure keeps too busy to be wise,
Whom Joys with soft varieties invite,
By day the frolick, and the dance by night,
Who frown with vanity, who smile with art,
And ask the latest fashion of the heart,
What care, what rules your heedless charms shall save,
Each nymph your rival, and each youth your slave?
Against your fame with fondness hate combines,
The rival batters, and the lover mines.
With distant voice neglected Virtue calls,
Less heard and less, the faint remonstrance falls;
Tir'd with contempt, she quits the slipp'ry reign,
And Pride and Prudence take her seat in vain.
In crowd at once, where none the pass defend,
The harmless Freedom, and the private Friend.
The guardians yield, by force superior ply'd;
By Int'rest, Prudence; and by Flatt'ry, Pride.
Now beauty falls betray'd, despis'd, distress'd,
And hissing Infamy proclaims the rest.

   Where then shall Hope and Fear their objects find?
Must dull Suspense corrupt the stagnant mind?
Must helpless man, in ignorance sedate,
Roll darkling down the torrent of his fate?
Must no dislike alarm, no wishes rise,
No cries attempt the mercies of the skies?
Enquirer, cease, petitions yet remain,
Which heav'n may hear, nor deem religion vain.
Still raise for good the supplicating voice,
But leave to heav'n the measure and the choice,
Safe in his pow'r, whose eyes discern afar
The secret ambush of a specious pray'r.
Implore his aid, in his decisions rest,
Secure whate'er he gives, he gives the best.
Yet when the sense of sacred presence fires,
And strong devotion to the skies aspires,

Pour forth thy fervours for a healthful mind,
Obedient passions, and a will resign'd;
For love, which scarce collective man can fill;
For patience sov'reign o'er transmuted ill;
For faith, that panting for a happier seat,
Counts death kind Nature's signal of retreat:
These goods for man the laws of heav'n ordain,
These goods he grants, who grants the pow'r to gain;
With these celestial wisdom calms the mind,
And makes the happiness she does not find.

Prologue at the Opening of the Theatre in Drury-Lane 1747

WHEN Learning's Triumph o'er her barb'rous Foes
First rear'd the Stage, immortal Shakespeare rose;
Each Change of many-colour'd Life he drew,
Exhausted Worlds, and then imagin'd new:
Existence saw him spurn her bounded Reign,
And panting Time toil'd after him in vain:
His pow'rful Strokes presiding Truth impress'd,
And unresisted Passion storm'd the Breast.

Then Johnson came, instructed from the School,
To please in Method, and invent by Rule;
His studious Patience, and laborious Art,
By regular Approach essay'd the Heart;
Cold Approbation gave the ling'ring Bays,
For those who durst not censure, scarce cou'd praise.
A Mortal born he met the general Doom,
But left, like Egypt's Kings, a lasting Tomb.

The Wits of Charles found easier Ways to Fame,
Nor wish'd for Johnson's Art, or Shakespeare's Flame;
Themselves they studied, as they felt, they writ,
Intrigue was Plot, Obscenity was Wit.
Vice always found a sympathetic friend;
They pleas'd their Age, and did not aim to mend.
Yet Bards like these aspir'd to lasting Praise,
And proudly hop'd to pimp in future days.
Their cause was gen'ral, their supports were strong,
Their slaves were willing, and their Reign was long;
Till Shame regain'd the Post that Sense betray'd,
And Virtue call'd Oblivion to her Aid.

Then crush'd by Rules, and weaken'd as refin'd,

For Years the Pow'r of Tragedy declin'd;
From Bard, to Bard, the frigid Caution crept,
Till Declamation roar'd, while Passion slept.
Yet still did Virtue deign the Stage to tread,
Philosophy remain'd, though Nature fled.
But forc'd at length her antient Reign to quit,
She saw great Faustus lay the Ghost of Wit:
Exulting Folly hail'd the joyful Day,
And Pantomine, and Song, confirm'd her Sway.

But who the coming Changes can presage,
And mark the future Periods of the Stage?—
Perhaps if Skill could distant Times explore,
New Behns, new Durfeys, yet remain in Store.
Perhaps, where Lear has rav'd, and Hamlet died,
On flying Cars new Sorcerers may ride.
Perhaps, for who can guess th' Effects of Chance?
Here Hunt may box, or Mahomet may dance.

Hard is his lot, that here by Fortune plac'd,
Must watch the wild Vicissitudes of Taste;
With ev'ry Meteor of Caprice must play,
And chase the new-blown Bubbles of the Day.
Ah! let not Censure term our Fate our Choice,
The Stage but echoes back the publick Voice.
The Drama's Laws the Drama's Patrons give,
For we that live to please, must please to live.

Then prompt no more the Follies you decry,
As Tyrants doom their Tools of Guilt to die;
'Tis yours this Night to bid the Reign commence
Of rescu'd Nature, and reviving Sense;
To chase the Charms of Sound, the Pomp of Show,
For useful Mirth, and salutary Woe;
Bid scenic Virtue form the rising Age,
And Truth diffuse her Radiance from the Stage.

Prologue to
'A Word to the Wise'

THIS night presents a play, which public rage,
Or right, or wrong, once hooted from the stage;
From zeal or malice now no more we dread,
For English vengeance *wars not with the dead.*
A generous foe regards, with pitying eye,
The man whom fate has laid, where all must lye.

To wit, reviving from its author's dust,
Be kind, ye judges, or at least be just:
Let no resentful petulance invade
Th' oblivious grave's inviolable shade.
Let one great payment every claim appease,
And him who cannot hurt, allow to please;
To please by scenes unconscious of offence,
By harmless merriment, or useful sense.
Where aught of bright, or fair, the piece displays,
Approve it only—'tis too late to praise.
If want of skill, or want of care appear,
Forbear to hiss—the Poet cannot hear.
By all, like him, must praise and blame be found;
At best, a fleeting gleam, or empty sound.
Yet then shall calm reflection bless the night,
When liberal pity dignify'd delight;
When pleasure fired her torch at Virtue's flame,
And mirth was bounty with a humbler name.

An Epitaph on Claudy Phillips,
a Musician

PHILLIPS! whose touch harmonious could remove
The pangs of guilty pow'r, and hapless love,
Rest here distrest by poverty no more,
Find here that calm thou gav'st so oft before;
Sleep undisturb'd within this peaceful shrine,
Till angels wake thee with a note like thine.

Verses in Baretti's Commonplace Book

AT sight of sparkling bowls or beauteous dames,
When fondness melts me, or when wine inflames,
I too can feel the rapture, fierce and strong;
I too can pour the extemporary song:
But though the numbers for a moment please,
Though music thrills, or sudden sallies seize,
Yet, lay the sonnet for an hour aside,
Its charms are fled and all its powers destroyed.
What soon is perfect, soon alike is past;
That slowly grows, which must for ever last.

Epitaph on Hogarth

THE Hand of Art here torpid lies
    That wav'd th' essential form of Grace,
Here death has clos'd the curious eyes
    That saw the manners in the Face.

If Genius warm thee, Reader, stay,
    If Merit touch thee, shed a tear,
Be Vice and Dulness far away
    Great Hogarth's honour'd Dust is here.

Parodies in the Ballad Style

I

THE tender infant, meek and mild,
    Fell down upon the stone;
The nurse took up the squealing child,
    But still the child squeal'd on.

II

I PUT my hat upon my head
    And walk'd into the Strand,
And there I met another man
    Who's hat was in his hand.

III

I THEREFORE pray thee, Renny dear,
    That thou wilt give to me,
With cream and sugar soften'd well,
    Another dish of tea.

IV

IF the man who turnips cries,
Cry not when his father dies,
'Tis a proof that he had rather
Have a turnip than his father.

SAMUEL JOHNSON

A Short Song of Congratulation

LONG-EXPECTED one and twenty
Ling'ring year at last is flown,
Pomp and Pleasure, Pride and Plenty
Great Sir John, are all your own.

Loosen'd from the Minor's tether,
Free to mortgage or to sell,
Wild as wind, and light as feather
Bid the slaves of thrift farewell.

Call the Bettys, Kates, and Jennys
Ev'ry name that laughs at Care,
Lavish of your Grandsire's guineas,
Show the Spirit of an heir.

All that prey on vice and folly
Joy to see their quarry fly,
Here the Gamester light and jolly
There the Lender grave and sly.

Wealth, Sir John, was made to wander,
Let it wander as it will;
See the Jocky, see the Pander,
Bid them come, and take their fill.

When the bonny Blade carouses,
Pockets full, and Spirits high,
What are acres? What are houses?
Only dirt, or wet or dry.

If the Guardian or the Mother
Tell the woes of wilful waste,
Scorn their counsel and their pother,
You can hang or drown at last.

On the Death of Dr. Robert Levet

CONDEMN'D to hope's delusive mine,
    As on we toil from day to day,
By sudden blasts, or slow decline,
    Our social comforts drop away.

Well tried through many a varying year,
   See Levet to the grave descend;
Officious, innocent, sincere,
   Of ev'ry friendless name the friend.

Yet still he fills affection's eye,
   Obscurely wise, and coarsely kind;
Nor, letter'd arrogance, deny
   Thy praise to merit unrefin'd.

When fainting nature call'd for aid,
   And hovering death prepar'd the blow,
His vig'rous remedy display'd
   The power of art without the show.

In misery's darkest caverns known,
   His useful care was ever nigh,
Where hopeless anguish pour'd his groan,
   And lonely want retir'd to die.

No summons mock'd by chill delay,
   No petty gain disdain'd by pride,
The modest wants of ev'ry day
   The toil of ev'ry day supplied.

His virtues walk'd their narrow round,
   Nor made a pause, nor left a void;
And sure th' Eternal Master found
   The single talent well employ'd.

The busy day, the peaceful night,
   Unfelt, uncounted, glided by;
His frame was firm, his powers were bright,
   Tho' now his eightieth year was nigh.

Then with no throbbing fiery pain,
   No cold gradations of decay,
Death broke at once the vital chain,
   And free'd his soul the nearest way.

WILLIAM SHENSTONE
1714—1763

Written at an Inn at Henley

To thee, fair freedom! I retire
  From flattery, cards, and dice, and din;
Nor art thou found in mansions higher
  Than the low cot, or humble inn.

'Tis here with boundless power I reign;
  And every health which I begin,
Converts dull port to bright champagne;
  Such freedom crowns it, at an inn.

I fly from pomp, I fly from plate!
  I fly from falsehood's specious grin;
Freedom I love, and form I hate,
  And choose my lodgings at an inn.

Here, waiter! take my sordid ore,
  Which lackeys else might hope to win;
It buys, what courts have not in store;
  It buys me freedom at an inn.

Whoe'er has travelled life's dull round,
  Where'er his stages may have been,
May sigh to think he still has found
  The warmest welcome at an inn.

THOMAS GRAY
1716–1771

Ode on a Distant Prospect of Eton College

YE distant spires, ye antique towers
  That crown the watery glade,
Where grateful Science still adores
  Her Henry's holy shade;

And ye, that from the stately brow
Of Windsor's heights th' expanse below
   Of grove, of lawn, of mead survey,
Whose turf, whose shade, whose flowers among
Wanders the hoary Thames along
   His silver-winding way:

Ah happy hills! ah pleasing shade!
   Ah fields beloved in vain!
Where once my careless childhood strayed,
   A stranger yet to pain!
I feel the gales that from ye blow
A momentary bliss bestow,
   As waving fresh their gladsome wing
My weary soul they seem to soothe,
And, redolent of joy and youth,
   To breathe a second spring.

Say, Father Thames, for thou hast seen
   Full many a sprightly race
Disporting on thy margent green
   The paths of pleasure trace;
Who foremost now delight to cleave
With pliant arm, thy glassy wave?
   The captive linnet which enthral?
What idle progeny succeed
To chase the rolling circle's speed
   Or urge the flying ball?

While some on earnest business bent
   Their murmuring labours ply
'Gainst graver hours, that bring constraint
   To sweeten liberty:
Some bold adventurers disdain
The limits of their little reign
   And unknown regions dare descry:
Still as they run they look behind,
They hear a voice in every wind,
   And snatch a fearful joy.

Gay hope is theirs by fancy fed,
   Less pleasing when possest;
The tear forgot as soon as shed,
   The sunshine of the breast:

Theirs buxom health, of rosy hue,
Wild wit, invention ever new,
   And lively cheer, of vigour born;
The thoughtless day, the easy night,
The spirits pure, the slumbers light
   That fly th' approach of morn.

Alas! regardless of their doom
   The little victims play!
No sense have they of ills to come
   Nor care beyond to-day:
Yet see how all around then wait
The Ministers of human fate
   And black Misfortune's baleful train!
Ah show them where in ambush stand
To seize their prey, the murderous band!
   Ah, tell them they are men!

These shall the fury Passions tear,
   The vultures of the mind,
Disdainful Anger, pallid Fear,
   And Shame that skulks behind,
Or pining Love shall waste their youth;
Or Jealousy with rankling tooth
   That inly gnaws the secret heart,
And Envy wan, and faded Care,
Grim-visaged comfortless Despair,
   And Sorrow's piercing dart.

Ambition this shall tempt to rise,
   Then whirl the wretch from high,
To bitter Scorn a sacrifice
   And grinning Infamy.
The stings of Falsehood those shall try,
And hard Unkindness' altered eye,
   That mocks the tear it forced to flow;
And keen Remorse with blood defiled,
And moody Madness laughing wild
   Amid severest woe.

Lo, in the vale of years beneath
   A griesly troop are seen,
The painful family of Death,
   More hideous than their Queen:

griesly] horrible

This racks the joints, this fires the veins,
That every labouring sinew strains,
   Those in the deeper vitals rage:
Lo, Poverty, to fill the band,
That numbs the soul with icy hand,
   And slow-consuming Age.

To each his sufferings: all are men,
   Condemned alike to groan;
The tender for another's pain,
   Th' unfeeling for his own.
Yet, ah! why should they know their fate,
Since sorrow never comes too late,
   And happiness too swiftly flies?
Thought would destroy their paradise.
No more;—where ignorance is bliss,
   'Tis folly to be wise.

Elegy Written in a Country Churchyard

THE curfew tolls the knell of parting day,
   The lowing herd wind slowly o'er the lea,
The plowman homeward plods his weary way,
   And leaves the world to darkness and to me.

Now fades the glimmering landscape on the sight,
   And all the air a solemn stillness holds,
Save where the beetle wheels his droning flight,
   And drowsy tinklings lull the distant folds;

Save that from yonder ivy-mantled tower
   The moping owl does to the moon complain
Of such as, wand'ring near her secret bower,
   Molest her ancient solitary reign.

Beneath those rugged elms, that yew-tree's shade,
   Where heaves the turf in many a mould'ring heap,
Each in his narrow cell for ever laid,
   The rude forefathers of the hamlet sleep.

The breezy call of incense-breathing morn,
   The swallow twitt'ring from the straw-built shed,
The cock's shrill clarion, or the echoing horn,
   No more shall rouse them from their lowly bed.

For them no more the blazing hearth shall burn,
 Or busy housewife ply her evening care:
No children run to lisp their sire's return,
 Or climb his knees the envied kiss to share.

Oft did the harvest to their sickle yield,
 Their furrow oft the stubborn glebe has broke:
How jocund did they drive their team afield!
 How bowed the woods beneath their sturdy stroke!

Let not Ambition mock their useful toil,
 Their homely joys, and destiny obscure;
Nor Grandeur hear with a disdainful smile
 The short and simple annals of the poor.

The boast of heraldry, the pomp of power,
 And all that beauty, all that wealth e'er gave,
Awaits alike th' inevitable hour:
 The paths of glory lead but to the grave.

Nor you, ye proud, impute to These the fault,
 If Memory o'er their tomb no trophies raise,
Where through the long-drawn aisle and fretted vault
 The pealing anthem swells the note of praise.

Can storied urn or animated bust
 Back to its mansion call the fleeting breath?
Can Honour's voice provoke the silent dust,
 Or Flatt'ry soothe the dull cold ear of death?

Perhaps in this neglected spot is laid
 Some heart once pregnant with celestial fire;
Hands, that the rod of empire might have swayed,
 Or waked to ecstasy the living lyre.

But Knowledge to their eyes her ample page
 Rich with the spoils of time did ne'er unroll;
Chill Penury repressed their noble rage,
 And froze the genial current of the soul.

Full many a gem of purest ray serene
 The dark unfathomed caves of ocean bear:
Full many a flower is born to blush unseen,
 And waste its sweetness on the desert air.

Some village Hampden that with dauntless breast
   The little tyrant of his fields withstood,
Some mute inglorious Milton here may rest,
   Some Cromwell guiltless of his country's blood.

Th' applause of list'ning senates to command,
   The threats of pain and ruin to despise,
To scatter plenty o'er a smiling land,
   And read their history in a nation's eyes,

Their lot forbade: nor circumscribed alone
   Their growing virtues, but their crimes confined;
Forbade to wade through slaughter to a throne.
   And shut the gates of mercy on mankind,

The struggling pangs of conscious truth to hide,
   To quench the blushes of ingenuous shame,
Or heap the shrine of Luxury and Pride
   With incense kindled at the Muse's flame.

Far from the madding crowd's ignoble strife
   Their sober wishes never learned to stray;
Along the cool sequestered vale of life
   They kept the noiseless tenor of their way.

Yet ev'n these bones from insult to protect
   Some frail memorial still erected nigh,
With uncouth rhymes and shapeless sculpture decked,
   Implores the passing tribute of a sigh.

Their name, their years, spelt by th' unlettered Muse,
   The place of fame and elegy supply:
And many a holy text around she strews,
   That teach the rustic moralist to die.

For who, to dumb Forgetfulness a prey,
   This pleasing anxious being e'er resigned,
Left the warm precincts of the cheerful day,
   Nor cast one longing ling'ring look behind?

On some fond breast the parting soul relies,
   Some pious drops the closing eye requires;
E'en from the tomb the voice of Nature cries,
   E'en in our Ashes live their wonted fires.

For thee, who, mindful of th' unhonoured dead,
   Dost in these lines their artless tale relate;
If chance, by lonely contemplation led,
   Some kindred spirit shall inquire thy fate,

Haply some hoary-headed Swain may say,
   'Oft have we seen him at the peep of dawn
Brushing with hasty steps the dews away
   To meet the sun upon the upland lawn.

'There at the foot of yonder nodding beech
   That wreathes its old fantastic roots so high,
His listless length at noontide would he stretch,
   And pore upon the brook that babbles by.

'Hard by yon wood, now smiling as in scorn,
   Mutt'ring his wayward fancies he would rove,
Now drooping, woeful wan, like one forlorn,
   Or crazed with care, or crossed in hopeless love.

'One morn I missed him on the customed hill,
   Along the heath and near his fav'rite tree;
Another came; nor yet beside the rill,
   Nor up the lawn, nor at the wood was he;

'The next with dirges due in sad array
   Slow through the church-way path we saw him borne.
Approach and read (for thou canst read) the lay
   Graved on the stone beneath yon aged thorn:'

THE EPITAPH

Here rests his head upon the lap of Earth
   A Youth to Fortune and to Fame unknown.
Fair Science frowned not on his humble birth,
   And Melancholy marked him for her own.

Large was his bounty, and his soul sincere,
   Heaven did a recompense as largely send:
He gave to Mis'ry all he had, a tear,
   He gained from Heaven ('twas all he wished) a friend.

No further seek his merits to disclose,
   Or draw his frailties from their dread abode,
(There they alike in trembling hope repose,)
   The bosom of his Father and his God.

On a Favourite Cat, Drowned in a Tub of Goldfishes

'Twas on a lofty vase's side,
Where China's gayest art had dyed
   The azure flowers that blow;
Demurest of the tabby kind,
The pensive Selima reclined,
   Gazed on the lake below.

Her conscious tail her joy declared;
The fair round face, the snowy beard,
   The velvet of her paws,
Her coat, that with the tortoise vies,
Her ears of jet, and emerald eyes.
   She saw; and purred applause.

Still had she gazed; but 'midst the tide
Two angel forms were seen to glide,
   The Genii of the stream:
Their scaly armour's Tyrian hue
Through richest purple to the view
   Betrayed a golden gleam.

The hapless Nymph with wonder saw:
A whisker first and then a claw,
   With many an ardent wish,
She stretched in vain to reach the prize.
What female heart can gold despise?
   What Cat's adverse to fish?

Presumptuous Maid! with looks intent
Again she stretched, again she bent,
   Nor knew the gulf between.
(Malignant Fate sat by, and smiled.)
The slipp'ry verge her feet beguiled,
   She tumbled headlong in.

Eight times emerging from the flood
She mewed to every watery god,
   Some speedy aid to send.
No Dolphin came, no Nereid stirred:
Nor cruel *Tom*, nor *Susan* heard.
   A Fav'rite has no friend!

From hence, ye Beauties, undeceived,
Know, one false step is ne'er retrieved,
   And be with caution bold.
Not all that tempts your wand'ring eyes
And heedless hearts, is lawful prize;
   Nor all that glisters, gold.

from *The Progress of Poesy*

IN climes beyond the solar road,
Where shaggy forms o'er ice-built mountains roam,
The Muse haes broke the twilight gloom
   To cheer the shiv'ring native's dull abode.
And oft, beneath the odorous shade
Of Chili's boundless forests laid,
She deigns to hear the savage youth repeat
In loose numbers wildly sweet
Their feather-cinctured chiefs, and dusky loves.
Her track, where'er the Goddess roves,
Glory pursue and generous Shame,
Th' unconquerable Mind, and Freedom's holy flame.

Woods, that wave o'er Delphi's steep,
Isles, that crown th' Ægean deep,
   Fields, that cool Ilissus laves,
   Or where Maeander's amber waves
In lingering lab'rinths creep,
   How do your tuneful echoes languish,
   Mute, but to the voice of anguish?
Where each old poetic mountain
   Inspiration breathed around:
Every shade and hallowed fountain
   Murmured deep a solemn sound:
Till the sad Nine, in Greece's evil hour,
   Left their Parnassus for the Latian plains.
Alike they scorn the pomp of tyrant Power,
   And coward Vice, that revels in her chains.
When Latium had her lofty spirit lost,
They sought, O Albion! next thy sea-encircled coast.

The Bard

A Pindaric Ode

'RUIN seize thee, ruthless King!
  Confusion on thy banners wait!
Though fanned by Conquest's crimson wing
  They mock the air with idle state.
Helm, nor hauberk's twisted mail,
Nor e'en thy virtues, tyrant, shall avail
To save thy secret soul from nightly fears,
From Cambria's curse, from Cambria's tears!'
—Such were the sounds that o'er the crested pride
  Of the first Edward scattered wild dismay,
As down the steep of Snowdon's shaggy side
  He wound with toilsome march his long array:—
Stout Glo'ster stood aghast in speechless trance;
'To arms!' cried Mortimer, and couched his quivering lance.

On a rock, whose haughty brow
Frowns o'er old Conway's foaming flood,
  Robed in the sable garb of woe,
With haggard eyes the poet stood;
(Loose his beard and hoary hair
Streamed like a meteor to the troubled air;)
And with a master's hand and prophet's fire
Struck the deep sorrows of his lyre:
'Hark, how each giant oak and desert cave
  Sighs to the torrent's awful voice beneath!
O'er thee, O King! their hundred arms they wave
  Revenge on thee in hoarser murmurs breathe;
Vocal no more, since Cambria's fatal day,
To high-born Hoel's harp, or soft Llewellyn's lay.

'Cold is Cadwallo's tongue,
  That hushed the stormy main:
Brave Urien sleeps upon his craggy bed:
  Mountains, ye mourn in vain
  Modred, whose magic song
Made huge Plinlimmon bow his cloud-topt head.
  On dreary Arvon's shore they lie
Smeared with gore and ghastly pale:

Far, far aloof the affrighted ravens sail;
    The famished eagle screams, and passes by.
Dear lost companions of my tuneful art,
    Dear as the light that visits these sad eyes,
Dear as the ruddy drops that warm my heart,
    Ye died amidst your dying country's cries—
No more I weep. They do not sleep;
    On yonder cliffs, a griesly band,
I see them sit; they linger yet,
    Avengers of their native land:
With me in dreadful harmony they join;
And weave with bloody hands the tissue of thy line.

' "Weave the warp and weave the woof,
    The winding-sheet of Edward's race:
Give ample room and verge enough
    The characters of hell to trace.
Mark the year and mark the night
When Severn shall re-echo with affright
The shrieks of death through Berkley's roof that ring,
Shrieks of an agonizing king!
    She-wolf of France, with unrelenting fangs
That tear'st the bowels of thy mangled mate,
    From thee be born, who o'er thy country hangs
The scourge of heaven! What terrors round him wait!
Amazement in his van, with flight combined,
And sorrow's faded form, and solitude behind.

' "Mighty victor, mighty lord,
    Low on his funeral couch he lies!
No pitying heart, no eye, afford
    A tear to grace his obsequies.
Is the sable warrior fled?
Thy son is gone. He rests among the dead.
The swarm that in thy noon-tide beam were born?
—Gone to salute the rising morn.
Fair laughs the morn, and soft the zephyr blows,
    While proudly riding o'er the azure realm
In gallant trim the gilded vessel goes:
    Youth on the prow, and Pleasure at the helm:
Regardless of the sweeping whirlwind's sway,
That, hushed in grim repose, expected his evening prey.

'"Fill high the sparkling bowl,
The rich repast prepare;
    Reft of a crown, he yet may share the feast:
Close by the regal chair
    Fell Thirst and Famine scowl
    A baleful smile upon their baffled guest.
Heard ye the din of battle bray,
    Lance to lance, and horse to horse?
    Long years of havoc urge their destined course.
And through the kindred squadrons mow their way.
    Ye towers of Julius, London's lasting shame,
With many a foul and midnight murder fed,
    Revere his consort's faith, his father's fame,
And spare the meek usurper's holy head!
Above, below, the rose of snow,
    Twined with her blushing foe, we spread:
The bristled boar in infant-gore
    Wallows beneath the thorny shade.
Now, brothers, bending o'er the accursèd loom,
Stamp we our vengeance deep, and ratify his doom.

'"Edward, lo! to sudden fate
    (Weave we the woof; The thread is spun;)
Half of thy heart we consecrate.
    (The web is wove; The work is done.)"
Stay, O stay! nor thus forlorn
Leave me unblessed, unpitied, here to mourn:
In yon bright track that fires the western skies
They melt, they vanish from my eyes.
But O! what solemn scenes on Snowdon's height
    Descending slow their glittering skirts unroll?
Visions of glory, spare my aching sight,
    Ye unborn ages, crowd not on my soul!
No more our long-lost Arthur we bewail:—
All hail, ye genuine kings! Britannia's issue, hail!

    'Girt with many a baron bold
Sublime their starry fronts they rear;
    And gorgeous dames, and statesmen old
In bearded majesty, appear.
In the midst a form divine!
Her eye proclaims her of the Briton-line:
Her lion-port, her awe-commanding face
Attempered sweet to virgin-grace.

What strings symphonious tremble in the air,
    What strains of vocal transport round her play!
Hear from the grave, great Taliessin, hear;
    They breathe a soul to animate thy clay.
Bright Rapture calls, and soaring as she sings,
Waves in the eye of heaven her many-coloured wings.

    'The verse adorn again
    Fierce war, and faithful love,
And Truth severe, by fairy Fiction drest.
    In buskined measures move
Pale grief, and pleasing pain,
With horror, tyrant of the throbbing breast.
A voice as of the cherub-choir
    Gales from blooming Eden bear,
    And distant warblings lesson on my ear,
That lost in long futurity expire.
Fond impious man, think'st thou yon sanguine cloud
    Raised by thy breath, has quenched the orb of day?
To-morrow he repairs the golden flood
    And warms the nations with redoubled ray.
Enough for me: with joy I see
    The different doom our fates assign:
Be thine despair and sceptred care;
    To triumph and to die are mine.'
—He spoke, and headlong from the mountain's height
Deep in the roaring tide he plunged to endless night.

The Descent of Odin

UPROSE the King of Men with speed,
And saddled strait his coal-black steed:
Down the yawning steep he rode
That leads to Hela's drear abode.
Him the Dog of darkness spied:
His shaggy throat he open'd wide,
While from his jaws with carnage fill'd
Foam & human gore distill'd:
Hoarse he bays with hideous din,
Eyes, that glow, & fangs, that grin,
And long pursues with fruitless yell
The Father of the powerful spell.

Onward still his way he takes,
(The groaning earth beneath him shakes)
Till full before his fearless eyes
The portals nine of hell arise.

    Right against the eastern gate
By the moss-grown pile he sate,
Where long of yore to sleep was laid
The dust of the prophetic Maid.
Facing to the northern clime
Thrice he traced the runic rhyme,
Thrice pronounc'd in accents dread
The thrilling verse, that wakes the Dead,
Till from out the hollow ground
Slowly breath'd a sullen sound.

    Pr: What call unknown, what charms presume
To break the quiet of the tomb?
Who thus afflicts my troubled sprite,
And drags me from the realms of night?
Long on these mould'ring bones have beat
The winter's snow, the summer's heat
The drenching dews, & driving rain!
Let me, let me sleep again.
Who is he with voice unblest,
That calls me from the bed of rest?

    O: A Traveller to thee unknown
Is he, that calls, a Warriour's Son.
Thou the deeds of light shalt know,
Tell me what is done below,
For whom yon glitt'ring board is spread,
Drest for whom yon golden bed.

    Pr: Mantling in the goblet see
The pure bev'rage of the bee,
O'er it hangs the shield of gold;
'Tis the drink of *Balder* bold:
Balder's head to death is giv'n.
Pain can reach the Sons of heav'n!
Unwilling I my lips unclose,
Leave me, leave me to repose.

    O: Once again my call obey.
Prophetess, arise & say,
What dangers *Odin*'s Child await,
Who the Author of his fate.

    Pr: In *Hoder*'s hand the Heroe's doom:
His Brother sends him to the tomb.

Now my weary lips I close.
Leave me, leave me to repose.
  O: Prophetess, my spell obey,
Once again arise & say,
Who th' Avenger of his guilt,
By whom shall *Hoder*'s blood be spilt.
  Pr: In the caverns of the west
By *Odin*'s fierce embrace comprest
A wond'rous Boy shall *Rinda* bear,
Who ne'er shall comb his raven-hair,
Nor wash his visage in the stream,
Nor see the sun's departing beam:
Till he on *Hoder*'s coarse shall smile
Flaming on the fun'ral pile.
Now my weary lips I close;
Leave me, leave me to repose.
  O: Yet a while my call obey.
Prophetess, awake & say,
What Virgins these in speechless woe,
That bend to earth their solemn brow,
That their flaxen tresses tear,
And snowy veils, that float in air.
Tell me, whence their sorrows rose:
Then I leave thee to repose.
  Pr: Ha! no Traveller art thou,
King of Men, I know thee now,
Mightiest of a mighty line—
  O: No boding Maid of skill divine
Art thou, nor Prophetess of good;
But Mother of the giant-brood!
  Pr: Hie thee hence & boast at home,
That never shall Enquirer come
To break my iron-sleep again:
Till *Lok* has burst his tenfold chain.
Never, till substantial Night
Has reassum'd her ancient right;
Till wrap'd in flames, in ruin hurl'd,
Sinks the fabrick of the world.

WILLIAM COLLINS

1721–1759

Ode to Evening

IF aught of oaten stop, or pastoral song,
May hope, chaste eve, to soothe thy modest ear,
   Like thy own solemn springs,
   Thy springs and dying gales;

O nymph reserved, while now the bright-haired sun
Sits in yon western tent, whose cloudy skirts,
   With brede ethereal wove,
   O'er hang his wavy bed:

Now air is hushed, save where the weak-eyed bat
With short shrill shriek flits by on leathern wing,
   Or where the beetle winds
   His small but sullen horn,

As oft he rises, 'midst the twilight path
Against the pilgrim borne in heedless hum:
   Now teach me, maid composed
   To breathe some softened strain,

Whose numbers, stealing through thy darkening vale,
May not unseemly with its stillness suit,
   As, musing slow, I hail
   Thy genial loved return!

For when thy folding-star arising shows
His paly circlet, at his warning lamp
   The fragrant hours, and elves
   Who slept in buds the day,

And many a nymph who wreathes her brows with sedge,
And sheds the freshening dew, and lovelier still,
   The pensive pleasures sweet,
   Prepare thy shadowy car:

brede] braid, embroidery

Then lead, calm votaress, where some sheety lake
Cheers the lone heath, or some time-hallowed pile
  Or upland fallows grey
  Reflect its last cool gleam.

Or if chill blustering winds, or driving rain,
Prevent my willing feet, be mine the hut
  That from the mountain's side
  Views wilds and swelling floods,

And hamlets brown, and dim-discovered spires,
And hears their simple bell, and marks o'er all
  Thy dewy fingers draw
  The gradual dusky veil.

While spring shall pour his show'rs, as oft he wont,
And bathe thy breathing tresses, meekest eve!
  While summer loves to sport
  Beneath thy lingering light;

While sallow autumn fills thy lap with leaves,
Or winter, yelling through the troublous air,
  Affrights thy shrinking train,
  And rudely rends thy robes:

So long, regardful of thy quiet rule,
Shall fancy, friendship, science, rose-lipped health
  Thy gentlest influence own,
  And hymn thy favourite name!

An Ode on the Popular Superstitions of the Highlands of Scotland, Considered as the Subject of Poetry

HOME, thou return'st from Thames, whose naiads long
  Have seen thee ling'ring, with a fond delay,
Mid those soft friends, whose hearts, some future day,
  Shall melt, perhaps, to hear thy tragic song.
Go, not unmindful of that cordial youth,
  Whom, long endeared, thou leav'st by Lavant's side;
Together let us wish him lasting truth,
  And joy untainted with his destined bride.
Go! nor regardless, while these numbers boast
  My short-lived bliss, forget my social name;

But think far off how, on the southern coast,
    I met thy friendship with an equal flame!
Fresh to that soil thou turn'st, whose every vale
    Shall prompt the poet, and his song demand:
To thee thy copious subjects ne'er shall fail;
    Thou need'st but take the pencil to thy hand,
And paint what all believe who own thy genial land.

II

There must thou wake perforce thy Doric quill,
    'Tis Fancy's land to which thou sett'st thy feet,
Where still, 'tis said, the fairy people meet
    Beneath each birken shade or mead or hill.
There each trim lass that skims the milky store
    To the swart tribes their creamy bowl allots;
By night they sip it round the cottage-door,
    While airy minstrels warble jocund notes.
There every herd, by sad experience, knows
    How, winged with fate, their elf-shot arrows fly.
When the sick ewe her summer food foregoes,
    Or, stretched on earth, the heart-smit heifers lie.
Such airy beings awe th' untutored swain:
    Nor thou, though learned, his homelier thoughts neglect;
Let thy sweet muse the rural faith sustain:
    These are the themes of simple, sure effect,
That add new conquests to her boundless reign,
And fill, with double force, her heart-commanding strain.

III

Ev'n yet preserved, how often may'st thou hear,
    Where to the pole the Boreal mountains run,
Taught by the father to his list'ning son
    Strange lays, whose power had charmed a Spenser's ear.
At every pause, before thy mind possessed,
    Old Runic bards shall seem to rise around,
With uncouth lyres, in many-coloured vest,
    Their matted hair with boughs fantastic crowned:
Whether thou bid'st the well-taught hind repeat
    The choral dirge that mourns some chieftain brave,
When every shrieking maid her bosom beat,
    And strewed with choicest herbs his scented grave;

Or whether, sitting in the shepherd's shiel,
　Thou hear'st some sounding tale of war's alarms;
When, at the bugle's call, with fire and steel,
　The sturdy clans poured forth their bony swarms,
And hostile brothers met to prove each other's arms.

IV

'Tis thine to sing, how framing hideous spells
　In Sky's lone isle the gifted wizard seer,
Lodged in the wintry cave with ——,
　Or in the depth of Uist's dark forests dwells:
How they, whose sight such dreary dreams engross,
　With their own visions oft astonished droop,
When o'er the wat'ry strath or quaggy moss
　They see the gliding ghosts unbodied troop.
Or if in sports, or on the festive green,
　Their —— glance some fated youth descry,
Who, now perhaps in lusty vigour seen
　And rosy health, shall soon lamented die.
For them the viewless forms of air obey,
　Their bidding heed, and at their beck repair.
They know what spirit brews the stormful day,
　And heartless, oft like moody madness stare
To see the phantom train their secret work prepare.

[25 lines lost.]

VI

What though far off, from some dark dell espied
　His glimm'ring mazes cheer th' excursive sight,
Yet turn, ye wand'rers, turn your steps aside,
　Nor trust the guidance of that faithless light;
For watchful, lurking 'mid th' unrustling reed,
　At those mirk hours the wily monster lies,
And listens oft to hear the passing steed,
　And frequent round him rolls his sullen eyes,
If chance his savage wrath may some weak wretch surprise.

VII

Ah, luckless swain, o'er all unblest indeed!
　Whom late bewildered in the dank, dark fen,
Far from his flocks and smoking hamlet then!
　To that sad spot ————:

shiel] hut

On him enraged, the fiend, in angry mood,
Shall never look with pity's kind concern,
But instant, furious, raise the whelming flood
    O'er its drowned bank, forbidding all return.
Or, if he meditate his wished escape
    To some dim hill that seems uprising near,
To his faint eye the grim and grisly shape,
    In all its terrors clad, shall wild appear.
Meantime, the wat'ry surge shall around him rise,
    Poured sudden forth from every swelling source.
What now remains but tears and hopeless sighs!
    His fear-shook limbs have lost their youthly force,
And down the waves he floats, a pale and breathless corse.

VIII

For him, in vain, his anxious wife shall wait,
    Or wander forth to meet him on his way;
For him, in vain, at to-fall of the day,
    His babes shall linger at th' unclosing gate!
Ah, ne'er shall he return! Alone, if night
    Her travelled limbs in broken slumbers steep,
With dropping willows dressed, his mournful sprite
    Shall visit sad, perchance, her silent sleep:
Then he, perhaps, with moist and wat'ry hand,
    Shall fondly seem to press her shudd'ring cheek
And with his blue swoln face before her stand,
    And shiv'ring cold, these piteous accents speak:
'Pursue, dear wife, thy daily toils pursue
    At dawn or dusk, industrious as before;
Nor e'er of me one hapless thought renew,
    While I lie welt'ring on the oziered shore,
Drowned by the kelpie's wrath, nor e'er shall aid thee more!'

IX

Unbounded is thy range; with varied style
    Thy muse may, like those feath'ry tribes which spring
From their rude rocks, extend her skirting wing
    Round the moist marge of each cold Hebrid isle,
To that hoar pile which still its ruin shows:
    In whose small vaults a pigmy-folk is found,
Whose bones the delver with his spade upthrows,
    And culls them, wond'ring from the hallowed ground!

kelpie] a malignant water sprite

Or thither where beneath the show'ry west
   The mighty kings of three fair realms are laid;
Once foes, perhaps, together now they rest.
   No slaves revere them, and no wars invade:
Yet frequent now, at midnight's solemn hour,
   The rifted mounds their yawning cells unfold,
And forth the monarchs stalk with sov'reign power
   In pageant robes, and wreathed with sheeny gold,
And on their twilight tombs aerial council hold.

X

But O! o'er all, forget not Kilda's race,
   On whose bleak rocks, which brave the wasting tides,
Fair nature's daughter, virtue, yet abides.
   Go, just, as they, their blameless manners traced
Then to my ear transmit some gentle song
   Of those whose lives are yet sincere and plain,
Their bounded walks the rugged cliffs along,
   And all their prospect but the wintry main.
With sparing temp'rance, at the needful time,
   They drain the sainted spring, or, hunger-prest,
Along th' Atlantic rock undreading climb,
   And of its eggs despoil the solan's nest.
Thus blest in primal innocence they live,
   Sufficed and happy with that frugal fare
Which tasteful toil and hourly danger give.
   Hard is their shallow soil, and bleak and bare;
Nor ever vernal bee was heard to murmur there!

XI

Nor need'st thou blush, that such false themes engage
   Thy gentle mind, of fairer stores possessed;
For not alone they touch the village breast,
   But filled in elder time th' historic page,
There Shakespeare's self, with every garland crowned,

  . . . .

   In musing hour, his wayward sisters found,
And with their terrors dressed the magic scene.
   From them he sung, when mid his bold design,
Before the Scot afflicted and aghast,
   The shadowy kings of Banquo's fated line,
Through the dark cave in gleamy pageant past.
   Proceed, nor quit the tales which, simply told,

Could once so well my answ'ring bosom pierce;
   Proceed, in forceful sounds and colours bold
The native legends of thy land rehearse;
To such adapt thy lyre and suit thy powerful verse.

XII

In scenes like these, which, daring to depart
   From sober truth, are still to nature true,
And call forth fresh delight to fancy's view,
   Th' heroic muse employed her Tasso's art!
How have I trembled, when at Tancred's stroke,
   Its gushing blood the gaping cypress poured;
When each live plant with mortal accents spoke,
   And the wild blast up-heaved the vanished sword!
How have I sat, when piped the pensive wind,
   To hear his harp, by British Fairfax strung.
Prevailing poet, whose undoubting mind
   Believed the magic wonders which he sung!
Hence at each sound imagination glows;

. . . .

Hence his warm lay with softest sweetness flows;
Melting it flows, pure, num'rous, strong and clear,
And fills th' impassioned heart, and wins th' harmonious ear.

XIII

All hail, ye scenes that o'er my soul prevail,
   Ye ——— friths and lakes which, far away,
Are by smooth Annan filled, or past'ral Tay,
   Or Don's romantic springs, at distance, hail!
The time shall come when I, perhaps, may tread
   Your lowly glens, o'erhung with spreading broom,
Or o'er your stretching heaths by fancy led:

. . . .

Then will I dress once more the faded bower,
   Where Jonson sat in Drummond's [classic] shade,
Or crop from Tiviots dale each [lyric flower],
   And mourn on Yarrow's banks [where Willy's laid].
Meantime, ye pow'rs, that on the plains which bore,
   The cordial youth, on Lothian's plains attend,
Where'er he dwell, on hill, or lowly muir,
   To him I lose, your kind protection lend,
And, touched with love like mine, preserve my absent friend.

How Sleep the Brave

HOW sleep the brave, who sink to rest
By all their country's wishes blest!
When Spring, with dewy fingers cold,
Returns to deck their hallowed mould,
She there shall dress a sweeter sod
Than Fancy's feet have ever trod.
By fairy hands their knell is rung;
By forms unseen their dirge is sung;
There Honour comes, a pilgrim grey,
To bless the turf that wraps their clay;
And Freedom shall awhile repair
To dwell, a weeping hermit, there!

Ode to Simplicity

O THOU, by Nature taught
To breathe her genuine thought
In numbers warmly pure and sweetly strong:
Who first on mountains wild,
In fancy, loveliest child,
Thy babe and pleasure's, nursed the pow'rs of song.

Thou, who with hermit heart
Disdain'st the wealth of art,
And gauds, and pageant weeds, and trailing pall:
But com'st a decent maid,
In Attic robe arrayed,
O chaste, unboastful nymph, to thee I call!

By all the honeyed store
On Hybla's thymy shore,
By all her blooms and mingled murmurs dear,
By her whose love-lorn woe,
In evening musings slow,
Soothed sweetly sad Electra's poet's ear:

By old Cephisus deep,
Who spread his wavy sweep
In warbled wand'rings round thy green retreat;
On whose enamelled side,
When holy Freedom died,
No equal haunt allured thy future feet!

O sister meek of truth,
   To my admiring youth
Thy sober aid and native charms infuse!
   The flow'rs that sweetest breathe,
   Though beauty culled the wreath,
Still ask thy hand to range their ordered hues.

   While Rome could none esteem,
   But virtue's patriot theme,
You loved her hills, and led her laureate band;
   But stayed to sing alone
   To one distinguished throne,
And turned thy face, and fled her altered land.

   No more, in hall or bower,
   The passions own thy power.
Love, only Love her forceless numbers mean;
   For thou hast left her shrine,
   Nor olive more, nor vine,
Shall gain thy feet to bless the servile scene.

   Though taste, though genius bless
   To some divine excess,
Faint's the cold work till thou inspire the whole;
   What each, what all supply,
   May court, may charm our eye,
Thou, only thou, canst raise the meeting soul!

   Of these let others ask,
   To aid some mighty task,
I only seek to find thy temperate vale;
   Where oft my reed might sound
   To maids and shepherds round,
And all thy sons, O Nature, learn my tale.

CHRISTOPHER SMART

1722–1771

from *The Song to David*

O THOU, that sit'st upon a throne,
With harp of high majestic tone,
   To praise the King of Kings;
And voice of heaven-ascending swell,
Which, while its deeper notes excel,
   Clear, as a clarion, rings:

To bless each valley, grove, and coast,
And charm the cherubs to the post
   Of gratitude in throngs;
To keep the days on Zion's mount,
And send the year to his account,
   With dances and with songs:

O Servant of God's holiest charge,
The minister of praise at large,
   Which thou may'st now receive;
From thy blest mansion hail and hear,
From topmost eminence appear
   To this the wreath I weave.

He sang of God—the mighty source
Of all things—the stupendous force
   On which all strength depends;
From whose right arm, beneath whose eyes,
All period, power, and enterprise
   Commences, reigns, and ends.

Angels—their ministry and meed,
Which to and fro with blessings speed,
   Or with their citterns wait;
Where Michael with his millions bows,
Where dwells the seraph and his spouse,
   The cherub and her mate.

Of man—the semblance and effect
Of God and Love—the Saint elect
   For infinite applause—
To rule the land, and briny broad,
To be laborious in his laud,
   And heroes in his cause.

The world, the clustering spheres, He made;
The glorious light, the soothing shade,
   Dale, champaign, grove, and hill;
The multitudinous abyss,
Where Secrecy remains in bliss,
   And Wisdom hides her skill.

Trees, plants, and flowers—of virtuous root;
Gem yielding blossom, yielding fruit,
   Choice gums and precious balm;
Bless ye the nosegay in the vale,
And with the sweetness of the gale
   Enrich the thankful psalm.

Of fowl—e'en every beak and wing
Which cheer the winter, hail the spring,
   That live in peace or prey;
They that make music, or that mock,
The quail, the brave domestic cock,
   The raven, swan, and jay.

Of fishes—every size and shape,
Which nature frames of light escape,
   Devouring man to shun:
The shells are in the wealthy deep,
The shoals upon the surface leap,
   And love the glancing sun.

Of beasts—the beaver plods his task;
While the sleek tigers roll and bask,
   Nor yet the shades arouse:
Her cave the mining coney scoops;
Where o'er the mead the mountain stoops,
   The kids exult and browse.

Of gems—their virtue and their price,
Which hid in earth from man's device,
    Their darts of lustre sheathe;
The jasper of the master's stamp,
The topaz blazing like a lamp
    Among the mines beneath.

Blest was the tenderness he felt
When to his graceful harp he knelt,
    And did for audience call;
When Satan with his hand he quelled,
And in serene suspense he held
    The frantic throes of Saul.

His furious foes no more maligned
As he such melody divined,
    And sense and soul detained;
Now striking strong, now soothing soft,
He sent the godly sounds aloft,
    Or in delight refrained.

When up to heaven his thoughts he piled,
From fervent lips fair Michal smiled,
    As blush to blush she stood;
And chose herself the queen, and gave
Her utmost from her heart, 'so brave,
    And plays his hymns so good.'

The pillars of the Lord are seven,
Which stand from earth to topmost heaven;
    His wisdom drew the plan;
His Word accomplished the design,
From brightest gem to deepest mine,
    From Christ enthroned to man.

Thou art—to give and to confirm,
For each his talent and his term;
    All flesh thy bounties share:
Thou shalt not call thy brother fool;
The porches of the Christian school
    Are meekness, peace, and prayer.

Open, and naked of offence,
Man's made of mercy, soul, and sense;
   God armed the snail and wilk;
Be good to him who pulls thy plough;
Due food and care, due rest, allow
   For her that yields thee milk.

Rise up before the hoary head,
And God's benign commandment dread,
   Which says thou shalt not die:
'Not as I will, but as thou wilt,'
Prayed He whose conscience knew no guilt;
   With whose blessed pattern vie.

Use all thy passions!—love is thine,
And joy, and jealousy divine;
   Thine hope's eternal fort,
And care thy leisure to disturb,
With fear concupiscence to curb,
   And rapture to transport.

Act simply, as occasion asks;
Put mellow wine in seasoned casks;
   Till not with ass and bull:
Remember thy baptismal bond;
Keep from commixtures foul and fond,
   Nor work thy flax with wool.

Distribute: pay the Lord his tithe,
And make the widow's heart-strings blithe;
   Resort with those that weep:
As you from all and each expect,
For all and each thy love direct,
   And render as you reap.

The slander and its bearer spurn,
And propagating praise sojourn
   To make thy welcome last;
Turn from old Adam to the New;
By hope futurity pursue;
   Look upwards to the past.

Control thine eye, salute success,
Honour the wiser, happier bless,
   And for thy neighbour feel;
Grudge not of mammon and his leaven,
Work emulation up to heaven
   By knowledge and by zeal.

O David, highest in the list
   Of worthies, on God's ways insist,
   The genuine word repeat:
Vain are the documents of men,
And vain the flourish of the pen
   That keeps the fool's conceit.

from *Jubilate Agno*

FOR I will consider my Cat Jeoffry.

For he is the servant of the Living God duly and daily serving him.

For at the first glance of the glory of God in the East he worships in his way.

For is this done by wreathing his body seven times round with elegant quickness.

For then he leaps up to catch the musk, which is the blessing of God upon his prayer.

For he rolls upon prank to work it in.

For having done duty and received blessing he begins to consider himself.

For this he performs in ten degrees.

For first he looks upon his fore-paws to see if they are clean.

For secondly he kicks up behind to clear away there.

For thirdly he works it upon stretch with the fore paws extended.

For fourthly he sharpens his paws by wood.

For fifthly he washes himself.

For Sixthly he rolls upon wash.

For Seventhly he fleas himself, that he may not be interrupted upon the beat.

For Eighthly he rubs himself against a post.

For ninthly he rubs himself against a post.

For tenthly he goes in quest of food.

For having consider'd God and himself he will consider his neighbour.

For if he meets another cat he will kiss her in kindness.

For when he takes his prey he plays with it to give it a chance.

For one mouse in seven escapes by his dallying.

For when his day's work is done his business more properly begins.

For he keeps the Lord's watch in the night against the adversary.

For he counteracts the powers of darkness by his electrical skin & glaring eyes.

For he counteracts the Devil, who is death, by brisking about the life.

For in his morning orisons he loves the sun and the sun loves him.

For he is of the tribe of Tiger.

For the Cherub Cat is a term of the Angel Tiger.

For he has the subtlety and hissing of a serpent, which in goodness he suppresses.

For he will not do destruction if he is well-fed, neither will he spit without provocation.

For he purrs in thankfulness, when God tells him he's a good Cat.

For he is an instrument for the children to learn benevolence upon.

For every house is incompleat without him & a blessing is lacking in the spirit.

For the Lord commanded Moses concerning the cats at the departure of the Children of Israel from Egypt.

For every family had one cat at least in the bag.

For the English Cats are the best in Europe.

For he is the cleanest in the use of his fore-paws of any quadrupede.

For the dexterity of his defence is an instance of the love of God to him exceedingly.

For he is the quickest to his mark of any creature.

For he is tenacious of his point.

For he is a mixture of gravity and waggery.

For he knows that God is his Saviour.

For there is nothing sweeter than his peace when at rest.

For there is nothing brisker than his life when in motion.

For he is of the Lord's poor and so indeed is he called by benevolence perpetually—Poor Jeoffry! poor Jeoffry! the rat has bit thy throat.

For I bless the name of the Lord Jesus that Jeoffry is better.

For the divine spirit comes about his body to sustain it in compleat cat.

For his tongue is exceeding pure so that it has in purity what it wants in musick.

For he is docile and can learn certain things.

For he can set up with gravity which is patience upon approbation.

For he can fetch and carry, which is patience in employment.

For he can jump over a stick which is patience upon proof positive.

For he can spraggle upon waggle at the word of command.

For he can jump from an eminence into his master's bosom.

For he can catch the cork and toss it again.

For he is hated by the hypocrite and miser.

For the former is afraid of detection.

For the latter refuses the charge.
For he camels his back to bear the first notion of business.
For he is good to think on, if a man would express himself neatly.
For he made a great figure in Egypt for his signal services.
For he killed the Icneumon-rat very pernicious by land.
For his ears are so acute that they sting again.
For from this proceeds the passing quickness of his attention.
For by stroaking of him I have found out electricity.
For I have perceived God's light about him both wax and fire.
For the Electrical fire is the spiritual substance, which God sends from
    heaven to sustain the bodies both of man and beast.
For God has blessed him in the variety of his movements.
For, tho he cannot fly, he is an excellent clamberer.
For his motions upon the face of the earth are more than any other
    quadrupede.
For he can tread to all the measures upon the musick.
For he can swim for life.
For he can creep.

JOSEPH WARTON

1722–1800

The Dying Indian

THE dart of Izdabel prevails! 'twas dipt
In double poison—I shall soon arrive
At the blest island, where no tigers spring
On heedless hunters; where ananas bloom
Thrice in each moon; where rivers smoothly glide,
Nor thund'ring torrents whirl the light canoe
Down to the sea; where my forefathers feast
Daily on hearts of Spaniards! O my son,
I feel the venom busy in my breast;
Approach and bring my crown, deck'd with the teeth
Of that bold Christian who first dar'd deflow'r
The virgins of the Sun; and, dire to tell!
Robb'd Pachacamac's altar of its gems!
I mark'd the spot where they interr'd this traitor,
And once at midnight stole I to his tomb,
And tore his carcass from the earth, and left it
A prey to poisonous flies. Preserve this crown

With sacred secrecy; if e'er returns
Thy much lov'd mother from the desert woods,
Where, as I hunted late, I hapless lost her,
Cherish her age. Tell her, I ne'er have worshipp'd
With those that eat their God. And when disease
Preys on her languid limbs, then kindly stab her
With thine own hands, nor suffer her to linger,
Like Christian cowards, in a life of pain.
I go! great Copac beckons me! Farewell!

Ode to Evening

HAIL, meek-eyed maiden, clad in sober grey,
Whose soft approach the weary woodman loves,
As, homeward bent to kiss his prattling babes,
He jocund whistles through the twilight groves.

When Phœbus sinks beneath the gilded hills,
You lightly o'er the misty meadows walk,
The drooping daisies bathe in dulcet dews,
And nurse the nodding violet's slender stalk.

The panting Dryads, that in day's fierce heat
To inmost bow'rs and cooling caverns ran,
Return to trip in wanton evening dance,
Old Sylvan, too, returns, and laughing Pan.

To the deep wood the clam'rous rooks repair,
Light skims the swallow o'er the watery scene,
And from the sheep-cotes and fresh furrow'd field,
Stout ploughmen meet to wrestle on the green.

The swain that artless sings on yonder rock,
His nibbling sheep and length'ning shadow spies,
Pleas'd with the cool, the calm, refreshful hour,
And with hoarse hummings of unnumber'd flies.

Now ev'ry passion sleeps; desponding Love,
And pining Envy, ever-restless Pride;
An holy calm creeps o'er my peaceful soul,
Anger and mad ambition's storms subside.

O modest Evening, oft let me appear
A wand'ring votary in thy pensive train,
List'ning to ev'ry wildly warbling throat
That fills with farewell notes the darkening plain.

OLIVER GOLDSMITH
1728–1774

The Deserted Village

SWEET Auburn! loveliest village of the plain,
Where health and plenty cheered the labouring swain,
Where smiling spring its earliest visit paid,
And parting summer's lingering blooms delayed:
Dear lovely bowers of innocence and ease,
Seats of my youth, when every sport could please,
How often have I loitered o'er thy green,
Where humble happiness endeared each scene;
How often have I paused on every charm,
The sheltered cot, the cultivated farm,
The never-failing brook, the busy mill,
The decent church that topped the neighbouring hill,
The hawthorn bush, with seats beneath the shade,
For talking age and whisp'ring lovers made;
How often have I blessed the coming day,
When toil remitting lent its turn to play,
And all the village train, from labour free,
Led up their sports beneath the spreading tree;
While many a pastime circled in the shade,
The young contending as the old surveyed;
And many a gambol frolicked o'er the ground,
And sleights of art and feats of strength went round;
And still as each repeated pleasure tired,
Succeeding sports the mirthful band inspired;
The dancing pair that simply sought renown,
By holding out to tire each other down;
The swain mistrustless of his smutted face,
While secret laughter tittered round the place;
The bashful virgin's side-long looks of love,
The matron's glance that would those looks reprove,
These were thy charms, sweet village; sports like these,
With sweet succession, taught e'en toil to please;
These round thy bowers their cheerful influence shed,
These were thy charms—But all these charms are fled.

Sweet smiling village, loveliest of the lawn,
Thy sports are fled, and all thy charms withdrawn;

Amidst thy bowers the tyrant's hand is seen,
And desolation saddens all thy green:
One only master grasps the whole domain,
And half a tillage stints thy smiling plain:
No more thy glassy brook reflects the day,
But choked with sedges, works its weedy way.
Along thy glades, a solitary guest,
The hollow-sounding bittern guards its nest;
Amidst thy desert walks the lapwing flies,
And tires their echoes with unvaried cries.
Sunk are thy bowers in shapeless ruin all,
And the long grass o'ertops the mould'ring wall;
And trembling, shrinking from the spoiler's hand,
Far, far away, thy children leave the land.

Ill fares the land, to hast'ning ills a prey,
Where wealth accumulates, and men decay:
Princes and lords may flourish, or may fade;
A breath can make them, as a breath has made;
But a bold peasantry, their country's pride,
When once destroyed, can never be supplied.

A time there was, ere England's griefs began,
When every rood of ground maintained its man;
For him light labour spread her wholesome store,
Just gave what life required, but gave no more:
His best companions, innocence and health;
And his best riches, ignorance of wealth.

But times are altered; trade's unfeeling train,
Usurp the land and dispossess the swain;
Along the lawn, where scattered hamlets rose,
Unwieldy wealth and cumbrous pomp repose;
And every want to opulence allied,
And every pang that folly pays to pride.
Those gentle hours that plenty bade to bloom,
Those calm desires that asked but little room,
Those healthful sports that graced the peaceful scene,
Lived in each look, and brightened all the green;
These, far departing, seek a kinder shore,
And rural mirth and manners are no more.

Sweet Auburn! parent of the blissful hour,
Thy glades forlorn confess the tyrant's power.

Here as I take my solitary rounds,
Amidst thy tangling walks and ruined grounds,
And, many a year elapsed, return to view
Where once the cottage stood, the hawthorn grew,
Remembrance wakes with all her busy train,
Swells at my breast, and turns the past to pain.

In all my wand'rings round this world of care,
In all my griefs—and God has given my share—
I still had hopes my latest hours to crown,
Amidst these humble bowers to lay me down;
To husband out life's taper at the close,
And keep the flame from wasting by repose.
I still had hopes, for pride attends us still,
Amidst the swains to show my book-learned skill,
Around my fire an evening group to draw,
And tell of all I felt, and all I saw;
And, as a hare, whom hounds and horns pursue,
Pants to the place from whence at first she flew,
I still had hopes, my long vexations passed,
Here to return—and die at home at last.

O blest retirement, friend to life's decline,
Retreats from care, that never must be mine,
How happy he who crowns in shades like these,
A youth of labour with an age of ease;
Who quits a world where strong temptations try
And, since 'tis hard to combat, learns to fly!
For him no wretches, born to work and weep,
Explore the mine, or tempt the dangerous deep;
No surly porter stands in guilty state
To spurn imploring famine from the gate;
But on he moves to meet his latter end,
Angels around befriending Virtue's friend;
Bends to the grave with unperceived decay,
While resignation gently slopes the way;
And, all his prospects bright'ning to the last,
His Heaven commences ere the world be passed!

Sweet was the sound, when oft at evening's close
Up yonder hill the village murmur rose;
There, as I passed with careless steps and slow,
The mingling notes came softened from below;

157

The swain responsive as the milk-maid sung,
The sober herd that lowed to meet their young;
The noisy geese that gabbled o'er the pool,
The playful children just let loose from school;
The watchdog's voice that bayed the whisp'ring wind,
And the loud laugh that spoke the vacant mind;
These all in sweet confusion sought the shade,
And filled each pause the nightingale had made.
But now the sounds of population fail,
No cheerful murmurs fluctuate in the gale,
No busy steps the grass-grown foot-way tread,
For all the bloomy flush of life is fled.
All but yon widowed, solitary thing
That feebly bends beside the plashy spring;
She, wretched matron, forced, in age, for bread,
To strip the brook with mantling cresses spread,
To pick her wintry faggot from the thorn,
To seek her nightly shed, and weep till morn;
She only left of all the harmless train,
The sad historian of the pensive plain.

Near yonder copse, where once the garden smiled,
And still where many a garden flower grows wild:
There, where a few torn shrubs the place disclose,
The village preacher's modest mansion rose.
A man he was to all the country dear,
And passing rich with forty pounds a year;
Remote from towns he ran his godly race,
Nor e'er had changed, nor wished to change his place;
Unpractised he to fawn, or seek for power,
By doctrines fashioned to the varying hour;
For other aims his heart had learned to prize,
More skilled to raise the wretched than to rise.
His house was known to all the vagrant train,
He chid their wand'rings, but relieved their pain;
The long-remembered beggar was his guest,
Whose beard descending swept his aged breast;
The ruined spendthrift, now no longer proud,
Claimed kindred there, and had his claims allowed;
The broken soldier, kindly bade to stay,
Sat by his fire, and talked the night away;
Wept o'er his wounds, or tales of sorrow done,
Shouldered his crutch, and showed how fields were won.

Pleased with his guests, the good man learned to glow,
And quite forgot their vices in their woe;
Careless their merits, or their faults to scan,
His pity gave ere charity began.

    Thus to relieve the wretched was his pride,
And e'en his failings leaned to virtue's side;
But in his duty prompt at every call,
He watched and wept, he prayed and felt, for all.
And, as a bird each fond endearment tries
To tempt its new-fledged offspring to the skies,
He tried each art, reproved each dull delay,
Allured to brighter worlds, and led the way.

    Beside the bed where parting life was laid,
And sorrow, guilt, and pain, by turns dismayed,
The reverend champion stood. At his control,
Despair and anguish fled the struggling soul;
Comfort came down the trembling wretch to raise,
And his last falt'ring accents whispered praise.

    At church, with meek and unaffected grace,
His looks adorned the venerable place;
Truth from his lips prevailed with double sway,
And fools, who came to scoff, remained to pray.
The service passed, around the pious man,
With steady zeal, each honest rustic ran;
E'en children followed with endearing wile,
And plucked his gown, to share the good man's smile.
His ready smile a parent's warmth expressed,
Their welfare pleased him, and their cares distressed;
To them his heart, his love, his griefs were given,
But all his serious thoughts had rest in Heaven.
As some tall cliff, that lifts its awful form,
Swells from the vale, and midway leaves the storm,
Though round its breast the rolling clouds are spread,
Eternal sunshine settles on its head.

    Beside yon straggling fence that skirts the way,
With blossomed furze unprofitably gay,
There, in his noisy mansion, skilled to rule,
The village master taught his little school;

A man severe he was, and stern to view;
I knew him well, and every truant knew;
Well had the boding tremblers learned to trace
The day's disasters in his morning face;
Full well they laughed, with counterfeited glee,
At all his jokes, for many a joke had he;
Full well the busy whisper, circling round,
Conveyed the dismal tidings when he frowned;
Yet he was kind; or if severe in aught
The love he bore to learning was in fault;
The village all declared how much he knew;
'Twas certain he could write, and cypher too;
Lands he could measure, terms and tides presage,
And e'en the story ran that he could gauge.
In arguing too, the parson owned his skill,
For e'en though vanquished, he could argue still;
While words of learned length and thund'ring sound
Amazed the gazing rustics ranged around,
And still they gazed, and still the wonder grew,
That one small head could carry all he knew.

But past is all his fame. The very spot
Where many a time he triumphed, is forgot.
Near yonder thorn, that lifts its head on high,
Where once the sign-post caught the passing eye,
Low lies that house where nut-brown draughts inspired,
Where grey-beard mirth and smiling toil retired,
Where village statesmen talked with looks profound,
And news much older than their ale went round.
Imagination fondly stoops to trace
The parlour splendours of that festive place;
The white-washed wall, the nicely sanded floor,
The varnished clock that clicked behind the door;
The chest contrived a double debt to pay,
A bed by night, a chest of drawers by day;
The pictures placed for ornament and use,
The twelve good rules, the royal game of goose;
The hearth, except when winter chilled the day,
With aspen boughs, and flowers, and fennel gay;
While broken tea-cups, wisely kept for show,
Ranged o'er the chimney, glistened in a row.

Vain, transitory splendours! Could not all
Reprieve the tottering mansion from its fall!

Obscure it sinks, nor shall it more impart
An hour's importance to the poor man's heart;
Thither no more the peasant shall repair
To sweet oblivion of his daily care;
No more the farmer's news, the barber's tale,
No more the wood-man's ballad shall prevail;
No more the smith his dusky brow shall clear,
Relax his pond'rous strength, and lean to hear;
The host himself no longer shall be found
Careful to see the mantling bliss go round;
Nor the coy maid, half willing to be pressed,
Shall kiss the cup to pass it to the rest.

Yes! let the rich deride, the proud disdain,
These simple blessings of the lowly train;
To me more dear, congenial to my heart,
One native charm, than all the gloss of art;
Spontaneous joys, where Nature has its play,
The soul adopts, and owns their first-born sway;
Lightly they frolic o'er the vacant mind,
Unenvied, unmolested, unconfined:
But the long pomp, the midnight masquerade,
With all the freaks of wanton wealth arrayed,
In these, ere triflers half their wish obtain,
The toiling pleasure sickens into pain;
And, e'en while fashion's brightest arts decoy,
The heart distrusting asks, if this be joy.

Ye friends to truth, ye statesmen, who survey
The rich man's joys increase, the poor's decay,
'Tis yours to judge, how wide the limits stand
Between a splendid and a happy land.
Proud swells the tide with loads of freighted ore,
And shouting Folly hails them from her shore;
Hoards, e'en beyond the miser's wish abound,
And rich men flock from all the world around.
Yet count our gains. This wealth is but a name
That leaves our useful products still the same.
Not so the loss. The man of wealth and pride
Takes up a space that many poor supplied;
Space for his lake, his park's extended bounds,
Space for his horses, equipage, and hounds;
The robe that wraps his limbs in silken sloth

Has robbed the neighbouring fields of half their growth,
His seat, where solitary sports are seen,
Indignant spurns the cottage from the green;
Around the world each needful product flies,
For all the luxuries the world supplies:
While thus the land adorned for pleasure, all
In barren splendour feebly waits the fall.

As some fair female unadorned and plain,
Secure to please while youth confirms her reign,
Slights every borrowed charm that dress supplies,
Nor shares with art the triumph of her eyes:
But when those charms are passed, for charms are frail,
When time advances, and when lovers fail,
She then shines forth, solicitous to bless,
In all the glaring impotence of dress.
Thus fares the land, by luxury betrayed,
In nature's simplest charms at first arrayed;
But verging to decline, its splendours rise,
Its vistas strike, its palaces surprise;
While scourged by famine from the smiling land,
The mournful peasant leads his humble band;
And while he sinks, without one arm to save,
The country blooms—a garden, and a grave.

Where then, ah! where, shall poverty reside,
To 'scape the pressure of contiguous pride?
If to some common's fenceless limits strayed,
He drives his flock to pick the scanty blade,
Those fenceless fields the sons of wealth divide,
And e'en the bare-worn common is denied.

If to the city sped—What waits him there?
To see profusion that he must not share;
To see ten thousand baneful arts combined
To pamper luxury, and thin mankind;
To see those joys the sons of pleasure know
Extorted from his fellow creature's woe.
Here, while the courtier glitters in brocade,
There the pale artist plies the sickly trade;
Here, while the proud their long-drawn pomps display,
There the black gibbet glooms beside the way.
The dome where Pleasure holds her midnight reign
Here, richly decked, admits the gorgeous train;

Tumultuous grandeur crowds the blazing square,
The rattling chariots clash, the torches glare.
Sure scenes like these no troubles e'er annoy!
Sure these denote one universal joy!
Are these thy serious thoughts?—Ah, turn thine eyes
Where the poor houseless shiv'ring female lies.
She once, perhaps, in village plenty bless'd,
Has wept at tales of innocence distress'd;
Her modest looks the cottage might adorn,
Sweet as the primrose peeps beneath the thorn;
Now lost to all; her friends, her virtue fled,
Near her betrayer's door she lays her head,
And, pinched with cold, and shrinking from the shower.
With heavy heart deplores that luckless hour,
When idly first, ambitious of the town,
She left her wheel and robes of country brown.

Do thine, sweet Auburn, thine, the loveliest train,
Do thy fair tribes participate her pain?
E'en now, perhaps, by cold and hunger led,
At proud men's doors they ask a little bread!

Ah, no. To distant climes, a dreary scene,
Where half the convex world intrudes between,
Through torrid tracts with fainting steps they go,
Where wild Altama murmurs to their woe.
Far different there from all that charmed before,
The various terrors of that horrid shore;
Those blazing suns that dart a downward ray,
And fiercely shed intolerable day;
Those matted woods where birds forget to sing,
But silent bats in drowsy clusters cling;
Those pois'nous fields with rank luxuriance crowned,
Where the dark scorpion gathers death around;
Where at each step the stranger fears to wake
The rattling terrors of the vengeful snake;
Where crouching tigers wait their hapless prey,
And savage men more murd'rous still than they;
While oft in whirls the mad tornado flies,
Mingling the ravaged landscape with the skies.
Far different these from every former scene,
The cooling brook, the grassy-vested green,
The breezy covert of the warbling grove,
That only sheltered thefts of harmless love.

Good heaven! what sorrows gloomed that parting day,
That called them from their native walks away;
When the poor exiles, every pleasure passed,
Hung round their bowers, and fondly looked their last,
And took a long farewell, and wished in vain
For seats like these beyond the western main;
And shudd'ring still to face the distant deep,
Returned and wept, and still returned to weep.
The good old sire, the first prepared to go
To new-found worlds, and wept for others' woe;
But for himself, in conscious virtue brave,
He only wished for worlds beyond the grave.
His lovely daughter, lovelier in her tears,
The fond companion of his helpless years,
Silent went next, neglectful of her charms,
And left a lover's for a father's arms.
With louder plaints the mother spoke her woes,
And bless'd the cot where every pleasure rose
And kissed her thoughtless babes with many a tear,
And clasped them close, in sorrow doubly dear;
Whilst her fond husband strove to lend relief
In all the silent manliness of grief.

O Luxury! thou curs'd by Heaven's decree,
How ill exchange are things like these for thee!
How do thy potions, with insidious joy
Diffuse their pleasures only to destroy!
Kingdoms, by thee, to sickly greatness grown,
Boast of a florid vigour not their own;
At every draught more large and large they grow,
A bloated mass of rank unwieldy woe;
Till sapped their strength, and every part unsound,
Down, down they sink, and spread a ruin round.

E'en now the devastation is begun,
And half the business of destruction done;
E'en now, methinks, as pond'ring here I stand,
I see the rural virtues leave the land:
Down where yon anchoring vessel spreads the sail,
That idly waiting flaps with every gale,
Downward they move, a melancholy band,
Pass from the shore, and darken all the strand.
Contented toil, and hospitable care,
And kind connubial tenderness, are there;

And piety, with wishes placed above,
And steady loyalty, and faithful love.
And thou, sweet Poetry, thou loveliest maid,
Still first to fly where sensual joys invade;
Unfit in these degenerate times of shame,
To catch the heart, or strike for honest fame;
Dear charming nymph, neglected and decried,
My shame in crowds, my solitary pride;
Thou source of all my bliss, and all my woe,
That found'st me poor at first, and keep'st me so;
Thou guide by which the nobler arts excel,
Thou nurse of every virtue, fare thee well!
Farewell, and Oh! where'er thy voice be tried,
On Torno's cliffs, or Pambamarca's side,
Whether where equinoctial fervours glow,
Or winter wraps the polar world in snow,
Still let thy voice, prevailing over time,
Redress the rigours of th' inclement clime;
Aid slighted truth; with thy persuasive strain
Teach erring man to spurn the rage of gain;
Teach him, that states of native strength possess'd,
Though very poor, may still be very bless'd;
That trade's proud empire hastes to swift decay,
As ocean sweeps the laboured mole away;
While self-dependent power can time defy,
As rocks resist the billows and the sky.

Elegy on the Death of a Mad Dog

GOOD people all, of every sort,
    Give ear unto my song;
And if you find it wond'rous short,
    It cannot hold you long.

In Islington there was a man,
    Of whom the world might say,
That still a godly race he ran,
    Whene'er he went to pray.

A kind and gentle heart he had,
    To comfort friends and foes;
The naked every day he clad,
    When he put on his clothes.

And in that town a dog was found,
   As many dogs there be,
Both mongrel, puppy, whelp, and hound,
   And curs of low degree.

This dog and man at first were friends;
   But when a pique began,
The dog, to gain some private ends,
   Went mad and bit the man.

Around from all the neighbouring streets
   The wond'ring neighbours ran,
And swore the dog had lost his wits,
   To bite so good a man.

The wound it seemed both sore and sad
   To every Christian eye;
And while they swore the dog was mad,
   They swore the man would die.

But soon a wonder came to light,
   That showed the rogues they lied:
The man recovered of the bite,
   The dog it was that died.

from *The Vicar of Wakefield*

Song

WHEN lovely woman stoops to folly,
   And finds too late that men betray,
What charm can soothe her melancholy,
   What art can wash her guilt away?

The only art her guilt to cover,
   To hide her shame from every eye,
To give repentance to her lover,
   And wring his bosom, is—to die.

THOMAS WARTON THE YOUNGER
1728–1790

To the River Lodon

AH! what a weary race my feet have run,
Since first I trod thy banks with alders crowned,
And thought my way was all through fairy ground,
Beneath thy azure sky, and golden sun:
Where first my Muse to lisp her notes begun!
While pensive Memory traces back the round,
Which fills the varied interval between;
Much pleasure, more of sorrow, marks the scene.
Sweet native stream! those skies and suns so pure
No more return, to cheer my evening road;
Yet still one joy remains, that not obscure,
Nor useless, all my vacant days have flowed,
From youth's gay dawn to manhood's prime mature;
Nor with the Muse's laurel unbestowed.

from *The Pleasures of Melancholy*

BENEATH yon ruin'd abbey's moss-grown piles
Oft let me sit, at twilight hour of eve,
Where through some western window the pale moon
Pours her long-levell'd rule of streaming light;
While sullen sacred silence reigns around,
Save the lone screech-owl's note, who builds his bow'r
Amid the mould'ring caverns dark and damp,
Or the calm breeze, that rustles in the leaves
Of flaunting ivy, that with mantle green
Invests some wasted tow'r. Or let me tread
Its neighbouring walk of pines, where mus'd of old
The cloister'd brothers: through the gloomy void
That far extends beneath their ample arch,
As on I pace, religious horror wraps
My soul in dread repose. But when the world
Is clad in midnight's raven-colour'd robe,
'Mid hollow charnel let me watch the flame
Of taper dim, shedding a livid glare
O'er the wan heaps; while airy voices talk

Along the glimm'ring walls; or ghostly shape
At distance seen, invites with beck'ning hand
My lonesome steps, through the far-winding vaults.
Nor undelightful is the solemn noon
Of night, when haply wakeful from my couch
I start: Lo, all is motionless around!
Roars not the rushing wind; the sons of men
And ev'ry beast in mute oblivion lie;
All nature's husht in silence and in sleep.
O, then how fearful is it to reflect
That through the still globe's awful solitude,
No being wakes but me! till stealing sleep
My drooping temples bathes in opiate dews.
Nor then let dreams, of wanton folly born,
My senses lead through flow'ry paths of joy;
But let the sacred Genius of the night
Such mystic visions send, as Spenser saw,
When thro' bewilder'd Fancy's magic maze,
To the fell house of Busyrane he led
Th' unshaken Britomart; or Milton knew,
When in abstracted thought he first conceived
All heav'n in tumult, and the Seraphim
Came tow'ring, arm'd in adamant and gold . . .
    Few know that elegance of soul refin'd,
Whose soft sensation feels a quicker joy
From Melancholy's scenes, than the dull pride
Of tasteless splendour and magnificence
Can e'er afford. Thus Elöise, whose mind
Had languished to the pangs of melting love,
More genuine transport found, as on some tomb
Reclin'd, she watch'd the tapers of the dead;
Or through the pillar'd aisles, and pale shrines
Of imaged saints and intermingled graves,
Mus'd a veil'd votaress; than Flavia feels,
As thro' the mazes of the festive ball,
Proud of her conquering charms, and beauty's blaze,
She floats amid the silken sons of dress,
And shines the fairest of th' assembled fair.
    When azure noontide cheers the dædal globe,
And the blest regent of the golden day
Rejoices in his bright meridian tower,
How oft my wishes ask the night's return
That best befriends the melancholy mind!
Hail, sacred Night! Thou too shalt share my song!

Sister of ebon-sceptred Hecate, hail!
Whether in congregated clouds thou wrap'st
Thy viewless chariot, or with silver crown
Thy beaming head encirclest, ever hail!
What tho' beneath thy gloom the sorceress-train,
Far in obscured haunt of Lapland moors,
With rhymes uncouth the bloody cauldron bless;
Tho' Murder wan beneath thy shrouding shade
Summons her slow-ey'd vot'ries to devise
Of secret slaughter, while by one blue lamp
In hideous conference sits the list'ning band,
And starts at each low wind or wakeful sound;
What tho' thy stay the pilgrim curseth oft,
As all benighted in Arabian wastes
He hears the wilderness around him howl
With roaming monsters, while on his hoar head
The black-descending tempest ceaseless beats;
Yet more delightful to my pensive mind
Is thy return, than blooming morn's approach,
Ev'n then, in youthful pride of op'ning May,
When from the portals of the saffron east
She sheds fresh roses, and ambrosial dews. . . .
Yet not ungrateful is the morn's approach,
When dropping wet she comes, and clad in clouds,
While thro' the damp air scowls the louring south,
Black'ning the landscape's face, that grove and hill
In formless vapours undistinguish'd swim:
Th' afflicted songsters of the sadden'd groves
Hail not the sullen gloom; the waning elms
That, hoar thro' time, and rang'd in thick array,
Enclose with stately row some rural hall,
Are mute, nor echo with the clamours hoarse
Of rooks, rejoicing in their airy boughs;
While to the shed the dripping poultry crowd,
A mournful train; secure the village hind
Hangs o'er the crackling blaze, nor tempts the storm;
Fix'd in the unfinish'd furrow rests the plough:
Rings not the high wood with enliven'd shouts
Of early hunter; all is silence drear;
And deepest sadness wraps the face of things.

WILLIAM COWPER

1731–1800

Loss of the 'Royal George'

TOLL for the brave—
The brave! that are no more:
    All sunk beneath the wave,
Fast by their native shore.

    Eight hundred of the brave,
Whose courage well was tried,
    Had made the vessel heel
And laid her on her side;

    A land-breeze shook the shrouds,
And she was overset;
    Down went the *Royal George*
With all her crew complete.

    Toll for the brave—
Brave Kempenfelt is gone,
    His last sea-fight is fought,
His work of glory done.

    It was not in the battle,
No tempest gave the shock,
    She sprang no fatal leak,
She ran upon no rock;

    His sword was in the sheath,
His fingers held the pen,
    When Kempenfelt went down
With twice four hundred men.

    Weigh the vessel up,
Once dreaded by our foes,
    And mingle with your cup
The tears that England owes;

    Her timbers yet are sound,
And she may float again,
    Full charged with England's thunder,
And plough the distant main;

    But Kempenfelt is gone,
His victories are o'er;
    And he and his eight hundred
Must plough the wave no more.

WILLIAM COWPER

On the Receipt of My Mother's Picture out of Norfolk, the gift of my cousin Ann Bodham

OH that those lips had language! Life has passed
With me but roughly since I heard thee last.
Those lips are thine—thy own sweet smiles I see,
The same that oft in childhood solaced me;
Voice only fails, else, how distinct they say,
'Grieve not, my child, chase all thy fears away!'
The meek intelligence of those dear eyes
(Blest be the art that can immortalize,
The art that baffles time's tyrannic claim
To quench it) here shines on me still the same.
    Faithful remembrancer of one so dear,
Oh welcome guest, though unexpected, here!
Who bidd'st me honour with an artless song,
Affectionate, a mother lost so long,
I will obey, not willingly alone,
But gladly, as the precept were her own;
And, while that face renews my filial grief,
Fancy shall weave a charm for my relief—
Shall steep me in Elysian reverie,
A momentary dream, that thou art she.
    My mother! when I learned that thou wast dead,
Say, wast thou conscious of the tears I shed?
Hovered thy spirit o'er thy sorrowing son,
Wretch even then, life's journey just begun?
Perhaps thou gav'st me, though unseen, a kiss;
Perhaps a tear, if souls can weep in bliss—
Ah that maternal smile! it answers—Yes.
I heard the bell tolled on thy burial day,
I saw the hearse that bore thee slow away,
And, turning from my nurs'ry window, drew
A long, long sigh, and wept a last adieu!
But was it such?—It was.—Where thou art gone
Adieus and farewells are a sound unknown.
May I but meet thee on that peaceful shore,
The parting sound shall pass my lips no more!
Thy maidens grieved themselves at my concern,
Oft gave me promise of a quick return.
What ardently I wished, I long believed,
And, disappointed still, was still deceived;

By disappointment every day beguiled,
Dupe of *to-morrow* even from a child.
Thus many a sad to-morrow came and went,
Till, all my stock of infant sorrow spent,
I learned at last submission to my lot;
But, though I less deplored thee, ne'er forgot.
Where once we dwelt our name is heard no more,
Children not thine have trod my nurs'ry floor;
And where the gard'ner Robin, day by day,
Drew me to school along the public way,
Delighted with my bauble coach, and wrapped
In scarlet mantle warm, and velvet capped,
'Tis now become a history little known,
That once we called the past'ral house our own.
Short-lived possession! but the record fair
That mem'ry keeps of all thy kindness there,
Still outlives many a storm that has effaced
A thousand other themes less deeply traced.
Thy nightly visits to my chamber made,
That thou might'st know me safe and warmly laid.
Thy morning bounties ere I left my home,
The biscuit, or confectionary plum;
The fragrant waters on my cheeks bestowed
By thy own hand, till fresh they shone and glowed.
All this, and more endearing still than all,
Thy constant flow of love, that knew no fall,
Ne'er roughened by those cataracts and brakes
That humour interposed too often makes;
All this still legible in mem'ry's page,
And still to be so, to my latest age,
Adds joy to duty, makes me glad to pay
Such honours to thee as my numbers may;
Perhaps a frail memorial, but sincere,
Not scorned in heaven, though little noticed here.
Could time, his flight reversed, restore the hours,
When, playing with thy vesture's tissued flowers,
The violet, the pink, and jessamine,
I pricked them into paper with a pin,
(And thou wast happier than myself the while,
Would'st softly speak, and stroke my head and smile)
Could those few pleasant hours again appear,
Might one wish bring them, would I wish them here?
I would not trust my heart—the dear delight
Seems so to be desired, perhaps I might.—

But no—what here we call our life is such,
So little to be loved, and thou so much,
That I should ill requite thee to constrain
Thy unbound spirit into bonds again.
   Thou, as a gallant bark from Albion's coast
(The storms all weathered and the ocean crossed)
Shoots into port at some well-havened isle,
Where spices breathe and brighter seasons smile,
There sits quiescent on the floods that show
Her beauteous form reflected clear below,
While airs impregnated with incense play
Around her, fanning light her streamers gay;
So thou, with sails how swift! hast reached the shore
'Where tempests never beat nor billows roar,'
And thy loved consort on the dang'rous tide
Of life, long since, has anchored at thy side.
But me, scarce hoping to attain that rest,
Always from port withheld, always distressed—
Me howling winds drive devious, tempest tossed,
Sails ripped, seams op'ning wide, and compass lost,
And day by day some current's thwarting force
Sets me more distant from a prosp'rous course.
But oh the thought, that thou art safe, and he!
That thought is joy, arrive what may to me.
My boast is not that I deduce my birth
From loins enthroned, and rulers of the earth;
But higher far my proud pretensions rise—
The son of parents passed into the skies.
And now, farewell—time, unrevoked, has run
His wonted course, yet what I wished is done.
By contemplation's help, not sought in vain,
I seem t' have lived my childhood o'er again;
To have renewed the joys that once were mine,
Without the sin of violating thine:
And, while the wings of fancy still are free,
And I can view this mimic show of thee,
Time has but half succeeded in his theft—
Thyself removed, thy power to soothe me left.

WILLIAM COWPER

from *The Winter Morning Walk*

ACQUAINT thyself with God, if thou wouldst taste
His works. Admitted once to his embrace,
Thou shalt perceive that thou wast blind before:
Thine eye shall be instructed; and thine heart
Made pure shall relish, with divine delight,
Till then unfelt, what hands divine have wrought.
Brutes graze the mountain-top, with faces prone,
And eyes intent upon the scanty herb
It yields them; or, recumbent on its brow,
Ruminate heedless of the scene outspread
Beneath, beyond, and stretching far away
From inland regions to the distant main.
Man views it, and admires; but rests content
With what he views. The landscape has his praise,
But not its Author. Unconcerned who formed
The paradise he sees, he finds it such,
And, such well pleased to find it, asks no more.
Not so the mind that has been touched from Heaven,
And in the school of sacred wisdom taught
To read his wonders, in whose thought the world,
Fair as it is, existed ere it was.
Not for its own sake merely, but for His
Much more who fashioned it, he gives it praise,
Praise that, from earth resulting, as it ought,
To earth's acknowledged Sovereign, finds at once
Its only just proprietor in Him.
The soul that sees him or receives sublimed
New faculties, or learns at least to employ
More worthily the powers she owned before;
Discerns in all things what, with stupid gaze
Of ignorance, till then she overlooked,
A ray of heavenly light, gilding all forms
Terrestrial in the vast and the minute—
The unambiguous footsteps of the God
Who gives its lustre to an insect's wing,
And wheels his throne upon the rolling worlds.

WILLIAM FALCONER

1732–1769

from *The Shipwreck*

The ship sets out

THE sun's bright orb, declining all serene,
Now glanc'd obliquely o'er the woodland scene.
Creation smiles around; on every spray
The warbling birds exalt their evening lay.
Blithe skipping o'er yon hill, the fleecy train
Join the deep chorus of the lowing plain:
The golden lime and orange there were seen,
On fragrant branches of perpetual green.
The crystal streams that velvet meadows lave,
To the green ocean roll with chiding wave.
The glassy ocean hush'd forgets to roar,
But trembling murmurs on the sandy shore:
And lo! his surface, lovely to behold!
Glows in the west a sea of living gold!
While, all above, a thousand liveries gay
The skies with pomp ineffable array.
Arabian sweets perfume the happy plains;
Above, beneath, around enchantment reigns!
While yet the shades on Time's eternal scale,
With long vibration deepen o'er the vale;
While yet the songsters of the vocal grove,
With dying numbers tune the soul to love;
With joyful eyes th' attentive master sees
Th' auspicious omens of an eastern breeze—
Now radiant Vesper leads the starry train,
And Night slow draws her veil o'er land and main;
Round the charg'd bowl the sailors form a ring;
By turns recount the wondrous tale, or sing;
As love or battle, hardships of the main,
Or genial wine, awake the homely strain:
Then some the watch of night alternate keep,
The rest lie buried in oblivious sleep.

Deep midnght now involves the livid skies,
While infant breezes from the shore arise.
The waning moon, behind a watery shroud,

Pale glimmer'd o'er the long protracted cloud.
A mighty ring around her silver throne,
With parting meteors cross'd, portentous shone.
This in the troubled sky full oft prevails;
Oft deem'd a signal of tempestuous gales.—
While young ARION sleeps, before his sight
Tumultuous swim the visions of the night.
Now blooming ANNA with her happy swain
Approach'd the sacred Hymeneal fane:
Anon tremendous lightnings flash between;
And funeral pomp, and weeping loves are seen!
Now with PALEMON up a rocky steep,
Whose summit trembles o'er the roaring deep,
With painful step he climb'd; while far above
Sweet ANNA charm'd them with the voice of love.
Then sudden from the slippery height they fell,
While dreadful yawn'd beneath the jaws of Hell.—
Amid this fearful trance a thundering sound
He hears—and thrice the hollow decks rebound.
Upstarting from his couch, on deck he sprung;
Thrice with shrill note the boatswain's whistle rung.
All hands unmoor! proclaims a boisterous cry:
All hands unmoor! the cavern'd rocks reply.
Rous'd from repose, aloft the sailors swarm,
And with their levers soon the windlass arm.
The order given, up springing with a bound,
They lodge the bars, and wheel their engine round; }
At every turn the clanging pauls resound.
Up-torn reluctant from its oozy cave,
The ponderous anchor rises o'er the wave.
Along their slippery masts the yards ascend,
And high in air the canvass wings extend:
Redoubling cords the lofty canvass guide,
And thro' inextricable mazes glide.
The lunar rays with long reflection gleam,
To light the vessel o'er the silver stream:
Along the glassy plain serene she glides,
While azure radiance trembles on her sides.
From east to north the transient breezes play,
And in the Egyptian quarter soon decay.
A calm ensues; they dread the adjacent shore;
The boats with rowers arm'd are sent before:
With cordage fasten'd to the lofty prow,
Aloof to sea the stately ship they tow.

The nervous crew their sweeping oars extend,
And pealing shouts the shore of Candia rend.
Success attends their skill; the danger's o'er;
The port is doubled and beheld no more.

 Now Morn, her lamp pale glimmering on the sight,
Scatter'd before her van reluctant Night.
She comes not in refulgent pomp array'd,
But sternly frowning, wrapt in sullen shade.
Above incumbent vapours, Ida's height,
Tremendous rock! emerges on the sight.
North-east the guardian isle of Standia lies,
And westward Freschin's woody capes arise.

 With whining postures now the wanton sails
Spread all their snares to charm th' inconstant gales.
The swelling stud-sails now their wings extend,
Then stay-sails sidelong to the breeze ascend:[1]
While all to court the wandering breeze are plac'd;
With yards now thwarting, now obliquely brac'd.

 The dim horizon lowering vapours shroud,
And blot the sun yet struggling in the cloud:
Thro' the wide atmosphere, condens'd with haze,
His glaring orb emits a sanguine blaze.
The pilots now their rules of art apply,
The mystic needle's devious aim to try.
The compass plac'd to catch the rising ray,[2]
The quadrant's shadows studious they survey!
Along the arch the gradual index slides.
While Phœbus down the vertic-circle glides.
Now seen on ocean's utmost verge to swim,
He sweeps it vibrant with his nether limb.
Their sage experience thus explores the height,
And polar distance of the source of light:
Then thro' the chiliad's triple maze they trace
Th' analogy that proves the magnet's place,
The wayward steel, to truth thus reconcil'd,
No more th' attentive pilot's eye beguil'd.

 The natives, while the ship departs the land,
Ashore with admiration gazing stand.

---

[1] Studding-sails are long narrow sails, which are only used in fine weather and fair winds, on the outside of the larger square-sails. Stay-sails are three-cornered sails, which are hoisted up on the stays, when the wind crosses the ship's course, either directly or obliquely. (*Author*)

[2] The operation of taking the sun's azimuth, in order to discover the eastern or western variation of the magnetic needle. (*Author*).

Majestically slow, before the breeze,
In silent pomp she marches on the seas.
Her milk-white bottom casts a softer gleam,
While trembling thro' the green translucent stream.
The wales, that close above in contrast shone,
Clasp the long fabric with a jetty zone.
BRITANNIA, riding awful on the prow,
Gaz'd o'er the vassal waves that roll'd below;
Where'er she mov'd, the vassal waves were seen
To yield obsequious and confess their queen.
Th' imperial trident grac'd her dexter hand,
Of power to rule the surge like Moses' wand,
Th' eternal empire of the main to keep,
And guide her squadrons o'er the trembling deep.

The ship is lost

And now, lash'd on by destiny severe,
With horror fraught, the dreadful scene drew near!
The ship hangs hovering on the verge of death,
Hell yawns, rocks rise, and breakers roar beneath!—
In vain, alas! the sacred shades of yore
Would arm the mind with philosophic lore;
In vain they'd teach us, at the latest breath,
To smile serene amid the pangs of death.
Even Zeno's self, and Epictetus old,
This fell abyss had shudder'd to behold.
Had Socrates, for godlike virtue fam'd,
And wisest of the sons of men proclaim'd,
Beheld this scene of phrenzy and distress,
His soul had trembled to its last recess!—
O yet confirm my heart, ye Powers above,
This last tremendous shock of Fate to prove.
The tottering frame of reason yet sustain!
Nor let this total ruin whirl my brain!

In vain the cords and axes were prepar'd,
For now th' audacious seas insult the yard;
High o'er the ship they throw a horrid shade,
And o'er her burst in terrible cascade.
Uplifted on the surge, to heaven she flies,
Her shatter'd top half-buried in the skies,
Then headlong plunging thunders on the ground,
Earth groans! air trembles! and the deeps resound!

Her giant bulk the dread concussion feels,
And quivering with the wound in torment reels.
So reels, convuls'd with agonizing throes,
The bleeding bull beneath the murd'rer's blows—
Again she plunges! hark! a second shock
Tears her strong bottom on the marble rock:
Down on the vale of Death, with dismal cries,
The fated victims shuddering roll their eyes
In wild despair; while yet another stroke,
With deep convulsion, rends the solid oak:
Till like the mine, in whose infernal cell
The lurking demons of destruction dwell,
At length asunder torn, her frame divides;
And crashing spreads in ruin o'er the tides.

Oh were it mine with tuneful Maro's art
To wake to sympathy the feeling heart;
Like him the smooth and mournful verse to dress
In all the pomp of exquisite distress!
Then too, severely taught by cruel Fate,
To share in all the perils I relate,
Then might I, with unrivall'd strains deplore
Th' impervious horrors of a leeward shore.—

As o'er the surge the stooping main-mast hung,
Still on the rigging thirty seamen clung;
Some, struggling, on a broken crag were cast,
And there by oozy tangles grappled fast,
Awhile they bore th' o'erwhelming billows' rage,
Unequal combat with their fate to wage;
Till all benumb'd and feeble they forego
Their slippery hold, and sink to shades below.
Some, from the main-yard-arm impetuous thrown
On marble ridges, die without a groan.
Three with PALEMON on their skill depend,
And from the wreck on oars and rafts descend.
Now on the mountain-wave on high they ride,
Then downward plunge beneath th' involving tide;
Till one, who seems in agony to strive,
The whirling breakers heave on shore alive;
The rest a speedier end of anguish knew,
And prest the stony beach, a lifeless crew!

WILLIAM JULIUS MICKLE

1735–1788

There's Nae Luck About The House[1]

AND are ye sure the news is true?
   And are ye sure he's weel?
Is this a time to think o' wark?
   Ye jades, lay by your wheel;
Is this the time to spin a thread,
   When Colin's at the door?
Reach down my cloak, I'll to the quay,
   And see him come ashore.
For there's nae luck about the house,
   There's nae luck at a';
There's little pleasure in the house
   When our gudeman's awa'.

And gie to me my bigonet,
   My bishop's satin gown;
For I maun tell the baillie's wife
   That Colin's in the town.
My Turkey slippers maun gae on,
   My stockins pearly blue;
It's a' to pleasure our gudeman,
   For he's baith leal and true.

Rise, lass, and mak a clean fireside,
   Put on the muckle pot;
Gie little Kate her button gown
   And Jock his Sunday coat;
And mak their shoon as black as slaes,
   Their hose as white as snaw;
It's a' to please my ain gudeman,
   For he's been long awa'.

bigonet] head-dress

---

[1] The above song is sometimes attributed to Jean Adam, who died in 1765, but the evidence points almost conclusively to Mickle's authorship.

There's twa fat hens upo' the coop
    Been fed this month and mair;
Mak haste and thraw their necks about
    That Colin weel may fare;
And spread the table neat and clean,
    Gar ilka thing look braw,
For wha can tell how Colin fared
    When he was far awa'?

Sae true his heart, sae smooth his speech,
    His breath like caller air;
His very foot has music in 't
    As he comes up the stair—
And will I see his face again?
    And will I hear him speak?
I'm downright dizzy wi' the thought,
    In troth I'm like to greet!

If Colin's weel, and weel content,
    I hae nae mair to crave:
And gin I live to keep him sae,
    I'm blest aboon the lave:
And will I see his face again,
    And will I hear him speak?
I'm downright dizzy wi' the thought,
    In troth I'm like to greet.
For there's nae luck about the house,
    There's nae luck at a';
There's little pleasure in the house
    When our gudeman's awa'.

thraw] twist   caller] fresh, cool   lave] remainder

JAMES BEATTIE

1735–1803

Edwin, The Minstrel

THERE lived in Gothic days, as legends tell,
A shepherd-swain, a man of low degree;
Whose sires, perchance, in Fairyland might dwell,
Sicilian groves, or vales of Arcady;
But he, I ween, was of the north countrie;
A nation famed for song, and beauty's charms;
Zealous, yet modest; innocent, though free;
Patient of toil; serene amidst alarms;
Inflexible in faith; invincible in arms.

The shepherd-swain of whom I mention made,
On Scotia's mountains fed his little flock;
The sickle, scythe, or plough he never swayed;
An honest heart was almost all his stock;
His drink the living water from the rock:
The milky dams supplied his board, and lent
Their kindly fleece to baffle winter's shock;
And he, though oft with dust and sweat besprent,
Did guide and guard their wanderings, wheresoe'er they went....

And yet poor Edwin was no vulgar boy;
Deep thought oft seemed to fix his infant eye,
Dainties he heeded not, nor gaud, nor toy,
Save one short pipe of rudest minstrelsy.
Silent when glad; affectionate, though shy;
And now his look was most demurely sad,
And now he laughed aloud, yet none knew why.
The neighbours stared and sighed, yet blessed the lad;
Some deemed him wonderous wise, and some believed him mad.

But why should I his childish feats display?
Concourse, and noise, and toil he ever fled;
Nor cared to mingle in the clamorous fray
Of squabbling imps; but to the forest sped,
Or roamed at large the lonely mountain's head,
Or where the maze of some bewildered stream
To deep untrodden groves his footsteps led,

There would he wander wild, till Phoebus' beam,
Shot from the western cliff, released the weary team.

Th' exploit of strength, dexterity, or speed,
   To him nor vanity nor joy could bring.
His heart, from cruel sport estranged, would bleed
   To work the woe of any living thing,
   By trap, or net, by arrow, or by sling;
   These he detested; those he scorned to wield:
   He wished to be the guardian, not the king,
   Tyrant far less, or traitor of the field.
And sure the sylvan reign unbloody joy might yield.

Lo! where the stripling wrapt in wonder, roves
   Beneath the precipice o'erhung with pine;
And sees on high, amidst th' encircling groves,
   From cliff to cliff the foaming torrents shine;
   While waters, woods, and winds in concert join,
   And echo swells the chorus to the skies.
   Would Edwin this majestic scene resign
   For aught the huntsman's puny craft supplies?
Ah! no: he better knows great Nature's charms to prize.

And oft he traced the uplands, to survey,
   When o'er the sky advanced the kindling dawn,
The crimson cloud, blue main, and mountain gray,
   And lake, dim-gleaming on the smoky lawn:
   Far to the west the long, long vale withdrawn,
   Where twilight loves to linger for a while,
   And now he faintly kens the bounding fawn,
   And villager abroad at early toil.
But, lo! the sun appears! and heaven, earth, ocean, smile.

And oft the craggy cliff he loved to climb,
   When all in mist the world below was lost.
What dreadful pleasure! there to stand sublime,
   Like shipwrecked mariner on desert coast,
   And view th' enormous waste of vapour, tost
   In billows, lengthening to th' horizon round,
   Now scooped in gulfs, with mountains now embossed!
   And hear the voice of mirth and song rebound,
Flocks, herds, and waterfalls, along the hoar profound!

In truth he was a strange and wayward wight,
Fond of each gentle and each dreadful scene.
In darkness, and in storm, he found delight;
Nor less, than when on ocean-wave serene,
The southern sun diffused his dazzling sheen.
Even sad vicissitude amused his soul:
And if a sigh would sometimes intervene,
And down his cheek a tear of pity roll,
A sigh, a tear, so sweet, he wished not to control.

ISOBEL PAGAN

1740–1821

Ca' the Yowes to the Knowes

CA' the yowes to the knowes,
Ca' them where the heather grows,
Ca' them where the burnie rows,
   My bonnie dearie.

As I gaed down the water side,
There I met my shepherd lad;
He rowed me sweetly in his plaid,
   And he ca'd me his dearie.

'Will ye gang down the water side,
And see the waves sae sweetly glide
Beneath the hazels spreading wide?
   The moon it shines fu' clearly.'

'I was bred up at nae sic school,
My shepherd lad, to play the fool,
And a' the day to sit in dool,
   And naebody to see me.'

'Ye sall get gowns and ribbons meet,
Cauf-leather shoon upon your feet,
And in my arms ye'se lie and sleep,
   And ye sall be my dearie.'

vowes] ewes   knowes] hillocks   rows] rolls   rowed] wrapped
dool] sorrow   lift] sky

'If ye'll but stand to what ye've said,
I'se gang wi' you, my shepherd lad,
And ye may row me in your plaid,
   And I sall be your dearie.'

'While waters wimple to the sea,
While day blinks in the lift sae hie,
Till clay-cauld death sall blin' my e'e,
   Ye aye sall be my dearie!'

ANNA LETITIA BARBAULD

1743–1825

Life

LIFE ! I know not what thou art,
But know that thou and I must part;
And when, or how, or where we met,
I own to me 's a secret yet.
But this I know, when thou art fled,
Where'er they lay these limbs, this head,
No clod so valueless shall be
As all that then remains of me.

O whither, whither dost thou fly?
Where bend unseen thy trackless course?
   And in this strange divorce,
Ah, tell where I must seek this compound I?
To the vast ocean of empyreal flame
   From whence thy essence came
Dost thou thy flight pursue, when freed
From matter's base encumbering weed?
   Or dost thou, hid from sight,
   Wait, like some spell-bound knight,
Through blank oblivious years th' appointed hour
To break thy trance and reassume thy power?
Yet canst thou without thought or feeling be?
O say, what art thou, when no more thou'rt thee?

Life! we've been long together,
Through pleasant and through cloudy weather;

'Tis hard to part when friends are dear;
Perhaps 'twill cost a sigh, a tear;—
    Then steal away, give little warning,
        Choose thine own time;
    Say not Good-night, but in some brighter clime
        Bid me Good-morning!

Ode to Spring

SWEET daughter of a rough and stormy sire,
Hoar Winter's blooming child, delightful Spring!
    Whose unshorn locks with leaves
    And swelling buds are crowned;

From the green islands of eternal youth
(Crowned with fresh blooms, and ever-springing shade)
    Turn, hither turn thy step,
    O thou, whose powerful voice,

More sweet than softest touch of Doric reed,
Or Lydian flute, can soothe the madding winds,
    And through the stormy deep
    Breathe thine own tender calm.

Thee, best beloved! the virgin train await
With songs and festal rites, and joy to rove
    Thy blooming wilds among,
    And vales and dewy lawns,

With untired feet; and cull thy earliest sweet,
To weave fresh garlands for the glowing brow
    Of him, the favoured youth
    That prompts their whispered sigh.

Unlock thy copious stores,—those tender showers
That drop their sweetness on the infant buds;
    And silent dews that swell
    The milky ear's green stem,

And feed the flowering osier's early shoots;
And call those winds which through the whispering boughs
    With warm and pleasant breath
    Salute the bowing flowers.

Now let me sit beneath the whitening thorn
And mark thy spreading tints steal o'er the dale,
 And watch with patient eye
 Thy fair unfolding charms.

O nymph, approach! while yet the temperate sun
With bashful forehead through the cool moist air
 Throws his young maiden beams,
 And with chaste kisses woos

The earth's fair bosom; while the streaming veil
Of lucid clouds with wind and frequent shade
 Protects thy modest blooms
 From his severer blaze.

Sweet is thy reign, but short: the red dog-star
Shall scorch thy tresses, and the mower's scythe
 Thy greens, thy flowerets all,
 Remorseless shall destroy.

Reluctant shall I bid thee then farewell;
For O! not all that Autumn's lap contains,
 Nor Summer's ruddiest fruits,
 Can aught for thee atone,

Fair Spring! whose simplest promise more delights,
Then all their largest wealth, and through the heart
 Each joy and new-born hope
 With softest influence breathes.

THOMAS HOLCROFT

1745–1809

Gaffer Gray

 Ho, why dost thou shiver and shake,
  Gaffer Gray?
 And why does thy nose look so blue?
  ''Tis the weather that's cold,
  'Tis I'm grown very old,
 And my doublet is not very new,
  Well-a-day!'

Then line thy worn doublet with ale;
   Gaffer Gray;
And warm thy old heart with a glass.
    'Nay, but credit I've none,
    And my money's all gone;
Then say how may that come to pass?
    Well-a-day!'

Hie away to the house on the brow,
   Gaffer Gray;
And knock at the jolly priest's door.
    'The priest often preaches
    Against worldly riches,
But ne'er gives a mite to the poor,
    Well-a-day!'

The lawyer lives under the hill,
   Gaffer Gray;
Warmly fenced both in back and in front.
    'He will fasten his locks,
    And will threaten the stocks,
Should he ever more find me in want,
    Well-a-day!'

The squire has fat beeves and brown ale,
   Gaffer Gray;
And the season will welcome you there.
    'His fat beeves and his beer,
    And his merry new year,
Are all for the flush and the fair,
    Well-a-day!'

My keg is but low, I confess,
   Gaffer Gray;
What then? While it lasts, man, we'll live.
    'The poor man alone,
    When he hears the poor moan,
Of his morsel a morsel will give,
    Well-a-day!'

CHARLES DIBDIN

1745-1814

Tom Bowling

HERE, a sheer hulk, lies poor Tom Bowling,
The darling of our crew;
No more he'll hear the tempest howling,
For death has broached him to.
His form was of the manliest beauty,
His heart was kind and soft;
Faithful below Tom did his duty,
And now he's gone aloft. (*twice*)

Tom never from his word departed,
His virtues were so rare;
His friends were many, and true hearted,
His Poll was kind and fair.
And then he'd sing so blithe and jolly,
Ah! many's the time and oft;
But mirth is turned to melancholy,
For Tom is gone aloft.

Yet shall poor Tom find pleasant weather,
When He, Who all commands,
Shall give, to call life's crew together,
The word to pipe all hands.
Thus Death, who kings and tars dispatches,
In vain Tom's life has doffed;
For though his body's under hatches,
His soul is gone aloft.

The Jolly Young Waterman

AND did you not hear of a jolly young waterman,
   Who at Blackfriars Bridge used for to ply;
And he feathered his oars with such skill and dexterity,
   Winning each heart and delighting each eye:
He looked so neat and rowed so steadily,
The maidens all flocked to his boat so readily,
And he eyed the young rogues with so charming an air,
That this waterman ne'er was in want of a fare.

What sights of fine folks he oft rowed in his wherry,
   'Twas cleaned out so nice, and so painted withal,
He was always first oars when the fine city ladies
   In a party to Ranelagh went, or Vauxhall.
And oftentimes would they be giggling and leering,
But 'twas all one to Tom, their jibing and jeering.
For loving, or liking, he little did care,
For this waterman ne'er was in want of a fare.

And yet, but to see how strangely things happen;
   As he rowed along, thinking of nothing at all,
He was plied by a damsel so lovely and charming,
   That she smiled and so straightway in love he did fall.
And would this young damsel but banish his sorrow,
He'd wed her to-night before even to-morrow,
And how should this waterman ever know care,
When he's married and never in want of a fare?

ROBERT FERGUSSON

1750–1774

The Daft Days

Now mirk December's dowie face
Glowrs owr the rigs wi' sour grimace,
While, thro' his *minimum* o' space,
            The bleer-ey'd sun,
Wi' blinkin' light and stealin' pace,
            His race doth run.

Frae naked groves nae birdie sings;
To shepherd's pipe nae hillock rings;
The breeze nae od'rous flavour brings
            Frae Borean cave;
And dwynin' Nature, droops her wings,
            Wi' visage grave.

Mankind but scanty pleasure glean
Frae snawy hill or barren plain,
Whan Winter, 'midst his nipping train,
            Wi' frozen spear,
Sends drift owr a' his bleak domain,
            And guides the weir.

daft] mad   mirk] dark   dowie] sad   glowrs] stares
dwynin'] decaying

Auld Reikie! thou'rt the canty hole,
A bield for mony a cauldrife soul,
Wha snugly at thine ingle loll,
   Baith warm and couth;
While round they gar the bicker roll
   To weet their mouth.

When merry Yule-day comes I trow,
You'll scantlins find a hungry mou;
Sma' are our cares, our stamacks fou
   O' gusty gear,
And kickshaws, strangers to our view.
   Sin' fairn-year.

Ye browster wives! now busk ye bra,
And fling your sorrows far awa';
Then, come and gie's the tither blaw
   Of reaming ale,
Mair precious than the Well of Spa,
   Our hearts to heal.

Then, tho' at odds wi' a' the warl',
Amang oursells we'll never quarrel;
Tho' Discord gie a cankered snarl
   To spoil our glee,
As lang's there's pith into the barrel
   We'll drink and 'gree.

Fiddlers! your pins in temper fix,
And roset weel your fiddlesticks,
But banish vile Italian tricks
   From out your quorum,
Nor *fortes* wi' *pianos* mix—
   Gie's *Tullochgorum.*

For nought can cheer the heart sae weel
As can a canty Highland reel;
It even vivifies the heel
   To skip and dance:
Lifeless is he wha canna feel
   Its influence.

canty] jolly	bield] shelter	cauldrife] cold	couth] comfortable
gar] make	bicker] bowl, goblet	gusty] windy	fairn-year] last year
browster] brewer	busk] deck	bra] finely	blaw] draught
reaming] foaming	pins] pegs	roset] rosin	

Let mirth abound; let social cheer
Invest the dawning of the year;
Let blithesome innocence appear
        To crown our joy;
Nor envy, wi' sarcastic sneer,
          Our bliss destroy.

And thou, great god of *aqua vitæ*!
Wha sways the empire of this city—
When fou we're sometimes capernoity—
        Be thou prepared
To hedge us frae that black banditti,
          The City Guard.

Drinking Song

Tune: 'Lumps of Pudding'

HOLLO! keep it up, boys—and push around the glass,
Let each seize his bumper, and drink to his lass:
Away with dull thinking—'tis madness to think—
And let those be sober who've nothing to drink.
            Tal de ral, &c.

Silence that vile clock, with its iron tongu'd bell,
Of the hour that's departed still ringing the knell:
But what is't to us that the hours flie away;
'Tis only a signal to moisten the clay.

Huzza, boys! let each take a bumper in hand,
And stand—if there's any one able to stand.
How all things dance round me!—'tis life, tho' my boys:
Of drinking and spewing how great are the joys?

My head! oh my head!—but no matter, 'tis life;
Far better than mopping [*sic*] at home with one's wife.
The pleasures of drinking you're sure must be grand,
When I'm neither able to think, speak, nor stand.

THE DAFT DAYS: capernoity] peevish

JOHN PHILPOT CURRAN

1750–1817

The Deserter

If sadly thinking,
With spirits sinking,
Could more than drinking
　My cares compose,
A cure for sorrow
From sighs I'd borrow,
And hope to-morrow
　Would end my woes.
But as in wailing
There's nought availing,
And Death unfailing
　Will strike the blow,
Then for that reason,
And for a season,
Let us be merry
　Before we go.
To joy a stranger,
A way-worn ranger,
In every danger
　My course I've run;
Now hope all ending,
And Death befriending,
His last aid lending,
　My cares are done:
No more a rover,
Or hapless lover,
My griefs are over,
　My glass runs low;
Then for that reason,
And for a season,
Let us be merry
　Before we go!

RICHARD BRINSLEY SHERIDAN

1751–1816

Song from *The Duenna*
Oh, the days when I was young

OH, the days when I was young,
    When I laughed in fortune's spite;
Talked of love the whole day long,
    And with nectar crowned the night!
Then it was, old Father Care,
    Little recked I of thy frown;
Half thy malice youth could bear,
    And the rest a bumper drown.

Truth, they say, lies in a well,
    Why, I vow I ne'er could see;
Let the water-drinkers tell,
    There it always lay for me;
For when sparkling wine went round,
    Never saw I falsehood's mask;
But still honest truth I found
    In the bottom of each flask.

True, at length my vigour's flown,
    I have years to bring decay;
Few the locks that now I own,
    And the few I have are grey.
Yet, old Jerome, thou mayst boast
    While thy spirits do not tire,
Still beneath thy age's frost
    Glows a spark of youthful fire.

Song from *The School for Scandal*
Here's to the Maiden of Bashful Fifteen

HERE'S to the maiden of bashful fifteen;
    Here's to the widow of fifty;
Here's to the flaunting extravagant quean,
    And here's to the housewife that's thrifty.

Chorus

Let the toast pass,—
Drink to the lass,
I'll warrant she'll prove an excuse for the glass.

Here's to the charmer whose dimples we prize;
  Now to the maid who has none, sir:
Here's to the girl with a pair of blue eyes,
  And here's to the nymph with but *one*, sir.
    Chorus. Let the toast pass, &c.

Here's to the maid with a bosom of snow;
  Now to her that's as brown as a berry:
Here's to the wife with a face full of woe,
  And now to the girl that is merry.
    Chorus. Let the toast pass, &c.

For let 'em be clumsy, or let 'em be slim,
  Young or ancient, I care not a feather;
So fill a pint bumper quite up to the brim,
  And let us e'en toast them together.
    Chorus. Let the toast pass, &c.

THOMAS CHATTERTON

1752–1770

Mynstrelles Songe

O! SYNGE untoe mie roundelaie,
O! droppe the brynie teare wythe mee,
Daunce ne moe atte hallie daie,
Lycke a reynynge[1] ryver bee;
    Mie love ys dedde,
    Gon to hys death-bedde,
    Al under the wyllowe tree.

Blacke hys cryne[2] as the wyntere nyghte,
Whyte hys rode[3] as the sommer snowe,
Rodde hys face as the mornynge lyghte,
Cale he lyes ynne the grave belowe;

---

[1] running [2] hair [3] complexion. [Chatterton's notes.]   cale] cold.

Mie love ys dedde,
Gon to hys deathe-bedde,
Al under the wyllowe tree.
Swote hys tyngue as the throstles note,
Quycke ynn daunce as thoughte canne bee,
Defte hys taboure, codgelle stote,
O! hee lyes bie the wyllowe tree:
Mie love ys dedde,
Gonne to hys deathe-bedde,
Alle underre the wyllowe tree.

Harke! the ravenne flappes hys wynge,
In the briered delle belowe;
Harke! the dethe-owle loude dothe synge,
To the nyghte-mares as heie goe;
Mie love ys dedde,
Gone to hys deathe-bedde,
Al under the wyllowe tree.

See! the whyte moone sheenes onne hie;
Whyterre ys mie true loves shroude;
Whyterre yanne the mornynge skie,
Whyterre yanne the evenynge cloude;
Mie love ys dedde,
Gon to hys deathe-bedde,
Al under the wyllowe tree.

Heere, uponne mie true loves grave,
Schalle the baren fleurs be layde,
Nee one hallie Seyncte to save
Al the celness of a mayde.
Mie love ys dedde,
Gonne to hys death-bedde,
Alle under the wyllowe tree.

Wythe mie hondes I'lle dente the brieres
Rounde his hallie corse to gre,
Ouphante fairie, lyghte youre fyres,
Heere mie boddie stylle schalle bee.
Mie love ys dedde,
Gon to hys death-bedde,
Al under the wyllowe tree.

heie] they   celness] coldness   Ouphante] elfin

Comme, wythe acorne-coppe & thorne,
Drayne mie hartys blodde awaie;
Lyfe and all yttes goode I scorne,
Daunce bie nete, or feaste by daie.
  Mie love ys dedde,
  Gon to hys death-bedde,
  Al under the wyllowe tree.

Waterre wytches, crownede wythe reytes,[1]
Bere mee to yer leathalle tyde.
I die; I comme; mie true love waytes.
Thos the damselle spake, and dyed.

An Excelente Balade of Charitie

A wroten bie the gode prieste
Thomas Rowley[2], 1464

IN Virgyne the sweltrie sun gan sheene,
And hotte upon the mees[3] did caste his raie;
The apple rodded[4] from its palie greene,
And the mole[5] peare did bende the leafy spraie;
The peede chelandri[6] sunge the livelong daie;
'Twas nowe the pride, the manhode of the yeare,
And eke the grounde was dighte[7] in its mose defte[8] aumere[9]

The sun was glemeing in the midde of daie,
Deadde still the aire, and eke the welken[10] blue,
When from the sea arist[11] in drear arraie
A hepe of cloudes of sable sullen hue,
The which full fast unto the woodlande drewe,
Hiltring[12] attenes[13] the sunnis fetive[14] face,
And the blacke tempeste swolne and gatherd up apace.

---

[1] Water-flags [C.'s note]

AN EXCELENTE BALADE OF CHARITIE: [2] Thomas Rowley, the author, was born at Norton Malreward in Somersetshire, educated at the Convent of St. Kenna at Keyneham, and died at Westbury in Gloucestershire. [3] meads [4] reddened, ripened [5] soft [6] pied goldfinch [7] drest, arrayed [8] neat, ornamental [9] a loose robe or mantle [10] the sky, the atmosphere [11] arose [12] hiding, shrouding [13] at once [14] beauteous [C.'s notes.]

Beneathe an holme, faste by a pathwaie side,
Which dide unto Seyncte Godwine's covent[1] lede,
A hapless pilgrim moneynge did abide,
Pore in his viewe, ungentle[2] in his weede,
Longe bretful[3] of the miseries of neede,
Where from the hail-stone coulde the almer[4] flie?
He had no housen theere, ne anie covent nie.

Look in his glommed[5] face, his sprighte there scanne;
Howe woe-be-gone, how withered, forwynd[6], deade!
Haste to thie church-glebe-house[7], asshrewed[8] manne!
Haste to thie kiste[9], thie onlie dortoure[10] bedde.
Cale, as the claie whiche will gre on thie hedde,
Is Charitie and Love aminge highe elves;
Knightis and Barons live for pleasure and themselves.

The gatherd storme is rype; the bigge drops falle;
The forswat[11] meadowes smethe[12], and drenche[13] the raine;
The comyng ghastness do the cattle pall[14],
And the full flockes are drivynge ore the plaine;
Dashde from the cloudes the waters flott[15] againe;
The welkin opes; the yellow levynne[16] flies;
And the hot fierie smothe[17] in the wide lowings[18] dies.

Liste! now the thunder's rattling clymmynge[19] sound
Cheves[20] slowlie on, and then embollen[21] clangs,
Shakes the hie spyre, and losst, dispended, drown'd,
Still on the gallard[22] eare of terroure hanges;
The windes are up; the lofty elmen swanges;
Again the levynne and the thunder poures,
And the full cloudes are braste[23] attenes in stonen showers.

---

[1] It would have been *charitable*, if the author had not pointed at personal characters in this Ballad of Charity. The Abbot of St. Godwin's at the time of the writing of this was Ralph de Bellomont, a great stickler for the Lancastrian family. Rowley was a Yorkist   [2] beggarly   [3] filled with   [4] beggar   [5] clouded, dejected. A person of some note in the literary world is of opinion that *glum* and *glom* are modern cast words; and from this circumstance doubts the authenticity of Rowley's Manuscripts. Glum-mong in the Saxon signifies twilight, a dark or dubious light; and the modern word *gloomy* is derived from the Saxon *glum*   [6] dry, sapless   [7] the grave   [8] accursed, unfortunate   [9] coffin   [10] a sleeping room   [11] sun-burnt   [12] smoke   [13] drink   [14] *pall*, a contraction from *apall*, to fright   [15] fly   [16] lightning   [17] steam, or vapours   [18] flames   [19] noisy   [20] moves   [21] swelled, strengthened   [22] frighted   [23] burst [C.'s notes.]

Spurreynge his palfrie oere the watrie plaine,
The Abbote of Seyncte Godwynes convente came;
His chapournette[1] was drented with the reine,
And his pencte[2] gyrdle met with mickle shame;
He aynewarde tolde his bederoll[3] at the same;
The storme encreasen, and he drew aside,
With the mist[4] almes craver neere to the holme to bide.

His cope[5] was all of Lyncolne clothe so fyne,
With a gold button fasten'd neere his chynne;
His autremete[6] was edged with golden twynne,
And his shoone pyke a loverds[7] mighte have binne;
Full well is shewn he thoughten coste no sinne:
The trammels of the palfrye pleasde his sighte,
For the horse-millanare[8] his head with roses dighte.

An almes, sir prieste! the droppynge pilgrim saide,
O! let me waite within your covente dore,
Till the sunne sheneth hie above our heade,
And the loude tempeste of the aire is oer;
Helpless and ould am I alas! and poor;
No house, ne friend, ne moneie in my pouche;
All yatte I call my owne is this my silver crouche.

Varlet, replyd the Abbatte, cease your dinne;
This is no season almes and prayers to give;
Mie porter never lets a faitour[9] in;
None touch mie rynge who not in honour live.
And now the sonne with the blacke cloudes did stryve,
And shettynge on the grounde his glairie raie,
The Abbatte spurrde his steede, and eftsoones roadde awaie.

Once moe the skie was blacke, the thounder rolde;
Faste reyneynge oer the plaine a prieste was seen;
Ne dighte full proude, ne buttoned up in golde;
His cope and jape[10] were graie, and eke were clene;
A Limitoure he was of order seene;
And from the pathwaie side then turned hee,
Where the pore almer laie binethe the holmen tree.

. [1] a small round hat, not unlike the shapournette in heraldry, formerly worn by Ecclesiastics and Lawyers   [2] painted   [3] He told his beads backwards; a figurative expression to signify cursing   [4] poor, needy   [5] a cloke   [6] a loose white robe, worn by Priests   [7] a lord's   [8] I believe this trade is still in being, though but seldom employed   [9] a beggar, or vagabond   [10] a short surplice, worn by Friars of an inferior class, and secular priests [C.'s notes.]

An almes, sir priest! the droppynge pilgrim sayde,
For sweet Seyncte Marie and your order sake.
The Limitoure then loosen'd his pouche threade,
And did thereoute a groate of silver take;
The mister pilgrim dyd for halline[1] shake.
Here take this silver, it maie eathe[2] thie care;
We are Goddes stewards all, nete[3] of oure owne we bare.

But ah! unhailie[4] pilgrim, lerne of me,
Scathe anie give a rentrolle to their Lorde.
Here take my semecope[5], thou arte bare I see;
Tis thyne; the Seynctes will give me mie rewarde.
He left the pilgrim, and his waie aborde.
Virgynne and hallie Seyncte, who sitte yn gloure[6],
Or give the mittee[7] will, or give the gode man power.

There Lackethe Somethynge Stylle

THE boddynge flourettes bloshes atte the lyghte;
The mees be sprenged wyth the yellowe hue;
Yn daiseyd mantels ys the mountayne dyghte
The nesh[8] yonge cowslepe bendethe wyth the dewe;
The trees enlesed, yntoe Heavenne straughte,
Whenn gentle wyndes doe blowe, to whestling dynne ys
broughte.

The evenynge commes, and brynges the dewe alonge;
The roddie welkynne sheeneth to the eyne;
Arounde the alestake Mynstrells synge the songe;
Yonge ivie rounde the doore poste do entwyne;
I laie mee onn the grasse; yette, to mie wylle,
Albeytte all ys fayre, there lackethe somethynge stylle.

So Adam thoughtenne, whan, ynn Paradyse,
All Heavenn and Erthe dyd hommage to hys mynde;
Ynn Womman alleyne mannes pleasaunce lyes;
As Instrumentes joie were made the kynde.
Go, take a wyfe untoe thie armes, and see
Wynter, and brownie hylles, wyll have a charme for thee.

---

[1] joy   [2] ease   [3] nought   [4] unhappy   [5] a short under-cloke
[6] glory   [7] mighty, rich   [8] tender   [C.'s notes.]   Limitoure] A
licensed begging friar   aborde] went on   Albeytte] Albeit
    THERE LACKETHE SOMETHYNGE STYLLE: bloshes] blushes   sprenged] sprinkled
enlesed] enleafed

Whanne Autumpne blake[1] and sonne-brente doe appere,
With hys goulde honde guylteynge the falleynge lefe,
Bryngeynge oppe Wynterr to folfylle the yere,
Beerynge uponne hys backe the riped shefe;
Whan al the hyls wythe woddie sede ys whyte;
Whanne levynne-fyres and lemes do mete from far the syghte;

Angelles bee wrogte to bee of neidher kynde;
Angelles alleyne fromme chafe[2] desyre bee free;
Dheere ys a somwhatte evere yn the mynde,
Yatte, wythout wommanne, cannot stylled bee;
Ne seyncte yn celles, botte, havynge blodde and tere,[3]
Do fynde the spryte to joie on syghte of womanne fayre.

GEORGE CRABBE

1754–1832

The Village

BOOK II

No longer truth, though shown in verse, disdain,
But own the Village Life a life of pain.
I too must yield, that oft amid these woes
Are gleams of transient mirth and hours of sweet repose,
Such as you find on yonder sportive Green,
The 'squire's tall gate and churchway-walk between;
Where loitering stray a little tribe of friends,
On a fair Sunday when the sermon ends.
Then rural beaux their best attire put on,
To win their nymphs, as other nymphs are won;
While those long wed go plain, and, by degrees,
Like other husbands, quit their care to please.
Some of the sermon talk, a sober crowd,
And loudly praise, if it were preach'd aloud;
Some on the labours of the week look round,
Feel their own worth, and think their toil renown'd;
While some, whose hopes to no renown extend,
Are only pleased to find their labours end.

---

[1] naked   [2] hot.   [3] health.   [C.'s notes.]

Thus, as their hours glide on, with pleasure fraught,
Their careful masters brood the painful thought;
Much in their mind they murmur and lament,
That one fair day should be so idly spent;
And think that Heaven deals hard, to tithe their store
And tax their time for preachers and the poor.

Yet still, ye humbler friends, enjoy your hour,
This is your portion, yet unclaim'd of power;
This is Heaven's gift to weary men oppress'd,
And seems the type of their expected rest.
But yours, alas! are joys that soon decay;
Frail joys, begun and ended with the day;
Or yet, while day permits those joys to reign,
The village vices drive them from the plain.

See the stout churl, in drunken fury great,
Strike the bare bosom of his teeming mate!
His naked vices, rude and unrefined,
Exert their open empire o'er the mind;
But can we less the senseless rage despise,
Because the savage acts without disguise?

Yet here disguise, the city's vice, is seen,
And Slander steals along and taints the Green:
At her approach domestic peace is gone,
Domestic broils at her approach come on;
She to the wife the husband's crime conveys,
She tells the husband when his consort strays,
Her busy tongue through all the little state
Diffuses doubt, suspicion, and debate;
Peace, tim'rous goddess! quits her old domain,
In sentiment and song content to reign.

Nor are the nymphs that breathe the rural air
So fair as Cynthia's, nor so chaste as fair:
These to the town afford each fresher face,
And the clown's trull receives the peer's embrace;
From whom, should chance again convey her down,
The peer's disease in turn attacks the clown.

Here too the 'squire, or 'squire-like farmer, talk,
How round their regions nightly pilferers walk;
How from their ponds the fish are borne, and all
The rip'ning treasures from their lofty wall;
How meaner rivals in their sports delight,
Just rich enough to claim a doubtful right;
Who take a licence round their fields to stray,
A mongrel race! the poachers of the day.

And hark! the riots of the Green begin,
That sprang at first from yonder noisy inn;
What time the weekly pay was vanish'd all,
And the slow hostess scored the threat'ning wall;
What time they ask'd their friendly feast to close,
A final cup, and that will make them foes;
When blows ensue that break the arm of toil,
And rustic battle ends the boobies' broil.

Save when to yonder Hall they bend their way,
Where the grave justice ends the grievous fray;
He who recites, to keep the poor in awe,
The law's vast volume—for he knows the law:—
To him with anger or with shame repair
The injured peasant and deluded fair.

Lo! at his throne the silent nymph appears,
Frail by her shape, but modest in her tears;
And while she stands abash'd, with conscious eye,
Some favourite female of her judge glides by,
Who views with scornful glance the strumpet's fate,
And thanks the stars that made her keeper great;
Near her the swain, about to bear for life
One certain evil, doubts 'twixt war and wife;
But, while the falt'ring damsel takes her oath,
Consents to wed, and so secures them both.

Yet, why, you ask, these humble crimes relate,
Why make the poor as guilty as the great?
To show the great, those mightier sons of pride,
How near is vice the lowest are allied;
Such are their natures and their passions such,
But these disguise too little, those too much:
So shall the man of power and pleasure see
In his own slave as vile a wretch as he;
In his luxurious lord the servant find
His own low pleasures and degenerate mind:
And each in all the kindred vices trace
Of a poor, blind, bewilder'd, erring race;
Who, a short time in varied fortune past,
Die, and are equal in the dust at last.

And you, ye poor, who still lament your fate,
Forbear to envy those you call the great;
And know, amid those blessings they possess,
They are, like you, the victims of distress;
While sloth with many a pang torments her slave,
Fear waits on guilt, and danger shakes the brave.

Oh! if in life one noble chief appears,
Great in his name, while blooming in his years;
Born to enjoy whate'er delights mankind,
And yet to all you feel or fear resign'd;
Who gave up joys and hopes, to you unknown,
For pains and dangers greater than your own:
If such there be, then let your murmurs cease,
Think, think of him, and take your lot in peace.

And such there was:—Oh! grief, that checks our pride!
Weeping we say, there was—for Manners died:
Beloved of Heaven, these humble lines forgive,
That sing of Thee, and thus aspire to live.

As the tall oak, whose vigorous branches form
An ample shade and brave the wildest storm,
High o'er the subject wood is seen to grow,
The guard and glory of the trees below;
Till on its head the fiery bolt descends,
And o'er the plain the shatter'd trunk extends;
Yet then it lies, all wond'rous as before,
And still the glory, though the guard no more:

So THOU, when every virtue, every grace,
Rose in thy soul, or shone within thy face;
When, though the son of Granby, thou wert known
Less by thy father's glory than thy own;
When Honour loved and gave thee every charm,
Fire to thy eye and vigour to thy arm;
Then from our lofty hopes and longing eyes,
Fate and thy virtues call'd thee to the skies;
Yet still we wonder at thy tow'ring fame,
And, losing thee, still dwell upon thy name.

Oh! ever honour'd, ever valued! say,
What verse can praise thee, or what work repay?
Yet verse (in all we can) thy worth repays,
Nor trusts the tardy zeal of future days;—
Honours for thee thy country shall prepare,
Thee in their hearts, the good, the brave shall bear;
To deeds like thine shall noblest chiefs aspire,
The Muse shall mourn thee, and the world admire.

In future times, when, smit with Glory's charms,
The untried youth first quits a father's arms;—
'Oh! be like him,' the weeping sire shall say;
'Like Manners walk, who walk'd in Honour's way;
'In danger foremost, yet in death sedate,
'Oh! be like him in all things, but his fate!'

If for that fate such public tears be shed,
That Victory seems to die now THOU art dead;
How shall a friend his nearer hope resign,
That friend a brother, and whose soul was thine?
By what bold lines shall we his grief express,
Or by what soothing numbers make it less?

'Tis not, I know, the chiming of a song,
Nor all the powers that to the Muse belong,
Words aptly cull'd and meanings well express'd,
Can calm the sorrows of a wounded breast;
But Virtue, soother of the fiercest pains,
Shall heal that bosom, Rutland, where she reigns.

Yet hard the task to heal the bleeding heart,
To bid the still-recurring thoughts depart,
Tame the fierce grief and stem the rising sigh,
And curb rebellious passion with reply;
Calmly to dwell on all that pleased before,
And yet to know that all shall please no more—
Oh! glorious labour of the soul, to save
Her captive powers, and bravely mourn the brave.

To such these thoughts will lasting comfort give—
Life is not measured by the time we live:
'Tis not an even course of threescore years,
A life of narrow views and paltry fears,
Gray hairs and wrinkles and the cares they bring,
That take from death the terrors or the sting;
But 'tis the gen'rous spirit, mounting high
Above the world, that native of the sky;
The noble spirit, that, in dangers brave,
Calmly looks on, or looks beyond the grave:—
Such Manners was, so he resign'd his breath,
If in a glorious, then a timely death.

Cease then that grief, and let those tears subside;
If Passion rule us, be that passion pride;
If Reason, Reason bids us strive to raise
Our fallen hearts, and be like him we praise;
Or, if Affection still the soul subdue,
Bring all his virtues, all his worth in view,
And let Affection find its comfort too:
For how can Grief so deeply wound the heart,
When Admiration claims so large a part?

Grief is a foe; expel him, then, thy soul;
Let nobler thoughts the nearer views control!
Oh! make the age to come thy better care;

See other Rutlands, other Granbys there!
And, as thy thoughts through streaming ages glide,
See other heroes die as Manners died:
And, from their fate, thy race shall nobler grow,
As trees shoot upwards that are pruned below;
Or as old Thames, borne down with decent pride,
Sees his young streams run warbling at his side;
Though some, by art cut off, no longer run,
And some are lost beneath the summer's sun—
Yet the pure stream moves on, and, as it moves,
Its power increases and its use improves;
While plenty round its spacious waves bestow,
Still it flows on, and shall for ever flow.

from *The Lover's Journey*

The sun is in the heavens, and the proud day,
Attended with the pleasures of the world,
Is all too wanton.   *King John*, Act III, Scene 3

The lunatic, the lover, and the poet,
Are of imagination all compact.
        Midsummer Night's Dream, Act V, Scene 2

Oh! how the spring of love resembleth
    Th' uncertain glory of an April day,
Which now shows all her beauty to the sun,
    And by and by a cloud bears all away.

And happily I have arrived at last
Unto the wished haven of my bliss.
        Taming of the Shrew, Act V, Scene 1

IT is the soul that sees; the outward eyes
Present the object, but the mind descries;
And thence delight, disgust, or cool indiff'rence rise:
When minds are joyful, then we look around,
And what is seen is all on fairy ground;
Again they sicken, and on every view
Cast their own dull and melancholy hue;
Or, if absorb'd by their peculiar cares,
The vacant eye on viewless matter glares,
Our feelings still upon our views attend,
And their own natures to the objects lend;

Sorrow and joy are in their influence sure,
Long as the passion reigns th' effects endure;
But love in minds his various changes makes,
And clothes each object with the change he takes;
His light and shade on every view he throws,
And on each object, what he feels, bestows.

Fair was the morning, and the month was June,
When rose a lover; love awakens soon;
Brief his repose, yet much he dreamt the while
Of that day's meeting, and his Laura's smile;
Fancy and love that name assign'd to her,
Call'd Susan in the parish-register;
And he no more was John—his Laura gave
The name Orlando to her faithful slave.

Bright shone the glory of the rising day,
When the fond traveller took his favourite way;
He mounted gaily, felt his bosom light,
And all he saw was pleasing in his sight.

'Ye hours of expectation, quickly fly,
And bring on hours of blest reality;
When I shall Laura see, beside her stand,
Hear her sweet voice, and press her yielded hand.'

First o'er a barren heath beside the coast
Orlando rode, and joy began to boast.

'This neat low gorse,' said he, 'with golden bloom,
Delights each sense, is beauty, is perfume;
And this gay ling, with all its purple flowers,
A man at leisure might admire for hours;
This green-fringed cup-moss has a scarlet tip,
That yields to nothing but my Laura's lip;
And then how fine this herbage! men may say
A heath is barren; nothing is so gay:
Barren or bare to call such charming scene
Argues a mind possess'd by care and spleen.'

Onward he went, and fiercer grew the heat,
Dust rose in clouds before the horse's feet;
For now he pass'd through lanes of burning sand,
Bounds to thin crops or yet uncultured land;
Where the dark poppy flourish'd on the dry
And sterile soil, and mock'd the thin-set rye.

'How lovely this!' the rapt Orlando said;
With what delight is labouring man repaid!
The very lane has sweets that all admire,
The rambling suckling and the vigorous brier;

See! wholesome wormwood grows beside the way,
Where dew-press'd yet the dog-rose bends the spray;
Fresh herbs the fields, fair shrubs the banks adorn,
And snow-white bloom falls flaky from the thorn;
No fostering hand they need, no sheltering wall,
They spring uncultured and they bloom for all.'
    The lover rode as hasty lovers ride,
And reach'd a common pasture wild and wide;
Small black-legg'd sheep devour with hunger keen
The meagre herbage, fleshless, lank, and lean;
Such o'er thy level turf, Newmarket! stray,
And there, with other *black-legs* find their prey:
He saw some scatter'd hovels; turf was piled
In square brown stacks; a prospect bleak and wild!
A mill, indeed, was in the centre found,
With short sear herbage withering all around;
A smith's black shed opposed a wright's long shop,
And join'd an inn where humble travellers stop.
    'Ay, this is Nature,' said the gentle 'squire;
'This ease, peace, pleasure—who would not admire?
With what delight these sturdy children play,
And joyful rustics at the close of day;
Sport follows labour, on this even space
Will soon commence the wrestling and the race;
Then will the village-maidens leave their home,
And to the dance with buoyant spirits come;
No affectation in their looks is seen,
Nor know they what disguise or flattery mean;
Nor aught to move an envious pang they see,
Easy their service, and their love is free;
Hence early springs that love, it long endures,
And life's first comfort, while they live, ensures:
They the low roof and rustic comforts prize,
Nor cast on prouder mansions envying eyes:
Sometimes the news at yonder town they hear,
And learn what busier mortals feel and fear;
Secure themselves, although by tales amazed,
Of towns bombarded and of cities razed;
As if they doubted, in their still retreat,
The very news that makes their quiet sweet,
And their days happy—happier only knows
He on whom Laura her regard bestows.'
    On rode Orlando, counting all the while
The miles he pass'd and every coming mile;

Like all attracted things, he quicker flies,
The place approaching where th' attraction lies;
When next appear'd a *dam*—so call the place—
Where lies a road confined in narrow space;
A work of labour, for on either side
Is level fen, a prospect wild and wide,
With dikes on either hand by ocean's self supplied:
Far on the right the distant sea is seen,
And salt the springs that feed the marsh between;
Beneath an ancient bridge, the straiten'd flood
Rolls through its sloping banks of slimy mud;
Near it a sunken boat resists the tide,
That frets and hurries to th' opposing side;
The rushes sharp, that on the borders grow,
Bend their brown flow'rets to the stream below,
Impure in all its course, in all its progress slow:
Here a grave *Flora scarcely deigns to bloom,
Nor wears a rosy blush, nor sheds perfume;
The few dull flowers that o'er the place are spread
Partake the nature of their fenny bed;
Here on its wiry stem, in rigid bloom,
Grows the salt lavender that lacks perfume;
Here the dwarf sallows creep, the septfoil harsh,
And the soft slimy mallow of the marsh;
Low on the ear the distant billows sound,
And just in view appears their stony bound;
No hedge nor tree conceals the glowing sun,
Birds, save a wat'ry tribe, the district shun,
Nor chirp among the reeds where bitter waters run.
   'Various as beauteous, Nature, is thy face,'
Exclaim'd Orlando: 'all that grows has grace;
All are appropriate—bog, and marsh, and fen,

* The ditches of a fen so near the ocean are lined with irregular patches of a coarse and stained lava; a muddy sediment rests on the horse-tail and other perennial herbs, which in part conceal the shallowness of the stream; a fat-leaved pale-flowering scurvy-grass appears early in the year, and the razor-edged bull-rush in the summer and autumn. The fen itself has a dark and saline herbage; there are rushes and *arrow-head*, and in a few patches the flakes of the cotton-grass are seen, but more commonly the *sea-aster*, the dullest of that numerous and hardy genus; a *thrift*, blue in flower, but withering and remaining withered till the winter scatters it; the *saltwort*, both simple and shrubby; a few kinds of grass changed by their soil and atmosphere, and low plants of two or three denominations undistinguished in a general view of the scenery;—such is the vegetation of the fen when it is at a small distance from the ocean; and in this case there arise from it effluvia strong and peculiar, half-saline, half-putrid, which would be considered by most people as offensive, and by some as dangerous; but there are others to whom singularity of taste or association of ideas has rendered it agreeable and pleasant.

Are only poor to undiscerning men;
Here may the nice and curious eye explore
How Nature's hand adorns the rushy moor;
Here the rare moss in secret shade is found,
Here the sweet myrtle of the shaking ground;
Beauties are these that from the view retire,
But well repay th' attention they require;
For these my Laura will her home forsake,
And all the pleasures they afford partake.'
   Again the country was enclosed, a wide
And sandy road has banks on either side;
Where, lo! a hollow on the left appear'd,
And there a gipsy-tribe their tent had rear'd;
'Twas open spread, to catch the morning sun,
And they had now their early meal begun,
When two brown boys just left their grassy seat,
The early trav'ller with their pray'rs to greet:
While yet Orlando held his pence in his hand,
He saw their sister on her duty stand;
Some twelve years old, demure, affected, sly,
Prepared the force of early powers to try;
Sudden a look of languor he descries,
And well-feign'd apprehension in her eyes;
Train'd but yet savage, in her speaking face
He mark'd the features of her vagrant race;
When a light laugh and roguish leer express'd
The vice implanted in her youthful breast:
Forth from the tent her elder brother came,
Who seem'd offended, yet forbore to blame
The young designer, but could only trace
The looks of pity in the trav'ller's face:
Within, the father, who from fences nigh
Had brought the fuel for the fire's supply,
Watch'd now the feeble blaze, and stood dejected by:
On ragged rug, just borrow'd from the bed,
And by the hand of coarse indulgence fed,
In dirty patchwork negligently dress'd,
Reclined the wife, an infant at her breast;
In her wild face some touch of grace remain'd,
Of vigour palsied and of beauty stain'd;
Her bloodshot eyes on her unheeding mate
Were wrathful turn'd, and seem'd her wants to state,
Cursing his tardy aid—her mother there
With gipsy-state engrass'd the only chair;

Solemn and dull her look; with such she stands,
And reads the milk-maid's fortune in her hands,
Tracing the lines of life; assumed through years,
Each feature now the steady falsehood wears;
With hard and savage eye she views the food,
And grudging pinches their intruding brood;
Last in the group, the worn-out grandsire sits
Neglected, lost, and living but by fits;
Useless, despised, his worthless labours done,
And half protected by the vicious son,
Who half supports him; he with heavy glance
Views the young ruffians who around him dance;
And, by the sadness in his face, appears
To trace the progress of their future years
Through what strange course of misery, vice, deceit,
Must wildly wander each unpractised cheat!
What shame and grief, what punishment and pain,
Sport of fierce passions, must each child sustain—
Ere they like him approach their latter end,
Without a hope, a comfort, or a friend!

But this Orlando felt not; 'Rogues,' said he,
'Doubtless they are, but merry rogues they be;
They wander round the land, and be it true,
They break the laws—then let the laws pursue
The wanton idlers; for the life they live,
Acquit I cannot, but I can forgive.'
This said, a portion from his purse was thrown,
And every heart seem'd happy like his own.

He hurried forth, for now the town was nigh—
'The happiest man of mortal men am I.'
Thou art! but change in every state is near,
(So while the wretched hope, the blest may fear);
'Say, where is Laura?'—'That her words must show,'
A lass replied; 'read this, and thou shalt know!'

'What, gone!'—her friend insisted—forced to go:—
'Is vex'd, was teased, could not refuse her!—No?'
'But you can follow:' 'Yes:' 'The miles are few,
The way is pleasant; will you come?—Adieu!
Thy Laura!' 'No! I feel I must resign
The pleasing hope, thou hadst been here, if mine:
A lady was it?—Was no brother there?
But why should I afflict me if there were?'
'The way is pleasant:' 'What to me the way?
I cannot reach her till the close of day.

My dumb companion! is it thus we speed?
Not I from grief nor thou from toil art freed;
Still art thou doom'd to travel and to pine,
For my vexation—What a fate is mine!
    'Gone to a friend, she tells me; I commend
Her purpose; means she to a female freind?
By Heaven, I wish she suffer'd half the pain
Of hope protracted through the day in vain:
Shall I persist to see th' ungrateful maid?
Yes, I will see her, slight her, and upbraid:
What! in the very hour? She knew the time,
And doubtless chose it to increase her crime.'
    Forth rode Orlando by a river's side,
Inland and winding, smooth, and full and wide,
That roll'd majestic on, in one soft-flowing tide;
The bottom gravel, flow'ry were the banks,
Tall willows, waving in their broken ranks;
The road, now near, now distant, winding led
By lovely meadows which the waters fed;
He pass'd the way-side inn, the village spire,
Nor stopp'd to gaze, to question, or admire;
On either side the rural mansions stood,
With hedge-row trees, and hills high-crown'd with wood,
And many a devious stream that reach'd the nobler flood.
    'I hate these scenes,' Orlando angry cried,
'And these proud farmers! yes, I hate their pride:
See! that sleek fellow, how he strides along,
Strong as an ox, and ignorant as strong;
Can yon close crops a single eye detain
But his who counts the profits of the grain?
And these vile beans with deleterious smell,
Where is their beauty? can a mortal tell?
These deep fat meadows I detest; it shocks
One's feelings there to see the grazing ox;—
For slaughter fatted, as a lady's smile
Rejoices man, and means his death the while.
Lo! now the sons of labour! every day
Employ'd in toil, and vex'ed in every way;
Theirs is but mirth assumed, and they conceal,
In their affected joys, the ills they feel:
I hate these long green lanes; there's nothing seen
In this vile country but eternal green;
Woods! waters! meadows! Will they never end?
'Tis a vile prospect:—Gone to see a friend!'—

[The lovers clear up their misunderstanding; but, when 'Orlando' rides back the same way, his mind is engrossed in thoughts and the landscape has no effect on him, thus illustrating the third proposition set out in the opening lines. (J.W.)]

WILLIAM BLAKE

1757–1827

from *Songs of Innocence*

Introduction

PIPING down the valleys wild,
Piping songs of pleasant glee,
On a cloud I saw a child,
And he laughing said to me:

'Pipe a song about a Lamb!'
So I piped with merry chear.
'Piper, pipe that song again;'
So I piped: he wept to hear.

'Drop thy pipe, thy happy pipe;
'Sing thy songs of happy chear:'
So I sung the same again,
While he wept with joy to hear.

'Piper, sit thee down and write
'In a book that all may read.'
So he vanish'd from my sight.
And I pluck'd a hollow reed,

And I made a rural pen,
And I stain'd the water clear,
And I wrote my happy songs
Every child may joy to hear.

The Lamb

LITTLE Lamb, who made thee?
　　Dost thou know who made thee?
Gave thee life, & bid thee feed
By the stream & o'er the mead;
Gave thee clothing of delight,
Softest clothing, wooly, bright;
Gave thee such a tender voice,
Making all the vales rejoice?
　　Little Lamb, who made thee?
　　Dost thou know who made thee?

Little Lamb, I'll tell thee,
Little Lamb, I'll tell thee:
He is called by thy name,
For he calls himself a Lamb.
He is meek, & he is mild;
He became a little child.
I a child, & thou a lamb,
We are called by his name.
　　Little Lamb, God bless thee!
　　Little Lamb, God bless thee!

The Ecchoing Green

THE Sun does arise,
And make happy the skies;
The merry bells ring
To welcome the Spring;
The skylark and thrush,
The birds of the bush,
Sing louder around
To the bells' chearful sound,
While our sports shall be seen
On the Ecchoing Green.

Old John, with white hair,
Does laugh away care,
Sitting under the oak,
Among the old folk.
They laugh at our play,

And soon they all say:
'Such, such were the joys
'When we all, girls & boys,
'In our youth time were seen
'On the Ecchoing Green.'

Till the little ones, weary,
No more can be merry;
The sun does descend,
And our sports have an end.
Round the laps of their mothers
Many sisters and brothers,
Like birds in their nest,
Are ready for rest,
And sport no more seen
On the darkening Green.

The Chimney Sweeper

WHEN my mother died I was very young,
And my Father sold me while yet my tongue
Could scarcely cry ''weep! 'weep! 'weep! 'weep!'
So your chimneys I sweep, & in soot I sleep.

There's little Tom Dacre, who cried when his head,
That curl'd like a lamb's back, was shav'd: so I said
'Hush, Tom! never mind it, for when your head's bare
'You know that the soot cannot spoil your white hair.'

And so he was quiet, & that very night
As Tom was a-sleeping, he had such a sight!
That thousands of sweepers, Dick, Joe, Ned, & Jack,
Were all of them lock'd up in coffins of black.

And by came an Angel who had a bright key,
And he open'd the coffins & set them all free;
Then down a green plain leaping, laughing, they run,
And wash in a river, and shine in the Sun.

Then naked & white, all their bags left behind,
They rise upon clouds and sport in the wind;
And the Angel told Tom, if he'd be a good boy,
He'd have God for his father, & never want joy.

And so Tom awoke; and we rose in the dark,
And got with our bags & our brushes to work.
Tho' the morning was cold, Tom was happy & warm;
So if all do their duty they need not fear harm.

Infant Joy

'I HAVE no name:
'I am but two days old.'
What shall I call thee?
'I happy am,
'Joy is my name.'
Sweet joy befall thee!

Pretty joy!
Sweet joy but two days old,
Sweet joy I call thee:
Thou dost smile,
I sing the while,
Sweet joy befall thee!

On Another's Sorrow

CAN I see another's woe,
And not be in sorrow too?
Can I see another's grief,
And not seek for kind relief?

Can I see a falling tear,
And not feel my sorrow's share?
Can a father see his child
Weep, nor be with sorrow fill'd?

Can a mother sit and hear
An infant groan, an infant fear?
No, no! never can it be!
Never, never can it be!

And can he who smiles on all
Hear the wren with sorrows small,
Hear the small bird's grief & care,
Hear the woes that infants bear,

And not sit beside the nest,
Pouring pity in their breast;
And not sit the cradle near,
Weeping tear on infant's tear;

And not sit both night & day,
Wiping all our tears away?
O! no never can it be!
Never, never can it be!

He doth give his joy to all;
He becomes an infant small;
He becomes a man of woe;
He doth feel the sorrow too.

Think not thou canst sigh a sigh
And thy maker is not by;
Think not thou canst weep a tear
And thy maker is not near.

O! he gives to us his joy
That our grief he may destroy;
Till our grief is fled & gone
He doth sit by us and moan.

The School Boy

I LOVE to rise in a summer morn
When the birds sing on every tree;
The distant huntsman winds his horn,
And the sky-lark sings with me.
O! what sweet company.

But to go to school in a summer morn,
O! it drives all joy away;
Under a cruel eye outworn,
The little ones spend the day
In sighing and dismay.

Ah! then at times I drooping sit,
And spend many an anxious hour,
Nor in my book can I take delight,
Nor sit in learning's bower,
Worn thro' with the dreary shower.

How can the bird that is born for joy
Sit in a cage and sing?
How can a child, when fears annoy,
But droop his tender wing,
And forget his youthful spring?

O! father & mother, if buds are nip'd
And blossoms blown away,
And if the tender plants are strip'd
Of their joy in the springing day,
By sorrow and care's dismay,

How shall the summer arise in joy,
Or the summer fruits appear?
Or how shall we gather what griefs destroy,
Or bless the mellowing year,
When the blasts of winter appear?

from *Songs of Experience*

The Clod & the Pebble

'LOVE seeketh not Itself to please,
'Nor for itself hath any care,
'But for another gives its ease,
'And builds a Heaven in Hell's despair.'

So sang a little Clod of Clay
Trodden with the cattle's feet,
But a Pebble of the brook
Warbled out these metres meet:

'Love seeketh only Self to please,
'To bind another to Its delight,
'Joys in another's loss of ease,
'And builds a Hell in Heaven's despite.'

The Sick Rose

O ROSE, thou art sick!
The invisible worm
That flies in the night,
In the howling storm,

Has found out thy bed
Of crimson joy:
And his dark secret love
Does thy life destroy.

The Fly

LITTLE Fly,
Thy summer's play
My thoughtless hand
Has brush'd away.

Am not I
A fly like thee?
Or art not thou
A man like me?

For I dance,
And drink, & sing,
Till some blind hand
Shall brush my wing.

If thought is life
And strength & breath,
And the want
Of thought is death;

Then am I
A happy fly,
If I live
Or if I die.

The Tyger

TYGER! Tyger! burning bright
In the forests of the night,
What immortal hand or eye
Could frame thy fearful symmetry?

In what distant deeps or skies
Burnt the fire of thine eyes?
On what wings dare he aspire?
What the hand dare seize the fire?

And what shoulder, & what art,
Could twist the sinews of thy heart?
And when thy heart began to beat,
What dread hand? & what dread feet?

What the hammer? what the chain?
In what furnace was thy brain?
What the anvil? what dread grasp
Dare its deadly terrors clasp?

When the stars threw down their spears,
And water'd heaven with their tears,
Did he smile his work to see?
Did he who made the Lamb make thee?

Tyger! Tyger! burning bright
In the forests of the night,
What immortal hand or eye
Dare frame thy fearful symmetry?

The Garden of Love

I WENT to the Garden of Love,
And saw what I never had seen:
A Chapel was built in the midst,
Where I used to play on the green.

And the gates of this Chapel were shut,
And 'Thou shalt not' writ over the door;
So I turn'd to the Garden of Love
That so many sweet flowers bore;

And I saw it was filled with graves,
And tomb-stones where flowers should be;
And Priests in black gowns were walking their rounds,
And binding with briars my joys & desires.

London

I WANDER thro' each charter'd street,
Near where the charter'd Thames does flow,
And mark in every face I meet
Marks of weakness, marks of woe.

In every cry of every Man,
In every Infant's cry of fear,
In every voice, in every ban,
The mind-forg'd manacles I hear.

How the Chimney-sweeper's cry
Every black'ning Church appalls;
And the hapless Soldier's sigh
Runs in blood down Palace walls.

But most thro' midnight streets I hear
How the youthful Harlot's curse
Blasts the new born Infant's tear,
And blights with plagues the Marriage hearse.

The Human Abstract

PITY would be no more
If we did not make somebody Poor;
And Mercy no more could be
If all were as happy as we.

And mutual fear brings peace,
Till the selfish loves increase:
Then Cruelty knits a snare,
And spreads his baits with care.

He sits down with holy fears,
And waters the ground with tears;
Then Humility takes its root
Underneath his foot.

Soon spreads the dismal shade
Of Mystery over his head;
And the Catterpiller and Fly
Feed on the Mystery.

And it bears the fruit of Deceit,
Ruddy and sweet to eat;
And the Raven his nest has made
In its thickest shade.

The Gods of the earth and sea
Sought thro' Nature to find this Tree;
But their search was all in vain:
There grows one in the Human Brain.

Infant Sorrow

My mother groan'd! my father wept.
Into the dangerous world I leapt:
Helpless, naked, piping loud:
Like a fiend hid in a cloud.

Struggling in my father's hands,
Striving against my swadling bands,
Bound and weary I thought best
To sulk upon my mother's breast.

A Poison Tree

I was angry with my friend:
I told my wrath, my wrath did end.
I was angry with my foe:
I told it not, my wrath did grow.

And I water'd it in fears,
Night & morning with my tears;
And I sunned it with smiles,
And with soft deceitful wiles.

And it grew both day and night,
Till it bore an apple bright;
And my foe beheld it shine,
And he knew that it was mine,

And into my garden stole
When the night had veil'd the pole:
In the morning glad I see
My foe outstretch'd beneath the tree.

Auguries of Innocence

To see a World in a Grain of Sand
And a Heaven in a Wild Flower,
Hold Infinity in the palm of your hand
And Eternity in an hour.

A Robin Red breast in a Cage
Puts all Heaven in a Rage.
A dove house fill'd with doves & Pigeons
Shudders Hell thro' all its regions.
A dog starv'd at his Master's Gate
Predicts the ruin of the State.
A Horse misus'd upon the Road
Calls to Heaven for Human blood.
Each outcry of the hunted Hare
A fibre from the Brain does tear.
A Skylark wounded in the wing,
A Cherubim does cease to sing.
The Game Cock clip'd & arm'd for fight
Does the Rising Sun affright.
Every Wolf's & Lion's howl
Raises from Hell a Human Soul.
The wild deer, wand'ring here & there,
Keeps the Human Soul from Care.
The Lamb misus'd breeds Public strife
And yet forgives the Butcher's Knife.
The Bat that flits at close of Eve
Has left the Brain that won't Believe.
The Owl that calls upon the Night
Speaks the Unbeliever's fright.
He who shall hurt the little Wren
Shall never be belov'd by Men.
He who the Ox to wrath has mov'd
Shall never be by Woman lov'd.
The wanton Boy that kills the Fly
Shall feel the Spider's enmity.
He who torments the Chafer's sprite
Weaves a Bower in endless Night.
The Catterpiller on the Leaf
Repeats to thee thy Mother's grief.
Kill not the Moth nor Butterfly,
For the Last Judgment draweth nigh.
He who shall train the Horse to War
Shall never pass the Polar Bar.
The Begger's Dog & Widow's Cat,
Feed them & thou wilt grow fat.
The Gnat that sings his Summer's song
Poison gets from Slander's tongue.
The poison of the Snake & Newt
Is the sweat of Envy's Foot.

The Poison of the Honey Bee
Is the Artist's Jealousy.
The Prince's Robes & Beggar's Rags
Are Toadstools on the Miser's Bags.
A truth that's told with bad intent
Beats all the Lies you can invent.
It is right it should be so;
Man was made for Joy & Woe;
And when this we rightly know
Thro' the World we safely go.
Joy & Woe are woven fine,
A Clothing for the Soul divine;
Under every grief & pine
Runs a joy with silken twine.
The Babe is more than swadling Bands;
Throughout all these Human Lands
Tools were made, & Born were hands,
Every Farmer Understands.
Every Tear from Every Eye
Becomes a Babe in Eternity;
This is caught by Females bright
And return'd to its own delight.
The Bleat, the Bark, Bellow & Roar
Are Waves that Beat on Heaven's Shore.
The Babe that weeps the Rod beneath
Writes Revenge in realms of death.
The Beggar's Rags, fluttering in Air,
Does to Rags the Heavens tear.
The Soldier, arm'd with Sword & Gun,
Palsied strikes the Summer's Sun.
The poor Man's Farthing is worth more
Than all the Gold on Afric's Shore.
One Mite wrung from the Labrer's hands
Shall buy & sell the Miser's Lands:
Or, if protected from on high,
Does that whole Nation sell & buy.
He who mocks the Infant's Faith
Shall be mock'd in Age & Death.
He who shall teach the Child to Doubt
The rotting Grave shall ne'er get out.
He who respects the Infant's faith
Triumphs over Hell & Death.
The Child's Toys & the Old Man's Reasons
Are the Fruits of the Two seasons.

The Questioner, who sits so sly,
Shall never know how to Reply.
He who replies to words of Doubt
Doth put the Light of Knowledge out.
The Strongest Poison ever known
Came from Caesar's Laurel Crown.
Nought can deform the Human Race
Like to the Armour's iron brace.
When Gold & Gems adorn the Plow
To peaceful Arts shall Envy Bow.
A Riddle or the Cricket's Cry
Is to Doubt a fit Reply.
The Emmet's Inch & Eagle's Mile
Make Lame Philosophy to smile.
He who Doubts from what he sees
Will ne'er Believe, do what you Please.
If the Sun & Moon should doubt,
They'd immediately Go out.
To be in a Passion you Good may do,
But no Good if a Passion is in you.
The Whore & Gambler, by the State
Licenc'd, build that Nation's Fate.
The Harlot's cry from Street to Street
Shall weave Old England's winding Sheet.
The Winner's Shout, the Loser's Curse,
Dance before dead England's Hearse.
Every Night & every Morn
Some to Misery are Born.
Every Morn & every Night
Some are Born to sweet delight.
Some are Born to sweet delight,
Some are Born to Endless Night.
We are led to Believe a Lie
When we see [With *del.*] not Thro' the Eye
Which was Born in a Night to perish in a Night
When the Soul Slept in Beams of Light.
God Appears & God is Light
To those poor Souls who dwell in Night,
But does a Human Form Display
To those who Dwell in Realms of day.

WILLIAM BLAKE

from *Milton*

Jerusalem

AND did those feet in ancient time
Walk upon England's mountains green?
And was the holy Lamb of God
On England's pleasant pastures seen?

And did the Countenance Divine
Shine forth upon our clouded hills?
And was Jerusalem builded here
Among these dark Satanic Mills?

Bring me my Bow of burning gold:
Bring me my Arrows of desire:
Bring me my Spear: O clouds unfold!
Bring me my Chariot of fire.

I will not cease from Mental Fight,
Nor shall my Sword sleep in my hand
Till we have built Jerusalem
In England's green & pleasant Land.

'Would to God that all the Lord's people were Prophets.'
Numbers, xi. ch., 29 v.

*   *   *

BUT turning toward Ololon in terrible majesty Milton
Replied: 'Obey thou the Words of the Inspired Man.
'All that can (ann be) annihilated must be annihilated
'That the Children of Jersualem may be saved from slavery.
'There is a Negation, & there is a Contrary:
'The Negation must be destroy'd to redeem the Contraries.
'The Negation is the Spectre, the Reasoning Power in Man:
'This is a false Body, an Incrustation over my Immortal
'Spirit, a Selfhood which must be put off & annihilated alway.
'To cleanse the Face of my Spirit by Self-examination,

41

'To bathe in the Waters of Life, to wash off the Not Human,
'I come in Self-annihilation & the grandeur of Inspiration,
'To cast off Rational Demonstration by Faith in the Saviour,
'To cast off the rotten rags of Memory by Inspiration,

'To cast off Bacon, Locke & Newton from Albion's covering,
'To take off his filthy garments & clothe him with Imagination,
'To cast aside from Poetry all that is not Inspiration,
'That it no longer shall dare to mock with the aspersion of Madness
'Cast on the Inspired by the tame high finisher of paltry Blots
'Indefinite, or paltry Rhymes, or paltry Harmonies,
'Who creeps into State Government like a catterpiller to destroy;
'To cast off the idiot Questioner who is always questioning
'But never capable of answering, who sits with a sly grin
'Silent plotting when to question, like a thief in a cave,
'Who publishes doubt & calls it knowledge, whose Science is Despair,
'Whose pretence to knowledge is envy, whose whole Science is
'To destroy the wisdom of ages to gratify ravenous Envy
'That rages round him like a Wolf day & night without rest:
'He smiles with condescension, he talks of Benevolence & Virtue,
'And those who act with Benevolence & Virtue they murder time on
    time.
'These are the destroyers of Jerusalem, these are the murderers
'Of Jesus, who deny the Faith & mock at Eternal Life,
'Who pretend to Poetry that they may destroy Imagination
'By imitation of Nature's Images drawn from Remembrance.
'These are the Sexual Garments, the Abomination of Desolation,
'Hiding the Human Lineaments as with an Ark & Curtains
'Which Jesus rent & now shall wholly purge away with Fire
'Till Generation is swallow'd up in Regeneration.'

To Morning

O HOLY virgin! clad in purest white,
Unlock heav'n's golden gates, and issue forth;
Awake the dawn that sleeps in heaven; let light
Rise from the chambers of the east, and bring
The honied dew that cometh on waking day.
O radiant morning, salute the sun,
Rouz'd like a huntsman to the chace, and, with
Thy buskin'd feet, appear upon our hills.

from *Visions of the Daughters of Albion*

'INFANCY! fearless, lustful, happy, nestling for delight
'In laps of pleasure: Innocence! honest, open, seeking
'The vigorous joys of morning light; open to virgin bliss.

227

'Who taught thee modesty, subtil modesty, child of night & sleep?
'When thou awakest wilt thou dissemble all thy secret joys,
'Or wert thou not awake when all this mystery was disclos'd?
'Then com'st thou forth a modest virgin, knowing to dissemble,
'With nets found under thy night pillow, to catch virgin joy
'And brand it with the name of whore, & sell it in the night,
'In silence, ev'n without a whisper, and in seeming sleep.
'Religious dreams and holy vespers light thy smoky fires:
'Once were thy fires lighted by the eyes of honest morn.
'And does my Theotormon seek this hypocrite modesty,
'This knowing, artful, secret, fearful, cautious, trembling hypocrite?
'Then is Oothoon a whore indeed! and all the virgin joys
'Of life are harlots, and Theotormon is a sick man's dream;
'And Oothoon is the crafty slave of selfish holiness.

'But Oothoon is not so: a virgin fill'd with virgin fancies,
'Open to joy and to delight where ever beauty appears;
'If in the morning sun I find it, there my eyes are fix'd

PLATE 7

'In happy copulation; if in evening mild, wearied with work,
'Sit on a bank and draw the pleasures of this free born joy.

'The moment of desire! the moment of desire! The virgin
'That pines for man shall awaken her womb to enormous joys
'In the secret shadows of her chamber: the youth shut up from
'The lustful joy shall forget to generate & create an amorous image
'In the shadows of his curtains and in the folds of his silent pillow.
'Are not these the places of religion, the rewards of continence,
'The self enjoyings of self denial? why dost thou seek religion?
'Is it because acts are not lovely that thou seekest solitude
'Where the horrible darkness is impressed with reflections of desire?

'Father of Jealousy, be thou accursed from the earth!
'Why hast thou taught my Theotormon this accursed thing?
'Till beauty fades from off my shoulders, darken'd and cast out,
'A solitary shadow wailing on the margin of non-entity.

'I cry: Love! Love! Love! happy happy Love! free as the mountain
    wind!"

ROBERT BURNS

1759–1796

Auld Lang Syne

SHOULD auld acquaintance be forgot,
   And never brought to min'?
Should auld acquaintance be forgot,
   And auld lang syne?

   For auld lang syne, my dear.
     For auld lang syne,
   We'll tak a cup o' kindness yet,
     For auld lang syne.

We twa hae run about the braes,
   And pu'd the gowans fine;
But we've wandered mony a weary foot
   Sin' auld lang syne.

We twa hae paidled i' the burn,
   From morning sun till dine;
But seas between us braid hae roared
   Sin' auld lang syne.

And there's a hand, my trusty fiere,
   And gie's a hand o' thine;
And we'll tak a right guid-willie waught,
   For auld lang syne.

And surely ye'll be your pint-stowp,
   And surely I'll be mine;
And we'll tak a cup o' kindness yet
   For auld lang syne.

---

gowans] daisies   paidled] paddled   fiere] comrade   guid-willie] hearty
waught] draught

Green Grow the Rashes

GREEN grow the rashes O,
   Green grow the rashes O;
The sweetest hours that e'er I spend,
   Are spent amang the lasses O!

There's nought but care on ev'ry han',
   In ev'ry hour that passes O;
What signifies the life o' man,
   An' 'twere na for the lasses O.

The warly race may riches chase,
   An' riches still may fly them O;
An' tho' at last they catch them fast,
   Their hearts can ne'er enjoy them O.

But gie me a canny hour at e'en,
   My arms about my dearie O;
An' warly cares, an' warly men,
   May a' gae tapsalteerie O!

For you sae douce, ye sneer at this,
   Ye're nought but senseless asses O:
The wisest man the warl' saw,
   He dearly loved the lasses O.

Auld nature swears, the lovely dears
   Her noblest work she classes O;
Her prentice han's he tried on man,
   An' then she made the lasses O.

Coming Through the Rye

COMING through the rye, poor body,
   Coming through the rye,
She draiglet a' her petticoatie,
   Coming through the rye.

rashes] rushes   warly] worldly   canny] quiet   tapsalteerie] topsy-turvey
douce] grave, sober

Gin a body meet a body
   Coming through the rye;
Gin a body kiss a body,
   Need a body cry?

Gin a body meet a body
   Coming through the glen;
Gin a body kiss a body,
   Need the world ken?

Jenny's a' wat, poor body;
   Jenny's seldom dry;
She draiglet a' her petticoatie,
   Coming through the rye.

For A' That

Is there, for honest poverty,
   That hangs his head, and a' that?
The coward-slave, we pass him by,
   We dare be poor for a' that!
     For a' that, and a' that,
      Our toils obscure, and a' that;
     The rank is but the guinea stamp;
      The man's the gowd for a' that.

What tho' on hamely fare we dine,
   Wear hodden-grey, and a' that;
Gie fools their silks, and knaves their wine,
   A man's a man for a' that.
     For a' that, and a' that,
      Their tinsel show, and a' that;
     The honest man, tho' e'er sae poor,
      Is king o' men for a' that.

Ye see yon birkie, ca'd a lord,
   Wha struts, and stares, and a' that;
Tho' hundreds worship at his word,
   He's but a coof for a' that:
     For a' that, and a' that,
      His riband, star, an' a' that,
     The man of independent mind,
      He looks and laughs at a' that.

gowd] gold   hodden] coarse cloth   birkie] fellow   ca'd] called   coof] dolt

A prince can mak a belted knight,
  A marquis, duke, an' a' that;
But an honest man's aboon his might,
  Guid faith he mauna fa' that!
    For a' that, an' a' that,
      Their dignities, and a' that,
      The pith o' sense, and pride o' worth,
        Are higher rank than a' that.

Then let us pray that come it may,
  As come it will for a' that;
That sense and worth, o'er a' the earth,
  May bear the gree, an' a' that.
    For a' that, and a' that,
      It's comin' yet, for a' that,
      That man to man the warld o'er
        Shall brothers be for a' that.

Whistle, and I'll come to You, My Lad

  Chorus—
  O WHISTLE, and I'll come to you, my lad;
  O whistle, and I'll come to you, my lad:
  Tho' father and mither and a' should gae mad,
  O whistle, and I'll come to you, my lad.

But warily tent, when ye come to court me,
And come na unless the back-yett be a-jee;
Syne up the back-stile, and let naebody see,
And come as ye were na comin' to me.
And come as ye were na comin' to me.

At kirk, or at market, whene'er ye meet me,
Gang by me as tho' that ye cared na a flee:
But steal me a blink o' your bonnie black ee,
Yet look as ye were na lookin' at me.
Yet look as ye were na lookin' at me.

Aye vow and protest that ye care na for me,
And whiles ye may lightly my beauty a wee;
But court na anither, tho' jokin' ye be,
For fear that she wyle your fancy frae me.
For fear that she wyle your fancy frae me.

aboon] above   mauna] must not   fa'] manage   gree] prize, pre-eminence
WHISTLE, AND I'LL COME TO YOU, MY LAD: yett] gate   a-jee] ajar   syne] then

ROBERT BURNS

A Red, Red Rose

O MY Luve's like a red, red rose
   That's newly sprung in June:
O my Luve's like the melodie
   That's sweetly played in tune.

As fair art thou, my bonnie lass,
   So deep in luve am I:
And I will luve thee still, my dear,
   Till a' the seas gang dry:

Till a' the seas gang dry, my dear,
   And the rocks melt wi' the sun;
I will luve thee still, my dear,
   While the sands o' life shall run.

And fare thee weel, my only Luve!
   And fare thee weel a while!
And I will come again my Luve,
   Tho' it were ten thousand mile.

To a Mouse, on turning her up in her Nest with the Plough, November, 1785

WEE, sleekit, cow'rin', tim'rous beastie,
O what a panic's in thy breastie!
Thou need na start awa sae hasty,
       Wi' bickering brattle!
I wad be laith to rin an' chase thee
       Wi' murd'ring pattle!

I'm truly sorry man's dominion
Has broken Nature's social union,
An' justifies that ill opinion
       Which makes thee startle
At me, thy poor earth-born companion,
       An' fellow-mortal!

sleekit] sleek   bickering brattle] hurrying scamper   laith] loath   pattle]
plough-stick

I doubt na, whiles, but thou may thieve;
What then? poor beastie, thou maun live!
A daimen-icker in a thrave
       'S a sma' request:
I'll get a blessin' wi' the lave,
       And never miss 't!

Thy wee bit housie, too, in ruin!
Its silly wa's the win's are strewin'!
An' naething, now, to big a new ane,
       O' foggage green!
An' bleak December's winds ensuin',
       Baith snell an' keen!

Thou saw the fields laid bare and waste,
An' weary winter comin' fast,
An' cozie here, beneath the blast,
       Thou thought to dwell,
Till crash! the cruel coulter past
       Out-thro' thy cell.

That wee bit heap o' leaves an' stibble
Hast cost thee mony a weary nibble!
Now thou's turned out, for a' thy trouble,
       But house or hald,
To thole the winter's sleety dribble,
       An' cranreuch cauld!

But, Mousie, thou art no thy lane,
In proving foresight may be vain:
The best laid schemes o' mice an' men
       Gang aft a-gley,
An' lea'e us nought but grief an' pain
       For promised joy.

Still thou art blest compared wi' me!
The present only toucheth thee:
But oh! I backward cast my e'e
       On prospects drear!
An' forward tho' I canna see,
       I guess an' fear!

whiles] sometimes   maun] must   daimen-icker in a thrave] odd ear in a bundle.
A thrave is 24 sheaves   lave] rest   big] build   foggage] moss   snell] bitter
But house] Without house   hald] holding   thole] endure   cranreuch] hoar-frost
lane] alone   a-gley] askew

O Wert Thou in the Cauld Blast

O WERT thou in the cauld blast,
  On yonder lea, on yonder lea,
My plaidie to the angry airt,
  I'd shelter thee, I'd shelter thee;
Or did misfortune's bitter storms
  Around thee blaw, around thee blaw,
Thy bield should be my bosom,
  To share it a', to share it a'.

Or were I in the wildest waste,
  Sae black and bare, sae black and bare,
The desert were a paradise,
  If thou wert there, if thou wert there;
Or were I monarch o' the globe,
  Wi' thee to reign, wi' thee to reign,
The brightest jewel in my crown
  Wad be my queen, wad be my queen.

JOANNA BAILLIE
1762–1851

Hay Making

UPON the grass no longer hangs the dew;
Forth hies the mower, with his glittering scythe,
In snowy shirt bedight, and all unbraced,
He moves athwart the mead with sidling bend,
And lays the grass in many a swathey line:
In every field, in every lawn and meadow,
The rousing voice of industry is heard;
The haycock rises, and the frequent rake
Sweeps on the fragrant hay in heavy wreaths.
The old and young, the weak and strong, are there,
And, as they can, help on the cheerful work.
The father jeers his awkward half-grown lad,
Who trails his tawdry armful o'er the field,
Nor does he fear the jeering to repay.
The village oracle, and simple maid,

Jest in their turns and raise the ready laugh;
All are companions in the general glee;
Authority, hard-favoured, frowns not there.
Some, more advanced, raise up the lofty rick,
Whilst on its top doth stand the parish toast,
In loose attire, and swelling ruddy cheek.
With taunts and harmless mockery she receives
The tossed-up heaps from fork of simple youth,
Who, staring on her, takes his arm away,
While half the load falls back upon himself.
Loud is her laugh, her voice is heard afar:
The mower busied on the distant lawn,
The carter trudging on his dusty way,
The shrill sound know, their bonnets toss in air,
And roar across the field to catch her notice:
She waves her arm to them, and shakes her head,
And then renews her work with double spirit.
Thus do they jest and laugh away their toil
Till the bright sun, now past his middle course,
Shoots down his fiercest beams which none may brave.
The stoutest arm feels listless, and the swart
And brawny-shouldered clown begins to fail,
But to the weary, lo! there comes relief!
A troop of welcome children o'er the lawn
With slow and wary steps approach: some bear
In baskets oaten cakes or barley scones,
And gusty cheese and stoups of milk or whey.
Beneath the branches of a spreading tree,
Or by the shady side of the tall rick,
They spread their homely fare, and seated round,
Taste every pleasure that a feast can give.

WILLIAM LISLE BOWLES

1762–1850

Dover Cliffs

ON these white cliffs, that calm above the flood
Uplift their shadowy heads, and at their feet
Scarce hear the surge that has for ages beat,
Sure many a lonely wanderer has stood;

And while the distant murmur met his ear,
And o'er the distant billows the still eve
Sailed slow, has thought of all his heart must leave
To-morrow; of the friends he loved most dear;
Of social scenes from which he wept to part.
But if, like me, he knew how fruitless all
The thoughts that would full fain the past recall;
Soon would he quell the risings of his heart,
And brave the wild winds and unhearing tide,
The world his country, and his God his guide.

SAMUEL ROGERS

1763–1855

The Sleeping Beauty

SLEEP on, and dream of Heaven awhile—
    Though shut so close thy laughing eyes,
Thy rosy lips still wear a smile
    And move, and breathe delicious sighs!

Ah, now soft blushes tinge her cheeks
    And mantle o'er her neck of snow:
Ah, now she murmurs, now she speaks
    What most I wish—and fear to know!

She starts, she trembles, and she weeps!
    Her fair hands folded on her breast:
—And now, how like a saint she sleeps!
    A seraph in the realms of rest!

Sleep on secure! Above control
    Thy thoughts belong to Heaven and thee:
And may the secret of thy soul
    Remain within its sanctuary!

Ginevra

I F thou shouldst ever come by choice or chance
To Modena, where still religiously
Among her ancient trophies is preserved
Bologna's bucket (in its chain it hangs
Within that reverend tower, the Guirlandine)
Stop at a palace near the Reggio-gate,
Dwelt in of old by one of the Orsini.
Its noble gardens, terrace above terrace,
And rich in fountains, statues, cypresses,
Will long detain thee; through their arched walks,
Dim at noon-day, discovering many a glimpse
Of knights and dames, such as in old romance,
And lovers, such as in heroic song—
Perhaps the two, for groves were their delight,
That in the spring-time, as alone they sat,
Venturing together on a tale of love,
Read only part that day. A summer-sun,
Sets ere one half is seen; but, ere thou go,
Enter the house—prithee, forget it not—
And look awhile upon a picture there.

'Tis of a lady in her earliest youth,
The very last of that illustrious race,
Done by Zampieri—but by whom I care not.
He, who observes it, ere he passes on,
Gazes his fill, and comes and comes again,
That he may call it up, when far away.
She sits, inclining forward as to speak,
Her lips half-open, and her finger up,
As though she said 'Beware!' Her vest of gold
Broidered with flowers, and clasped from head to foot,
An emerald-stone in every golden clasp;
And on her brow fairer than alabaster,
A coronet of pearls. But then her face,
So lovely, yet so arch, so full of mirth,
The overflowings of an innocent heart—
It haunts me still, though many a year has fled,
Like some wild melody!
                                    Alone it hangs
Over a mouldering heir-loom, its companion,
An oaken-chest, half-eaten by the worm,
But richly carved by Antony of Trent

With Scripture-stories from the Life of Christ;
A chest that came from Venice, and had held
The ducal robes of some old ancestor.
That by the way—it may be true or false—
But don't forget the picture; and thou wilt not,
When thou hast heard the tale they told me there.

　She was an only child; from infancy
The joy, the pride of an indulgent sire.
Her mother dying of the gift she gave,
That precious gift, what else remained to him?
The young Ginevra was his all in life,
Still as she grew, for ever in his sight;
And in her fifteenth year became a bride,
Marrying an only son, Francesco Doria,
Her playmate from her birth, and her first love.

　Just as she looks there in her bridal dress,
She was all gentleness, all gaiety,
Her pranks the favourite theme of every tongue.
But now the day was come, the day, the hour;
Now, frowning, smiling, for the hundredth time,
The nurse, that ancient lady, preached decorum;
And, in the lustre of her youth, she gave
Her hand, with her heart in it, to Francesco.

　Great was the joy; but at the bridal feast,
When all sat down, the bride was wanting there.
Nor was she to be found! Her Father cried,
"'Tis but to make a trial of our love!'
And filled his glass to all; but his hand shook,
And soon from guest to guest the panic spread.
'Twas but that instant she had left Francesco,
Laughing and looking back and flying still,
Her ivory-tooth imprinted on his finger.
But now, alas, she was not to be found;
Nor from that hour could any thing be guessed
But that she was not!—Weary of his life,
Francesco flew to Venice, and forthwith
Flung it away in battle with the Turk.
Orsini lived; and long might'st thou have seen
An old man wandering as in quest of something,
Something he could not find—he knew not what.
When he was gone, the house remained a while
Silent and tenantless—then went to strangers.

　Full fifty years were past, and all forgot,
When on an idle day, a day of search

'Mid the old lumber in the gallery,
That mouldering chest was noticed; and 'twas said
By one as young, as thoughtless as Ginevra,
Why not remove it from its lurking place?
'Twas done as soon as said; but on the way
It burst, it fell; and lo, a skeleton,
With here and there a pearl, an emerald-stone,
A golden clasp, clasping a shred of gold.
All else had perished—save a nuptial ring,
And a small seal, her mother's legacy,
Engraven with a name, the name of both,
'Ginevra.'—There then had she found a grave!
Within that chest had she concealed herself,
Fluttering with joy, the happiest of the happy;
When a spring-lock that lay in ambush there,
Fastened her down for ever!

A Wish

Mine be a cot beside the hill;
    A bee-hive's hum shall soothe my ear;
A willowy brook, that turns a mill,
    With many a fall shall linger near.

The swallow oft beneath my thatch
    Shall twitter from her clay-built nest;
Oft shall the pilgrim lift the latch
    And share my meal, a welcome guest.

Around my ivied porch shall spring
    Each fragrant flower that drinks the dew,
And Lucy at her wheel shall sing
    In russet gown and apron blue.

The village church among the trees,
    Where first our marriage vows were given,
With merry peals shall swell the breeze
    And point with taper spire to Heaven.

JAMES HOGG

1770–1835

Kilmeny

BONNIE Kilmeny gaed up the glen;
But it wasna to meet Duneira's men,
Nor the rosy monk of the isle to see,
For Kilmeny was pure as pure could be.
It was only to hear the yorlin sing,
And pu' the cress-flower round the spring;
The scarlet hypp and the hindberrye,
And the nut that hung frae the hazel tree;
For Kilmeny was pure as pure could be.
But lang may her minny look o'er the wa',
And lang may she seek i' the green-wood shaw;
Lang the laird o' Duneira blame,
And lang, lang greet or Kilmeny come hame!

When many a day had come and fled,
When grief grew calm, and hope was dead,
When mess for Kilmeny's soul had been sung,
When the bedesman had prayed and the dead bell rung,
Late, late in gloamin' when all was still,
When the fringe was red on the westlin hill,
The wood was sere, the moon i' the wane,
The reek o' the cot hung over the plain,
Like a little wee cloud in the world its lane;
When the ingle lowed wi' an eiry leme,
Late, late in the gloamin' Kilmeny came hame!

'Kilmeny, Kilmeny, where have you been?
Lang hae we sought baith holt and den;
By linn, by ford, and green-wood tree,
Yet you are halesome and fair to see.
Where gat you that joup o' the lily scheen?
That bonnie snood of the birk sae green?
And these roses, the fairest that ever were seen?
Kilmeny, Kilmeny, where have you been?'

yorlin] yellow-hammer   hindberrye] blackberry   minny] mother   greet] weep
westlin] western   its lane] alone   ingle] hearth   lowed] flamed   eiry
leme] eery gleam   linn] waterfall   joup] skirt   scheen] bright

Kilmeny looked up with a lovely grace,
But nae smile was seen on Kilmeny's face;
As still was her look, and as still was her e'e,
As the stillness that lay on the emerant lea,
Or the mist that sleeps on a waveless sea.
For Kilmeny had been, she knew not where,
And Kilmeny had seen what she could not declare;
Kilmeny had been where the cock never crew,
Where the rain never fell, and the wind never blew.
But it seemed as the harp of the sky had rung,
And the airs of heaven played round her tongue,
When she spake of the lovely forms she had seen,
And a land where sin had never been;
A land of love and a land of light,
Withouten sun, or moon, or night;
Where the river swa'd a living stream,
And the light a pure celestial beam;
The land of vision, it would seem,
A still, an everlasting dream.

    In yon green-wood there is a waik,
And in that waik there is a wene,
    And in that wene there is a maike,
That neither has flesh, blood, nor bane;
And down in yon green-wood he walks his lane.

In that green wene Kilmeny lay,
Her bosom happed wi' flowerets gay;
But the air was soft and the silence deep,
And bonnie Kilmeny fell sound asleep.
She kenned nae mair, nor opened her e'e,
Till waked by the hymns of a far countrye.

She 'wakened on a couch of the silk sae slim,
All striped wi' the bars of the rainbow's rim;
And lovely beings round were rife,
Who erst had travelled mortal life;
And aye they smiled and 'gan to speer,
'What spirit has brought this mortal here?'—

'Lang have I journeyed, the world wide,'
A meek and reverend fere replied;
'Baith night and day I have watched the fair,
Eident a thousand years and mair.

swa'd] swelled   waik] glade   wene] recess   maike] mate   his
lane] alone   happed] covered   speer] ask   fere] comrade   eident]
diligently

Yes, I have watched o'er ilk degree,
Wherever blooms femenitye;
But sinless virgin, free of stain
In mind and body, fand I nane.
Never, since the banquet of time,
Found I a virgin in her prime,
Till late this bonnie maiden I saw
As spotless as the mornin snaw:
Full twenty years she has lived as free
As the spirits that sojourn in this countrye:
I have brought her away frae the snares of men,
That sin or death she never may ken.'—

They clasped her waist and her hands sae fair,
They kissed her cheek and they kemed her hair,
And round came many a blooming fere,
Saying, 'Bonnie Kilmeny, ye're welcome here!
Women are freed of the littand scorn:
O blest be the day Kilmeny was born!
Now shall the land of the spirits see,
Now shall it ken what a woman may be!
Many a lang year, in sorrow and pain,
Many a lang year through the world we've gane,
Commissioned to watch fair womankind,
For it's they who nurice the immortal mind.
We have watched their steps as the dawning shone
And deep in the green-wood walks alone;
By lily bower and silken bed,
The viewless tears have o'er them shed;
Have soothed their ardent minds to sleep,
Or left the couch of love to weep.
We have seen! we have seen! but the time must come,
And the angels will weep at the day of doom!

'O would the fairest of mortal kind
Aye keep the holy truths in mind,
That kindred spirits their motions see,
Who watch their ways with anxious e'e,
And grieve for the guilt of humanitye!
O, sweet to Heaven the maiden's prayer,
And the sigh that heaves a bosom sae fair!

kemed] combed

243

And dear to Heaven the words of truth,
And the praise of virtue frae beauty's mouth!
And dear to the viewless forms of air,
The minds that kyth as the body fair!

'O bonnie Kilmeny! free frae stain,
If ever you seek the world again,
That world of sin, of sorrow and fear,
O tell of the joys that are waiting here;
And tell of the signs you shall shortly see;
Of the times that are now, and the times that shall be.'—
They lifted Kilmeny, they led her away,
And she walked in the light of a sunless day;
The sky was a dome of crystal bright,
The fountain of vision, and fountain of light:
The emerald fields were of dazzling glow,
And the flowers of everlasting blow.
Then deep in the stream her body they laid,
That her youth and beauty never might fade;
And they smiled on heaven, when they saw her lie
In the stream of life that wandered by.
And she heard a song, she heard it sung,
She kenned not where; but sae sweetly it rung,
It fell on the ear like a dream of the morn:
'O, blest be the day Kilmeny was born!
Now shall the land of the spirits see,
Now shall it ken what a woman may be!
The sun that shines on the world sae bright,
A borrowed gleid frae the fountain of light;
And the moon that sleeks the sky sae dun,
Like a gouden bow, or a beamless sun,
Shall wear away, and be seen nae mair,
And the angels shall miss them travelling the air.
But lang, lang after baith night and day,
When the sun and the world have elyed away;
When the sinner has gane to his waesome doom,
Kilmeny shall smile in eternal bloom!'—

They bore her away, she wist not how,
For she felt not arm nor rest below;
But so swift they wained her through the light,
'Twas like the motion of sound or sight;

kyth] appear   kenned] knew   gleid] gleam   elyed] vanished

They seemed to split the gales of air,
And yet nor gale nor breeze was there.
Unnumbered groves below them grew,
They came, they passed, and backward flew,
Like floods of blossoms gliding on,
In moment seen, in moment gone.
O, never vales to mortal view
Appeared like those o'er which they flew!
That land to human spirits given,
The lowermost vales of the storied heaven;
From thence they can view the world below,
And heaven's blue gates with sapphires glow,
More glory yet unmeet to know.

They bore her far to a mountain green,
To see what mortal never had seen;
And they seated her high on a purple sward,
And bade her heed what she saw and heard,
And note the changes the spirits wrought,
For now she lived in the land of thought.
She looked, and she saw nor sun nor skies,
But a crystal dome of a thousand dyes:
She looked, and she saw nae land aright,
But an endless whirl of glory and light:
And radiant beings went and came,
Far swifter than wind, or the linkèd flame.
She hid her e'en frae the dazzling view;
She looked again, and the scene was new.

She saw a sun on a summer sky,
And clouds of amber sailing by;
A lovely land beneath her lay,
And that land had glens and mountains gray;
And that land had valleys and hoary piles,
And marlèd seas, and a thousand isles.
Its fields were speckled, its forests green,
And its lakes were all of the dazzling sheen,
Like magic mirrors, where slumbering lay
The sun and the sky and the cloudlet gray;
Which heaved and trembled, and gently swung,
On every shore they seemed to be hung;
For there they were seen on their downward plain

marlèd] variegated

A thousand times and a thousand again;
In winding lake and placid firth,
Little peaceful heavens in the bosom of earth.

Kilmeny sighed and seemed to grieve,
For she found her heart to that land did cleave;
She saw the corn wave on the vale,
She saw the deer run down the dale;
She saw the plaid and the broad claymore,
And the brows that the badge of freedom bore;
And she thought she had seen the land before.

She saw a lady sit on a throne,
The fairest that ever the sun shone on!
A lion licked her hand of milk,
And she held him in a leish of silk;
And a leifu' maiden stood at her knee,
With a silver wand and melting e'e;
Her sovereign shield till love stole in.
And poisoned all the fount within.

Then a gruff untoward bedesman came,
And hundit the lion on his dame;
And the guardian maid wi' the dauntless e'e,
She dropped a tear, and left her knee;
And she saw till the queen frae the lion fled,
Till the bonniest flower of the world lay dead;
A coffin was set on a distant plain,
And she saw the red blood fall like rain;
Then bonnie Kilmeny's heart grew sair,
And she turned away, and could look nae mair.

Then the gruff grim carle girned amain,
And they trampled him down, but he rose again:
And he baited the lion to deeds of weir,
Till he lapped the blood to the kingdom dear;
And weening his head was danger-preef,
When crowned with the rose and clover leaf,
He gowled at the carle, and chased him away
To feed wi' the deer on the mountain gray.
He gowled at the carle, and gecked at Heaven,
But his mark was set, and his arles given.
Kilmeny a while her e'en withdrew;
She looked again, and the scene was new.

leifu'] lone   girned] snarled   weir] war   gowled] bowled
gecked] mocked   arles] *lit*. earnest money given in confirmation of a bargain:
fig. a beating

She saw before her fair unfurled
One half of all the glowing world,
Where oceans rolled, and rivers ran,
To bound the aims of sinful man.
She saw a people, fierce and fell,
Burst frae their bounds like fiends of hell;
Their lilies grew, and the eagle flew;
And she herkèd on her ravening crew,
Till the cities and towers were wrapped in a blaze,
And the thunder it roared o'er the lands and the seas.
The widows they wailed, and the red blood ran,
And she threatened an end to the race of man;
She never lened, nor stood in awe,
Till caught by the lion's deadly paw.
O, then the eagle swinked for life,
And brainyelled up a mortal strife;
But flew she north, or flew she south,
She met wi' the gowl o' the lion's mouth.

With a mooted wing and waefu' maen,
The eagle sought her eiry again;
But lang may she cower in her bloody nest,
And lang, lang sleek her wounded breast,
Before she sey another flight,
To play wi', the norland lion's might.

But to sing the sights Kilmeny saw,
So far surpassing nature's law,
The singer's voice wad sink away,
And the string of his harp wad cease to play.
But she saw till the sorrows of man were by,
And all was love and harmony;
Till the stars of heaven fell calmly away,
Like flakes of snaw on a winter day.

Then Kilmeny begged again to see
The friends she had left in her own countrye;
To tell of the place where she had been,
And the glories that lay in the land unseen;
To warn the living maidens fair,
The loved of Heaven, the spirits' care,
That all whose minds unmeled remain
Shall bloom in beauty when time is gane.

lened] crouched   swinked] worked   brainyelled] beat   gowl] howl
mooted] moulted   sey] essay   unmeled] unblemished

With distant music, soft and deep,
They lulled Kilmeny sound asleep;
And when she awakened, she lay her lane,
All happed with flowers, in the green-wood wene.
When seven lang years had come and fled,
When grief was calm, and hope was dead;
When scarce was rememberd Kilmeny's name,
Late, late in a gloamin' Kilmeny came hame!
And O, her beauty was fair to see,
But still and steadfast was her e'e!
Such beauty bard may never declare,
For there was no pride nor passion there;
And the soft desire of maiden's e'en
In that mild face could never be seen.
Her seymar was the lily flower,
And her cheek the moss-rose in the shower;
And her voice like the distant melodye,
That floats along the twilight sea.
But she loved to raike the lanely glen,
And keepèd afar frae the haunts of men;
Her holy hymns unheard to sing,
To suck the flowers, and drink the spring.
But wherever her peaceful form appeared,
The wild beasts of the hill were cheered;
The wolf played blythly round the field,
The lordly bison lowed and kneeled;
The dun deer wooed with manner bland,
And cowered aneath her lily hand.
And when at even the woodlands rung,
When hymns of other worlds she sung
In ecstacy of sweet devotion,
O, then the glen was all in motion!
The wild beasts of the forest came,
Broke from their bughts and faulds the tame,
And goved around, charmed and amazed;
Even the dull cattle crooned and gazed,
And murmured and looked with anxious pain
For something the mystery to explain.
The buzzard came with the throstle-cock;
The corby left her houf in the rock;
The blackbird alang wi' the eagle flew;

her lane] alone   happed] covered   wene] recess   gloamin'] twilight
seymar] cymar, smock   raike] wander through   bughts] pens   faulds]
folds   goved] stared   corby] raven   houf] haunt

The hind came tripping o'er the dew;
The wolf and the kid their raike began,
And the tod, and the lamb, and the leveret ran;
The hawk and the hern attour them hung,
And the merle and the mavis forhooyed their young;
And all in a peaceful ring were hurled;
It was like an eve in a sinless world!

When a month and a day had come and gane,
Kilmeny sought the green-wood wene;
There laid her down on the leaves sae green,
And Kilmeny on earth was never mair seen.
But O, the words that fell from her mouth
Were words of wonder, and words of truth!
But all the land were in fear and dread,
For they kendna whether she was living or dead.
It wasna her hame, and she couldna remain;
She left this world of sorrow and pain,
And returned to the land of thought again.

A Boy's Song

WHERE the pools are bright and deep,
Where the grey trout lies asleep,
Up the river and over the lea,
That's the way for Billy and me.

Where the blackbird sings the latest,
Where the hawthorn blooms the sweetest,
Where the nestlings chirp and flee,
That's the way for Billy and me.

Where the mowers mow the cleanest,
Where the hay lies thick and greenest,
There to track the homeward bee,
That's the way for Billy and me.

Where the hazel bank is steepest,
Where the shadow falls the deepest,
Where the clustering nuts fall free,
That's the way for Billy and me.

raike] walk   tod] fox   hern] heron   attour] above   forhooyed]
forsook   hurled] drawn

Why the boys should drive away
Little sweet maidens from the play,
Or love to banter and fight so well,
That's the thing I never could tell.

But this I know, I love to play
Through the meadow, among the hay;
Up the water and over the lea,
That's the way for Billy and me.

WILLIAM WORDSWORTH

1770–1850

Lines
Composed a few miles above Tintern Abbey, on Revisiting the Banks of the Wye during a Tour. July 13, 1798

FIVE years have past; five summers, with the length
Of five long winters! and again I hear
These waters, rolling from their mountain-springs
With a soft inland murmur.—Once again
Do I behold these steep and lofty cliffs,
That on a wild secluded scene impress
Thoughts of more deep seclusion; and connect
The landscape with the quiet of the sky.
The day is come when I again repose
Here, under this dark sycamore, and view
These plots of cottage-ground, these orchard-tufts,
Which at this season, with their unripe fruits,
Are clad in one green hue, and lose themselves
'Mid groves and copses. Once again I see
These hedge-rows, hardly hedge-rows, little lines
Of sportive wood run wild: these pastoral farms,
Green to the very door; and wreaths of smoke
Sent up, in silence, from among the trees!
With some uncertain notice, as might seem
Of vagrant dwellers in the houseless woods,
Or of some Hermit's cave, where by his fire
The Hermit sits alone.

These beauteous forms,
Through a long absence, have not been to me
As is a landscape to a blind man's eye:
But oft, in lonely rooms, and 'mid the din
Of towns and cities, I have owed to them,
In hours of weariness, sensations sweet,
Felt in the blood, and felt along the heart;
And passing even into my purer mind,
With tranquil restoration:—feelings too
Of unremembered pleasure: such, perhaps,
As have no slight or trivial influence
On that best portion of a good man's life,
His little, nameless, unremembered, acts
Of kindness and of love. Nor less, I trust,
To them I may have owed another gift,
Of aspect more sublime; that blessed mood,
In which the burthen of the mystery,
In which the heavy and the weary weight
Of all this unintelligible world,
Is lightened:—that serene and blessed mood,
In which the affections gently lead us on,—
Until, the breath of this corporeal frame
And even the motion of our human blood
Almost suspended, we are laid asleep
In body, and become a living soul:
While with an eye made quiet by the power
Of harmony, and the deep power of joy,
We see into the life of things.
                              If this
Be but a vain belief, yet, oh! how oft—
In darkness and amid the many shapes
Of joyless daylight; when the fretful stir
Unprofitable, and the fever of the world,
Have hung upon the beatings of my heart—
How oft, in spirit, have I turned to thee,
O sylvan Wye! thou wanderer through the woods,
How often has my spirit turned to thee!

And now, with gleams of half-extinguished thought,
With many recognitions dim and faint,
And somewhat of a sad perplexity,
The picture of the mind revives again:
While here I stand, not only with the sense
Of present pleasure, but with pleasing thoughts

That in this moment there is life and food
For future years. And so I dare to hope,
Though changed, no doubt, from what I was when first
I came among these hills; when like a roe
I bounded o'er the mountains, by the sides
Of the deep rivers, and the lonely streams,
Wherever nature led: more like a man
Flying from something that he dreads than one
Who sought the thing he loved. For nature then
(The coarser pleasures of my boyish days,
And their glad animal movements all gone by)
To me was all in all.—I cannot paint
What then I was. The sounding cataract
Haunted me like a passion: the tall rock,
The mountain, and the deep and gloomy wood,
Their colours and their forms, were then to me
An appetite; a feeling and a love,
That had no need of a remoter charm,
By thought supplied, nor any interest
Unborrowed from the eye.—That time is past,
And all its aching joys are now no more,
And all its dizzy raptures. Not for this
Faint I, nor mourn nor murmur; other gifts
Have followed; for such loss, I would believe,
Abundant recompense. For I have learned
To look on nature, not as in the hour
Of thoughtless youth; but hearing oftentimes
The still, sad music of humanity,
Nor harsh nor grating, though of ample power
To chasten and subdue. And I have felt
A presence that disturbs me with the joy
Of elevated thoughts; a sense sublime
Of something far more deeply interfused,
Whose dwelling is the light of setting suns,
And the round ocean and the living air,
And the blue sky, and in the mind of man:
A motion and a spirit, that impels
All thinking things, all objects of all thought,
And rolls through all things. Therefore am I still
A lover of the meadows and the woods,
And mountains; and of all that we behold
From this green earth; of all the mighty world
Of eye, and ear,—both what they half create,
And what perceive; well pleased to recognize

In nature and the language of the sense
The anchor of my purest thoughts, the nurse,
The guide, the guardian of my heart, and soul
Of all my moral being.
                              Nor perchance,
If I were not thus taught, should I the more
Suffer my genial spirits to decay:
For thou art with me here upon the banks
Of this fair river; thou my dearest Friend,
My dear, dear Friend; and in thy voice I catch
The language of my former heart, and read
My former pleasures in the shooting lights
Of thy wild eyes. Oh! yet a little while
May I behold in thee what I was once,
My dear, dear Sister! and this prayer I make,
Knowing that Nature never did betray
The heart that loved her; 'tis her privilege,
Through all the years of this our life, to lead
From joy to joy: for she can so inform
The mind that is within us, so impress
With quietness and beauty, and so feed
With lofty thoughts, that neither evil tongues,
Rash judgments, nor the sneers of selfish men,
Nor greetings where no kindness is, nor all
The dreary intercourse of daily life,
Shall e'er prevail against us, or disturb
Our cheerful faith, that all which we behold
Is full of blessings. Therefore let the moon
Shine on thee in thy solitary walk;
And let the misty mountain-winds be free
To blow against thee: and, in after years,
When these wild ecstasies shall be matured
Into a sober pleasure; when thy mind
Shall be a mansion for all lovely forms,
Thy memory be as a dwelling-place
For all sweet sounds and harmonies; oh! then,
If solitude, or fear, or pain, or grief,
Should be thy portion, with what healing thoughts
Of tender joy wilt thou remember me,
And these my exhortations! Nor, perchance—
If I should be where I no more can hear
Thy voice, nor catch from thy wild eyes these gleams
Of past existence—wilt thou then forget
That on the banks of this delightful stream

We stood together; and that I, so long
A worshipper of Nature, hither came
Unwearied in that service: rather say
With warmer love—oh! with far deeper zeal
Of holier love. Nor wilt thou then forget
That after many wanderings, many years
Of absence, these steep woods and lofty cliffs,
And this green pastoral landscape, were to me
More dear, both for themselves and for thy sake!

Lucy Gray; or, Solitude

OFT I had heard of Lucy Gray:
And, when I crossed the wild,
I chanced to see at break of day
The solitary child.

No mate, no comrade Lucy knew;
She dwelt on a wide moor,
—The sweetest thing that ever grew
Beside a human door!

You yet may spy the fawn at play,
The hare upon the green;
But the sweet face of Lucy Gray
Will never more be seen.

'Tonight will be a stormy night—
You to the town must go;
And take a lantern, Child, to light
Your mother through the snow.'

'That, Father! will I gladly do:
Tis scarcely afternoon—
The minster-clock has just struck two,
And yonder is the moon!'

At this the Father raised his hook,
And snapped a faggot-band;
He plied his work;—and Lucy took
The lantern in her hand.

Not blither is the mountain roe:
With many a wanton stroke
Her feet disperse the powdery snow,
That rises up like smoke.

The storm came on before its time:
She wandered up and down;
And many a hill did Lucy climb:
But never reached the town.

The wretched parents all that night
Went shouting far and wide;
But there was neither sound nor sight
To serve them for a guide.

At day-break on a hill they stood
That overlooked the moor;
And thence they saw the bridge of wood,
A furlong from their door.

They wept—and, turning homeward, cried,
'In heaven we all shall meet;'
—When in the snow the mother spied
The print of Lucy's feet.

Then downwards from the steep hill's edge
They tracked the footmarks small;
And through the broken hawthorn hedge,
And by the long stone-wall;

And then an open field they crossed:
The marks were still the same;
They tracked them on, nor ever lost;
And to the bridge they came.

They followed from the snowy bank
Those footmarks, one by one,
Into the middle of the plank;
And further there were none!

—Yet some maintain that to this day
She is a living child;
That you may see sweet Lucy Gray
Upon the lonesome wild.

O'er rough and smooth she trips along,
And never looks behind;
And sings a solitary song
That whistles in the wind.

The Fountain

A Conversation

WE talked with open heart, and tongue
Affectionate and true,
A pair of friends, though I was young,
And Matthew seventy-two.

We lay beneath a spreading oak,
Beside a mossy seat;
And from the turf a fountain broke,
And gurgled at our feet.

'Now, Matthew!' said I, 'let us match
This water's pleasant tune
With some old border-song, or catch
That suits a summer's noon;

'Or of the church-clock and the chimes
Sing here beneath the shade,
That half-mad thing of witty rhymes
Which you last April made!'

In silence Matthew lay, and eyed
The spring beneath the tree;
And thus the dear old man replied,
The grey-haired man of glee:

'No check, no stay, this streamlet fears;
How merrily it goes!
'Twill murmur on a thousand years,
And flow as now it flows.

'And there, on this delightful day,
I cannot choose but think
How oft, a vigorous man, I lay
Beside this fountain's brink.

'My eyes are dim with childish tears,
My heart is idly stirred,
For the same sound is in my ears
Which in those days I heard.

'Thus fares it still in our decay:
And yet the wiser mind
Mourns less for what age takes away
Than what it leaves behind.

'The blackbird amid leafy trees,
The lark above the hill,
Let loose their carols when they please,
Are quiet when they will.

'With Nature never do *they* wage
A foolish strife; they see
A happy youth, and their old age
Is beautiful and free:

'But we are pressed by heavy laws;
And often, glad no more,
We wear a face of joy, because
We have been glad of yore.

'If there be one who need bemoan
His kindred laid in earth,
The household hearts that were his own;
It is the man of mirth.

'My days, my Friend, are almost gone,
My life has been approved,
And many love me! but by none
Am I enough beloved.'

'Now both himself and me he wrongs,
The man who thus complains!
I live and sing my idle songs
Upon these happy plains;

'And, Matthew, for thy children dead
I'll be a son to thee!'
At this he grasped my hand, and said,
'Alas! that cannot be.'

We rose up from the fountain-side;
And down the smooth descent
Of the green sheep-track did we glide;
And through the wood we went;

And, ere we came to Leonard's rock,
He sang those witty rhymes
About the crazy old church-clock,
And the bewildered chimes.

Michael

A Pastoral Poem

IF from the public way you turn your steps
Up the tumultuous brook of Green-head Ghyll,
You will suppose that with an upright path
Your feet must struggle; in such bold ascent
The pastoral mountains front you, face to face.
But, courage! for around that boisterous brook
The mountains have all opened out themselves,
And made a hidden valley of their own.
No habitation can be seen; but they
Who journey thither find themselves alone
With a few sheep, with rocks and stones, and kites
That overhead are sailing in the sky.
It is in truth an utter solitude;
Nor should I have made mention of this Dell
But for one object which you might pass by,
Might see and notice not. Beside the brook
Appears a straggling heap of unhewn stones!
And to that simple object appertains
A story—unenriched with strange events,
Yet not unfit, I deem, for the fireside,
Or for the summer shade. It was the first
Of those domestic tales that spake to me
Of Shepherds, dwellers in the valleys, men
Whom I already loved;—not verily
For their own sakes, but for the fields and hills
Where was their occupation and abode.
And hence this Tale, while I was yet a Boy
Careless of books, yet having felt the power

Of Nature, by the gentle agency
Of natural objects, led me on to feel
For passions that were not my own, and think
(At random and imperfectly indeed)
On man, the heart of man, and human life.
Therefore, although it be a history
Homely and rude, I will relate the same
For the delight of a few natural hearts;
And, with yet fonder feeling, for the sake
Of youthful Poets, who among these hills
Will be my second self when I am gone.

    Upon the forest-side in Grasmere Vale
There dwelt a Shepherd, Michael was his name;
An old man, stout of heart, and strong of limb.
His bodily frame had been from youth to age
Of an unusual strength: his mind was keen,
Intense, and frugal, apt for all affairs,
And in his shepherd's calling he was prompt
And watchful more than ordinary men.
Hence had he learned the meaning of all winds,
Of blasts of every tone; and oftentimes,
When others heeded not, He heard the South
Make subterraneous music, like the noise
Of bagpipers on distant Highland hills.
The Shepherd, at such warning, of his flock
Bethought him, and he to himself would say,
'The winds are now devising work for me!'
And, truly, at all times, the storm, that drives
The traveller to a shelter, summoned him
Up to the mountains: he had been alone
Amid the heart of many thousand mists,
That came to him, and left him, on the heights.
So lived he till his eightieth year was past.
And grossly that man errs, who should suppose
That the green valleys, and the streams and rocks,
Were things indifferent to the Shepherd's thoughts.
Fields, where with cheerful spirits he had breathed
The common air; hills, which with vigorous step
He had so often climbed; which had impressed
So many incidents upon his mind
Of hardship, skill or courage, joy or fear;
Which, like a book, preserved the memory
Of the dumb animals, whom he had saved,

Had fed or sheltered, linking to such acts
The certainty of honourable gain;
Those fields, those hills—what could they less? had laid
Strong hold on his affections, were to him
A pleasurable feeling of blind love,
The pleasure which there is in life itself.

His days had not been passed in singleness.
His Helpmate was a comely matron, old—
Though younger than himself full twenty years.
She was a woman of a stirring life,
Whose heart was in her house: two wheels she had
Of antique form; this large, for spinning wool;
That small, for flax; and, if one wheel had rest,
It was because the other was at work.
The Pair had but one inmate in their house,
An only Child, who had been born to them
When Michael, telling o'er his years, began
To deem that he was old,—in shepherd's phrase,
With one foot in the grave. This only Son,
With two brave sheep-dogs tried in many a storm,
The one of an inestimable worth,
Made all their household. I may truly say,
That they were as a proverb in the vale
For endless industry. When day was gone,
And from their occupations out of doors
The Son and Father were come home, even then,
Their labour did not cease; unless when all
Turned to the cleanly supper-board, and there,
Each with a mess of pottage and skimmed milk,
Sat round the basket piled with oaten cakes,
And their plain home-made cheese. Yet when the meal
Was ended, Luke (for so the Son was named)
And his old Father both betook themselves
To such convenient work as might employ
Their hands by the fire-side; perhaps to card
Wool for the Housewife's spindle, or repair
Some injury done to sickle, flail, or scythe,
Or other implement of house or field.

Down from the ceiling, by the chimney's edge,
That in our ancient uncouth country style
With huge and black projection overbrowed
Large space beneath, as duly as the light

Of day grew dim the Housewife hung a lamp;
An aged utensil, which had performed
Service beyond all others of its kind.
Early at evening did it burn—and late,
Surviving comrade of uncounted hours,
Which, going by from year to year, had found,
And left, the couple neither gay perhaps
Nor cheerful, yet with objects and with hopes,
Living a life of eager industry.
And now, when Luke had reached his eighteenth year,
There by the light of this old lamp they sate,
Father and Son, while far into the night
The Housewife plied her own peculiar work,
Making the cottage through the silent hours
Murmur as with the sound of summer flies.
This light was famous in its neighbourhood,
And was a public symbol of the life
That thrifty Pair had lived. For, as it chanced,
Their cottage on a plot of rising ground
Stood single, with large prospect, north and south,
High into Easedale, up to Dunmail-Raise,
And westward to the village near the lake;
And from this constant light, so regular,
And so far seen, the House itself, by all
Who dwelt within the limits of the vale,
Both old and young, was named THE EVENING STAR.

Thus living on through such a length of years,
The Shepherd, if he loved himself, must needs
Have loved his Helpmate; but to Michael's heart
This son of his old age was yet more dear—
Less from instinctive tenderness, the same
Fond spirit that blindly works in the blood of all—
Than that a child, more than all other gifts
That earth can offer to declining man,
Brings hope with it, and forward-looking thoughts,
And stirrings of inquietude, when they
By tendency of nature needs must fail.
Exceeding was the love he bare to him,
His heart and his heart's joy! For oftentimes
Old Michael, while he was a babe in arms,
Had done him female service, not alone
For pastime and delight, as is the use
Of fathers, but with patient mind enforced

To acts of tenderness; and he had rocked
His cradle, as with a woman's gentle hand.

    And in a later time, ere yet the Boy
Had put on boy's attire, did Michael love,
Albeit of a stern unbending mind,
To have the Young-one in his sight, when he
Wrought in the field, or on his shepherd's stool
Sate with a fettered sheep before him stretched
Under the large old oak, that near his door
Stood single, and, from matchless depth of shade,
Chosen for the Shearer's covert from the sun,
Thence in our rustic dialect was called
The CLIPPING TREE, a name which yet it bears.
There, while they two were sitting in the shade,
With others round them, earnest all and blithe,
Would Michael exercise his heart with looks
Of fond correction and reproof bestowed
Upon the Child, if he disturbed the sheep
By catching at their legs, or with his shouts
Scared them, while they lay still beneath the shears.

    And when by Heaven's good grace the boy grew up
A healthy lad, and carried in his cheek
Two steady roses that were five years old;
Then Michael from a winter coppice cut
With his own hand a sapling, which he hooped
With iron, making it throughout in all
Due requisites a perfect shepherd's staff,
And gave it to the Boy; wherewith equipped
He as a watchman oftentimes was placed
At gate or gap, to stem or turn the flock;
And, to his office prematurely called,
There stood the urchin, as you will divine,
Something between a hindrance and a help;
And for this cause not always, I believe,
Receiving from his Father hire of praise;
Though nought was left undone which staff, or voice,
Or looks, or threatening gestures, could perform.

    But soon as Luke, full ten years old, could stand
Against the mountain blasts; and to the heights,
Not fearing toil, nor length of weary ways,

He with his Father daily went, and they
Were as companions, why should I relate
That objects which the Shepherd loved before
Were dearer now? that from the Boy there came
Feelings and emanations—things which were
Light to the sun and music to the wind;
And that the old Man's heart seemed born again?

Thus in his Father's sight the Boy grew up:
And now, when he had reached his eighteenth year,
He was his comfort and his daily hope.
While in this sort the simple household lived
From day to day, to Michael's ear there came
Distressful tidings. Long before the time
Of which I speak, the Shepherd had been bound
In surety for his brother's son, a man
Of an industrious life, and ample means;
But unforeseen misfortunes suddenly
Had prest upon him; and old Michael now
Was summoned to discharge the forfeiture,
A grievous penalty, but little less
Than half his substance. This unlooked-for claim,
At the first hearing, for a moment took
More hope out of his life than he supposed
That any old man ever could have lost.
As soon as he had armed himself with strength
To look his trouble in the face, it seemed
The Shepherd's sole resource to sell at once
A portion of his patrimonial fields.
Such was his first resolve; he thought again,
And his heart failed him. 'Isabel,' said he,
Two evenings after he had heard the news,
'I have been toiling more than seventy years,
And in the open sunshine of God's love
Have we all lived; yet, if these fields of ours
Should pass into a stranger's hand, I think
That I could not lie quiet in my grave.
Our lot is a hard lot; the sun himself
Has scarcely been more diligent than I;
And I have lived to be a fool at last
To my own family. An evil man
That was, and made an evil choice, if he
Were false to us; and, if he were not false,
There are ten thousand to whom loss like this

Had been no sorrow. I forgive him;—but
'Twere better to be dumb than to talk thus.
   When I began, my purpose was to speak
Of remedies and of a cheerful hope.
Our Luke shall leave us, Isabel; the land
Shall not go from us, and it shall be free;
He shall possess it, free as is the wind
That passes over it. We have, thou know'st,
Another kinsman—he will be our friend
In this distress. He is a prosperous man,
Thriving in trade—and Luke to him shall go,
And with his kinsman's help and his own thrift
He quickly will repair this loss, and then
He may return to us. If here he stay,
What can be done? Where every one is poor,
What can be gained?'
                  At this the old Man paused,
And Isabel sat silent, for her mind
Was busy, looking back into past times.
There's Richard Bateman, thought she to herself,
He was a parish-boy—at the church-door
They made a gathering for him, shillings, pence,
And halfpennies, wherewith the neighbours bought
A basket, which they filled with pedlar's wares;
And, with this basket on his arm, the lad
Went up to London, found a master there,
Who, out of many, chose the trusty boy
To go and overlook his merchandize
Beyond the seas; where he grew wondrous rich,
And left estates and monies to the poor,
And, at his birth-place, built a chapel floored
With marble, which he sent from foreign lands.
These thoughts, and many others of like sort,
Passed quickly through the mind of Isabel,
And her face brightened. The old Man was glad,
And thus resumed:—'Well, Isabel! this scheme
These two days has been meat and drink to me.
Far more than we have lost is left us yet.
   We have enough—I wish indeed that I
Were younger;—but this hope is a good hope.
Make ready Luke's best garments, of the best
Buy for him more, and let us send him forth
To-morrow, or the next day, or to-night:
   If he *could* go, the Boy should go to-night.'

Here Michael ceased, and to the fields went forth
With a light heart. The Housewife for five days
Was restless morn and night, and all day long
Wrought on with her best fingers to prepare
Things needful for the journey of her son.
But Isabel was glad when Sunday came
To stop her in her work: for, when she lay
By Michael's side, she through the last two nights
Heard him, how he was troubled in his sleep:
And when they rose at morning she could see
That all his hopes were gone. That day at noon
She said to Luke, while they two by themselves
Were sitting at the door, 'Thou must not go:
We have no other Child but thee to lose,
None to remember—do not go away,
For if thou leave thy Father he will die.'
The Youth made answer with a jocund voice;
And Isabel, when she had told her fears,
Recovered heart. That evening her best fare
Did she bring forth, and all together sat
Like happy people round a Christmas fire.

With daylight Isabel resumed her work;
And all the ensuing week the house appeared
As cheerful as a grove in Spring: at length
The expected letter from their kinsman came,
With kind assurances that he would do
His utmost for the welfare of the Boy;
To which, requests were added, that forthwith
He might be sent to him. Ten times or more
The letter was read over; Isabel
Went forth to show it to the neighbours round;
Nor was there at that time on English land
A prouder heart than Luke's. When Isabel
Had to her house returned, the old Man said,
'He shall depart to-morrow.' To this word
The Housewife answered, talking much of things
Which, if at such short notice he should go,
Would surely be forgotten. But at length
She gave consent, and Michael was at ease.

Near the tumultuous brook of Greenhead Ghyll,
In that deep valley, Michael had designed
To build a Sheep-fold; and, before he heard

The tidings of his melancholy loss,
For this same purpose he had gathered up
A heap of stones, which by the streamlet's edge
Lay thrown together, ready for the work.
With Luke that evening thitherward he walked:
And soon as they had reached the place he stopped,
And thus the old Man spake to him:—'My son,
To-morrow thou wilt leave me: with full heart
I look upon thee, for thou art the same
That wert a promise to me ere thy birth,
And all thy life hast been my daily joy.
I will relate to thee some little part
Of our two histories; 'twill do thee good
When thou art from me, even if I should touch
On things thou canst not know of.——After thou
First cam'st into the world—as oft befalls
To new-born infants—thou didst sleep away
Two days, and blessings from thy Father's tongue
Then fell upon thee. Day by day passed on,
And still I loved thee with increasing love.
Never to living ear came sweeter sounds
Than when I heard thee by our own fire-side
First uttering, without words, a natural tune;
While thou, a feeding babe, didst in thy joy
Sing at thy Mother's breast. Month followed month,
And in the open fields my life was passed
And on the mountains; else I think that thou
Hadst been brought up upon thy Father's knees.
But we were playmates, Luke: among these hills,
As well thou knowest, in us the old and young
Have played together, nor with me didst thou
Lack any pleasure which a boy can know.'
Luke had a manly heart; but at these words
He sobbed aloud. The old Man grasped his hand,
And said, 'Nay, do not take it so—I see
That these are things of which I need not speak.
—Even to the utmost I have been to thee
A kind and a good Father: and herein
I but repay a gift which I myself
Received at others' hands; for, though now old
Beyond the common life of man, I still
Remember them who loved me in my youth.
Both of them sleep together: here they lived,
As all their Forefathers had done; and, when

At length their time was come, they were not loth
To give their bodies to the family mould.
I wished that thou shouldst live the life they lived,
But 'tis a long time to look back, my Son,
And see so little gain from threescore years.
These fields were burthened when they came to me;
Till I was forty years of age, not more
Than half of my inheritance was mine.
I toiled and toiled; God blessed me in my work,
And till these three weeks past the land was free.
—It looks as if it never could endure
Another Master. Heaven forgive me, Luke,
If I judge ill for thee, but it seems good
That thou shouldst go.'

                At this the old Man paused;
Then, pointing to the stones near which they stood,
Thus, after a short silence, he resumed:
'This was a work for us; and now, my Son,
It is a work for me. But, lay one stone—
Here, lay it for me, Luke, with thine own hands.
Nay, Boy, be of good hope;—we both may live
To see a better day. At eighty-four
I still am strong and hale;—do thou thy part;
I will do mine.—I will begin again
With many tasks that were resigned to thee:
Up to the heights, and in among the storms,
Will I without thee go again, and do
All works which I was wont to do alone,
Before I knew thy face.—Heaven bless thee, Boy!
Thy heart these two weeks has been beating fast
With many hopes; it should be so—yes—yes—
I knew that thou couldst never have a wish
To leave me, Luke: thou hast been bound to me
Only by links of love: when thou art gone,
What will be left to us!—But I forget
My purposes. Lay now the corner-stone,
As I requested; and hereafter, Luke,
When thou art gone away, should evil men
By thy companions, think of me, my Son,
And of this moment; hither turn thy thoughts,
And God will strengthen thee: amid all fear
And all temptation, Luke, I pray that thou
May'st bear in mind the life thy Fathers lived,
Who, being innocent, did for that cause

Bestir them in good deeds. Now, fare thee well—
When thou return'st, thou in this place wilt see
A work which is not here: a convenant
'Twill be between us; but, whatever fate
Befall thee, I shall love thee to the last,
And bear thy memory with me to the grave.'

    The Shepherd ended here; and Luke stooped down,
And, as his Father had requested, laid
The first stone of the Sheep-fold. At the sight
The old Man's grief broke from him; to his heart
He pressed his Son, he kissèd him and wept;
And to the house together they returned.
—Hushed was that House in peace, or seeming peace,
Ere the night fell:—with morrow's dawn the Boy
Began his journey, and, when he had reached
The public way, he put on a bold face;
And all the neighbours, as he passed their doors,
Came forth with wishes and with farewell prayers,
That followed him till he was out of sight.
    A good report did from their Kinsman come,
Of Luke and his well-doing; and the Boy
Wrote loving letters, full of wondrous news,
Which, as the Housewife phrased it, were throughout
'The prettiest letters that were ever seen.'
Both parents read them with rejoicing hearts.
So, many months passed on: and once again
The Shepherd went about his daily work
With confident and cheerful thoughts; and now
Sometimes when he could find a leisure hour
He to that valley took his way, and there
Wrought at the Sheep-fold. Meantime Luke began
To slacken in his duty; and, at length,
He in the dissolute city gave himself
To evil courses: ignominy and shame
Fell on him, so that he was driven at last
To seek a hiding-place beyond the seas.

    There is a comfort in the strength of love;
'Twill make a thing endurable, which else
Would overset the brain, or break the heart:
I have conversed with more than one who well
Remember the old Man, and what he was
Years after he had heard this heavy news.

His bodily frame had been from youth to age
Of an unusual strength. Among the rocks
He went, and still looked up to sun and cloud,
And listened to the wind; and, as before,
Performed all kinds of labour for his sheep,
And for the land, his small inheritance.
And to that hollow dell from time to time
Did he repair, to build the Fold of which
His flock had need. 'Tis not forgotten yet
The pity which was then in every heart
For the old Man—and 'tis believed by all
That many and many a day he thither went,
And never lifted up a single stone.

    There, by the Sheep-fold, sometimes was he seen
Sitting alone, or with his faithful Dog,
Then old, beside him, lying at his feet.
The length of full seven years, from time to time,
He at the building of this Sheep-fold wrought,
And left the work unfinished when he died.
Three years, or little more, did Isabel
Survive her Husband: at her death the estate
Was sold, and went into a stranger's hand.
The Cottage which was named the EVENING STAR
Is gone—the ploughshare has been through the ground
On which it stood; great changes have been wrought
In all the neighbourhood:—yet the oak is left
That grew beside their door; and the remains
Of the unfinished Sheep-fold may be seen
Beside the boisterous brook of Greenhead Ghyll.

Lucy

SHE dwelt among the untrodden ways
    Beside the springs of Dove,
A Maid whom there were none to praise
    And very few to love:

A violet by a mossy stone
    Half hidden from the eye!
—Fair as a star, when only one
    Is shining in the sky.

She lived unknown, and few could know
 When Lucy ceased to be;
But she is in her grave, and, oh,
 The difference to me!

Resolution and Independence

I

THERE was a roaring in the wind all night;
The rain came heavily and fell in floods;
But now the sun is rising calm and bright;
The birds are singing in the distant woods;
Over his own sweet voice the Stock-dove broods;
The Jay makes answer as the Magpie chatters;
And all the air is filled with pleasant noise of waters.

II

All things that love the sun are out of doors;
The sky rejoices in the morning's birth;
The grass is bright with rain-drops;—on the moors
The hare is running races in her mirth;
And with her feet she from the plashy earth
Raises a mist; that, glittering in the sun,
Runs with her all the way, wherever she doth run.

III

I was a Traveller then upon the moor;
I saw the hare that raced about with joy;
I heard the woods and distant waters roar;
Or heard them not, as happy as a boy:
The pleasant season did my heart employ:
My old remembrances went from me wholly;
And all the ways of men, so vain and melancholy.

IV

But, as it sometimes chanceth, from the might
Of joy in minds that can no farther go,
As high as we have mounted in delight
In our dejection do we sink as low;
To me that morning did it happen so;
And fears and fancies thick upon me came;
Did sadness—and blind thoughts, I knew not, nor could name.

V

I heard the sky-lark warbling in the sky;
And I bethought me of the playful hare:
Even such a happy Child of earth am I;
Even as these blissful creatures do I fare;
Far from the world I walk, and from all care;
But there may come another day to me—
Solitude, pain of heart, distress, and poverty.

VI

My whole life I have lived in pleasant thought,
As if life's business were a summer mood;
As if all needful things would come unsought
To genial faith, still rich in genial good;
But how can He expect that others should
Build for him, sow for him, and at his call
Love him, who for himself will take no heed at all!

VII

I thought of Chatterton, the marvellous Boy,
The sleepless Soul that perished in his pride;
Of Him who walked in glory and in joy
Following his plough, along the mountain-side:
By our own spirits are we deified:
We Poets in our youth begin in gladness;
But thereof come in the end despondency and madness.

VIII

Now, whether it were by peculiar grace,
A leading from above, a something given,
Yet it befell that, in this lonely place,
When I with these untoward thoughts had striven,
Beside a pool bare to the eye of heaven
I saw a Man before me unawares:
The oldest man he seemed that ever wore grey hairs.

IX

As a huge stone is sometimes seen to lie
Couched on the bald top of an eminence;
Wonder to all who do the same espy,
By what means it could thither come, and whence;
So that it seems a thing endued with sense:
Like a sea-beast crawled forth, that on a shelf
Of rock or sand reposeth, there to sun itself;

X

Such seemed this Man, not all alive nor dead,
Nor all asleep—in his extreme old age:
His body was bent double, feet and head
Coming together in life's pilgrimage;
As if some dire constraint of pain, or rage
Of sickness felt by him in times long past,
A more than human weight upon his frame had cast.

XI

Himself he propped, limbs, body, and pale face,
Upon a long grey staff of shaven wood:
And, still as I drew near with gentle pace,
Upon the margin of that moorish flood
Motionless as a cloud the old Man stood,
That heareth not the loud winds when they call;
And moveth all together, if it move at all.

XII

At length, himself unsettling, he the pond
Stirred with his staff, and fixedly did look
Upon the muddy water, which he conned,
As if he had been reading in a book:
And now a stranger's privilege I took;
And, drawing to his side, to him did say,
'This morning gives us promise of a glorious day.'

XIII

A gentle answer did the old Man make,
In courteous speech which forth he slowly drew:
And him with further words I thus bespake,
'What occupation do you there pursue?
This is a lonesome place for one like you.'
Ere he replied, a flash of mild surprise
Broke from the sable orbs of his yet-vivid eyes.

XIV

His words came feebly, from a feeble chest,
But each in solemn order followed each,
With something of a lofty utterance drest—
Choice word and measured phrase, above the reach
Of ordinary men; a stately speech;
Such as grave Livers do in Scotland use,
Religious men, who give to God and man their dues.

XV

He told, that to these waters he had come
To gather leeches, being old and poor:
Employment hazardous and wearisome!
And he had many hardships to endure:
From pond to pond he roamed, from moor to moor;
Housing, with God's good help, by choice or chance;
And in this way he gained an honest maintenance.

XVI

The old Man still stood talking by my side;
But now his voice to me was like a stream
Scarce heard; nor word from word could I divide;
And the whole body of the Man did seem
Like one whom I had met with in a dream;
Or like a man from some far region sent,
To give me human strength, by apt admonishment.

XVII

My former thoughts returned: the fear that kills;
And hope that is unwilling to be fed;
Cold, pain, and labour, and all fleshly ills;
And mighty Poets in their misery dead.
—Perplexed, and longing to be comforted,
My question eagerly did I renew,
'How is it that you live, and what is it you do?'

XVIII

He with a smile did then his words repeat;
And said that, gathering leeches, far and wide
He travelled; stirring thus about his feet
The waters of the pools where they abide.
'Once I could meet with them on every side;
But they have dwindled long by slow decay;
Yet still I persevere, and find them where I may.'

XIX

While he was talking thus, the lonely place,
The old Man's shape, and speech—all troubled me:
In my mind's eye I seemed to see him pace
About the weary moors continually,
Wandering about alone and silently.
While I these thoughts within myself pursued,
He, having made a pause, the same discourse renewed.

XX

And soon with this he other matter blended,
Cheerfully uttered, with demeanour kind,
But stately in the main; and, when he ended,
I could have laughed myself to scorn to find
In that decrepit Man so firm a mind.
'God,' said I, 'be my help and stay secure;
I'll think of the Leech-gatherer on the lonely moor!'

Sonnets

London, 1802

MILTON! thou shouldst be living at this hour:
England hath need of thee: she is a fen
Of stagnant waters: altar, sword, and pen,
Fireside, the heroic wealth of hall and bower,
Have forfeited their ancient English dower
Of inward happiness. We are selfish men;
Oh! raise us up, return to us again;
And give us manners, virtue, freedom, power.
Thy soul was like a Star, and dwelt apart;
Thou hadst a voice whose sound was like the sea:
Pure as the naked heavens, majestic, free,
So didst thou travel on life's common way,
In cheerful godliness; and yet thy heart
The lowliest duties on herself did lay.

It is a Beauteous Evening, Calm and Free

IT is a beauteous evening, calm and free,
The holy time is quiet as a Nun
Breathless with adoration; the broad sun
Is sinking down in its tranquillity;
The gentleness of heaven broods o'er the Sea:
Listen! the mighty Being is awake,
And doth with his eternal motion make
A sound like thunder—everlastingly.
Dear Child! dear Girl! that walkest with me here,
If thou appear untouched by solemn thought,
Thy nature is not therefore less divine:
Thou liest in Abraham's bosom all the year;
And worshipp'st at the Temple's inner shrine,
God being with thee when we know it not.

Composed upon Westminister Bridge, September 3, 1802

EARTH has not anything to show more fair:
Dull would he be of soul who could pass by
A sight so touching in its majesty:
This City now doth, like a garment, wear
The beauty of the morning: silent, bare,
Ships, towers, domes, theatres, and temples lie
Open unto the fields, and to the sky;
All bright and glittering in the smokeless air.
Never did sun more beautifully steep
In his first splendour, valley, rock, or hill;
Ne'er saw I, never felt, a calm so deep!
The river glideth at his own sweet will:
Dear God! the very houses seem asleep;
And all that mighty heart is lying still!

The Solitary Reaper

BEHOLD her, single in the field,
Yon solitary Highland Lass!
Reaping, and singing by herself;
Stop here, or gently pass!
Alone she cuts and binds the grain,
And sings a melancholy strain;
O listen! for the Vale profound
Is overflowing with the sound.

No Nightingale did ever chaunt
More welcome notes to weary bands
Of travellers in some shady haunt,
Among Arabian sands:
A voice so thrilling ne'er was heard
In spring-time from the Cuckoo-bird,
Breaking the silence of the seas
Among the farthest Hebrides.

Will no one tell me what she sings? —
Perhaps the plaintive numbers flow
For old, unhappy, far-off things,
And battles long ago:

Or is it some more humble lay,
Familiar matter of to-day?
Some natural sorrow, loss, or pain,
That has been, and may be again?

Whate'er the theme, the Maiden sang
As if her song could have no ending;
I saw her singing at her work,
And o'er the sickle bending;—
I listened, motionless and still;
And, as I mounted up the hill,
The music in my heart I bore,
Long after it was heard no more.

from *The Prelude*

Childhood and School-Time

FAIR seed-time had my soul, and I grew up
Foster'd alike by beauty and by fear;
Much favor'd in my birthplace, and no less
In that beloved Vale to which, erelong,
I was transplanted. Well I call to mind
('Twas at an early age, ere I had seen
Nine summers) when upon the mountain slope
The frost and breath of frosty wind had snapp'd
The last autumnal crocus, 'twas my joy
To wander half the night among the Cliffs
And the smooth Hollows, where the woodcocks ran
Along the open turf. In thought and wish
That time, my shoulder all with springes hung,
I was a fell destroyer. On the heights
Scudding away from snare to snare, I plied
My anxious visitation, hurrying on,
Still hurrying, hurrying onward; moon and stars
Were shining o'er my head; I was alone,
And seem'd to be a trouble to the peace
That was among them. Sometimes it befel
In these night-wanderings, that a strong desire
O'erpower'd my better reason, and the bird
Which was the captive of another's toils
Became my prey; and, when the deed was done
I heard among the solitary hills

Low breathings coming after me, and sounds
Of undistinguishable motion, steps
Almost as silent as the turf they trod.
Nor less in springtime when on southern banks
The shining sun had from his knot of leaves
Decoy'd the primrose flower, and when the Vales
And woods were warm, was I a plunderer then
In the high places, on the lonesome peaks
Where'er, among the mountains and the winds,
The Mother Bird had built her lodge. Though mean
My object, and inglorious, yet the end
Was not ignoble. Oh! when I have hung
Above the raven's nest, by knots of grass
And half-inch fissures in the slippery rock
But ill sustain'd, and almost, as it seem'd,
Suspended by the blast which blew amain,
Shouldering the naked crag; Oh! at that time,
While on the perilous ridge I hung alone,
With what strange utterance did the loud dry wind
Blow through my ears! the sky seem'd not a sky
Of earth, and with what motion mov'd the clouds!

    The mind of Man is fram'd even like the breath
And harmony of music. There is a dark
Invisible workmanship that reconciles
Discordant elements, and makes them move
In one society. Ah me! that all
The terrors, all the early miseries
Regrets, vexations, lassitudes, that all
The thoughts and feelings which have been infus'd
Into my mind, should ever have made up
The calm existence that is mine when I
Am worthy of myself! Praise to the end!
Thanks likewise for the means! But I believe
That Nature, oftentimes, when she would frame
A favor'd Being, from his earliest dawn
Of infancy doth open out the clouds,
As at the touch of lightning, seeking him
With gentlest visitation; not the less,
Though haply aiming at the self-same end,
Does it delight her sometimes to employ
Severer interventions, ministry
More palpable, and so she dealt with me.

One evening (surely I was led by her)
I went alone into a Shepherd's Boat,
A Skiff that to a Willow tree was tied
Within a rocky Cave, its usual home.
'Twas by the shores of Patterdale, a Vale
Wherein I was a Stranger, thither come
A School-boy Traveller, at the Holidays.
Forth rambled from the Village Inn alone
No sooner had I sight of this small Skiff,
Discover'd thus by unexpected chance,
Than I unloos'd her tether and embark'd.
The moon was up, the Lake was shining clear
Among the hoary mountains; from the Shore
I push'd, and struck the oars and struck again
In cadence, and my little Boat mov'd on
Even like a Man who walks with stately step
Though bent on speed. It was an act of stealth
And troubled pleasure; not without the voice
Of mountain-echoes did my Boat move on,
Leaving behind her still on either side
Small circles glittering idly in the moon,
Until they melted all into one track
Of sparkling light. A rocky Steep uprose
Above the Cavern of the Willow tree
And now, as suited one who proudly row'd
With his best skill, I fix'd a steady view
Upon the top of that same craggy ridge,
The bound of the horizon, for behind
Was nothing but the stars and the grey sky.
She was an elfin Pinnace, lustily
I dipp'd my oars into the silent Lake,
And, as I rose upon the stroke, my Boat
Went heaving through the water, like a Swan;
When from behind that craggy Steep, till then
The bound of the horizon, a huge Cliff,
As if with voluntary power instinct,
Uprear'd its head. I struck, and struck again,
And, growing still in stature, the huge Cliff
Rose up between me and the stars, and still,
With measur'd motion, like a living thing,
Strode after me. With trembling hands I turn'd,
And through the silent water stole my way
Back to the Cavern of the Willow tree.
There, in her mooring-place, I left my Bark,

And, through the meadows homeward went, with grave
And serious thoughts; and after I had seen
That spectacle, for many days, my brain
Work'd with a dim and undetermin'd sense
Of unknown modes of being; in my thoughts
There was a darkness, call it solitude,
Or blank desertion, no familiar shapes
Of hourly objects, images of trees,
Of sea or sky, no colours of green fields;
But huge and mighty Forms that do not live
Like living men mov'd slowly through my mind
By day and were the trouble of my dreams.

    Wisdom and Spirit of the universe!
Thou Soul that art the Eternity of Thought!
That giv'st to forms and images a breath
And everlasting motion! not in vain,
By day or star-light thus from my first dawn
Of Childhood didst Thou intertwine for me
The passions that build up our human Soul,
Not with the mean and vulgar works of Man,
But with high objects, with enduring things,
With life and nature, purifying thus
The elements of feeling and of thought,
And sanctifying, by such discipline,
Both pain and fear, until we recognize
A grandeur in the beatings of the heart.

    Nor was this fellowship vouchsaf'd to me
With stinted kindness. In November days,
When vapours, rolling down the valleys, made
A lonely scene more lonesome; among woods
At noon, and 'mid the calm of summer nights,
When, by the margin of the trembling Lake,
Beneath the gloomy hills I homeward went
In solitude, such intercourse was mine;
'Twas mine among the fields both day and night,
And by the waters all the summer long.

    And in the frosty season, when the sun
Was set, and visible for many a mile
The cottage windows through the twilight blaz'd,
I heeded not the summons:—happy time
It was, indeed, for all of us; to me

It was a time of rapture: clear and loud
The village clock toll'd six; I wheel'd about,
Proud and exulting, like an untired horse,
That cares not for its home.—All shod with steel,
We hiss'd along the polish'd ice, in games
Confederate, imitative of the chace
And woodland pleasures, the resounding horn,
The Pack loud bellowing, and the hunted hare.
So through the darkness and the cold we flew,
And not a voice was idle; with the din,
Meanwhile, the precipices rang aloud,
The leafless trees, and every icy crag
Tinkled like iron, while the distant hills
Into the tumult sent an alien sound
Of melancholy, not unnoticed, while the stars,
Eastward, were sparkling clear, and in the west
The orange sky of evening died away.

Not seldom from the uproar I retired
Into a silent bay, or sportively
Glanced sideway, leaving the tumultuous throng,
To cut across the image of a star
That gleam'd upon the ice: and oftentimes
When we had given our bodies to the wind,
And all the shadowy banks, on either side,
Came sweeping through the darkness, spinning still
The rapid line of motion; then at once
Have I, reclining back upon my heels,
Stopp'd short, yet still the solitary Cliffs
Wheeled by me, even as if the earth had roll'd
With visible motion her diurnal round;
Behind me did they stretch in solemn train
Feebler and feebler, and I stood and watch'd
Till all was tranquil as a dreamless sleep.

*   *   *

Nor should this, perchance
Pass unrecorded, that I still had lov'd
The exercise and produce of a toil
Than analytic industry to me
More pleasing, and whose character I deem
Is more poetic as resembling more
Creative agency. I mean to speak
Of that interminable building rear'd

By observation of affinities
In objects where no brotherhood exists
To common minds. My seventeenth year was come
And, whether from this habit, rooted now
So deeply in my mind, or from excess
Of the great social principle of life,
Coercing all things into sympathy,
To unorganic natures I transferr'd
My own enjoyments, or, the power of truth
Coming in revelation, I convers'd
With things that really are, I, at this time
Saw blessing spread around me like a sea.
Thus did my days pass on, and now at length
From Nature and her overflowing soul
I had receiv'd so much that all my thoughts
Were steep'd in feeling; I was only then
Contented when with bliss ineffable
I felt the sentiment of Being spread
O'er all that moves, and all that seemeth still,
O'er all, that, lost beyond the reach of thought
And human knowledge, to the human eye
Invisible, yet liveth to the heart,
O'er all that leaps, and runs, and shouts, and sings,
Or beats the gladsome air, o'er all that glides
Beneath the wave, yea, in the wave itself
And mighty depth of waters. Wonder not
If such my transports were; for in all things
I saw one life, and felt that it was joy.
One song they sang, and it was audible,
Most audible then when the fleshly ear,
O'ercome by grosser prelude of that strain,
Forgot its functions, and slept undisturb'd.

    If this be error, and another faith
Find easier access to the pious mind,
Yet were I grossly destitute of all
Those human sentiments which make this earth
So dear, if I should fail, with grateful voice
To speak of you, Ye Mountains and Ye Lakes,
And sounding Cataracts! Ye Mists and Winds
That dwell among the hills where I was born.
If, in my youth, I have been pure in heart,
If, mingling with the world, I am content
With my own modest pleasures, and have liv'd,

With God and Nature communing, remov'd
From little enmities and low desires,
The gift is yours; if in these times of fear,
This melancholy waste of hopes o'erthrown,
If, 'mid indifference and apathy
And wicked exultation, when good men,
On every side fall off we know not how,
To selfishness, disguis'd in gentle names
Of peace, and quiet, and domestic love,
Yet mingled, not unwillingly, with sneers
On visionary minds; if in this time
Of dereliction and dismay, I yet
Despair not of our nature; but retain
A more than Roman confidence, a faith
That fails not, in all sorrow my support,
The blessing of my life, the gift is yours,
Ye mountains! thine, O Nature! Thou hast fed
My lofty speculations; and in thee,
For this uneasy heart of ours I find
A never-failing principle of joy,
And purest passion.

Residence at Cambridge

I T was a dreary morning when the Chaise
Roll'd over the flat Plains of Huntingdon
And, through the open windows, first I saw
The long-back'd Chapel of King's College rear
His pinnacles above the dusky groves.

Soon afterwards, we espied upon the road,
A student cloth'd in Gown and tassell'd Cap;
He pass'd; nor was I master of my eyes
Till he was left a hundred yards behind.
The Place, as we approach'd, seem'd more and more
To have an eddy's force, and suck'd us in
More eagerly at every step we took.
Onward we drove beneath the Castle, down
By Magdalene Bridge we went and cross'd the Cam,
And at the *Hoop* we landed, famous Inn.

My spirit was up, my thoughts were full of hope;
Some Friends I had, acquaintances who there
Seem'd Friends, poor simple Schoolboys, now hung round
With honour and importance; in a world
Of welcome faces up and down I rov'd;
Questions, directions, counsel and advice
Flow'd in upon me from all sides, fresh day
Of pride and pleasure! to myself I seem'd
A man of business and expence, and went
From shop to shop about my own affairs,
To Tutors or to Tailors, as befel,
From street to street with loose and careless heart.

I was the Dreamer, they the Dream; I roam'd
Delighted, through the motley spectacle;
Gowns grave or gaudy, Doctors, Students, Streets,
Lamps, Gateways, Flocks of Churches, Courts and Towers:
Strange transformation for a mountain Youth,
A northern Village. As if by word
Of magic or some Fairy's power, at once
Behold me rich in monies, and attir'd
In splendid clothes, with hose of silk, and hair
Glittering like rimy trees when frost is keen.
My lordly Dressing-gown I pass it by,
With other signs of manhood which supplied
The lack of beard. — The weeks went roundly on,
With invitations, suppers, wine, and fruit,
Smooth housekeeping within, and all without
Liberal and suiting Gentleman's array!

The Evangelist St. John my Patron was,
Three gloomy Courts are his; and in the first
Was my abiding-place, a nook obscure!
Right underneath, the College kitchens made
A humming sound, less tuneable than bees,
But hardly less industrious; with shrill notes
Of sharp command and scolding intermix'd.
Near me was Trinity's loquacious Clock,
Who never let the Quarters, night or day,
Slip by him unproclaim'd, and told the hours
Twice over with a male and female voice.
Her pealing organ was my neighbour too;
And, from my Bedroom, I in moonlight nights

283

Could see, right opposite, a few yards off,
The Antechapel, where the Statue stood
Of Newton, with his Prism and silent Face.

* * *

  Beside the pleasant Mills of Trompington
I laugh'd with Chaucer; in the hawthorn shade
Heard him (while birds were warbling) tell his tales
Of amorous passion. And that gentle Bard,
Chosen by the Muses for their Page of State,
Sweet Spenser, moving through his clouded heaven
With the moon's beauty and the moon's soft pace,
I call'd him Brother, Englishman, and Friend.
Yea, our blind Poet, who, in his later day,
Stood almost single, uttering odious truth,
Darkness before, and danger's voice behind;
Soul awful! if the earth has ever lodg'd
An awful Soul, I seem'd to see him here
Familiarly, and in his Scholar's dress
Bounding before me, yet a stripling Youth,
A Boy, no better, with his rosy cheeks
Angelical, keen eye, courageous look,
And conscious step of purity and pride.

Summer Vacation

  WHILE thus I wander'd, step by step led on,
It chanced a sudden turning of the road
Presented to my view an uncouth shape
So near, that, slipping back into the shade
Of a thick hawthorn, I could mark him well,
Myself unseen. He was of stature tall,
A foot above man's common measure tall,
Still in his form, and upright, lank and lean;
A man more meagre, as it seem'd to me,
Was never seen abroad by night or day.
His arms were long, and bare his hands; his mouth
Shew'd ghastly in the moonlight: from behind
A milestone propp'd him, and his figure seem'd
Half-sitting, and half-standing. I could mark
That he was clad in military garb,
Though faded, yet entire. He was alone,
Had no attendant, neither Dog, nor Staff,

Nor knapsack; in his very dress appear'd
A desolation, a simplicity
That seem'd akin to solitude. Long time
Did I peruse him with a mingled sense
Of fear and sorrow. From his lips, meanwhile,
There issued murmuring sounds, as if of pain
Or of uneasy thought; yet still his form
Kept the same steadiness; and at his feet
His shadow lay, and mov'd not. In a Glen
Hard by, a Village stood, whose roofs and doors
Were visible among the scatter'd trees,
Scarce distant from the spot an arrow's flight;
I wish'd to see him move; but he remain'd
Fix'd to his place, and still from time to time
Sent forth a murmuring voice of dead complaint,
Groans scarcely audible. Without self-blame
I had not thus prolong'd my watch; and now,
Subduing my heart's specious cowardise
I left the shady nook where I had stood,
And hail'd him. Slowly from his resting-place
He rose, and with a lean and wasted arm
In measur'd gesture lifted to his head,
Return'd my salutation; then resum'd
His station as before: and when, erelong,
I ask'd his history, he in reply
Was neither slow nor eager; but unmov'd,
And with a quiet, uncomplaining voice,
A stately air of mild indifference,
He told, in simple words, a Soldier's tale,
That in the Tropic Islands he had serv'd,
Whence he had landed, scarcely ten days past,
That on his landing he had been dismiss'd,
And now was travelling to his native home.
At this, I turn'd and looked towards the Village
But all were gone to rest; the fires all out;
And every silent window to the Moon
Shone with a yellow glitter. 'No one there,'
Said I, 'is waking, we must measure back
The way which we have come: behind yon wood
A Labourer dwells; and, take it on my word
He will not murmur should we break his rest;
And with a ready heart will give you food
And lodging for the night.' At this he stoop'd,
And from the ground took up an oaken Staff,

By me yet unobserv'd, a Traveller's Staff;
Which, I suppose, from his slack hand had dropp'd,
And lain till now neglected in the grass.

   Towards the Cottage without more delay
We shap'd our course; as it appear'd to me,
He travell'd without pain, and I beheld
With ill-suppress'd astonishment his tall
And ghastly figure moving at my side;
Nor, while we journey'd thus could I forbear
To question him of what he had endured
From hardship, battle, or the pestilence.
He, all the while, was in demeanour calm,
Concise in answer; solemn and sublime
He might have seem'd, but that in all he said
There was a strange half-absence, and a tone
Of weakness and indifference, as of one
Remembering the importance of his theme
But feeling it no longer. We advanced
Slowly, and, ere we to the wood were come
Discourse had ceas'd. Together on we pass'd,
In silence, through the shades, gloomy and dark;
Then, turning up along an open field
We gain'd the Cottage. At the door I knock'd,
Calling aloud 'my Friend, here is a Man
By sickness overcome; beneath your roof
This night let him find rest, and give him food,
If food he need, for he is faint and tired.'
Assured, that now my Comrade would repose
In comfort, I entreated that henceforth
He would not linger in the public ways
But ask for timely furtherance and help
Such as his state requir'd. At this reproof,
With the same ghastly mildness in his look
He said 'my trust is in the God of Heaven
And in the eye of him that passes me.'
The Cottage door was speedily unlock'd,
And now the Soldier touch'd his hat again
With his lean hand; and in a voice that seem'd
To speak with a reviving interest,
Till then unfelt, he thank'd me; I return'd
The blessing of the poor unhappy Man;
And so we parted. Back I cast a look,

And linger'd near the door a little space;
Then sought with quiet heart my distant home.

Books

THIRTEEN years
Or haply less, I might have seen, when first
My ears began to open to the charm
Of words in tuneful order, found them sweet
For *their own sakes*, a passion and a power;
And phrases pleas'd me, chosen for delight,
For pomp, or love. Oft in the public roads,
Yet unfrequented, while the morning light
Was yellowing the hill-tops, with that dear Friend
The same whom I have mention'd heretofore,
I went abroad, and for the better part
Of two delightful hours we stroll'd along
By the still borders of the misty Lake,
Repeating favourite verses with one voice,
Or conning more; as happy as the birds
That round us chaunted. Well might we be glad,
Lifted above the ground by airy fancies
More bright than madness or the dreams of wine,
And, though full oft the objects of our love
Were false, and in their splendour overwrought,
Yet, surely, at such time no vulgar power
Was working in us, nothing less, in truth,
Than that most noble attribute of man,
Though yet untutor'd and inordinate,
That wish for something loftier, more adorn'd,
Than is the common aspect, daily garb
Of human life. What wonder then if sounds
Of exultation echoed through the groves!
For images, and sentiments, and words,
And everything with which we had to do
In that delicious world of poesy,
Kept holiday; a never-ending show,
With music, incense, festival, and flowers!

Cambridge and the Alps

I, TOO, have been a Wanderer; but, alas!
How different is the fate of different men
Though Twins almost in genius and in mind!
Unknown unto each other, yea, and breathing
As if in different elements, we were framed
To bend at last to the same discipline,
Predestin'd, if two Beings ever were,
To seek the same delights, and have one health,
One happiness. Throughout this narrative,
Else sooner ended, I have known full well
For whom I thus record the birth and growth
Of gentleness, simplicity, and truth,
And joyous loves that hallow innocent days
Of peace and self-command. Of Rivers, Fields,
And Groves, I speak to thee, my Friend*; to thee,
Who, yet a liveried School-Boy, in the depths
Of the huge City, on the leaded Roof
Of that wide Edifice, thy home and School,
Wast used to lie and gaze upon the clouds
Moving in Heaven; or haply, tired of this,
To shut thine eyes, and by internal light
See trees, and meadows, and thy native Stream
Far distant, thus beheld from year to year
Of thy long exile. Nor could I forget
In this late portion of my argument
That scarcely had I finally resign'd
My rights among those academic Bowers
When Thou wert thither guided. From the heart
Of London, and from Cloisters there Thou cam'st,
And didst sit down in temperance and peace,
A rigorous Student. What a stormy course
Then follow'd. Oh! it is a pang that calls
For utterance, to think how small a change
Of circumstances might to Thee have spared
A world of pain, ripen'd ten thousand hopes
For ever wither'd. Through this retrospect
Of my own College life I still have had
Thy after sojourn in the self-same place
Present before my eyes; I have play'd with times,
(I speak of private business of the thought)

* S. T. Coleridge

And accidents as children do with cards,
Or as a man, who, when his house is built,
A frame lock'd up in wood and stone, doth still,
In impotence of mind, by his fireside
Rebuild it to his liking. I have thought
Of Thee, thy learning, gorgeous eloquence
And all the strength and plumage of thy Youth,
Thy subtle speculations, toils abstruse
Among the Schoolmen, and platonic forms
Of wild ideal pageantry, shap'd out
From things well-match'd, or ill, and words for things,
The self-created sustenance of a mind
Debarr'd from Nature's living images,
Compell'd to be a life unto itself,
And unrelentingly possess'd by thirst
Of greatness, love, and beauty. Not alone,
Ah! surely not in singleness of heart
Should I have seen the light of evening fade
Upon the silent Cam, if we had met,
Even at that early time; I needs must hope,
Must feel, must trust, that my maturer age,
And temperature less willing to be mov'd,
My calmer habits and more steady voice
Would with an influence benign have sooth'd
Or chas'd away the airy wretchedness
That batten'd on thy youth. But thou has trod,
In watchful mediation thou hast trod
A march of glory, which doth put to shame
These vain regrets; health suffers in thee; else
Such grief for thee would be the weakest thought
That ever harbour'd in the breast of man.

Residence in London

THOSE days* are now
My theme; and, mid the numerous scenes which they
Have left behind them, foremost I am cross'd
Here by remembrance of two figures, One
A rosy Babe, who, for a twelvemonth's space
Perhaps, had been of age to deal about
Articulate prattle, Child as beautiful
As ever sate upon a Mother's knee;

* i.e. the period of Wordsworth's residence in London

The other was the Parent of that Babe;
But on the Mother's cheek the tints were false,
A painted bloom. 'Twas at a Theatre
That I beheld this Pair; the Boy had been
The pride and pleasure of all lookers-on
In whatsoever place; but seem'd in this
A sort of Alien scatter'd from the clouds.
Of lusty vigour, more than infantine,
He was in limbs, in face a Cottage rose
Just three parts blown; a Cottage Child, but ne'er
Saw I, by Cottage or elsewhere, a Babe
By Nature's gifts so honor'd. Upon a Board
Whence an attendant of the Theatre
Serv'd out refreshments, had this Child been placed,
And there he sate, environ'd with a Ring
Of chance Spectators, chiefly dissolute men
And shameless women; treated and caress'd,
Ate, drank, and with the fruit and glasses play'd,
While oaths, indecent speech, and ribaldry
Were rife about him as are songs of birds
In spring-time after showers. The Mother, too,
Was present! but of her I know no more
Then hath been said, and scarcely at this time
Do I remember her. But I behold
The lovely Boy as I beheld him then,
Among the wretched and the falsely gay,
Like one of those who walk'd with hair unsinged
Amid the fiery furnace. He hath since
Appear'd to me oft times as if embalm'd
By Nature; through some special privilege,
Stopp'd at the growth he had; destined to live,
To be, to have been, come and go, a Child
And nothing more, no partner in the years
That bear us forward to distress and guilt,
Pain and abasement, beauty in such excess
Adorn'd him in that miserable place.

Residence in France

I QUITTED, and betook myself to France,
Led thither chiefly by a personal wish
To speak the language more familiarly,
With which intent I chose for my abode
A City on the Borders of the Loire.

Through Paris lay my readiest path, and there
I sojourn'd a few days, and visited
In haste each spot of old and recent fame
The latter chiefly, from the Field of Mars
Down to the Suburbs of St. Anthony,
And from Mont Martyr southward, to the Dome
Of Geneviève. In both her clamorous Halls,
The National Synod and the Jacobins
I saw the revolutionary Power
Toss like a Ship at anchor, rock'd by storms;
The Arcades I traversed in the Palace huge
Of Orleans, coasted round and round the line
Of Tavern, Brothel, Gaming-house, and Shop,
Great rendezvous of worst and best, the walk
Of all who had a purpose, or had not;
I star'd and listen'd with a stranger's ears
To Hawkers and Haranguers, hubbub wild!
And hissing Factionists with ardent eyes,
In knots, or pairs, or single, ant-like swarms
Of Builders and Subverters, every face
That hope or apprehension could put on,
Joy, anger, and vexation in the midst
Of gaiety and dissolute idleness.

*　　*　　*

For, born in a poor District, and which yet
Retaineth more of ancient homeliness,
Manners erect, and frank simplicity,
Than any other nook of English Land,
It was my fortune scarcely to have seen
Through the whole tenor of my School-day time
The face of one, who, whether Boy or Man,
Was vested with attention or respect
Through claims of wealth or blood; nor was it least
Of many debts which afterwards I owed
To Cambridge, and an academic life
That something there was holden up to view
Of a Republic, where all stood thus far
Upon equal ground, that they were brothers all
In honour, as in one community,
Scholars and Gentlemen, where, furthermore,
Distinction lay open to all that came,
And wealth and titles were in less esteem
Than talents and successful industry.

Residence in France and French Revolution

It was a beautiful and silent day
That overspread the countenance of earth,
Then fading, with unusual quietness,
When from the Loire I parted, and through scenes
Of vineyard, orchard, meadow-ground and tilth,
Calm waters, gleams of sun, and breathless trees
Towards the fierce Metropolis turn'd my steps
Their homeward way to England. From his Throne
The King had fallen; the congregated Host,
Dire cloud upon the front of which was written
The tender mercies of the dismal wind
That bore it, on the Plains of Liberty
Had burst innoculously, say more, the swarm
That came elate and jocund, like a Band
Of Eastern Hunters, to enfold in ring
Narrowing itself by moments and reduce
To the last punctual spot of their despair
A race of victims, so they seem'd, *themselves*
Had shrunk from sight of their own task, and fled
In terror; desolation and dismay
Remained for them whose fancies had grown rank
With evil expectations, confidence
And perfect triumph to the better cause.
The State, as if to stamp the final seal
On her security, and to the world
Shew what she was, a high and fearless soul,
Or rather in a spirit of thanks to those
Who had stirr'd up her slackening faculties
To a new transition, had assumed with joy
The body and the venerable name
Of a Republic: lamentable crimes
'Tis true had gone before this hour, the work
Of massacre, in which the senseless sword
Was pray'd to as a judge; but these were past,
Earth free from them for ever, as was thought,
Ephemeral monsters, to be seen but once;
Things that could only shew themselves and die.

This was the time in which enflam'd with hope,
To Paris I returned. Again I rang'd
More eagerly than I had done before
Through the wide City, and in progress pass'd

The Prison where the unhappy Monarch lay,
Associate with his Children and his Wife
In bondage; and the Palace lately storm'd
With roar of cannon, and a numerous Host.
I cross'd (a blank and empty area then)
The Square of the Carousel, few weeks back
Heap'd up with dead and dying, upon these
And other sights looking as doth a man
Upon a volume whose contents he knows
Are memorable, but from him lock'd up,
Being written in a tongue he cannot read,
So that he questions the mute leaves with pain
And half upbraids their silence. But that night
When on my bed I lay, I was most mov'd
And felt most deeply in what world I was;
My room was high and lonely, near the roof
Of a large Mansion or Hotel, a spot
That would have pleas'd me in more quiet times,
Nor was it wholly without pleasure then.
With unextinguish'd taper I kept watch,
Reading at intervals; the fear gone by
Press'd on me almost like a fear to come;
I thought of those September Massacres,
Divided from me by a little month,
And felt and touch'd them, a substantial dread;
The rest was conjured up from tragic fictions,
And mournful Calendars of true history,
Remembrances and dim admonishments.
'The horse is taught his manage, and the wind
Of heaven wheels round and treads in his own steps,
Year follows year, the tide returns again,
Day follows day, all things have second birth;
The earthquake is not satisfied at once.'
And in such way I wrought upon myself,
Until I seem'd to hear a voice that cried,
To the whole City, 'Sleep no more.' To this
Add comments of a calmer mind, from which
I could not gather full security,
But at the best it seem'd a place of fear
Unfit for the repose of night [   ],
Defenceless as a wood where tigers roam.

   Betimes next morning to the Palace Walk
Of Orleans I repair'd and entering there

Was greeted, among divers other notes,
By voices of the Hawkers in the crowd
Bawling, *Denunciation of the crimes*
Of Maximilian Robespierre; the speech
Which in their hands they carried was the same
Which had been recently pronounced, the day
When Robespierre, well knowing for what mark
Some words of indirect reproof had been
Intended, rose in hardihood, and dared
The Man who had an ill surmise of him
To bring his charge in openness, whereat
When a dead pause ensued, and no one stirr'd,
In silence of all present, from his seat
Louvet walked singly through the avenue
And took his station in the Tribune, saying,
'I, Robespierre, accuse thee!' 'Tis well known
What was the issue of that charge, and how
Louvet was left alone without support
Of his irresolute Friends; but these are things
Of which I speak, only as they were storm
Or sunshine to my individual mind,
No further. Let me then relate that now
In some sort seeing with my proper eyes
That Liberty, and Life, and Death would soon
To the remotest corners of the land
Lie in the arbitrement of those who ruled
The capital City, what was struggled for,
And by what combatants victory must be won,
The indecision on their part whose aim
Seem'd best, and the straightfoward path of those
Who in attack or in defence alike
Were strong through their impiety, greatly I
Was agitated; yea I could almost
Have pray'd that throughout earth upon all souls
Worthy of liberty, upon every soul
Matured to live in plainness and in truth
The gift of tongues might fall, and men arrive
From the four quarters of the winds to do
For France what without help she could not do,
A work of honour; think not that to this
I added, work of safety; from such thought
And the least fear about the end of things
I was as far as Angels are from guilt.

Yet did I grieve, nor only griev'd, but thought
Of opposition and of remedies,
An insignificant Stranger, and obscure,
Mean as I was, and little graced with power
Of eloquence even in my native speech,
And all unfit for tumult and intrigue,
Yet would I willingly have taken up
A service at this time for cause so great,
However dangerous. Inly I revolved
How much the destiny of man had still
Hung upon single persons, that there was,
Transcendent to all local patrimony,
One Nature as there is one Sun in heaven,
That objects, even as they are great, thereby
Do come within the reach of humblest eyes,
That Man was only weak through his mistrust
And want of hope, where evidence divine
Proclaim'd to him that hope should be most sure,
That, with desires heroic and firm sense,
A Spirit thoroughly faithful to itself,
Unquenchable, unsleeping, undismay'd,
Was as an instinct among men, a stream
That gather'd up each petty straggling rill
And vein of water, glad to be roll'd on
In safe obedience, that a mind whose rest
Was where it ought to be, in self-restraint,
In circumspection and simplicity,
Fell rarely in entire discomfiture
Below its aim, or met with from without
A treachery that defeated it or foil'd.

On the other side, I call'd to mind those truths
Which are the common-places of the Schools,
A theme for Boys, too trite even to be felt,
Yet, with a revelation's liveliness,
In all their comprehensive bearings known
And visible to Philosophers of old,
Men who, to business of the world untrain'd,
Liv'd in the Shade, and to Harmodius known
And his Compeer Aristogiton, known
To Brutus, that tyrannic Power is weak,
Hath neither gratitude, nor faith, nor love,
Nor the support of good or evil men
To trust in, that the Godhead which is ours

Can never utterly be charm'd or still'd,
That nothing hath a natural right to last
But equity and reason, that all else
Meets foes irreconcilable, and at best
Doth live but by variety of disease.

   Well might my wishes be intense, my thoughts
Strong and perturb'd, not doubting at that time,
Creed which ten shameful years have not annull'd,
But that the virtue of one paramount mind
Would have abash'd those impious crests, have quell'd
Outrage and bloody power, and in despite
Of what the People were through ignorance
And immaturity, and, in the teeth
Of desperate opposition from without,
Have clear'd a passage for just government,
And left a solid birthright to the State,
Redeem'd according to example given
By ancient Lawgivers.
                In this frame of mind,
Reluctantly to England I return'd,
Compell'd by nothing less than absolute want
Of funds for my support, else, well assured
That I both was and must be of small worth,
No better than an alien in the Land,
I doubtless should have made a common cause
With some who perish'd, haply perish'd, too,
A poor mistaken and bewilder'd offering,
Should to the breast of Nature have gone back
With all my resolutions, all my hopes,
A Poet only to myself, to Men
Useless, and even, beloved Friend! a soul
To thee unknown.
          When to my native Land
(After a whole year's absence) I return'd
I found the air yet busy with the stir
Of a contention which had been rais'd up
Against the Traffickers in Negro blood,
An effort, which though baffled, nevertheless
Had call'd back old forgotten principles
Dismiss'd from service, had diffus'd some truths
And more of virtuous feeling through the heart
Of the English People. And no few of those
So numerous (little less in verity

Than a whole Nation crying with one voice)
Who had been cross'd in this their just intent
And righteous hope, thereby were well prepared
To let that journey sleep awhile, and join
Whatever other Caravan appear'd
To travel forward towards Liberty
With more success. For me that strife had ne'er
Fasten'd on my affections, nor did now
Its unsuccessful issue much excite
My sorrow, having laid this faith to heart,
That, if France prosper'd, good Men would not long
Pay fruitless worship to humanity,
And this most rotten branch of human shame,
Object, as seem'd, of a superfluous pains
Would fall together with its parent tree.

Such was my then belief, that there was one,
And only one solicitude for all;
And now the strength of Britain was put forth
In league with the confederated Host,
Not in my single self alone I found,
But in the minds of all ingenuous Youth,
Change and subversion from this hour. No shock
Given to my moral nature had I known
Down to that very moment; neither lapse
Nor turn of sentiment that might be nam'd
A revolution, save at this one time,
All else was progress on the self-same path
On which with a diversity of pace
I had been travelling; this a stride at once
Into another region. True it is,
'Twas not conceal'd with what ungracious eyes
Our native Rulers from the very first
Had look'd upon regenerated France
Nor had I doubted that this day would come.
But in such contemplation I had thought
Of general interests only, beyond this
Had [never] once foretasted the event.
Now had I other business for I felt
The ravage of this most unnatural strife
In my own heart; there lay it like a weight
At enmity with all the tenderest springs
Of my enjoyments. I, who with the breeze
Had play'd, a green leaf on the blessed tree

Of my beloved Country; nor had wish'd
For happier fortune than to whither there,
Now from my pleasant station was cut off,
And toss'd about in whirlwinds. I rejoiced,
Yea, afterwards, truth painful to record!
Exulted in the triumph of my soul
When Englishmen by thousands were o'erthrown,
Left without glory on the Field, or driven,
Brave hearts, to shameful flight. It was a grief,
Grief call it not, 'twas anything but that,
A conflict of sensations without name,
Of which he only who may love the sight
Of a Village Steeple as I do can judge
When in the Congregation, bending all
To their great Father, prayers were offer'd up,
Or praises for our Country's Victories,
And 'mid the simple worshippers, perchance,
I only, like an uninvited Guest
Whom no one owned sate silent, shall I add,
Fed on the day of vengeance yet to come?

*　　*　　*

But from these bitter truths I must return
To my own History. It hath been told
That I was led to take an eager part
In arguments of civil polity
Abruptly, and indeed before my time:
I had approach'd, like other Youth, the Shield
Of human nature from the golden side
And would have fought, even to the death, to attest
The quality of the metal which I saw.
What there is best in individual Man,
Of wise in passion, and sublime in power,
What there is strong and pure in household love,
Benevolent in small societies,
And great in large ones also, when call'd forth
By great occasions, these were things of which
I something knew, yet even these themselves,
Felt deeply, were not thoroughly understood
By Reason; nay, far from it, they were yet,
As cause was given me afterwards to learn,
Not proof against the injuries of the day,
Lodged only at the Sanctuary's door,
Not safe within its bosom. Thus prepared,

And with such general insight into evil,
And of the bounds which sever it from good,
As books and common intercourse with life
Must needs have given; to the noviciate mind,
When the world travels in a beaten road,
Guide faithful as is needed, I began
To think with fervour upon management
Of Nations, what it is and ought to be,
And how their worth depended on their Laws
And on the Constitution of the State.

O pleasant exercise of hope and joy!
For great were the auxiliars which then stood
Upon our side, we who were strong in love;
Bliss was it in that dawn to be alive,
But to be young was very heaven; O times,
In which the meagre, stale, forbidding ways
Of custom, law, and statute took at once
The attraction of a Country in Romance;
When Reason seem'd the most to assert her rights
When most intent on making of herself
A prime Enchanter to assist the work,
Which then was going forwards in her name.
Not favour'd spots alone, but the whole earth
The beauty wore of promise, that which sets,
To take an image which was felt, no doubt,
Among the bowers of paradise itself,
The budding rose above the rose full blown.
What temper at the prospect did not wake
To happiness unthought of? The inert
Were rouz'd, and lively natures rapt away:
They who had fed their childhood upon dreams,
The Play-fellows of Fancy, who had made
All powers of swiftness, subtlety, and strength
Their ministers, used to stir in lordly wise
Among the grandest objects of the sense,
And deal with whatsoever they found there
As if they had within some lurking right
To wield it; they too, who, of gentle mood
Had watch'd all gentle motions, and to those
Had fitted their own thoughts, schemers more mild,
And in the region of their peaceful selves,
Did now find helpers to their hearts' desire,
And stuff at hand, plastic as they could wish,

Were call'd upon to exercise their skill,
Not in Utopia, subterraneous Fields,
Or some secreted Island, Heaven knows where,
But in the very world which is the world
Of all of us, the place on which, in the end,
We find our happiness, or not at all.

   Why should I not confess that earth was then
To me what an inheritance new-fallen
Seems, when the first time visited, to one
Who thither comes to find in it his home?
He walks about and looks upon the place
With cordial transport, moulds it, and remoulds,
And is half pleased with things that are amiss,
'Twill be such joy to see them disappear.

Conclusion

IN one of these excursions, travelling then
Through Wales on foot, and with a youthful Friend,
I left Bethkelet's huts at couching-time,
And westward took my way to see the sun
Rise from the top of Snowdon. Having reach'd
The Cottage at the Mountain's foot, we there
Rouz'd up the Shepherd, who by ancient right
Of office is the Stranger's usual Guide;
And after short refreshment sallied forth.

   It was a Summer's night, a close warm night,
Wan, dull and glaring, with a dripping mist
Low-hung and thick that cover'd all the sky,
Half threatening storm and rain; but on we went
Uncheck'd, being full of heart and having faith
In our tried Pilot. Little could we see
Hemm'd round on every side with fog and damp,
And, after ordinary travellers' chat
With our Conductor, silently we sank
Each into commerce with his private thoughts:
Thus did we breast the ascent, and by myself
Was nothing either seen or heard the while
Which took me from my musings, save that once

The Shepherd's Cur did to his own great joy
Unearth a hedgehog in the mountain crags
Round which he made a barking turbulent.
This small adventure, for even such it seemed
In that wild place and at the dead of night,
Being over and forgotten, on we wound
In silence as before. With forehead bent
Earthward, as if in opposition set
Against an enemy, I panted up
With eager pace, and no less eager thoughts.
Thus might we wear perhaps an hour away,
Ascending at loose distance each from each,
And I, as chanced, the foremost of the Band;
When at my feet the ground appear'd to brighten,
And with a step or two seem'd brighter still;
Nor had I time to ask the cause of this,
For instantly a Light upon the turf
Fell like a flash: I look'd about, and lo!
The Moon stood naked in the Heavens, at height
Immense above my head, and on the shore
I found myself of a huge sea of mist,
Which, meek and silent, rested at my feet:
A hundred hills their dusky backs upheaved
All over this still Ocean, and beyond,
Far, far beyond, the vapours shot themselves,
In headlands, tongues, and promontory shapes,
Into the Sea, the real Sea, that seem'd
To dwindle, and give up its majesty,
Usurp'd upon as far as sight could reach.
Meanwhile, the Moon look'd down upon this shew
In single glory, and we stood, the mist
Touching our very feet; and from the shore
At distance not the third part of a mile
Was a blue chasm; a fracture in the vapour,
A deep and gloomy breathing-place thro' which
Mounted the roar of waters, torrents, streams
Innumerable, roaring with one voice.
The universal spectacle throughout
Was shaped for admiration and delight,
Grand in itself alone, but in that breach
Through which the homeless voice of waters rose,
That dark deep thoroughfare had Nature lodg'd
The Soul, the Imagination of the whole.

SIR WALTER SCOTT

1771–1832

from *The Lay of the Last Minstrel*

The Minstrel

THE way was long, the wind was cold,
The Minstrel was infirm and old;
His withered cheek, and tresses grey,
Seemed to have known a better day;
The harp, his sole remaining joy,
Was carried by an orphan boy.
The last of all the Bards was he,
Who sung of Border chivalry;
For, welladay! their date was fled,
His tuneful brethren all were dead;
And he, neglected and oppressed,
Wished to be with them, and at rest.
No more on prancing palfrey borne,
He carolled, light as lark at morn;
No longer courted and caressed,
High placed in hall, a welcome guest,
He poured to lord and lady gay
The unpremeditated lay:
Old times were changed, old manners gone;
A stranger filled the Stuarts' throne;
The bigots of the iron time
Had called his harmless art a crime.
A wandering Harper, scorned and poor,
He begged his bread from door to door,
And tuned, to please a peasant's ear,
The harp a king had loved to hear.

He passed where Newark's stately tower
Looks out from Yarrow's birchen bower:
The Minstrel gazed with wishful eye—
No humbler resting-place was nigh;
With hesitating step at last
The embattled portal arch he passed,
Whose ponderous grate and massy bar
Had oft rolled back the tide of war,

But never closed the iron door
Against the desolate and poor.
The Duchess marked his weary pace,
His timid mien, and reverend face,
And bade her page the menials tell
That they should tend the old man well:
For she had known adversity,
Though born in such a high degree;
In pride of power, in beauty's bloom,
Had wept o'er Monmouth's bloody tomb!

When kindness had his wants supplied,
And the old man was gratified,
Began to rise his minstrel pride:
And he began to talk anon
Of good Earl Francis, dead and gone,
And of Earl Walter, rest him, God!
A braver ne'er to battle rode;
And how full many a tale he knew
Of the old warriors of Buccleuch:
And, would the noble Duchess deign
To listen to an old man's strain,
Though stiff his hand, his voice though weak,
He thought even yet, the sooth to speak,
That, if she loved the harp to hear,
He could make music to her ear.

The humble boon was soon obtained;
The aged Minstrel audience gained.
But, when he reached the room of state,
Where she with all her ladies sate,
Perchance he wished his boon denied:
For, when to tune his harp he tried,
His trembling hand had lost the ease,
Which marks security to please;
And scenes long past, of joy and pain,
Came wildering o'er his aged brain—
He tried to tune his harp in vain!
The pitying Duchess praised its chime,
And gave him heart, and gave him time,
Till every string's according glee
Was blended into harmony.
And then, he said, he would full fain

He could recall an ancient strain
He never thought to sing again.
It was not framed for village churls,
But for high dames and mighty earls;
He had played it to King Charles the Good,
When he kept court in Holyrood;
And much he wished, yet feared, to try
The long-forgotten melody.
Amid the strings his fingers strayed,
And an uncertain warbling made,
And oft he shook his hoary head.
But when he caught the measure wild,
The old man raised his face and smiled;
And lightened up his faded eye
With all a poet's ecstasy.
In varying cadence, soft or strong,
He swept the sounding chords along:
The present scene, the future lot,
His toils, his wants, were all forgot;
Cold diffidence, and age's frost,
In the full tide of song were lost;
Each blank, in faithless memory void,
The poet's glowing thought supplied;
And, while his harp responsive rung,
'Twas thus the LATEST MINSTREL sung.

Melrose Abbey

IF thou would'st view fair Melrose aright,
Go visit it by the pale moonlight;
For the gay beams of lightsome day
Gild, but to flout, the ruins grey.
When the broken arches are black in night,
And each shafted oriel glimmers white;
When the cold light's uncertain shower
Streams on the ruined central tower;
When buttress and buttress, alternately,
Seem framed of ebon and ivory;
When silver edges the imagery,
And the scrolls that teach thee to live and die;
When distant Tweed is heard to rave,
And the owlet to hoot o'er the dead man's grave,

Then go—but go alone the while—
Then view St. David's ruined pile;
And, home returning, soothly swear,
Was never scene so sad and fair!

Love

I

AND said I that my limbs were old,
And said I that my blood was cold,
And that my kindly fire was fled,
And my poor withered heart was dead,
    And that I might not sing of love?—
How could I to the dearest theme,
That ever warmed a minstrel's dream,
    So foul, so false a recreant prove!
How could I name love's very name,
Nor wake my heart to notes of flame!

II

In peace, Love tunes the shepherd's reed;
In war, he mounts the warrior's steed;
In halls, in gay attire is seen;
In hamlets, dances on the green,
Love rules the court, the camp, the grove,
And men below, and saints above;
For love is heaven, and heaven is love.

Nature's Sympathy with the Poet

I

CALL it not vain; they do not err,
    Who say, that when the Poet dies,
Mute Nature mourns her worshipper,
    And celebrates his obsequies:
Who say, tall cliff and cavern lone
For the departed Bard make moan;
That mountains weep in crystal rill;
That flowers in tears of balm distil;
Through his loved groves that breezes sigh,
And oaks, in deeper groan, reply;
And rivers teach their rushing wave
To murmur dirges round his grave.

II

Not that, in sooth, o'er mortal urn
Those things inanimate can mourn;
But that the stream, the wood, the gale,
Is vocal with the plaintive wail
Of those, who, else forgotten long,
Lived in the poet's faithful song,
And, with the poet's parting breath,
Whose memory feels a second death.
The Maid's pale shade, who wails her lot,
That love, true love, should be forgot,
From rose and hawthorn shakes the tear
Upon the gentle Minstrel's bier:
The phantom Knight, his glory fled,
Mourns o'er the field he heaped with dead;
Mounts the wild blast that sweeps amain,
And shrieks along the battle-plain.
The Chief, whose antique crownlet long
Still sparkled in the feudal song,
Now, from the mountain's misty throne,
Sees, in the thanedom once his own,
His ashes, undistinguished lie,
His place, his power, his memory die:
His groans the lonely caverns fill,
His tears of rage impel the rill:
All mourn the Minstrel's harp unstrung,
Their name unknown, their praise unsung.

Patriotism

I

BREATHES there the man, with soul so dead,
Who never to himself hath said,
    This is my own, my native land!
Whose heart hath ne'er within him burned,
As home his footsteps he hath turned,
    From wandering on a foreign strand!
If such there breathe, go, mark him well;
For him no Minstrel raptures swell;
High though his titles, proud his name,
Boundless his wealth as wish can claim;
Despite those titles, power, and pelf,

The wretch, concentred all in self,
Living, shall forfeit fair renown,
And, doubly dying, shall go down
To the vile dust, from whence he sprung,
Unwept, unhonoured, and unsung.

II

O Caledonia! stern and wild,
Meet nurse for a poetic child!
Land of brown heath and shaggy wood,
Land of the mountain and the flood,
Land of my sires! what mortal hand
Can e'er untie the filial band,
That knits me to thy rugged strand!
Still as I view each well-known scene,
Think what is now, and what hath been,
Seems as, to me, of all bereft,
Sole friends thy woods and streams were left;
And thus I love them better still,
Even in extremity of ill.
By Yarrow's stream still let me stray,
Though none should guide my feeble way;
Still feel the breeze down Ettrick break,
Although it chill my withered cheek;
Still lay my head by Teviot Stone,
Though there, forgotten and alone,
The Bard may draw his parting groan.

Lochinvar

O, YOUNG Lochinvar is come out of the west,
Through all the wide Border his steed was the best;
And save his good broadsword he weapons had none,
He rode all unarmed, and he rode all alone.
So faithful in love, and so dauntless in war,
There never was knight like the young Lochinvar.

He staid not for brake, and he stopped not for stone.
He swam the Eske river where ford there was none;
But ere he alighted at Netherby gate,
The bride had consented, the gallant came late:
For a laggard in love, and a dastard in war,
Was to wed the fair Ellen of brave Lochinvar.

So boldly he entered the Netherby Hall,
Among bride's-men, and kinsmen, and brothers, and all:
Then spoke the bride's father, his hand on his sword,
(For the poor craven bridegroom said never a word,)
'O come ye in peace here, or come ye in war,
Or to dance at our bridal, young Lord Lochinvar?

'I long wooed your daughter, my suit you denied;—
Love swells like the Solway, but ebbs like its tide—
And now am I come, with this lost love of mine,
To lead but one measure, drink one cup of wine.
There are maidens in Scotland more lovely by far,
That would gladly be bride to the young Lochinvar.'

The bride kissed the goblet: the knight took it up,
He quaffed off the wine, and he threw down the cup.
She looked down to blush, and she looked up to sigh,
With a smile on her lips, and a tear in her eye.
He took her soft hand, ere her mother could bar,—
'Now tread we a measure!' said young Lochinvar.

So stately his form, and so lovely her face,
That never a hall such a galliard did grace;
While her mother did fret, and her father did fume.
And the bridegroom stood dangling his bonnet and plume;
And the bride-maidens whispered ''Twere better by far,
To have matched our fair cousin with young Lochinvar.'

One touch to her hand, and one word in her ear,
When they reached the hall-door, and the charger stood near;
So light to the croupe the fair lady he swung,
So light to the saddle before her he sprung!
'She is won! we are gone, over bank, bush, and scaur;
They'll have fleet steeds that follow,' quoth young Lochinvar.

There was mounting 'mong Græmes of the Netherby clan;
Forsters, Fenwicks, and Musgraves, they rode and they ran:
There was racing and chasing on Cannobie Lee,
But the lost bride of Netherby ne'er did they see.
So daring in love, and so dauntless in war,
Have ye e'er heard of gallant like young Lochinvar?—

from *The Lady of the Lake*

Flowers and Trees

BOON nature scattered, free and wild,
Each plant or flower, the mountain's child.
Here eglantine embalmed the air,
Hawthorn and hazel mingled there;
The primrose pale, and violet flower,
Found in such cliff a narrow bower;
Fox-glove and night-shade, side by side,
Emblems of punishment and pride,
Grouped their dark hues with every stain
The weather-beaten crags retain.
With boughs that quaked at every breath,
Grey birch and aspen wept beneath;
Aloft, the ash and warrior oak
Cast anchor in the rifted rock;
And, higher yet, the pine-tree hung
His shattered trunk, and frequent flung,
Where seemed the cliffs to meet on high,
His boughs athwart the narrowed sky.
Highest of all, where white peaks glanced,
Where glistening streamers waved and danced.
The wanderer's eye could barely view
The summer heaven's delicious blue;
So wonderous wild, the whole might seem
The scenery of a fairy dream.

Boat Song

'HAIL to the chief who in triumph advances!
  Honoured and blessed be the evergreen Pine!
Long may the tree, in his banner that glances,
  Flourish, the shelter and grace of our line!
    Heaven send it happy dew,
    Earth lend it sap anew,
Gayly to bourgeon, and broadly to grow,
    While every Highland glen
    Sends our shout back agen,
Roderigh Vich Alpine, dhu, ho! ieroe!

'Ours is no sapling, chance-sown by the fountain,
  Blooming at Beltane, in winter to fade;

When the whirlwind has stripped every leaf on the mountain,
   The more shall Clan-Alpine exult in her shade.
      Moored in the rifted rock,
      Proof to the tempest's shock,
Firmer he roots him the ruder it blow;
      Menteith and Breadalbane, then,
      Echo his praise agen,
Roderigh Vich Alpine dhu, ho! ieroe!

'Proudly our pibroch has thrilled in Glen Fruin,
   And Bannochar's groans to our slogan replied;
Glen Luss and Ross-dhu, they are smoking in ruin,
   And the best of Loch Lomond lie dead on her side.
      Widow and Saxon maid
      Long shall lament our raid,
Think of Clan-Alpine with fear and with woe;
      Lennox and Leven-glen
      Shake when they hear agen,
Roderigh Vich Alpine dhu, ho! ieroe!

'Row, vassals, row, for the pride of the Highlands!
   Stretch to your oars, for the evergreen Pine!
O! that the rose-bud that graces yon islands
   Were wreathed in a garland around him to twine!
      O that some seedling gem,
      Worthy such noble stem,
Honoured and blessed in their shadow might grow!
      Loud should Clan-Alpine then
      Ring from her deepmost glen,
Roderigh Vich Alpine dhu, ho! ieroe!'

Coronach

      HE is gone on the mountain,
         He is lost to the forest,
     Like a summer-dried fountain,
         When our need was the sorest.
     The font, reappearing,
         From the rain-drops shall borrow,
     But to us comes no cheering,
         To Duncan no morrow!

BOAT SONG: Beltane] a festival held early in May

The hand of the reaper
　Takes the ears that are hoary,
But the voice of the weeper
　Wails manhood in glory.
The autumn winds rushing
　Waft the leaves that are searest,
But our flower was in flushing,
　When blighting was nearest.

Fleet foot on the corrie,
　Sage counsel in cumber,
Red hand in the foray,
　How sound is thy slumber!
Like the dew on the mountain,
　Like the foam on the river,
Like the bubble on the fountain,
　Thou art gone, and for ever!

Ballad: Alice Brand

MERRY it is in the good greenwood
　When the mavis and merle are singing,
When the deer sweeps by, and the hounds are in cry,
　And the hunter's horn is ringing.

'O Alice Brand, my native land
　Is lost for love of you;
And we must hold by wood and wold,
　As outlaws wont to do.

'O Alice, 'twas all for thy locks so bright,
　And 'twas all for thine eyes so blue,
That on the night of our luckless flight
　Thy brother bold I slew.

'Now must I teach to hew the beech
　The hand that held the glaive,
For leaves to spread our lowly bed,
　And stakes to fence our cave.

'And for vest of pall, thy fingers small,
　That wont on harp to stray,
A cloak must shear from the slaughtered deer,
　To keep the cold away.'

BALLAD: ALICE BRAND: mavis] song thrush　　　merle] the blackbird

'O Richard! if my brother died,
   'Twas but a fatal chance;
For darkling was the battle tried,
   And fortune sped the lance.

'If pall and vair no more I swear,
   Nor thou the crimson sheen,
As warm, we'll say, is the russet grey,
   As gay the forest-green.

'And, Richard, if our lot be hard,
   And lost thy native land,
Still Alice has her own Richard,
   And he his Alice Brand.'

'Tis merry, 'tis merry, in good greenwood,
   So blithe Lady Alice is singing;
On the beech's pride, and oak's brown side,
   Lord Richard's axe is ringing.

Up spoke the moody Elfin King,
   Who woned within the hill;
Like wind in the porch of a ruined church,
   His voice was ghostly shrill.

'Why sounds yon stroke on beech and oak,
   Our moonlight circle's screen?
Or who comes here to chase the deer,
   Beloved of our Elfin Queen?
Or who may dare on wold to wear
   The fairies' fatal green?

'Up, Urgan, up! to yon mortal hie,
   For thou wert christened man:
For cross or sign thou wilt not fly,
   For muttered word or ban.

'Lay on him the curse of the withered heart,
   The curse of the sleepless eye;
Till he wish and pray that his life would part,
   Nor yet find leave to die.'

'Tis merry, 'tis merry, in good greenwood,
   Though the birds have stilled their singing;
The evening blaze doth Alice raise,
   And Richard is fagots bringing.

Up Urgan starts, that hideous dwarf,
   Before Lord Richard stands,
And, as he crossed and blessed himself,
'I fear not sign,' quoth the grisly elf,
   'That is made with bloody hands.'

But out then spoke she, Alice Brand,
   That woman, void of fear,—
'And if there's blood upon his hand,
   'Tis but the blood of deer.'

'Now loud thou liest, thou bold of mood!
   It cleaves unto his hand,
The stain of thine own kindly blood,
   The blood of Ethert Brand.'

Then forward stepped she, Alice Brand,
   And made the holy sign,—
'And if there's blood on Richard's hand,
   A spotless hand is mine.

'And I conjure thee, Demon elf,
   By him whom Demons fear,
To show us whence thou art thyself,
   And what thine errand here?'

''Tis merry, 'tis merry, in Fairy-land,
   When fairy birds are singing,
When the court doth ride by their monarch's side,
   With bit and bridle ringing:

'And gaily shines the Fairy-land—
   But all is glistening show,
Like the idle gleam that December's beam
   Can dart on ice and snow.

'And fading, like that varied gleam,
   Is our inconstant shape,
Who now like knight and lady seem,
   And now like dwarf and ape.

'It was between the night and day,
   When the Fairy King has power,
That I sunk down in a sinful fray,
And, 'twixt life and death, was snatched away
   To the joyless Elfin bower.

'But wist I of a woman bold,
　Who thrice my brow durst sign,
I might regain my mortal mold,
　As fair a form as thine.'

She crossed him once, she crossed him twice,
　That lady was so brave;
The fouler grew his goblin hue,
　The darker grew the cave.

She crossed him thrice, that lady bold;
　He rose beneath her hand
The fairest knight on Scottish mold,
　Her brother, Ethert Brand!

Merry it is in good greenwood,
　When the mavis and merle are singing,
But merrier were they in Dumfermline grey,
　When all the bells were ringing.

Harp of the North, Farewell!

HARP of the North, farewell! The hills grow dark,
　On purple peaks a deeper shade descending;
In twilight copse the glow-worm lights her spark,
　The deer, half-seen, are to the covert wending.
Resume thy wizard elm! the fountain lending,
　And the wild breeze, thy wilder minstrelsy;
Thy numbers sweet with nature's vespers blending,
　With distant echo from the fold and lea,
And herd-boy's evening pipe, and hum of housing bee.

Yet once again farewell, thou Minstrel harp!
　Yet once again forgive my feeble sway,
And little reck I of the censure sharp
　May idly cavil at an idle lay.
Much have I owed thy strains on life's long way,
　Through secret woes the world has never known,
When on the weary night dawned wearier day,
　And bitterer was the grief devoured alone.
That I o'erlived such woes, Enchantress! is thine own.

Hark! as my lingering footsteps slow retire,
   Some Spirit of the Air has waked thy string!
'Tis now a seraph bold, with touch of fire,
   'Tis now the brush of Fairy's frolic wing.
Receding now, the dying numbers ring
   Fainter and fainter down the rugged dell,
And now the mountain breezes scarcely bring
   A wandering witch-note of the distant spell—
And now, 'tis silent all!—Enchantress, fare thee well!

from *Rokeby*

Song: Brignall Banks

O, BRIGNALL banks are wild and fair,
   And Greta woods are green,
And you may gather garlands there
   Would grace a summer queen.
And as I rode by Dalton-hall,
   Beneath the turrets high,
A maiden on the castle wall
   Was singing merrily,—
'O, Brignall banks are fresh and fair,
   And Greta woods are green;
I'd rather rove with Edmund there,
   Than reign our English queen.'

'If, maiden, thou wouldst wend with me,
   To leave both tower and town,
Thou first must guess what life lead we,
   That dwell by dale and down.
And if thou canst that riddle read,
   As read full well you may,
Then to the greenwood shalt thou speed,
   As blithe as Queen of May.'
Yet sung she, 'Brignall banks are fair,
   And Greta woods are green;
I'd rather rove with Edmund there,
   Than reign our English queen.

I read you, by your bugle-horn,
   And by your palfrey good,
I read you for a ranger sworn,

To keep the king's greenwood.'
'A ranger, lady, winds his horn,
   And 'tis at peep of light;
His blast is heard at merry morn,
   And mine at dead of night.'
Yet sung she, 'Brignall banks are fair,
   And Greta woods are gay;
I would I were with Edmund there,
   To reign his Queen of May!

With burnished brand and musketoon,
   So gallantly you come,
I read you for a bold dragoon,
   That lists the tuck of drum.'
'I list no more the tuck of drum,
   No more the trumpet hear;
But when the beetle sounds his hum,
   My comrades take the spear.
And O! though Brignall banks be fair,
   And Greta woods be gay,
Yet mickle must the maiden dare,
   Would reign my Queen of May!

Maiden! a nameless life I lead,
   A nameless death I'll die;
The fiend, whose lantern lights the mead,
   Were better mate than I!
And when I'm with my comrades met
   Beneath the greenwood bough,
What once we were we all forget,
   Nor think what we are now.
Yet Brignall banks are fresh and fair,
   And Greta woods are green,
And you may gather garlands there
   Would grace a summer queen.'

Songs from the Novels

Hie Away, Hie Away

HIE away, hie away,
Over bank and over brae,
Where the copsewood is the greenest,
Where the fountains glisten sheenest,

Where the lady-fern grows strongest,
Where the morning dew lies longest,
Where the black-cock sweetest sips it,
Where the fairy latest trips it:
Hie to haunts right seldom seen,
Lovely, lonesome, cool, and green,
Over bank and over brae,
Hie away, hie away.

from *Waverley*

Lucy Ashton's Song

LOOK not thou on beauty's charming,
Sit thou still when kings are arming,
Taste not when the wine-cup glistens,
Speak not when the people listens,
Stop thine ear against the singer,
From the red gold keep thy finger;
Vacant heart and hand and eye,
Easy live and quiet die.

from *The Bride of Lammermoor*

Sound, Sound the Clarion

SOUND, sound the clarion, fill the fife!
To all the sensual world proclaim,
One crowded hour of glorious life
Is worth an age without a name.

from *Old Mortality*

SAMUEL TAYLOR COLERIDGE

1772–1834

The Rime of the Ancient Mariner

PART I

An ancient
Mariner
meeteth
three Gal-
lants bid-
den to a
wedding-
feast, and
detaineth
one.

IT is an ancient Mariner,
And he stoppeth one of three.
'By thy long grey beard and glittering eye,
Now wherefore stopp'st thou me?

'The Bridegroom's doors are opened wide,
And I am next of kin;
The guests are met, the feast is set:
May'st hear the merry din.'

He holds him with his skinny hand,
'There was a ship,' quoth he.
'Hold off! unhand me, greybeard loon!'
Eftsoons his hand dropt he.

The Wed-
ding-Guest
is spell-
bound by
the eye of
the old sea-
faring man,
and con-
strained to
hear his
tale.

He holds him with his glittering eye—
The Wedding-Guest stood still,
And listens like a three years' child:
The Mariner hath his will.

The Wedding-Guest sat on a stone:
He cannot choose but hear;
And thus spake on that ancient man,
The bright-eyed Mariner:

'The ship was cheered, the harbour cleared,
Merrily did we drop
Below the kirk, below the hill,
Below the lighthouse top.

The Mari-
ner tells
how the
ship sailed
southward
with a good
wind and fair

The sun came up upon the left,
Out of the sea came he!
And he shone bright, and on the right
Went down into the sea.

weather, till it reached the Line.

318

Higher and higher every day,
Till over the mast at noon—'
The Wedding-Guest here beat his breast,
For he heard the loud bassoon.

The Wed-
ding-Guest
heareth the
bridal
music; but
the Mari-
ner con-
tinueth his
tale.

The bride hath paced into the hall,
Red as a rose is she;
Nodding their heads before her goes
The merry minstrelsy.

The Wedding-Guest he beat his breast,
Yet he cannot choose but hear;
And thus spake on that ancient man,
The bright-eyed Mariner.

The ship
drawn by
a storm to-
ward the
South Pole.

'And now the Storm-blast came, and he
Was tyrannous and strong:
He struck with his o'ertaking wings,
And chased us south along.

With sloping masts and dipping prow,
As who pursued with yell and blow
Still treads the shadow of his foe,
And forward bends his head,
The ship drove fast, loud roared the blast,
And southward aye we fled.

And now there came both mist and snow
And it grew wonderous cold:
And ice, mast-high, came floating by,
As green as emerald.

The land of
ice, and of
fearful
sounds,
where no
living thing
was to be
seen.

And through the drifts the snowy clifts
Did send a dismal sheen:
Nor shapes of men nor beasts we ken—
The ice was all between.

The ice was here, the ice was there,
The ice was all around:
It cracked and growled, and roared and howled,
Like noises in a swound!

Till a great sea-bird, called the Albatross, came through the snow-fog, and was received with great joy and hospitality.

At length did cross an Albatross:
Thorough the fog it came;
As if it had been a Christian soul,
We hailed it in God's name.

It ate the food it ne'er had eat,
And round and round it flew.
The ice did split with a thunder-fit;
The helmsman steered us through!

And lo! the Albatross proveth a bird of good omen, and followeth the ship as it returned northward through fog and floating ice.

And a good south wind sprung up behind;
The Albatross did follow,
And every day, for food or play,
Came to the mariners' hollo!

In mist or cloud, on mast or shroud,
It perched for vespers nine;
Whiles all the night, through fog-smoke white,
Glimmered the white moonshine.'

The ancient Mariner inhospitably killeth the pious bird of good omen.

'God save thee, ancient Mariner!
From the fiends, that plague thee thus!—
Why look'st thou so?'—'With my crossbow
I shot the Albatross.'

PART II

'The Sun now rose upon the right:
Out of the sea came he,
Still hid in mist, and on the left
Went down into the sea.

And the good south wind still blew behind,
But no sweet bird did follow,
Nor any day for food or play
Came to the mariners' hollo!

His shipmates cry out against the ancient Mariner, for killing the bird of good luck.

And I had done an hellish thing,
And it would work 'em woe:
For all averred, I had killed the bird
That made the breeze to blow.
Ah wretch! said they, the bird to slay,
That made the breeze to blow!

But when
the fog
cleared off,
they justify
the same,
and thus
make
themselves
accomplices in the crime.

Nor dim nor red, like God's own head,
The glorious Sun uprist:
Then all averred, I had killed the bird
That brought the fog and mist.
'Twas right, said they, such birds to slay,
That bring the fog and mist.

The fair
breeze con-
tinues; the
ship enters
the Pacific
Ocean and
sails northward, even till it reaches the Line.

The fair breeze blew, the white foam flew,
The furrow followed free;
We were the first that ever burst
Into that silent sea.

The ship
hath been
suddenly
becalmed.

Down dropt the breeze, the sails dropt down,
'Twas sad as sad could be;
And we did speak only to break
The silence of the sea!

All in a hot and copper sky,
The bloody Sun, at noon,
Right up above the mast did stand,
No bigger than the Moon.

Day after day, day after day,
We stuck, nor breath nor motion:
As idle as a painted ship
Upon a painted ocean.

And the
Albatross
begins to
be avenged.

Water, water, everywhere,
And all the boards did shrink;
Water, water, everywhere,
Nor any drop to drink.

The very deep did rot: O Christ!
That ever this should be!
Yea, slimy things did crawl with legs
Upon the slimy sea.

About, about, in reel and rout
The death-fires danced at night;
The water, like a witch's oils,
Burnt green, and blue and white.

A spirit had
followed
them; one

And some in dreams assured were
Of the spirit that plagued us so;

of the invi-
sible inha-
bitants of
Nine fathom deep he had followed us
From the land of mist and snow.

this planet, neither departed souls nor angels; concerning whom the learned Jew, Josephus,
and the Platonic Constantinopolitan, Michael Psellus, may be consulted. They are very
numerous, and there is no climate or element without one or more.

And every tongue, through utter drought,
Was withered at the root;
We could not speak, no more than if
We had been choked with soot.

The ship-
mates, in
their sore
distress,
would fain
throw the
Ah! well-a-day! what evil looks
Had I from old and young!
Instead of the cross, the Albatross
About my neck was hung.

whole guilt on the ancient Mariner: in sign whereof they hang the
dead sea-bird round his neck.

PART III

'There passed a weary time. Each throat
Was parched, and glazed each eye.
A weary time! a weary time!
How glazed each weary eye,

The ancient
Mariner be-
holdeth a
sign in the
element
afar off.
When looking westward, I beheld
A something in the sky.

At first it seemed a little speck,
And then it seemed a mist;
It moved and moved, and took at last
A certain shape, I wist.

A speck, a mist, a shape, I wist!
And still it neared and neared:
As if it dodged a water-sprite,
It plunged and tacked and veered.

At its
nearer ap-
proach, it
seemeth
him to be
a ship; and
at a dear
ransom he
freeth his
speech
from the
bonds of
thirst.
With throats unslaked, with black lips baked,
We could nor laugh nor wail;
Through utter drought all dumb we stood!
I bit my arm, I sucked the blood,
And cried, "A sail! a sail!"

With throats unslaked, with black lips baked,
Agape they heard me call:
Gramercy! they for joy did grin,

A flash of
joy.
And all at once their breath drew in,
As they were drinking all.

And horror
follows. For
can it be a
ship that
comes on-
ward with-
out wind or
tide?

See! See! (I cried) she tacks no more!
Hither to work us weal:
Without a breeze, without a tide,
She steadies with upright keel!

The western wave was all a-flame.
The day was wellnigh done!
Almost upon the western wave
Rested the broad bright Sun;
When that strange shape drove suddenly
Betwixt us and the Sun.

It seemeth
him but the
skeleton of
a ship.

And straight the Sun was flecked with bars,
(Heaven's Mother send us grace!)
As if through a dungeon-grate he peered
With broad and burning face.

Alas! (thought I, and my heart beat loud)
How fast she nears and nears!
Are those her sails that glance in the Sun,
Like restless gossameres?

And its ribs
are seen as
bars on the
face of the
setting Sun.
The spectre-
woman and
her death-
mate and no
other on
board the
skeleton-
ship.
Like vessel,
like crew!

Are those her ribs through which the Sun
Did peer, as through a grate?
And is that Woman all her crew?
Is that a Death? and are there two?
Is Death that woman's mate?

Her lips were red, her looks were free,
Her locks were yellow as gold:
Her skin was as white as leprosy,
The Nightmare Life-in-Death was she,
Who thicks man's blood with cold.

Death and
Life-in-
Death have
diced for
the ship's
crew, and
she (the latter) winneth the ancient Mariner.

The naked hulk alongside came,
And the twain were casting dice;
"The game is done! I've won, I've won!"
Quoth she, and whistles thrice.

No twilight
within the
courts of
the sun.

The Sun's rim dips; the stars rush out:
At one stride comes the dark;
With far-heard whisper, o'er the sea,
Off shot the spectre-bark.

We listened and looked sideways up!
Fear at my heart, as at a cup,
My life-blood seemed to sip!
The stars were dim, and thick the night,
The steersman's face by his lamp gleamed white;
From the sails the dew did drip—

Till clomb above the eastern bar
The horned Moon, with one bright star
Within the nether tip.

One after one, by the star-dogged Moon,
Too quick for groan or sigh,
Each turned his face with a ghastly pang,
And cursed me with his eye.

Four times fifty living men,
(And I heard nor sigh nor groan)
With heavy thump, a lifeless lump,
They dropped down one by one.

The souls did from their bodies fly,—
They fled to bliss or woe!
And every soul, it passed me by,
Like the whizz of my cross-bow!'

PART IV

'I fear thee, ancient Mariner!
I fear thy skinny hand!
And thou art long, and lank, and brown,
As is the ribbed sea-sand.

I fear thee and thy glittering eye,
And thy skinny hand, so brown.'—

'Fear not, fear not, thou Wedding-Guest!
This body dropt not down.

Alone, alone, all, all alone,
Alone on a wide wide sea!
And never a saint took pity on
My soul in agony.

The many men, so beautiful!
And they all dead did lie:
And a thousand thousand slimy things
Lived on; and so did I.

And envi-
eth that
they should
live, and so
many lie
dead.

I looked upon the rotting sea,
And drew my eyes away;
I looked upon the rotting deck,
And there the dead men lay.

I looked to heaven, and tried to pray;
But or ever a prayer had gusht,
A wicked whisper came, and made
My heart as dry as dust.

I closed my lids, and kept them close,
And the balls like pulses beat;
For the sky and the sea, and the sea and the sky
Lay like a load on my weary eye,
And the dead were at my feet.

But the
curse liveth
for him in
the eye of
the dead
men.

The cold sweat melted from their limbs,
Nor rot nor reek did they;
The look with which they looked on me
Had never passed away.

An orphan's curse would drag to hell
A spirit from on high;
But oh! more horrible than that
Is a curse in a dead man's eye!
Seven days, seven nights, I saw that curse,
And yet I could not die.

In his lone-
liness and
fixedness
he yearneth
towards the
journeying

The moving Moon went up the sky,
And nowhere did abide:
Softly she was going up,
And a star or two beside—

Moon, and the stars that still sojourn, yet still move onward; and everywhere the blue sky
belongs to them, and is their appointed rest, and their native country and their own natural
homes, which they enter unannounced, as lords that are certainly expected and yet there is a
silent joy at their arrival.

Her beams bemocked the sultry main,
Like April hoar-frost spread;
But where the ship's huge shadow lay,
The charmed water burnt alway
A still and awful red.

By the
light of the
Moon he
beholdeth
God's
creatures of
the great
calm.

Beyond the shadow of the ship,
I watched the water-snakes:
They moved in tracks of shining white,
And when they reared, the elfish light
Fell off in hoary flakes.

Within the shadow of the ship
I watched their rich attire:
Blue, glossy green, and velvet black,
They coiled and swam; and every track
Was a flash of golden fire.

Their
beauty and
their hap-
piness.

He blesseth
them in his
heart.

O happy living things! no tongue
Their beauty might declare:
A spring of love gushed from my heart,
And I blessed them unaware:
Sure my kind saint took pity on me,
And I blessed them unaware.

The spell
begins to
break.

The selfsame moment I could pray;
And from my neck so free
The Albatross fell off, and sank
Like lead into the sea.

PART V

'Oh sleep! it is a gentle thing,
Beloved from pole to pole!
To Mary Queen the praise be given!
She sent the gentle sleep from Heaven,
That slid into my soul.

By grace of
the holy
Mother, the
ancient
Mariner is
refreshed
with rain.

The silly buckets on the deck,
That had so long remained,
I dreamt that they were filled with dew;
And when I awoke, it rained.

My lips were wet, my throat was cold,
My garments all were dank;
Sure I had drunken in my dreams,
And still by body drank.

I moved, and could not feel my limbs:
I was so light—almost
I thought that I had died in sleep,
And was a blessed ghost.

He heareth
sounds and
seeth
strange
sights and
commo-
tions in the
sky and the
element.

And soon I heard a roaring wind:
It did not come anear;
But with its sound it shook the sails,
That were so thin and sere.

The upper air burst into life!
And a hundred fire-flags sheen,
To and fro they were hurried about!
And to and fro, and in and out,
The wan stars danced between.

And the coming wind did roar more loud,
And the sails did sigh like sedge;
And the rain poured down from one black cloud;
The Moon was at its edge.

The thick black cloud was cleft, and still
The Moon was at its side:
Like waters shot from some high crag,
The lightning fell with never a jag,
A river steep and wide.

The bodies
of the
ship's crew
are in-
spired, and
the ship
moves on;

The loud wind never reached the ship,
Yet now the ship moved on!
Beneath the lightning and the Moon
The dead men gave a groan.

They groaned, they stirred, they all uprose,
Nor spake, nor moved their eyes;
It had been strange, even in a dream,
To have seen those dead men rise.

The helmsman steered, the ship moved on;
Yet never a breeze up blew;
The mariners all 'gan work the ropes,
Where they were wont to do;
They raised their limbs like lifeless tools—
We were a ghastly crew.

The body of my brother's son
Stood by me, knee to knee:
The body and I pulled at one rope,
But he said nought to me.'

327

but not by
the souls of
the men
nor by
daemons of
earth or
middle air,
but by a
blessed
troop of
angelic
spirits, sent
down by
the invoca-
tion of the
guardian
saint.

'I fear thee, ancient Mariner!'
'Be calm, thou Wedding-Guest!
'Twas not those souls that fled in pain,
Which to their corses came again,
But a troop of spirits blest:

For when it dawned—they dropt their arms,
And clustered round the mast;
Sweet sounds rose slowly through their mouths,
And from their bodies passed.

Around, around, flew each sweet sound,
Then darted to the Sun;
Slowly the sounds came back again,
Now mixed, now one by one.

Sometimes a-dropping from the sky
I heard the skylark sing;
Sometimes all little birds that are,
How they seemed to fill the sea and air
With their sweet jargoning!

And now 'twas like all instruments,
Now like a lonely flute;
And now it is an angel's song,
That makes the heavens be mute.

It ceased; yet still the sails made on
A pleasant noise till noon,
A noise like of a hidden brook
In the leafy month of June,
That to the sleeping woods all night
Singeth a quiet tune.

Till noon we quietly sailed on,
Yet never a breeze did breathe:
Slowly and smoothly went the ship,
Moved onward from beneath.

The
lonesome
Spirit from
the South
Pole carries
on the ship
as far as
the Line, in

Under the keel nine fathom deep,
From the land of mist and snow,
The spirit slid: and it was he
That made the ship to go.
The sails at noon left off their tune,
And the ship stood still also.

328

obedience to the angelic troop, but still requireth vengeance.

The Sun, right up above the mast,
Had fixed her to the ocean:
But in a minute she 'gan stir,
With a short uneasy motion—
Backwards and forwards half her length
With a short uneasy motion.

Then, like a pawing horse let go,
She made a sudden bound:
It flung the blood into my head,
And I fell down in a swound.

The Polar Spirit's fellow-daemons, the invisible inhabitants of the element, take part in his wrong; and two of them relate, one to the other, that penance long and heavy for the ancient mariner hath been accorded to the Polar Spirit, who returneth southward.

How long in that same fit I lay,
I have not to declare;
But ere my living life returned,
I heard and in my soul discerned
Two voices in the air.

"Is it he?" quoth one, "Is this the man?
By him who died on cross,
With his cruel bow he laid full low
The harmless Albatross.

"The spirit who bideth by himself
In the land of mist and snow,
He loved the bird that loved the man
Who shot him with his bow."

The other was a softer voice,
As soft as honeydew:
Quoth he, "The man hath penance done,
And penance more will do."

PART VI

First Voice

'"But tell me, tell me! speak again,
Thy soft response renewing—
What makes that ship drive on so fast?
What is the Ocean doing?"

Second Voice

"Still as a slave before his lord,
The Ocean hath no blast;
His great bright eye most silently
Up to the Moon is cast—

"If he may know which way to go;
For she guides him smooth or grim.
See, brother, see! how graciously
She looketh down on him."

First Voice

The Mari-
ner hath
been cast
into a
trance; for
the angelic
power
causeth the
vessel to
drive
northward
faster than
human life
could en-
dure.

"But why drives on that ship so fast,
Without or wave or wind?"

Second Voice

"The air is cut away before,
And closes from behind.

"Fly, brother, fly! more high, more high!
Or we shall be belated:
For slow and slow that ship will go,
When the Mariner's trance is abated."

The super-
natural
motion is
retarded;
the Mari-
ner awakes
and his
penance
begins
anew.

I woke, and we were sailing on
As in a gentle weather:
'Twas night, calm night, the Moon was high;
The dead men stood together.

All stood together on the deck,
For a charnel-dungeon fitter:
All fixed on me their stony eyes,
That in the Moon did glitter.

The pang, the curse, with which they died,
Had never passed away:
I could not draw my eyes from theirs,
Nor turn them up to pray.

The curse
is finally
expiated.

And now this spell was snapt: once more
I viewed the ocean green,
And looked far forth, yet little saw
Of what had else been seen—

Like one, that on a lonesome road
Doth walk in fear and dread,
And having once turned round walks on,
And turns no more his head;
Because he knows, a frightful fiend
Doth close behind him tread.

330

But soon there breathed a wind on me,
Nor sound nor motion made:
Its path was not upon the sea,
In ripple or in shade.

It raised my hair, it fanned my cheek
Like a meadow-gale of spring—
It mingled strangely with my fears,
Yet it felt like a welcoming.

Swiftly, swiftly flew the ship,
Yet she sailed softly too:
Sweetly, sweetly blew the breeze—
On me alone it blew.

And the
ancient
Mariner be-
holdeth his
native
country.

Oh! dream of joy! is this indeed
The lighthouse top I see?
Is this the hill? is this the kirk?
Is this mine own countree?

We drifted o'er the harbour-bar,
And I with sobs did pray—
O let me be awake, my God!
Or let me sleep alway.

The harbour-bay was clear as glass,
So smoothly it was strewn!
And on the bay the moonlight lay,
And the shadow of the Moon.

The rock shone bright, the kirk no less,
That stands above the rock:
The moonlight steeped in silentness
The steady weathercock.

And the bay was white with silent light,
Till rising from the same,

The angelic
spirits
leave the
dead
bodies, and
appear in
their own .
forms of
light.

Full many shapes, that shadows were,
In crimson colours came.

A little distance from the prow
Those crimson shadows were:
I turned my eyes upon the deck—
Oh, Christ! what saw I there!

331

Each corse lay flat, lifeless and flat,
And, by the holy rood!
A man all light, a seraph-man,
On every corse there stood.

This seraph-band, each waved his hand:
It was a heavenly sight!
They stood as signals to the land.
Each one a lovely light;

This seraph-band, each waved his hand,
No voice did they impart—
No voice; but oh! the silence sank
Like music on my heart.

But soon I heard the dash of oars,
I heard the Pilot's cheer;
My head was turned perforce away,
And I saw a boat appear.

The Pilot and the Pilot's boy,
I heard them coming fast:
Dear Lord in Heaven! it was a joy
The dead men could not blast.

I saw a third—I heard his voice:
It is the Hermit good!
He singeth loud his godly hymns
That he makes in the wood.
He'll shrive my soul, he'll wash away
The Albatross's blood.

PART VII

The Hermit of the Wood   'This Hermit good lives in that wood
Which slopes down to the sea.
How loudly his sweet voice he rears!
He loves to talk with marineres
That come from a far countree.

He kneels at morn, and noon, and eve—
He hath a cushion plump:
It is the moss that wholly hides
The rotted old oak-stump.

The skiff-boat neared: I heard them talk,
"Why this is strange, I trow!
Where are those lights so many and fair,
That signal made but now?"

approach-
eth the
ship with
wonder.

"Strange, by my faith!" the Hermit said—
"And they answered not our cheer!
The planks look warped! and see those sails,
How thin they are and sere!
I never saw aught like to them,
Unless perchance it were

"Brown skeletons of leaves that lag
My forest-brook along;
When the ivy-tod is heavy with snow,
And the owlet whoops to the wolf below,
That eats the she-wolf's young."

"Dear Lord! it hath a fiendish look—"
(The Pilot made reply)
"I am a-feared"—"Push on, push on!"
Said the Hermit cheerily.

The boat came closer to the ship,
But I nor spake nor stirred;
The boat came close beneath the ship,
And straight a sound was heard.

Under the water it rumbled on,
Still louder and more dread:
The ship
suddenly
sinketh.
It reached the ship, it split the bay;
The ship went down like lead.

The ancient
Mariner is
saved in
the Pilot's
boat.
Stunned by that loud and dreadful sound,
Which sky and ocean smote,
Like one that hath been seven days drowned
My body lay afloat;
But swift as dreams, myself I found
Within the Pilot's boat.

Upon the whirl, where sank the ship,
The boat spun round and round;
And all was still, save that the hill
Was telling of the sound.

I moved my lips—the Pilot shrieked
And fell down in a fit;
The holy Hermit raised his eyes,
And prayed where he did sit.

I took the oars: the Pilot's boy,
Who now doth crazy go.
Laughed loud and long, and all the while
His eyes went to and fro.
"Ha! ha!" quoth he, "full plain I see,
The Devil knows how to row."

And now, all in my own countree,
I stood on the firm land!
The Hermit stepped forth from the boat,
And scarcely he could stand.

The ancient
Mariner
earnestly
entreateth
the Hermit
to shrive
him; and
the penance
of life falls
on him.

"O shrive me, shrive me, holy man!"
The Hermit crossed his brow.
"Say quick," quoth he, "I bid thee say—
What manner of man art thou?"

Forthwith this frame of mine was wrenched
With a woeful agony,
Which forced me to begin my tale;
And then it left me free.

And ever
and anon
through-
out his
future life
an agony
constrain-
eth him to
travel from
land to
land,

Since then, at an uncertain hour,
That agony returns:
And till my ghastly tale is told,
This heart within me burns.

I pass, like night, from land to land;
I have strange power of speech;
That moment that his face I see,
I know the man that must hear me:
To him my tale I teach.

What loud uproar bursts from that door!
The wedding-guests are there:
But in the garden-bower the bride
And bride-maids singing are:
And hark the little vesper bell,
Which biddeth me to prayer!

O Wedding-Guest! this soul hath been
Alone on a wide wide sea:

So lonely 'twas, that God Himself
Scarce seemed there to be.

O sweeter than the marriage-feast,
'Tis sweeter far to me,
To walk together to the kirk
With a goodly company!—

To walk together to the kirk,
And all together pray,
While each to his great Father bends,
Old men, and babes, and loving friends,
And youths and maidens gay!

*and to
teach, by
his own
example,
love and
reverence
to all things
that God
made and
loveth.*

Farewell, farewell! but this I tell
To thee, thou Wedding-Guest!
He prayeth well, who loveth well
Both man and bird and beast.

He prayeth best, who loveth best
All things both great and small;
For the dear God who loveth us,
He made and loveth all.'

The Mariner, whose eye is bright,
Whose beard with age is hoar,
Is gone: and now the Wedding-Guest
Turned from the bridegroom's door.

He went like one that hath been stunned,
And is of sense forlorn:
A sadder and a wiser man,
He rose the morrow morn.

Dejection: an Ode

> Late, late yestreen I saw the new moon,
> With the old moon in her arms;
> And I fear, I fear, my Master dear!
> We shall have a deadly storm.
> BALLAD OF SIR PATRICK SPENCE

I

WELL! If the Bard was weather-wise, who made
   The grand old ballad of Sir Patrick Spence,

335

This night, so tranquil now, will not go hence
Unroused by winds, that ply a busier trade
Than those which mould yon cloud in lazy flakes,
Or the dull sobbing draft, that moans and rakes
  Upon the strings of this Aeolian lute,
  Which better far were mute.
  For lo! the new moon winter-bright!
  And overspread with phantom light,
 (With swimming phantom light o'erspread
 But rimm'd and circled by a silver thread)
I see the old moon in her lap, foretelling
 The coming-on of rain and squally blast.
And oh! that even now the gust were swelling,
 And the slant night-shower driving loud and fast!
Those sounds which oft have raised me, whilst they awed,
  And sent my soul abroad,
Might now perhaps their wonted impulse give,
Might startle this dull pain, and make it move and live!

II

A grief without a pang, void, dark, and drear,
 A stifled, drowsy, unimpassioned grief,
 Which finds no natural outlet, no relief,
  In word, or sigh, or tear—
O Lady! in this wan and heartless mood,
To other thoughts by yonder throstle woo'd,
 All this long eve, so balmy and serene,
Have I been gazing on the western sky,
 And its peculiar tint of yellow green:
And still I gaze—and with how blank an eye!
And those thin clouds above, in flakes and bars,
That give away their motion to the stars;
Those stars, that glide behind them or between,
Now sparkling, now bedimmed, but always seen:
Yon crescent moon, as fixed as if it grew
In its own cloudless, starless lake of blue;
I see them all so excellently fair,
I see, not feel, how beautiful they are!

III

 My genial spirits fail,
 And what can these avail
To lift the smothering weight from off my breast?

It were a vain endeavour,
Though I should gaze for ever
On that green light that lingers in the west:
I may not hope from outward forms to win
The passion and the life, whose fountains are within.

IV

O Lady! we receive but what we give,
And in our life alone does nature live:
Ours is her wedding-garment, ours her shroud!
    And would we aught behold, of higher worth,
Than that inanimate cold world allowed
To the poor loveless ever-anxious crowd,
    Ah! from the soul itself must issue forth
A light, a glory, a fair luminous cloud
        Enveloping the Earth—
And from the soul itself must there be sent
    A sweet and potent voice, of its own birth,
Of all sweet sounds the life and element!

V

O pure of heart! thou need'st not ask of me
What this strong music in the soul may be!
What, and wherein it doth exist,
This light, this glory, this fair luminous mist,
This beautiful and beauty-making power.
    Joy, virtuous Lady! Joy that ne'er was given,
Save to the pure, and in their purest hour,
Life, and Life's Effluence, cloud at once and shower,
Joy, Lady! is the spirit and the power,
Which wedding nature to us gives in dower,
    A new Earth and new Heaven,
Undreamt of by the sensual and the proud—
Joy is the sweet voice, Joy the luminous cloud—
        We in ourselves rejoice!
And thence flows all that charms or ear or sight,
    All melodies the echoes of that voice,
All colours a suffusion from that light.

VI

There was a time when, though my path was rough,
    This joy within me dallied with distress,
And all misfortunes were but as the stuff
    Whence Fancy made me dreams of happiness:

For hope grew round me, like the twining vine,
And fruits, and foliage, not my own, seemed mine,
But now afflictions bow me down to earth:
Nor care I that they rob me of my mirth,
  But oh! each visitation
Suspends what nature gave me at my birth,
 My shaping spirit of Imagination.
For not to think of what I needs must feel,
 But to be still and patient, all I can;
And haply by abstruse research to steal
 From my own nature all the natural man—
 This was my sole resource, my only plan:
Till that which suits a part infects the whole,
And now is almost grown the habit of my soul.

VII

Hence, viper thoughts, that coil around my mind,
  Reality's dark dream!
I turn from you, and listen to the wind,
 Which long has raved unnoticed. What a scream
Of agony by torture lengthened out
That lute sent forth! Thou wind, that ravest without,
 Bare crag, or mountain-tairn, or blasted tree,
Or pine-grove whither woodman never clomb,
Or lonely house, long held the witches' home,
 Methinks were fitter instruments for thee,
Mad Lutanist! who in this month of showers,
Of dark brown gardens, and of peeping flowers,
Makest Devils' yule, with worse than wintry song,
The blossoms, buds, and timorous leaves among.
 Thou Actor, perfect in all tragic sounds!
Thou mighty Poet, e'en to Frenzy bold!
  What tell'st thou now about?
  'Tis of the rushing of an host in rout,
 With groans of trampled men, with smarting wounds—
At once they groan with pain, and shudder with the cold!
But hush! there is a pause of deepest silence!
 And all that noise, as of a rushing crowd,
With groans, and tremulous shudderings—all is over—
 It tells another tale, with sounds less deep and loud!
  A tale of less affright,
  And tempered with delight,

As Otway's self had framed the tender lay,
   'Tis of a little child
   Upon a lonesome wild,
Not far from home, but she hath lost her way:
And now moans low in bitter grief and fear,
And now screams loud, and hopes to make her mother hear.

VIII

'Tis midnight, but small thoughts have I of sleep:
Full seldom may my friend such vigils keep!
Visit her, gentle Sleep! with wings of healing,
   And may this storm be but a mountain-birth,
May all the stars hang bright above her dwelling,
   Silent as though they watched the sleeping Earth!
     With light heart may she rise,
     Gay fancy, cheerful eyes,
  Joy lift her spirit, joy attune her voice:
To her may all things live, from Pole to Pole,
Their life the eddying of her living soul!
  O simple spirit, guided from above,
Dear Lady! friend devoutest of my choice,
Thus may'st thou ever, evermore rejoice.

Work Without Hope

ALL Nature seems at work. Slugs leave their lair—
The bees are stirring—birds are on the wing—
And Winter slumbering in the open air,
Wears on his smiling face a dream of Spring!
And I, the while, the sole unbusy thing,
Nor honey make, nor pair, nor build, nor sing.

Yet well I ken the banks where Amaranths blow,
Have traced the fount whence streams of nectar flow.
Bloom, O ye Amaranths! bloom for whom ye may.
For me ye bloom not! Glide, rich streams, away!
With lips unbrightened, wreathless brow, I stroll:
And would you learn the spells that drowse my soul?
Work without Hope draws nectar in a sieve,
And Hope without an object cannot live.

Kubla Khan

IN Xanadu did Kubla Khan
A stately pleasure-dome decree:
Where Alph, the sacred river, ran
Through caverns measureless to man
  Down to a sunless sea.
So twice five miles of fertile ground
With walls and towers were girdled round:
And here were gardens bright with sinuous rills,
Where blossomed many an incense-bearing tree;
And here were forests ancient as the hills,
Enfolding sunny spots of greenery.

But oh! that deep romantic chasm which slanted
Down the green hill athwart a cedarn cover!
A savage place! as holy and enchanted
As e'er beneath a waning moon was haunted
By woman wailing for her demon-lover!
And from this chasm, with ceaseless turmoil seething
As if this earth in fast thick pants were breathing,
A mighty fountain momently was forced:
Amid whose swift half-intermitted burst
Huge fragments vaulted like rebounding hail
Or chaffy grain beneath the thresher's flail:
And mid these dancing rocks at once and ever
It flung up momently the sacred river.
Five miles meandering with a mazy motion
Through wood and dale the sacred river ran,
Then reached the caverns measureless to man,
And sank in tumult to a lifeless ocean:
And 'mid this tumult Kubla heard from far
Ancestral voices prophesying war!

    The shadow of the dome of pleasure
    Floated midway on the waves;
    Where was heard the mingled measure
    From the fountain and the caves.
  It was a miracle of rare device,
  A sunny pleasure-dome with caves of ice!

    A damsel with a dulcimer
    In a vision once I saw:

It was an Abyssinian maid,
And on her dulcimer she played,
Singing of Mount Abora.
Could I revive within me
Her symphony and song,
To such a deep delight 'twould win me,
That with music loud and long,
I would build that dome in air,
That sunny dome! those caves of ice!
And all who heard should see them there,
And all should cry, Beware! Beware!
His flashing eyes, his floating hair!
Weave a circle round him thrice,
And close your eyes with holy dread,
For he on honey-dew hath fed,
And drunk the milk of Paradise.

To a Young Ass,
Its mother being tethered near it

POOR little Foal of an oppressed race!
I love the languid patience of thy face:
And oft with gentle hand I give thee bread,
And clap thy ragged coat, and pat thy head.
But what thy dulled spirits hath dismay'd,
That never thou dost sport along the glade?
And (most unlike the nature of things young)
That earthward still thy moveless head is hung?
Do thy prophetic fears anticipate,
Meek Child of Misery! thy future fate?
The starving meal, and all the thousand aches
'Which patient Merit of the Unworthy takes'?
Or is thy sad heart thrill'd with filial pain
To see thy wretched mother's shorten'd chain?
And truly, very pieteous is *her* lot—
Chain'd to a log within a narrow spot,
Where the close-eaten grass is scarcely seen,
While sweet around her waves the tempting green!

Poor Ass! thy master should have learnt to show
Pity—best taught by fellowship of Woe!
For much I fear me that *He* lives like thee,

Half famish'd in a land of Luxury!
How *askingly* its footsteps hither bend?
It seems to say, 'And have I then *one* friend?'
Innocent foal! thou poor despis'd forlorn!
I hail thee *Brother*—spite of the fool's scorn!
And fain would take thee with me, in the Dell
Of Peace and mild Equality to dwell,
Where Toil shall call the charmer Health his bride,
And Laughter tickle Plenty's ribless side!
How thou wouldst toss thy heels in gamesome play,
And frisk about, as lamb or kitten gay!
Yea! and more musically sweet to me
Thy dissonant harsh bray of joy would be,
Than warbled melodies that soothe to rest
The aching of pale Fashion's vacant breast!

This Lime-Tree Bower My Prison

WELL, they are gone, and here must I remain,
This lime-tree bower my prison! I have lost
Beauties and feelings, such as would have been
Most sweet to my remembrance even when age
Had dimm'd mine eyes to blindness! They, meanwhile,
Friends, whom I never more may meet again,
On springy heath, along the hill-top edge,
Wander in gladness, and wind down, perchance,
To that still roaring dell, of which I told;
The roaring dell, o'erwooded, narrow, deep,
And only speckled by the mid-day sun;
Where its slim trunk the ash from rock to rock
Flings arching like a bridge;—that branchless ash,
Unsunn'd and damp, whose few poor yellow leaves
Ne'er tremble in the gale, yet tremble still,
Fann'd by the water-fall! and there my friends
Behold the dark green file of long lank weeds,
That all at once (a most fantastic sight!)
Still nod and drip beneath the dripping edge
Of the blue clay-stone.

                              Now, my friends emerge
Beneath the wide wide Heaven—and view again
The many-steepled tract magnificent
Of hilly fields and meadows, and the sea,

With some fair bark, perhaps, whose sails light up
The slip of smooth clear blue betwixt two Isles
Of purple shadow! Yes! they wander on
In gladness all; but thou, methinks, most glad,
My gentle-hearted Charles! for thou hast pined
And hunger'd after Nature, many a year,
In the great City pent, winning thy way
With sad yet patient soul, through evil and pain
And strange calamity! Ah! slowly sink
Behind the western ridge, thou glorious Sun!
Shine in the slant beams of the sinking orb,
Ye purple heath-flowers! richlier burn, ye clouds!
Live in the yellow light, ye distant groves!
And kindle, thou blue Ocean! So my friend
Struck with deep joy may stand, as I have stood,
Silent with swimming sense; yea, gazing round
On the wide landscape, gaze till all doth seem
Less gross than bodily; and of such hues
As veil the Almighty Spirit, when yet he makes
Spirits perceive his presence.

              A delight
Comes sudden on my heart, and I am glad
As I myself were there! Nor in this bower,
This little lime-tree bower, have I not mark'd
Much that has sooth'd me. Pale beneath the blaze
Hung the transparent foliage; and I watch'd
Some broad and sunny leaf, and lov'd to see
The shadow of the leaf and stem above
Dappling its sunshine! And that walnut-tree
Was richly ting'd, and a deep radiance lay
Full on the ancient ivy, which usurps
Those fronting elms, and now, with blackest mass
Makes their dark branches gleam a lighter hue
Through the late twilight: and though now the bat
Wheels silent by, and not a swallow twitters,
Yet still the solitary humble-bee
Sings in the bean-flower! Henceforth I shall know
That Nature ne'er deserts the wise and pure;
No plot so narrow, be but Nature there,
No waste so vacant, but may well employ
Each faculty of sense, and keep the heart
Awake to Love and Beauty! and sometimes
'Tis well to be bereft of promis'd good,

That we may lift the soul, and contemplate
With lively joy the joys we cannot share.
My gentle-hearted Charles! when the last rook
Beat its straight path along the dusky air
Homewards, I blest it! deeming its black wing
(Now a dim speck, now vanishing in light)
Had cross'd the mighty Orb's dilated glory,
While thou stood'st gazing; or, when all was still,
Flew creeking o'er thy head, and had a charm
For thee, my gentle-hearted Charles, to whom
No sound is dissonant which tells of Life.

The Homeric Hexameter

STRONGLY it bears us along in swelling and limitless billows,
Nothing before and nothing behind but the sky and the ocean.

ROBERT SOUTHEY

1774–1843

After Blenheim

IT was a summer evening,
   Old Kaspar's work was done,
And he before his cottage door
   Was sitting in the sun;
And by him sported on the green
His little grandchild Wilhelmine.

She saw her brother Peterkin
   Roll something large and round
Which he beside the rivulet
   In playing there had found;
He came to ask what he had found
That was so large and smooth and round.

Old Kaspar took it from the boy
   Who stood expectant by;
And then the old man shook his head,

And with a natural sigh
''Tis some poor fellow's skull,' said he,
'Who fell in the great victory.

'I find them in the garden,
    For there's many here about,
And often when I go to plough
    The ploughshare turns them out,
For many thousand men,' said he
'Were slain in that great victory.'

'Now tell us what 'twas all about,'
    Young Peterkin he cries;
And little Wilhelmine looks up
    With wonder-waiting eyes;
'Now tell us all about the war,
And what they fought each other for.'

'It was the English,' Kaspar cried,
    'Who put the French to rout;
But what they fought each other for
    I could not well make out.
But everybody said,' quoth he,
'That 'twas a famous victory.

'My father lived at Blenheim then,
    Yon little stream hard by;
They burnt his dwelling to the ground,
    And he was forced to fly:
So with his wife and child he fled,
Nor had he where to rest his head.

'With fire and sword the country round
    Was wasted far and wide,
And many a childing mother then
    And new-born baby died:
But things like that, you know, must be
At every famous victory.

'They say it was a shocking sight
    After the field was won;
For many thousand bodies here
    Lay rotting in the sun:
But things like that, you know, must be
After a famous victory.

'Great praise the Duke of Marlbro' won
   And our good Prince Eugene;'
'Why, 'twas a very wicked thing!'
   Said little Wilhelmine;
'Nay . . nay . . my little girl,' quoth he,
'It was a famous victory.

'And everybody praised the Duke
   Who this great fight did win.'
'But what good came of it at last?'
   Quoth little Peterkin:—
'Why, that I cannot tell,' said he,
'But 'twas a famous victory.'

Among His Books

MY days among the Dead are past;
   Around me I behold,
Where'er these casual eyes are cast,
   The mighty minds of old:
My never-failing friends are they,
With whom I converse day by day.

With them I take delight in weal
   And seek relief in woe;
And while I understand and feel
   How much to them I owe,
My cheeks have often been bedewed
With tears of thoughtful gratitude.

My thoughts are with the Dead; with them
   I live in long-past years,
Their virtues love, their faults condemn,
   Partake their hopes and fears,
And from their lessons seek and find
Instruction with an humble mind.

My hopes are with the Dead; anon
   My place with them will be,
And I with them shall travel on
   Through all Futurity;
Yet leaving here a name, I trust,
That will not perish in the dust.

346

The Inchcape Rock

No stir in the air, no stir in the sea,
The ship was still as she could be,
Her sails from heaven received no motion,
Her keel was steady in the ocean.

Without either sign or sound of their shock
The waves flowed over the Inchcape Rock;
So little they rose, so little they fell,
They did not move the Inchcape Bell.

The worthy Abbot of Aberbrothok
Had placed that bell on the Inchcape Rock;
On a buoy in the storm it floated and swung,
And over the waves its warning rung.

When the Rock was hid by the surge's swell,
The mariners heard the warning bell;
And then they knew the perilous Rock,
And blessed the Abbot of Aberbrothok.

The Sun in heaven was shining gay,
All things were joyful on that day;
The sea-birds screamed as they wheeled round,
And there was joyaunce in the sound.

The buoy of the Inchcape Bell was seen
A darker speck on the ocean green;
Sir Ralph the Rover walked his deck,
And he fixed his eye on the darker speck.

He felt the cheering power of spring,
It made him whistle, it made him sing;
His heart was mirthful to excess,
But the Rover's mirth was wickedness.

His eye was on the Inchcape float,
Quoth he, 'My men, put out the boat,
And row me to the Inchcape Rock,
And I'll plague the Abbot of Aberbrothok'.

The boat is lowered, the boatmen row,
And to the Inchcape Rock they go;
Sir Ralph bent over from the boat,
And he cut the Bell from the Inchcape float.

Down sunk the Bell with a gurgling sound,
The bubbles rose and burst around:
Quoth Sir Ralph, 'The next who comes to the Rock
Won't bless the Abbot of Aberbrothok.'

Sir Ralph the Rover sailed away,
He scoured the seas for many a day;
And now grown rich with plundered store,
He steers his course for Scotland's shore.

So thick a haze o'erspreads the sky
They cannot see the Sun on high;
The wind hath blown a gale all day,
At evening it hath died away.

On deck the Rover takes his stand,
So dark it is they see no land;
Quoth Sir Ralph, 'It will be lighter soon,
For there is the dawn of the rising Moon.'

'Canst hear,' said one, 'the breakers roar?
For methinks we should be near the shore.'
'Now where we are I cannot tell,
But I wish I could hear the Inchcape Bell.'

They hear no sound, the swell is strong;
Though the wind hath fallen they drift along,
Till the vessel strikes with a shivering shock, —
'Oh Christ! it is the Inchcape Rock!'

Sir Ralph the Rover tore his hair;
He curst himself in his despair;
The waves rush in on every side,
The ship is sinking beneath the tide.

But even in his dying fear
One dreadful sound could the Rover hear,
A sound as if with the Inchcape Bell
The Devil below was ringing his knell.

Bishop Hatto and the Rats

THE summer and autumn had been so wet,
That in winter the corn was growing yet,
'Twas a piteous sight to see all around
The grain lie rotting on the ground.

Every day the starving poor
Crowded around Bishop Hatto's door,
For he had a plentiful last-year's store,
And all the neighbourhood could tell
His granaries were furnished well.

At last Bishop Hatto appointed a day
To quiet the poor without delay;
He bade them to his great Barn repair,
And they should have food for the winter there.

Rejoiced such tidings good to hear,
The poor folk flocked from far and near;
The great Barn was full as it could hold
Of women and children, and young and old.

Then when he saw it could hold no more,
Bishop Hatto he made fast the door;
And while for mercy on Christ they call,
He set fire to the Barn and burnt them all.

'I'faith 'tis an excellent bonfire!' quoth he,
'And the country is greatly obliged to me,
For ridding it in these times forlorn
Of Rats that only consume the corn.'

So then to his palace returned he,
And he sat down to supper merrily,
And he slept that night like an innocent man;
But Bishop Hatto never slept again.

In the morning as he entered the hall
Where his picture hung against the wall,
A sweat like death all over him came,
For the Rats had eaten it out of the frame.

As he looked there came a man from his farm—
He had a countenance white with alarm;
'My Lord, I opened your granaries this morn,
And the Rats had eaten all your corn.'

Another came running presently,
And he was pale as pale could be,
'Fly! my Lord Bishop, fly,' quoth he,
'Ten thousand Rats are coming this way, . .
The Lord forgive you for yesterday!'

'I'll go to my tower on the Rhine,' replied he,
''Tis the safest place in Germany;
The walls are high and the shores are steep,
And the stream is strong and the water deep.'·

Bishop Hatto fearfully hastened away,
And he crossed the Rhine without delay,
And reached his tower, and barred with care
All the windows, doors, and loop-holes there.

He laid him down and closed his eyes; . .
But soon a scream made him arise,
He started and saw two eyes of flame
On his pillow from whence the screaming came.

He listened and looked; . . it was only the Cat;
But the Bishop he grew more fearful for that,
For she sat screaming, mad with fear
At the Army of Rats that were drawing near.

For they have swum over the river so deep,
And they have climbed the shores so steep,
And up the Tower their way is bent,
To do the work for which they were sent.

They are not to be told by the dozen or score,
By thousands they come, and by myriads and more,
Such numbers had never been heard of before,
Such a judgement had never been witnessed of yore.

Down on his knees the Bishop fell,
And faster and faster his beads did he tell,
As louder and louder drawing near
The gnawing of their teeth he could hear.

And in at the windows and in at the door,
And through the walls helter-skelter they pour,
And down from the ceiling and up through the floor,
From the right and the left, from behind and before,
From within and without, from above and below,
And all at once to the Bishop they go.

They have whetted their teeth against the stones,
And now they pick the Bishop's bones;
They gnawed the flesh from every limb,
For they were sent to do judgement on him!

CHARLES LAMB

1775–1834

The Old Familiar Faces

I HAVE had playmates, I have had companions
In my days of childhood, in my joyful school-days;
    All, all are gone, the old familiar faces.

I have been laughing, I have been carousing,
Drinking late, sitting late, with my bosom cronies;
    All, all are gone, the old familiar faces.

I loved a love once, fairest among women:
Closed are her doors on me, I must not see her—
    All, all are gone, the old familiar faces.

I have a friend, a kinder friend has no man;
Like an ingrate, I left my friend abruptly;
    Left him, to muse on the old familiar faces.

Ghost-like I paced round the haunts of my childhood;
Earth seemed a desert I was bound to traverse,
    Seeking to find the old familiar faces.

Friend of my bosom, thou more than a brother,
Why wert not thou born in my father's dwelling!
    So might we talk of the old familiar faces,

How some they have died, and some they have left me,
And some are taken from me; all are departed;
   All, all are gone, the old familiar faces.

The Triumph of the Whale

Io! Pæan! Io! sing
To the finny people's King.
Not a mightier whale than this
In the vast Atlantic is;
Not a fatter fish than he
Flounders round the polar sea.
See his blubbers—at his gills
What a world of drink he swills,
From his trunk, as from a spout,
Which next moment he pours out.
Such his person—next declare,
Muse, who his companions are.
Every fish of generous kind
Scuds aside, or slinks behind:
But about his presence keep
All the Monsters of the Deep;
Mermaids, with their tails and singing
His delighted fancy stinging;
Crooked Dolphins, they surround him.
Dog-like Seals, they fawn around him.
Following hard, the progress mark
Of the intolerant salt sea shark.
For his solace and relief,
Flat fish are his courtiers chief.
Last and lowest in his train,
Ink-fish (libellers of the main)
Their black liquor shed in spite:
(Such on earth the things *that write*.)
In his stomach, some do say,
No good thing can ever stay.
Had it been the fortune of it
To have swallowed that old Prophet,
Three days there he'd not have dwell'd,
But in one have been expell'd.
Hapless mariners are they,
Who beguil'd (as seamen say),
Deeming him some rock or island,

Footing sure, safe spot, and dry land,
Anchor in his scaly rind;
Soon the difference they find;
Sudden plumb, he sinks beneath them;
Does to ruthless seas bequeath them.

Name or title what has he?
Is he Regent of the Sea?
From this difficulty free us,
Buffon, Banks or sage Linnæus.
With his wondrous attributes
Say what appellation suits.
By his bulk, and by his size,
By his oily qualities,
This (or else my eyesight fails),
This should be the PRINCE OF WHALES.

JOSEPH BLANCO WHITE

1775–1841

To Night

MYSTERIOUS Night! when our first parent knew
Thee from report divine, and heard thy name,
Did he not tremble for this lovely frame,
This glorious canopy of light and blue?
Yet 'neath a curtain of translucent dew,
Bathed in the rays of the great setting flame,
Hesperus with the host of heaven came,
And lo! Creation widened in man's view.

Who could have thought such darkness lay concealed
Within thy beams, O sun! or who could find,
Whilst fly and leaf and insect stood revealed,
That to such countless orbs thou mad'st us blind!
Why do we then shun death with anxious strife?
If Light can thus deceive, wherefore not Life?

WALTER SAVAGE LANDOR

1775-1864

Rose Aylmer

AH what avails the sceptred race!
  Ah what the form divine!
What every virtue, every grace!
  Rose Aylmer, all were thine.
Rose Aylmer, whom these wakeful eyes
  May weep, but never see,
A night of memories and of sighs
  I consecrate to thee.

On His Seventy-fifth Birthday

I STROVE with none, for none was worth my strife;
  Nature I loved, and, next to Nature, Art;
I warmed both hands before the fire of life;
  It sinks, and I am ready to depart.

Dirce

STAND close around, ye Stygian set,
  With Dirce in one boat conveyed!
Or Charon, seeing, may forget
  That he is old and she a shade.

JAMES SMITH

1775-1839

Playhouse Musings

By S. T. C.[1]

Ille velut fidis arcana sodalibus olim
Credebat libris; neque si male cesserat, usquam
Decurrens alio, neque si bene.

HORACE

[1] Samuel Taylor Coleridge

My pensive Public, wherefore look you sad?
I had a grandmother, she kept a donkey
To carry to the mart her crockery ware,
And when that donkey looked me in the face,
His face was sad! and you are sad, My Public!

  Joy should be yours: this tenth day of October
Again assembles us in Drury Lane.
Long wept my eye to see the timber planks
That hid our ruins; many a day I cried,
Ah me! I fear they never will rebuild it!
Till on one eve, one joyful Monday eve,
As along Charles Street I prepared to walk,
Just at the corner, by the pastrycook's,
I heard a trowel tick against a brick.
I looked me up, and straight a parapet
Uprose at least seven inches o'er the planks.
Joy to thee, Drury! to myself I said:
He of Blackfriars' Road, who hymned thy downfall
In loud Hosannahs, and who prophesied
That flames, like those from prostrate Solyma,
Would scorch the hand that ventured to rebuild thee,
Has proved a lying prophert. From that hour,
As leisure offered, close to Mr. Spring's
Box-office door, I've stood and eyed the builders.
They had a plan to render less their labours;
Workmen in olden times would mount a ladder
With hodded heads, but these stretched forth a pole
From the wall's pinnacle, they placed a pulley
Athwart the pole, a rope athwart the pulley;
To this a basket dangled; mortar and bricks
Thus freighted, swung securely to the top,
And in the empty basket workmen twain
Precipitate, unhurt, accosted earth.

  Oh! 'twas a goodly sound, to hear the people
Who watched the work, express their various thoughts!
While some believed it never would be finished,
Some, on the contrary, believed it would.

  I've heard our front that faces Drury Lane
Much criticized; they say 'tis vulgar brick-work,
A mimic manufactory of floor-cloth.
One of the morning papers wished that front

355

Cemented like the front in Brydges Street;
As it now looks, they call it Wyatt's Mermaid,
A handsome woman with a fish's tail.

 White is the steeple of St. Bride's in Fleet Street;
The Albion (as its name denotes) is white;
Morgan and Saunders' shop for chairs and tables
Gleams like a snow-ball in the setting sun;
White is Whitehall. But not St. Bride's in Fleet Street,
The spotless Albion, Morgan, no, nor Saunders,
Nor white Whitehall, is white as Drury's face.

 Oh, Mr. Whitbread! fie upon you, sir!
I think you should have built a colonnade;
When tender Beauty, looking for her coach,
Protrudes her gloveless hand, perceives the shower,
And draws the tippet closer round her throat,
Perchance her coach stands half a dozen off,
And, ere she mounts the step, the oozing mud
Soaks through her pale kid slipper. On the morrow,
She coughs at breakfast, and her gruff papa
Cries, 'There you go! this comes of playhouses!'
To build no portico is penny wise:
Heaven grant it prove not in the end pound foolish!

 Hail to thee, Drury! Queen of Theatres!
What is the Regency in Tottenham Street,
The Royal Amphitheatre of Arts,
Astley's, Olympic, or the Sans Pareil,
Compared with thee? Yet when I view thee pushed
Back from the narrow street that christened thee,
I know not why they call thee Drury Lane.

 Amid the freaks that modern fashion sanctions,
It grieves me much to see live animals
Brought on the stage. Grimaldi has his rabbit,
Laurent his cat, and Bradbury his pig;
Fie on such tricks! Johnson, the machinist
Of former Drury, imitated life
Quite to the life. The elephant in Blue Beard,
Stuffed by his hand, wound round his lithe proboscis,
As spruce as he who roared in Padmanaba.
Nought born on earth should die. On hackney stands
I reverence the coachman who cries 'Gee',

And spares the lash. When I behold a spider
Prey on a fly, a magpie on a worm,
Or view a butcher with horn-handled knife
Slaughter a tender lamb as dead as mutton,
Indeed, indeed, I'm very, very, sick!

THOMAS CAMPBELL
1777-1844

Ye Mariners of England

Y E Mariners of England
   That guard our native seas,
Whose flag has braved, a thousand years,
   The battle and the breeze,

Your glorious standard launch again
   To match another foe:
And sweep through the deep,
   While the stormy winds do blow;
While the battle rages loud and long
   And the stormy winds do blow.

The spirits of your fathers
   Shall start from every wave—
For the deck it was their field of flame,
   And Ocean was their grave.
Where Blake and mighty Nelson fell
   Your manly hearts shall glow,
As ye sweep through the deep,
   While the stormy winds do blow;
While the battle rages loud and long
   And the stormy winds do blow.

Britannia needs no bulwarks,
   No towers along the steep;
Her march is o'er the mountain waves,
   Her home is on the deep.
With thunders from her native oak
   She quells the floods below—
As they roar on the shore,

When the stormy winds do blow;
When the battle rages loud and long,
And the stormy winds do blow.

The meteor flag of England
Shall yet terrific burn;
Till danger's troubled night depart
And the star of peace return.
Then, then, ye ocean warriors!
Our song and feast shall flow
To the fame of your name,
When the storm has ceased to blow;
When the fiery fight is heard no more,
And the storm has ceased to blow.

The Soldier's Dream

OUR bugles sang truce, for the night-cloud had lowered,
And the sentinel stars set their watch in the sky;
And thousands had sunk on the ground over-powered
The weary to sleep, and the wounded to die.

When reposing that night on my pallet of straw
By the wolf-scaring faggot that guarded the slain,
At the dead of the night a sweet vision I saw;
And thrice ere the morning I dreamt it again.

Methought from the battle-field's dreadful array
Far, far I had roamed on a desolate track:
'Twas autumn,—and sunshine arose on the way
To the home of my fathers, that welcomed me back.

I flew to the pleasant fields traversed so oft
In life's morning march, when my bosom was young;
I heard my own mountain-goats bleating aloft,
And knew the sweet strain that the corn-reapers sung.

Then pledged we the wine-cup, and fondly I swore
From my home and my weeping friends never to part;
My little ones kissed me a thousand times o'er,
And my wife sobbed aloud in her fullness of heart.

'Stay—stay with us!—rest!—thou art weary and worn!'—
　　And fain was their war-broken soldier to stay;—
But sorrow returned with the dawning of morn,
　　And the voice in my dreaming ear melted away.

THOMAS MOORE

1779–1852

The Minstrel Boy

THE Minstrel Boy to the war is gone,
　　In the ranks of death you'll find him;
His father's sword he has girded on,
　　And his wild harp slung behind him.—
'Land of song!' said the warrior-bard,
　　'Though all the world betrays thee,
One sword, at least, thy rights shall guard,
　　One faithful harp shall praise thee!'

The Minstrel fell!—but the foeman's chain
　　Could not bring his proud soul under;
The harp he loved ne'er spoke again,
　　For he tore its chords asunder;
And said, 'No chains shall sully thee,
　　Thou soul of love and bravery!
Thy songs were made for the pure and free,
　　They shall never sound in slavery.'

She is Far from the Land

SHE is far from the land where her young hero sleeps,
　　And lovers are round her, sighing:
But coldly she turns from their gaze, and weeps,
　　For her heart in his grave is lying.

She sings the wild song of her dear native plains,
　　Every note which he loved awaking;—
Ah! little they think who delight in her strains,
　　How the heart of the Minstrel is breaking.

He had lived for his love, for his country he died,
    They were all that to life had entwined him;
Nor soon shall the tears of his country be dried,
    Nor long will his love stay behind him.

Oh! make her a grave where the sunbeams rest,
    When they promise a glorious morrow;
They'll shine o'er her sleep, like a smile from the West,
    From her own loved island of sorrow.

Pro Patria Mori

WHEN he who adores thee has left but the name
    Of his fault and his sorrows behind,
O! say wilt thou weep, when they darken the fame
    Of a life that for thee was resigned?
Yes, weep, and however my foes may condemn,
    Thy tears shall efface their decree;
For, Heaven can witness, though guilty to them,
    I have been but too faithful to thee.

With thee were the dreams of my earliest love,
    Every thought of my reason was thine:
In my last humble prayer to the Spirit above
    Thy name shall be mingled with mine!
O! blest are the lovers and friends who shall live
    The days of thy glory to see;
But the next dearest blessing that Heaven can give
    Is the pride of thus dying for thee.

Echoes

HOW sweet the answer Echo makes
    To Music at night,
When, roused by lute or horn, she wakes,
And far away o'er lawns and lakes
    Goes answering light!

Yet Love hath echoes truer far
    And far more sweet
Than e'er, beneath the moonlight's star,
Of horn or lute or soft guitar
    The songs repeat.

'Tis when the sigh,—in youth sincere
   And only then—
The sigh that's breathed for one to hear,
Is by that one, that only Dear
   Breathed back again.

The Journey Onwards

As slow our ship her foamy track
   Against the wind was cleaving,
Her trembling pennant still look'd back
   To that dear isle 'twas leaving.
So loth we part from all we love,
   From all the links that bind us;
So turn our hearts, as on we rove,
   To those we've left behind us!

When, round the bowl, of vanished years
   We talk with joyous seeming—
With smiles that might as well be tears,
   So faint, so sad their beaming;
While memory brings us back again
   Each early tie that twined us,
O, sweet's the cup that circles then
   To those we've left behind us!

And when in other climes we meet
   Some isle or vale enchanting,
Where all looks flowery, wild, and sweet,
   And nought but love is wanting;
We think how great had been our bliss
   If Heaven had but assign'd us
To live and die in scenes like this,
   With some we've left behind us!

As travellers oft look back at eve
   When eastward darkly going,
To gaze upon that light they leave
   Still faint behind them glowing,—
So, when the close of pleasure's day
   To gloom hath near consign'd us,
We turn to catch one fading ray
   Of joy that's left behind us.

EBENEZER ELLIOT
1781–1849

Battle Song

DAY, like our souls, is fiercely dark;
　　What then? 'Tis day!
We sleep no more; the cock crows—hark!
　　To arms! away!
They come! they come! the knell is rung
　　Of us or them;
Wide o'er their march the pomp is flung
　　Of gold and gem.
What collared hound of lawless sway,
　　To famine dear—
What pensioned slave of Attila,
　　Leads in the rear?
Come they from Scythian wilds afar,
　　Our blood to spill?
Wear they the livery of the Czar?
　　They do his will.
Nor tasselled silk, nor epaulet,
　　Nor plume, nor torse—
No splendour gilds, all sternly met,
　　Our foot and horse.
But, dark and still, we inly glow,
　　Condensed in ire!
Strike, tawdry slaves, and ye shall know
　　Our gloom is fire.
In vain your pomp, ye evil powers,
　　Insults the land;
Wrongs, vengeance, and the Cause are ours,
　　And God's right hand!
Madmen! they trample into snakes
　　The wormy clod!
Like fire, beneath their feet awakes
　　The sword of God!
Behind, before, above, below,
　　They rouse the brave;
Where'er they go, they make a foe,
　　Or find a grave.

When Wilt Thou Save the People?

WHEN wilt thou save the people?
 O God of mercy, when?
The people, Lord, the people,
 Not thrones and crowns, but men!
Flowers of thy heart, O God, are they;
Let them not pass, like weeds, away—
Their heritage a sunless day.
  God save the people!

Shall crime bring crime for ever,
 Strength aiding still the strong?
Is it thy will, O Father.
 That man shall toil for wrong?
'No,' say thy mountains; 'No,' thy skies;
Man's clouded sun shall brightly rise,
And songs be heard instead of sighs.
  God save the people!

When wilt thou save the people?
 O God of mercy, when?
The people, Lord, the people,
 Not thrones and crowns, but men!
God save the people; thine they are,
Thy children, as thy Angels fair;
From vice, oppression, and despair,
  God save the people!

Spring

AGAIN the violet of our early days
Drinks beauteous azure from the golden sun,
And kindles into fragrance at his blaze;
The streams, rejoiced that winter's work is done,
Talk of to-morrow's cowslips, as they run.
Wild apple, thou art bursting into bloom!
Thy leaves are coming, snowy-blossomed thorn!
Wake, buried lily! spirit, quit thy tomb;
And thou, shade-loving hyacinth, be born!
Then, haste, sweet rose! sweet woodbine, hymn the morn,
Whose dew-drops shall illume with pearly light

Each grassy blade that thick embattled stands
From sea to sea, while daisies infinite
Uplift in praise their little glowing hands,
O'er every hill that under heaven expands.

Song

WHEN working blackguards come to blows,
And give or take a bloody nose,
Shall juries try such dogs as those,
   Now Nap lies at Saint Helena?

No—let the Great Unpaid decide,
Without appeal, on tame bull's hide,
Ash-planted well, or fistified,
   Since Nap died at Saint Helena.

When Sabbath stills the dizzy mill,
Shall Cutler Tom, or Grinder Bill,
On footpaths wander where they will,
   Now Nap lies at Saint Helena?

No—let them curse, but *feel* our power;
Dogs! let them spend their idle hour
Where burns the highway's dusty shower;
   For Nap died at Saint Helena.

Huzza! the rascal Whiglings work
For better men than Hare and Burke,
And envy Algerine and Turk,
   Since Nap died at Saint Helena.

Then close each path that sweetly climbs
Suburban hills, where village chimes
Remind the rogues of other times,
   Ere Nap died at Saint Helena.

We tax their bread, restrict their trade;
To toil for us, their hands were made;
Their doom is sealed, their prayer is prayed;
   Nap perished at Saint Helena.

Dogs! would they toil and fatten too?
They grumble still, as dogs will do;
We conquered *them* at Waterloo:
   And Nap lies at Saint Helena.

But shall the villains meet and prate,
In crowds about affairs of State?
Ride, yeomen, ride! act, magistrate!
   Nap perished at Saint Helena.

ALLAN CUNNINGHAM
1784–1842

A WET sheet and a flowing sea,
   A wind that follows fast
And fills the white and rustling sail
   And bends the gallant mast;
And bends the gallant mast, my boys,
   While like the eagle free
Away the good ship flies, and leaves
   Old England on the lee.

O for a soft and gentle wind!
   I heard a fair one cry;
But give to me the snoring breeze
   And white waves heaving high;
And white waves heaving high, my lads,
   The good ship tight and free—
The world of waters is our home,
   And merry men are we.

There's tempest in yon hornéd moon,
   And lightning in yon cloud;
But hark the music, mariners!
   The wind is piping loud;
The wind is piping loud, my boys,
   The lightning flashes free—
While the hollow oak our palace is,
   Our heritage the sea.

JAMES HENRY LEIGH HUNT

1784–1859

Abou Ben Adhem

ABOU BEN ADHEM (may his tribe increase!)
Awoke one night from a deep dream of peace,
And saw, within the moonlight in his room,
Making it rich, and like a lily in bloom,
An angel writing in a book of gold:—
Exceeding peace had made Ben Adhem bold,
And to the presence in the room he said,
   'What writest thou?'—The vision raised its head,
And with a look made of all sweet accord,
Answered, 'The names of those that love the Lord.'
   'And is mine one?' said Abou. 'Nay, not so,'
Replied the angel. Abou spoke more low,
But cheerly still; and said, 'I pray thee, then,
Write me as one that loves his fellow men.'
   The angel wrote, and vanished. The next night
It came again with a great wakening light,
And showed the names whom love of God had blessed,
And lo! Ben Adhem's name led all the rest.

Jenny Kissed Me

JENNY kissed me when we met,
   Jumping from the chair she sat in;
Time, you thief, who love to get
   Sweets into your list, put that in!

Say I'm weary, say I'm sad,
   Say that health and wealth have missed me,
Say I'm growing old, but add,
      Jenny kissed me.

The Grasshopper and the Cricket

GREEN little vaulter in the sunny grass,
   Catching your heart up at the feel of June,
   Sole voice that's heard amidst the lazy noon,
When even the bees lag at the summoning brass;—
And you, warm little housekeeper, who class
   With those who think the candles come too soon,
   Loving the fire, and with your tricksome tune
Nick the glad silent moments as they pass;—

O sweet and tiny cousins, that belong,
   One to the fields, the other to the hearth,
Both have your sunshine; both, though small, are strong
   At your clear hearts; and both seem given to earth
To sing in thoughtful ears this natural song—
   Indoors and out,—summer and winter,—Mirth.

THOMAS LOVE PEACOCK
1785–1866

The Grave of Love

I DUG, beneath the cypress shade,
   What well might seem an elfin's grave;
And every pledge in earth I laid.
   That erst thy false affection gave.

I pressed them down the sod beneath;
   I placed one mossy stone above;
And twined the rose's fading wreath
   Around the sepulchre of love.

Frail as thy love, the flowers were dead,
   Ere yet the evening sun was set:
But years shall see the cypress spread,
   Immutable as my regret.

from *Nightmare Abbey*

Three Men of Gotham

SEAMEN three! What men be ye?
　Gotham's three wise men we be.
Whither in your bowl so free?
　To rake the moon from out the sea.
The bowl goes trim. The moon doth shine.
And our ballast is old wine.
And your ballast is old wine.

Who art thou, so fast adrift?
　I am he they call Old Care.
Here on board we will thee lift.
　No: I may not enter there.
Wherefore so? 'Tis Jove's decree,
In a bowl Care may not be.
In a bowl Care may not be.

Fear ye not the waves that roll?
　No: in charmèd bowl we swim.
What the charm that floats the bowl?
　Water may not pass the brim.
The bowl goes trim. The moon doth shine.
And our ballast is old wine.
And your ballast is old wine.

from *Maid Marian*

Robin Hood and the Grey Friars

BOLD Robin has robed him in ghostly attire,
And forth he is gone like a holy friar,
　Singing, hey down, ho down, down, derry down:
And of two grey friars he soon was aware,
Regaling themselves with dainty fare,
　All on the fallen leaves so brown.

'Good morrow, good brothers,' said bold Robin Hood,
'And what make you in the good greenwood,
　Singing hey down, ho down, down, derry down!
Now give me, I pray you, wine and food;
For none can I find in the good greenwood,
　All on the fallen leaves so brown.'

'Good brother,' they said, 'we would give you full fain,
But we have no more than enough for twain,
   Singing hey down, ho down, down, derry down.'
'Then give me some money,' said bold Robin Hood,
'For none can I find in the good greenwood,
   All on the fallen leaves so brown.'

'No money have we, good brother,' said they:
'Then,' said he, 'we three for money will pray:
   Singing, hey down, ho down, down, derry down:
And whatever shall come at the end of our prayer,
We three holy friars will piously share,
   All on the fallen leaves so brown.'

'We will not pray with thee, good brother. God wot:
For truly, good brother, thou pleasest us not,
   Singing, hey down, ho down, down, derry down:'
Then up they both started from Robin to run,
But down on their knees Robin pulled them each one,
   All on the fallen leaves so brown.

The grey friars prayed with a doleful face,
But bold Robin prayed with a right merry grace,
   Singing, hey down, ho down, down, derry down:
And when they had prayed, their portmanteau he took,
And from it a hundred good angels he shook,
   All on the fallen leaves so brown.

'The saints,' said bold Robin, 'have hearkened our prayer,
And here's a good angel apiece for your share:
If more you would have, you must win ere you wear:
   Singing, hey down, ho down, down, derry down:'
Then he blew his good horn with a musical cheer,
And fifty green bowmen came trooping full near,
And away the grey friars they bounded like deer,
   All on the fallen leaves so brown.

Over, Over

A DAMSEL came in midnight rain,
   And called across the ferry:
The weary wight she called in vain,
   Whose senses sleep did bury.

At evening, from her father's door
   She turned to meet her lover:
At midnight, on the lonely shore,
   She shouted, 'Over, over!'

She had not met him by the tree
   Of their accustomed meeting,
And sad and sick at heart was she,
   Her heart all wildly beating.
In chill suspense the hours went by,
   The wild storm burst above her:
She turned her to the river nigh,
   And shouted, 'Over, over!'

A dim, discoloured, doubtful light
   The moon's dark veil permitted,
And thick before her troubled sight
   Fantastic shadows flitted.
Her lover's form appeared to glide,
   And beckon o'er the water:
Alas! his blood that morn had dyed
   Her brother's sword with slaughter.

Upon a little rock she stood,
   To make her invocation:
She marked not that the rain-swoll'n flood
   Was islanding her station.
The tempest mocked her feeble cry:
   No saint his aid would give her:
The flood swelled high and yet more high,
   And swept her down the river.

Yet oft beneath the pale moonlight,
   When hollow winds are blowing,
The shadow of that maiden bright
   Glides by the dark stream's flowing.
And when the storms of midnight rave,
   While clouds the broad moon cover,
The wild gusts waft across the wave
   The cry of, 'Over, over!'

from *Crotchet Castle*

The Priest and the Mulberry Tree

DID you hear of the curate who mounted his mare,
And merrily trotted along to the fair?
Of creature more tractable none ever heard,
In the height of her speed she would stop at a word;
And again with a word, when the curate said Hey,
She put forth her mettle, and galloped away.

As near to the gates of the city he rode,
While the sun of September all brilliantly glowed,
The good priest discovered, with eyes of desire,
A mulberry tree in a hedge of wild briar;
On boughs long and lofty, in many a green shoot,
Hung large, black, and glossy, the beautiful fruit.

The curate was hungry and thirsty to boot;
He shrunk from the thorns, though he longed for the fruit;
With a word he arrested the courser's keen speed,
And he stood up erect on the back of his steed;
On the saddle he stood, while the creature stood still,
And he gathered the fruit, till he took his good fill.

'Sure never,' he thought, 'was a creature so rare,
So docile, so true, as my excellent mare.
Lo, here, how I stand' (and he gazed all around),
'As safe and as steady as if on the ground,
Yet how had it been, if some traveller this way,
Had, dreaming no mischief, but chanced to cry Hey?'

He stood with his head in the mulberry tree,
And he spoke out aloud in his fond reverie:
At the sound of the word, the good mare made a push,
And down went the priest in the wild-briar bush.
He remembered too late, on his thorny green bed,
Much that well may be thought, cannot wisely be said.

The War Song of Dinas Vawr

THE mountain sheep are sweeter,
But the valley sheep are fatter;
We therefore deemed it meeter
To carry off the latter.
We made an expedition;
We met a host, and quelled it;
We forced a strong position,
And killed the men who held it.

On Dyfed's richest valley,
Where herds of kine were brousing,
We made a mighty sally,
To furnish our carousing.
Fierce warriors rushed to meet us;
We met them, and o'erthrew them:
They struggled hard to beat us;
But we conquered them, and slew them.

As we drove our prize at leisure,
The king marched forth to catch us:
His rage surpassed all measure,
But his people could not match us.
He fled to his hall-pillars;
And, ere our force we led off,
Some sacked his house and cellars,
While others cut his head off.

We there, in strife bewildering,
Spilt blood enough to swim in:
We orphaned many children,
And widowed many women.
The eagles and the ravens
We glutted with our foemen;
The heroes and the cravens,
The spearmen and the bowmen.

We brought away from battle,
And much their land bemoaned them,
Two thousand head of cattle,
And the head of him who owned them:
Ednyfed, king of Dyfed,
His head was borne before us;
His wine and beasts supplied our feasts,
And his overthrow, our chorus.

BRYAN WALLER PROCTER
('BARRY CORNWALL')
1787–1874

The Leveller

THE king he reigns on a throne of gold,
   Fenced round by his 'right divine';
The baron he sits in his castle old,
   Drinking his ripe red wine:
But below, below, in his ragged coat,
The beggar he tuneth a hungry note,
And the spinner is bound to his weary thread,
And the debtor lies down with an aching head.

> *So the world goes!*
> *So the stream flows!*
> *Yet there is a fellow, whom nobody knows,*
> *Who maketh all free*
> *On land and sea,*
> *And forceth the rich like the poor to flee!*

The lady lies down in her warm white lawn,
   And dreams of her pearlèd pride;
The milkmaid sings, to the wild-eyed dawn,
   Sad songs on the cold hill-side:
And the bishop smiles, as on high he sits,
On the scholar who writes and starves by fits;
And the girl who her nightly needle plies,
Looks out for the summer of life,—and dies!

> *So the world goes!*
> *So the stream flows!*
> *Yet there is a fellow, whom nobody knows,*
> *Who maketh all free*
> *On land and sea,*
> *And forceth the rich like the poor to flee!*

GEORGE GORDON, LORD BYRON

1788–1824

She Walks in Beauty

I

SHE walks in beauty, like the night
  Of cloudless climes and starry skies;
And all that's best of dark and bright
  Meet in her aspect and her eyes:
Thus mellowed to that tender light
  Which heaven to gaudy day denies.

II

One shade the more, one ray the less,
  Had half impaired the nameless grace
Which waves in every raven tress,
  Or softly lightens o'er her face;
Where thoughts serenely sweet express
  How pure, how dear their dwelling-place.

III

And on that cheek, and o'er that brow,
  So soft, so calm, yet eloquent,
The smiles that win, the tints that glow,
  But tell of days in goodness spent,
A mind at peace with all below,
  A heart whose love is innocent!

The Destruction of Sennacherib

I

THE Assyrian came down like the wolf on the fold,
And his cohorts were gleaming in purple and gold;
And the sheen of their spears was like stars on the sea,
When the blue wave rolls nightly on deep Galilee.

II

Like the leaves of the forest when Summer is green,
That host with their banners at sunset were seen:
Like the leaves of the forest when Autumn hath blown,
That host on the morrow lay withered and strown.

III

For the Angel of Death spread his wings on the blast,
And breathed in the face of the foe as he passed;
And the eyes of the sleepers waxed deadly and chill,
And their hearts but once heaved, and for ever grew still!

IV

And there lay the steed with his nostril all wide,
But through it there rolled not the breath of his pride;
And the foam of his gasping lay white on the turf,
And cold as the spray of the rock-beating surf.

V

And there lay the rider distorted and pale,
With the dew on his brow, and the rust on his mail:
And the tents were all silent, the banners alone,
The lances unlifted, the trumpet unblown.

VI

And the widows of Asshur are loud in their wail,
And the idols are broke in the temple of Baal;
And the might of the Gentile, unsmote by the sword,
Hath melted like snow in the glance of the Lord!

from *Childe Harold's Pilgrimage*

from *Canto III*

THERE was a sound of revelry by night,
And Belgium's capital had gathered then
Her Beauty and her Chivalry, and bright
The lamps shone o'er fair women and brave men;
A thousand hearts beat happily; and when
Music arose with its voluptuous swell,
Soft eyes looked love to eyes which spake again,
And all went merry as a marriage bell;
But hush! hark! a deep sound strikes like a rising knell!

Did ye not hear it?—No; 'twas but the wind,
Or the car rattling o'er the stony street;
On with the dance! let joy be unconfined;
No sleep till morn, when Youth and Pleasure meet
To chase the glowing Hours with flying fleet—

But hark!—that heavy sound breaks in once more,
As if the clouds its echo would repeat;
And nearer, clearer, deadlier than before!
Arm! Arm! it is—it is—the cannon's opening roar!

Within a windowed niche of that high hall
Sate Brunswick's fated chieftain; he did hear
That sound the first amidst the festival,
And caught its tone with Death's prophetic ear;
And when they smiled because he deemed it near,
His heart more truly knew that peal too well
Which stretched his father on a bloody bier,
And roused the vengeance blood alone could quell;
He rushed into the field, and, foremost fighting, fell.

Ah! then and there was hurrying to and fro,
And gathering tears, and tremblings of distress,
And cheeks all pale, which but an hour ago
Blushed at the praise of their own loveliness;
And there were sudden partings, such as press
The life from out young hearts, and choking sighs
Which ne'er might be repeated; who could guess
If ever more should meet those mutual eyes,
Since upon night so sweet such awful morn could rise!

And there was mounting in hot haste: the steed,
The mustering squadron, and the clattering car,
Went pouring forward with impetuous speed,
And swiftly forming in the ranks of war;
And the deep thunder peal on peal afar;
And near, the beat of the alarming drum
Roused up the soldier ere the morning star;
While thronged the citizens with terror dumb,
Or whispering, with white lips—'The foe! they come! they come!'

And wild and high the 'Cameron's gathering' rose!
The war-note of Lochiel, which Albyn's hills
Have heard, and heard, too, have her Saxon foes:—
How in the noon of night that pibroch thrills,
Savage and shrill! But with the breath which fills
Their mountain-pipe, so fill the mountaineers
With the fierce native daring which instils
The stirring memory of a thousand years,
And Evan's, Donald's fame rings in each clansman's ears!

And Ardennes waves above them her green leaves,
Dewy with nature's tear-drops as they pass,
Grieving, if aught inanimate e'er grieves,
Over the unreturning brave,—alas!
Ere evening to be trodden like the grass
Which now beneath them, but above shall grow
In its next verdure, when this fiery mass
Of living valour, rolling on the foe
And burning with high hope, shall moulder cold and low.

Last noon beheld them full of lusty life,
Last eve in Beauty's circle proudly gay,
The midnight brought the signal-sound of strife,
The morn the marshalling in arms,—the day
Battle's magnificently stern array!
The thunder-clouds close o'er it, which when rent
The earth is covered thick with other clay,
Which her own clay shall cover, heaped and pent,
Rider and horse,—friend, foe,—in one red burial blent!

from *Canto IV*

THERE is a pleasure in the pathless woods,
There is a rapture on the lonely shore,
There is society, where none intrudes,
By the deep Sea, and music in its roar:
I love not Man the less, but Nature more,
From these our interviews, in which I steal
From all I may be, or have been before,
To mingle with the Universe, and feel
What I can ne'er express, yet cannot all conceal.

Roll on, thou deep and dark blue Ocean—roll!
Ten thousand fleets sweep over thee in vain;
Man marks the earth with ruin—his control
Stops with the shore; upon the watery plain
The wrecks are all thy deed, nor doth remain
A shadow of man's ravage, save his own,
When, for a moment, like a drop of rain,
He sinks into thy depths with bubbling groan,
Without a grave, unknelled, uncoffined, and unknown.

His steps are not upon thy paths,—thy fields
Are not a spoil for him,—thou dost arise
And shake him from thee; the vile strength he wields
For earth's destruction thou dost all despise,
Spurning him from thy bosom to the skies,
And send'st him, shivering in thy playful spray
And howling, to his Gods, where haply lies
His petty hope in some near port or bay,
And dashest him again to earth:—there let him lay.

The armaments which thunderstrike the walls
Of rock-built cities, bidding nations quake,
And monarchs tremble in their capitals,
The oak leviathans, whose huge ribs make
Their clay creator the vain title take
Of lord of thee, and arbiter of war—
These are thy toys, and, as the snowy flake,
They melt into thy yeast of waves, which mar
Alike the Armada's pride or spoils of Trafalgar.

Thy shores are empires, changed in all save thee—
Assyria, Greece, Rome, Carthage, what are they?
Thy waters washed them power while they were free,
And many a tyrant since; their shores obey
The stranger, slave, or savage; their decay
Had dried up realms to deserts:—not so thou;—
Unchangeable, save to thy wild waves' play,
Time writes no wrinkle on thine azure brow:
Such as creation's dawn beheld, thou rollest now.

Thou glorious mirror, where the Almighty's form
Glasses itself in tempests; in all time,—
Calm or convulsed, in breeze, or gale, or storm,
Icing the pole, or in the torrid clime
Dark-heaving—boundless, endless, and sublime,
The image of eternity, the throne
Of the Invisible; even from out thy slime
The monsters of the deep are made; each zone
Obeys thee; thou goest forth, dread, fathomless, alone.

GEORGE GORDON, LORD BYRON

Lines on Hearing that Lady Byron was Ill

AND thou wert sad—yet I was not with thee;
  And thou wert sick, and yet I was not near;
Methought that joy and health alone could be
  Where I was *not*—and pain and sorrow here!
And is it thus?—it is as I foretold,
  And shall be more so; for the mind recoils
Upon itself, and the wreck'd heart lies cold,
  While heaviness collects the shatter'd spoils.
It is not in the storm nor in the strife
  We feel benumb'd, and wish to be no more,
  But in the after-silence on the shore,
When all is lost, except a little life.
I am too well avenged!—but 'twas my right:
  Whate'er my sins might be, *thou* wert not sent
To be the Nemesis who should requite—
  Nor did Heaven choose so near an instrument.
Mercy is for the merciful!—if thou
Has been of such, 'twill be accorded now.
Thy nights are banish'd from the realms of sleep!—
  Yes! they may flatter thee, but thou shalt feel
  A hollow agony which will not heal,
For thou art pillow'd on a curse too deep;
Thou hast sown in my sorrow, and must reap
  The bitter harvest in a woe as real!
I have had many foes, but none like thee;
  For 'gainst the rest myself I could defend,
  And be avenged, or turn them into friend;
But thou in safe implacability
Hadst nought to dread—in thy own weakness shielded,
And in my love, which hath but too much yielded,
  And spared, for thy sake, some I should not spare;
And thus upon the world—trust in thy truth,
And the wild fame of my ungovern'd youth—
  On things that were not, and on things that are—
Even upon such a basis hast thou built
A monument, whose cement hath been guilt!
  The moral Clytemnestra of thy lord,
  And hew'd down, with an unsuspected sword,
Fame, peace, and hope—and all the better life,
  Which, but for this cold treason of thy heart,
Might still have risen from out the grave of strife,

And found a nobler duty than to part.
But of thy virtues didst thou make a vice,
   Trafficking with them in a purpose cold,
   For present anger, and for future gold—
And buying others' grief at any price.
And thus once enter'd into crooked ways,
The earthly truth, which was thy proper praise,
Did not still walk beside thee—but at times,
And with a breast unknowing its own crimes,
Deceit, averments incompatible,
Equivocations, and the thoughts which dwell
   In Janus-spirits—the significant eye
Which learns to lie with silence—the pretext
Of prudence, with advantages annex'd—
The acquiescence in all things which tend,
No matter how, to the desired end—
   All found a place in thy philosophy.
The means were worthy, and the end is won—
I would not do by thee as thou hast done!

from *Stanzas*

WHEN a man hath no freedom to fight for at home,
   Let him combat for that of his neighbours;
Let him think of the glories of Greece and of Rome,
   And get knock'd on the head for his labours.
To do good to mankind is the chivalrous plan,
   And is always as nobly requited;
Then battle for freedom wherever you can,
   And, if not shot or hang'd, you'll get knighted.

Prometheus

I

TITAN! to whose immortal eyes
   The sufferings of mortality,
   Seen in their sad reality,
Were not as things that gods despise;
What was thy pity's recompense?
A silent suffering, and intense;
The rock, the vulture, and the chain,
All that the proud can feel of pain,

The agony they do not show,
The suffocating sense of woe,
    Which speaks but in its loneliness,
And then is jealous lest the sky
Should have a listener, nor will sigh
    Until its voice is echoless.

II

Titan! to thee the strife was given
    Between the suffering and the will,
    Which torture where they cannot kill;
And the inexorable Heaven,
And the deaf tyranny of Fate,
The ruling principle of Hate,
Which for its pleasure doth create
The things it may annihilate,
Refused thee even the boon to die:
The wretched gift eternity
Was thine—and thou hast borne it well.
All that the Thunderer wrung from thee
Was but the menace which flung back
On him the torments of thy rack;
The fate thou didst so well forsee,
But would not to appease him tell;
And in thy Silence was his Sentence,
And in his Soul a vain repentance,
And evil dread so ill dissembled,
That in his hand the lightnings trembled.

III

Thy Godlike crime was to be kind,
    To render with thy precepts less
    The sum of human wretchedness,
And strengthen Man with his own mind;
But baffled as thou wert from high,
Still in thy patient energy,
In the endurance, and repulse
    Of thine impenetrable Spirit,
Which Earth and Heaven could not convulse,
    A mighty lesson we inherit:
Thou art a symbol and a sign
    To Mortals of their fate and force;
Like thee, Man is in part divine,
    A troubled stream from a pure source;

381

And Man in portions can foresee
His own funereal destiny;
His wretchedness and his resistance,
And his sad unallied existence:
To which his Spirit may oppose
Itself—and equal to all woes,
    And a firm will, and a deep sense,
Which even in torture can descry
    Its own concenter'd recompense,
Triumphant where it dares defy,
And making Death a Victory.

from *Don Juan*

CVIII

THERE, breathless, with his digging nails he clung
    Fast to the sand, lest the returning wave,
From whose reluctant roar his life he wrung,
    Should suck him back to her insatiate grave:
And there he lay, full length, where he was flung,
    Before the entrance of a cliff-worn cave,
With just enough of life to feel its pain,
And deem that it was saved, perhaps in vain.

CIX

With slow and staggering effort he arose,
    But sunk again upon his bleeding knee
And quivering hand; and then he look'd for those
    Who long had been his mates upon the sea;
But none of them appear'd to share his woes,
    Save one, a corpse, from out the famish'd three,
Who died two days before, and now had found
An unknown barren beach for burial-ground.

CX

And as he gazed, his dizzy brain spun fast,
    And down he sunk; and as he sunk, the sand
Swam round and round, and all his senses pass'd:
    He fell upon his side, and his stretch'd hand
Droop'd dripping on the oar (their jury-mast),
    And, like a wither'd lily, on the land
His slender frame and pallid aspect lay,
As fair a thing as e'er was form'd of clay.

CXI

How long in his damp trance young Juan lay
  He knew not, for the earth was gone for him,
And time had nothing more of night nor day
  For his congealing blood, and senses dim;
And how this heavy faintness pass'd away
  He knew not, till each painful pulse and limb,
And tingling vein, seem'd throbbing back to life,
For Death, though vanquish'd, still retired with strife.

CXII

His eyes he open'd, shut, again unclosed,
  For all was doubt and dizziness; he thought
He still was in the boat, and had but dozed,
  And felt again with his despair o'erwrought,
And wish'd it death in which he had reposed,
  And then once more his feelings back were brought,
And slowly by his swimming eyes was seen
A lovely female face of seventeen.

CXIII

'Twas bending close o'er his, and the small mouth
  Seem'd almost prying into his for breath;
And chafing him, the soft warm hand of youth
  Recall'd his answering spirits back from death;
And, bathing his chill temples, tried to soothe
  Each pulse to animation, till beneath
Its gentle touch and trembling care, a sigh
To these kind efforts made a low reply.

CXIV

Then was the cordial pour'd, and mantle flung
  Around his scarce-clad limbs; and the fair arm
Raised higher the faint head which o'er it hung;
  And her transparent cheek, all pure and warm,
Pillow'd his death-like forehead; then she wrung
  His dewy curls, long drench'd by every storm;
And watch'd with eagerness each throb that drew
A sigh from his heaved bosom—and hers, too.

CXV

And lifting him with care into the cave,
  The gentle girl, and her attendant,—one
Young, yet her elder, and of brow less grave,

And more robust of figure—then begun
To kindle fire, and as the new flames gave
   Light to the rocks that roof'd them, which the sun
Had never seen, the maid, or whatsoe'er
She was, appear'd distinct, and tall, and fair.

CXVI

Her brow was overhung with coins of gold,
   That sparkled o'er the auburn of her hair,
Her clustering hair, whose longer locks were roll'd
   In braids behind; and though her stature were
Even of the highest for a female mould,
   They nearly reach'd her heel; and in her air
There was a something which bespoke command,
As one who was a lady in the land.

CXVII

Her hair, I said, was auburn; but her eyes
   Were black as death, their lashes the same hue,
Of downcast length, in whose silk shadow lies
   Deepest attraction; for when to the view
Forth from its raven fringe the full glance flies,
   Ne'er with such force the swiftest arrow flew;
'Tis as the snake late coil'd, who pours his length,
And hurls at once his venom and his strength.

CXVIII

Her brow was white and low, her cheek's pure dye
   Like twilight rosy still with the set sun;
Short upper lip—sweet lips! that make us sigh
   Ever to have seen such; for she was one
Fit for the model of a statuary
   (A race of mere impostors, when all's done—
I've seen much finer women, ripe and real,
Than all the nonsense of their stone ideal).

CXIX

I'll tell you why I say so, for 'tis just
   One should not rail without a decent cause:
There was an Irish lady, to whose bust
   I ne'er saw justice done, and yet she was
A frequent model; and if e'er she must
   Yield to stern Time and Nature's wrinkling laws,
They will destroy a face which mortal thought
Ne'er compass'd, nor less mortal chisel wrought.

CXX

And such was she, the lady of the cave:
 Her dress was very different from the Spanish,
Simpler, and yet of colours not so grave;
 For, as you know, the Spanish women banish
Bright hues when out of doors, and yet, while wave
 Around them (what I hope will never vanish)
The basquina and the mantilla, they
Seem at the same time mystical and gay.

CXXI

But with our damsel this was not the case:
 Her dress was many-colour'd, finely spun;
Her locks curl'd negligently round her face,
 But through them gold and gems profusely shone:
Her girdle sparkled, and the richest lace
 Flow'd in her veil, and many a precious stone
Flash'd on her little hand; but, what was shocking,
Her small snow feet had slippers, but no stocking.

CXXII

The other female's dress was not unlike,
 But of inferior materials: she
Had not so many ornaments to strike,
 Her hair had silver only, bound to be
Her dowry; and her veil, in form alike,
 Was coarser; and her air, though firm, less free;
Her hair was thicker, but less long; her eyes
As black, but quicker, and of smaller size.

CXXIII

And these two tended him, and cheer'd him both
 With food and raiment, and those soft attentions,
Which are—(as I must own)—of female growth,
 And have ten thousand delicate inventions:
They made a most superior mess of broth,
 A thing which poesy but seldom mentions,
But the best dish that e'er was cook'd since Homer's
Achilles order'd dinner for new comers.

* * *

CXLVII

For still he lay, and on his thin worn cheek
   A purple hectic play'd like dying day
On the snow-tops of distant hills; the streak
   Of sufferance yet upon his forehead lay,
Where the blue veins look'd shadowy, shrunk, and weak;
   And his black curls were dewy with the spray,
Which weigh'd upon them yet, all damp and salt,
Mix'd with the stony vapours of the vault.

CXLVIII

And she bent o'er him, and he lay beneath,
   Hush'd as the babe upon its mother's breast,
Droop'd as the willow when no winds can breathe,
   Lull'd like the depth of ocean when at rest,
Fair as the crowning rose of the whole wreath,
   Soft as the callow cygnet in its nest;
In short, he was a very pretty fellow,
Although his woes had turn'd him rather yellow.

CXLIX

He woke and gazed, and would have slept again,
   But the fair face which met his eyes forbade
Those eyes to close, though weariness and pain
   Had further sleep a further pleasure made;
For woman's face was never form'd in vain
   For Juan, so that even when he pray'd
He turn'd from grisly saints, and martyrs hairy,
To the sweet portraits of the Virgin Mary.

CL

And thus upon his elbow he arose,
   And look'd upon the lady, in whose cheek
The pale contended with the purple rose,
   As with an effort she began to speak;
Her eyes were eloquent, her words would pose,
   Although she told him, in good modern Greek,
With an Ionian accent, low and sweet,
That he was faint, and must not talk, but eat.

CLI

Now Juan could not understand a word,
   Being no Grecian; but he had an ear,

And her voice was the warble of a bird,
    So soft, so sweet, so delicately clear,
That finer, simpler music ne'er was heard;
    The sort of sound we echo with a tear,
Without knowing why—an overpowering tone,
Whence melody descends as from a throne.

CLII

And Juan gazed as one who is awoke
    By a distant organ, doubting if he be
Not yet a dreamer, till the spell is broke
    By the watchman, or some such reality,
Or by one's early valet's cursed knock;
    At least it is a heavy sound to me,
Who like a morning slumber—for the night
Shows stars and women in a better light.

CLIII

And Juan, too, was help'd out from his dream,
    Or sleep, or whatsoe'er it was, by feeling
A most prodigious appetite; the steam
    Of Zoe's cookery no doubt was stealing
Upon his senses, and the kindling beam
    Of the new fire, which Zoe kept up, kneeling,
To stir her viands, made him quite awake
And long for food, but chiefly a beef-steak.

CLIV

But beef is rare within these oxless isles;
    Goat's flesh there is, no doubt, and kid, and mutton,
And, when a holiday upon them smiles,
    A joint upon their barbarous spits they put on:
But this occurs but seldom, between whiles,
    For some of these are rocks with scarce a hut on;
Others are fair and fertile, among which
This, though not large, was one of the most rich.

CLV

I say that beef is rare, and can't help thinking
    That the old fable of the Minotaur—
From which our modern morals, rightly shrinking,
    Condemn the royal lady's taste who wore
A cow's shape for a mask—was only (sinking

The allegory) a mere type, no more,
That Pasiphae promoted breeding cattle,
To make the Cretans bloodier in battle.

CLVI

For we all know that English people are
    Fed upon beef—I won't say much of beer,
Because 'tis liquor only, and being far
    From this my subject, has no business here;
We know, too, they are very fond of war,
    A pleasure—like all pleasures—rather dear;
So were the Cretans—from which I infer
That beef and battles both were owing to her.

CLVII

But to resume. The languid Juan raised
    His head upon his elbow, and he saw
A sight on which he had not lately gazed,
    As all his latter meals had been quite raw,
Three or four things, for which the Lord he praised,
    And, feeling still the famish'd vulture gnaw,
He fell upon whate'er was offer'd, like
A priest, a shark, an alderman, or pike.

CLVIII

He ate, and he was well supplied; and she,
    Who watch'd him like a mother, would have fed
Him past all bounds, because she smiled to see
    Such appetite in one she had deem'd dead:
But Zoe, being older than Haidée,
    Knew (by tradition, for she ne'er had read)
That famish'd people must be slowly nurst,
And fed by spoonfuls, else they always burst.

CLIX

And so she took the liberty to state,
    Rather by deeds than words, because the case
Was urgent, that the gentleman, whose fate
    Had made her mistress quit her bed to trace
The sea-shore at this hour, must leave his plate,
    Unless he wish'd to die upon the place—
She snatch'd it, and refused another morsel,
Saying, he had gorged enough to make a horse ill.

CLX

Next they—he being naked, save a tatter'd
  Pair of scarce decent trowsers—went to work,
And in the fire his recent rags they scatter'd,
  And dress'd him, for the present, like a Turk,
Or Greek—that is, although it not much matter'd,
  Omitting turban, slippers, pistols, dirk,—
They furnish'd him, entire, except some stitches,
With a clean shirt, and very spacious breeches.

* * *

CLXXI

When Juan woke he found some good things ready,
  A bath, a breakfast, and the finest eyes
That ever made a youthful heart less steady,
  Besides her maid's, as pretty for their size;
But I have spoken of all this already—
  And repetition's tiresome and unwise,—
Well—Juan, after bathing in the sea,
Came always back to coffee and Haidée.

CLXXII

Both were so young, and one so innocent,
  That bathing pass'd for nothing: Juan seem'd
To her, as 'twere, the kind of being sent,
  Of whom these two years she had nightly dream'd,
A something to be loved, a creature meant
  To be her happiness, and whom she deem'd
To render happy: all who joy would win
Must share it,—Happiness was born a twin.

CLXXIII

It was such pleasure to behold him, such
  Enlargement of existence to partake
Nature with him, to thrill beneath his touch,
  To watch him slumbering, and to see him wake;
To live with him for ever were too much;
  But then the thought of parting made her quake:
He was her own, her ocean-treasure, cast
Like a rich wreck—her first love, and her last.

* * *

CLXXXIII

It was the cooling hour, just when the rounded
   Red sun sinks down behind the azure hill,
Which then seems as if the whole earth it bounded,
   Circling all nature, hush'd, and dim, and still,
With the far mountain-crescent half surrounded
   On one side, and the deep sea calm and chill,
Upon the other, and the rosy sky,
With one star sparkling through it like an eye.

CLXXXIV

And thus they wander'd forth, and hand in hand,
   Over the shining pebbles and the shells,
Glided along the smooth and harden'd sand,
   And in the worn and wild receptacles
Work'd by the storms, yet work'd as it were plann'd,
   In hollow halls, with sparry roofs and cells,
They turn'd to rest; and, each clasp'd by an arm,
Yielded to the deep twilight's purple charm.

CLXXXV

They look'd up to the sky, whose floating glow
   Spread like a rosy ocean, vast and bright;
They gazed upon the glittering sea below,
   Whence the broad moon rose circling into sight;
They heard the waves splash, and the wind so low,
   And saw each other's dark eyes darting light
Into each other—and, beholding this,
Their lips drew near, and clung into a kiss;

CLXXXVI

A long, long kiss, a kiss of youth, and love,
   And beauty, all concentrating like rays
Into one focus, kindled from above;
   Such kisses as belong to early days,
Where heart, and soul, and sense, in concert move,
   And the blood's lava, and the pulse a blaze,
Each kiss a heart-quake,—for a kiss's strength,
I think it must be reckon'd by its length.

CLXXXVII

By length I mean duration; theirs endured
   Heaven knows how long—no doubt they never reckon'd;
And if they had, they could not have secured

The sum of their sensations to a second:
They had not spoken; but they felt allured,
   As if their souls and lips each other beckon'd,
Which, being join'd, like swarming bees they clung—
Their hearts the flowers from whence the honey sprung.

CLXXXVIII

They were alone, but not alone as they
   Who shut in chambers think it loneliness;
The silent ocean, and the starlight bay,
   The twilight glow, which momently grew less,
The voiceless sands, and dropping caves, that lay
   Around them, made them to each other press,
As if there were no life beneath the sky
Save theirs, and that their life could never die.

CLXXXIX

They fear'd no eyes nor ears on that lone beach,
   They felt no terrors from the night; they were
All in all to each other; though their speech
   Was broken words, they *thought* a language there,—
And all the burning tongues the passions teach
   Found in one sigh the best interpreter
Of nature's oracle—first love,—that all
Which Eve has left her daughters since her fall.

CXC

Haidée spoke not of scruples, ask'd no vows,
   Nor offer'd any; she had never heard
Of plight and promises to be a spouse,
   Or perils by a loving maid incurr'd;
She was all which pure ignorance allows,
   And flew to her young mate like a young bird,
And never having dreamt of falsehood, she
Had not one word to say of constancy.

CXCI

She loved, and was beloved—she adored,
   And she was worshipp'd; after nature's fashion,
Their intense souls, into each other pour'd,
   If souls could die, had perish'd in that passion,—
But by degrees their senses were restored,
   Again to be o'ercome, again to dash on;
And, beating 'gainst *his* bosom, Haidée's heart
Felt as if never more to beat apart.

CXCII

Alas! they were so young, so beautiful,
　　So lonely, loving, helpless, and the hour
Was that in which the heart is always full,
　　And, having o'er itself no further power,
Prompts deeds eternity cannot annul,
　　But pays off moments in an endless shower
Of hell-fire—all prepared for people giving
Pleasure or pain to one another living.

CXCIII

Alas! for Juan and Haidée! they were
　　So loving and so lovely—till then never,
Excepting our first parents, such a pair
　　Had run the risk of being damn'd for ever;
And Haidée, being devout as well as fair,
　　Had, doubtless, heard about the Stygian river,
And hell and purgatory—but forgot
Just in the very crisis she should not.

CXCIV

They look upon each other, and their eyes
　　Gleam in the moonlight; and her white arm clasps
Round Juan's head, and his around her lies
　　Half buried in the tresses which it grasps;
She sits upon his knee, and drinks his sighs,
　　He hers, until they end in broken gasps;
And thus they form a group that's quite antique,
Half naked, loving, natural, and Greek.

CXCV

And when those deep and burning moments pass'd,
　　And Juan sunk to sleep within her arms,
She slept not, but all tenderly, though fast,
　　Sustain'd his head upon her bosom's charms;
And now and then her eye to heaven is cast,
　　And then on the pale cheek her breast now warms,
Pillow'd on her o'erflowing heart, which pants
With all it granted, and with all it grants.

CXCVI

An infant when it gazes on a light,
　　A child the moment when it drains the breast,
A devotee when soars the Host in sight,

An Arab with a stranger for a guest,
A sailor when the prize has struck in fight,
  A miser filling his most hoarded chest,
Feel rapture; but not such true joy are reaping
As they who watch o'er what they love while sleeping.

*   *   *

from *Canto III*

1

The isles of Greece, the isles of Greece!
  Where burning Sappho loved and sung,
Where grew the arts of war and peace,
  Where Delos rose, and Phœbus sprung!
Eternal summer gilds them yet,
But all, except their sun, is set.

2

The Scian and the Teian muse,
  The hero's harp, the lover's lute,
Have found the fame your shores refuse:
  Their place of birth alone is mute
To sounds which echo further west
Than your sires' 'Islands of the Blest.'

3

The mountains look on Marathon—
  And Marathon looks on the sea;
And musing there an hour alone,
  I dream'd that Greece might still be free;
For standing on the Persians' grave,
I could not deem myself a slave.

4

A king sate on the rocky brow
  Which looks o'er sea-born Salamis;
And ships, by thousands, lay below,
  And men in nations;—all were his!
He counted them at break of day—
And when the sun set where were they?

from *Canto IX*

I

OH, Wellington (or 'Vilainton'—for Fame
 Sounds the heroic syllables both ways;
France could not even conquer your great name,
 But punn'd it down to this facetious phrase—
Beating or beaten she will laugh the same)
 You have obtain'd great pensions and much praise:
Glory like yours should any dare gainsay,
Humanity would rise, and thunder 'Nay!'

II

I don't think that you used Kinnaird quite well
 In Marinet's affair—in fact 'twas shabby,
And like some other things won't do to tell
 Upon your tomb in Westminster's old abbey,
Upon the rest 'tis not worth while to dwell,
 Such tales being for the tea-hours of some tabby;
But though your years as *man* tend fast to *zero*,
In fact your grace is still but a *young hero*.

III

Though Britain owes (and pays you too) so much
 Yet Europe's doubtless owes you greatly more:
You have repair'd Legitimacy's crutch,
 A prop not quite so certain as before:
The Spanish, and the French, as well as Dutch,
 Have seen, and felt, how strongly you *restore*;
And Waterloo has made the world your debtor
(I wish your bards would sing it rather better).

IV

You are 'the best of cut-throats':—do not start;
 The phrase is Shakspeare's, and not misapplied:—
War's a brain-spattering, windpipe-slitting art,
 Unless her cause by right be sanctified.
If you have acted *once* a generous part,
 The world, not the world's masters, will decide,
And I shall be delighted to learn who,
Save you and yours, have gain'd by Waterloo?

V

I am no flatterer—you've supp'd full of flattery:
   They say you like it too—'tis no great wonder.
He whose whole life has been assault and battery,
   At last may get a little tired of thunder;
And swallowing eulogy much more than satire, he
   May like being praised for every lucky blunder,
Call'd 'Saviour of the Nations'—not yet saved,
And 'Europe's Liberator'—still enslaved.

VI

I've done. Now go and dine from off the plate
   Presented by the Prince of the Brazils,
And send the sentinel before your gate
   A slice or two from your luxurious meals:
He fought, but has not fed so well of late.
   Some hunger, too, they say the people feels:—
There is no doubt that you deserve your ration,
But pray give back a little to the nation.

VII

I don't mean to reflect—a man so great as
   You, my lord duke! is far above reflection:
The high Roman fashion, too, of Cincinnatus,
   With modern history has but small connexion:
Though as an Irishman you love potatoes,
   You need not take them under your direction;
And half a million for your Sabine farm
Is rather dear!—I'm sure I mean no harm.

VIII

Great men have always scorn'd great recompenses:
   Epaminondas saved his Thebes, and died,
Not leaving even his funeral expenses:
   George Washington had thanks, and nought beside,
Except the all-cloudless glory (which few men's is)
   To free his country: Pitt too had his pride,
And as a high-soul'd minister of state is
Renown'd for ruining Great Britain gratis.

IX

Never had mortal man such opportunity,
   Except Napoleon, or abused it more:
You might have freed fallen Europe from the unity

Of tyrants, and been blest from shore to shore:
And *now*—what *is* your fame? Shall the Muse tune it ye?
    Now—that the rabble's first vain shouts are o'er?
Go! hear it in your famish'd country's cries!
Behold the world! and curse your victories!

The Vision of Judgment

I

SAINT PETER sat by the celestial gate:
    His keys were rusty, and the lock was dull,
So little trouble had been given of late;
    Not that the place by any means was full,
But since the Gallic era 'eighty-eight'
    The devils had ta'en a longer, stronger pull,
And 'a pull altogether,' as they say
At sea—which drew most souls another way.

II

The angels all were singing out of tune,
    And hoarse with having little else to do,
Excepting to wind up the sun and moon,
    Or curb a runaway young star or two,
Or wild colt of a comet, which too soon
    Broke out of bounds o'er th' ethereal blue,
Splitting some planet with its playful tail,
As boats are sometimes by a wanton whale.

III

The guardian seraphs had retired on high,
    Finding their charges past all care below;
Terrestrial business fill'd nought in the sky
    Save the recording angel's black bureau;
Who found, indeed, the facts to multiply
    With such rapidity of vice and woe,
That he had stripp'd off both his wings in quills,
And yet was in arrear of human ills.

IV

His business so augmented of late years,
    That he was forced, against his will no doubt,
(Just like those cherubs, earthly ministers,)

For some resource to turn himself about,
And claim the help of his celestial peers,
   To aid him ere he should be quite worn out
By the increased demand for his remarks:
Six angels and twelve saints were named his clerks.

V

This was a handsome board—at least for heaven;
   And yet they had even then enough to do,
So many conquerors' cars were daily driven,
   So many kingdoms fitted up anew;
Each day too slew its thousands six or seven,
   Till at the crowning carnage, Waterloo,
They threw their pens down in divine disgust—
The page was so besmear'd with blood and dust.

VI

This by the way; 'tis not mine to record
   What angels shrink from: even the very devil
On this occasion his own work abhorr'd,
   So surfeited with the infernal revel:
Though he himself had sharpen'd every sword,
   It almost quench'd his innate thirst of evil.
(Here Satan's sole good work deserves insertion—
'Tis, that he has both generals in reversion.)

VII

Let's skip a few short years of hollow peace,
   Which peopled earth no better, hell as wont,
And heaven none—they form the tyrant's lease,
   With nothing but new names subscribed upon't;
'Twill one day finish: meantime they increase,
   'With seven heads and ten horns,' and all in front,
Like Saint John's foretold beast; but ours are born
Less formidable in the head than horn.

VIII

In the first year of freedom's second dawn
   Died George the Third; although no tyrant, one
Who shielded tyrants, till each sense withdrawn
   Left him nor mental nor external sun:
A better farmer ne'er brush'd dew from lawn,
   A worse king never left a realm undone!
He died—but left his subjects still behind,
One half as mad—and t'other no less blind.

397

IX

He died! his death made no great stir on earth:
    His burial made some pomp; there was profusion
Of velvet, gilding, brass, and no great dearth
    Of aught but tears—save those shed by collusion.
For these things may be bought at their true worth;
    Of elegy there was the due infusion—
Bought also; and the torches, cloaks, and banners,
Heralds, and relics of old Gothic manners,

X

Form'd a sepulchral melodrame. Of all
    The fools who flock'd to swell or see the show,
Who cared about the corpse? The funeral
    Made the attraction, and the black the woe.
There throbb'd not there a thought which pierced the pall;
    And when the gorgeous coffin was laid low,
It seem'd the mockery of hell to fold
The rottenness of eighty years in gold.

XI

So mix his body with the dust! It might
    Return to what it *must* far sooner, were
The natural compound left alone to fight
    Its way back into earth, and fire, and air;
But the unnatural balsams merely blight
    What nature made him at his birth, as bare
As the mere million's base unmummied clay—
Yet all his spices but prolong decay.

XII

He's dead—and upper earth with him was done;
    He's buried; save the undertaker's bill,
Or lapidary scrawl, the world is gone
    For him, unless he left a German will:
But where's the proctor who will ask his son?
    In whom his qualities are reigning still:
Except that household virtue, most uncommon,
Of constancy to a bad, ugly woman.

XIII

'God save the king!' It is a large economy
    In God to save the like; but if he will
Be saving, all the better; for not one am I

398

Of those who think damnation better still;
I hardly know too if not quite alone am I
  In this small hope of bettering future ill
By circumscribing, with some slight restriction,
The eternity of hell's hot jurisdiction.

XIV

I know this is unpopular; I know
  'Tis blasphemous; I know one may be damn'd
For hoping no one else may e'er be so;
  I know my catechism; I know we're cramm'd
With the best doctrines till we quite o'er-flow;
  I know that all save England's church have shamm'd,
And that the other twice two hundred churches
And synagogues have made a *damn'd* bad purchase.

XV

God help us all! God help me too! I am,
  God knows, as helpless as the devil can wish,
And not a whit more difficult to damn,
  Than is to bring to land a late-hook'd fish,
Or to the butcher to purvey the lamb;
  Not that I'm fit for such a noble dish,
As one day will be that immortal fry
Of almost everybody born to die.

XVI

Saint Peter sat by the celestial gate,
  And nodded o'er his keys; when, lo! there came
A wonderous noise he had not heard of late—
  A rushing sound of wind, and stream, and flame;
In short, a roar of things extremely great,
  Which would have made aught save a saint exclaim;
But he, with first a start and then a wink,
Said, 'There's another star gone out, I think!'

XVII

But ere he could return to his repose,
  A cherub flapp'd his right wing o'er his eyes—
At which St. Peter yawn'd, and rubb'd his nose:
  'Saint porter,' said the angel, 'prithee rise!'
Waving a goodly wing, which glow'd, as glows
  An earthly peacock's tail, with heavenly dyes:
To which the saint replied, 'Well, what's the matter?
'Is Lucifer come back with all this clatter?'

XVIII

'No,' quoth the cherub; 'George the Third is dead.'
    'And who *is* George the Third?' replied the apostle:
'What George? what Third?' 'The king of England,' said
    The angel. 'Well! he won't find kings to jostle
Him on his way; but does he wear his head?
    Because the last we saw here had a tustle,
And ne'er would have got into heaven's good graces,
Had he not flung his head in all our faces.

XIX

'He was, if I remember, king of France;
    That head of his, which could not keep a crown
On earth, yet ventured in my face to advance
    A claim to those of martyrs—like my own:
If I had had my sword, as I had once
    When I cut ears off, I had cut him down;
But having, but my *keys*, and not my brand,
I only knock'd his head from out his hand.

XX

'And then he set up such a headless howl,
    That all the saints came out and took him in;
And there he sits by St. Paul, cheek by jowl;
    That fellow Paul—the parvenù! The skin
Of St. Bartholomew, which makes his cowl
    In heaven, and upon earth redeem'd his sin,
So as to make a martyr, never sped
Better than did this weak and wooden head.

XXI

'But had it come up here upon its shoulders,
    There would have been a different tale to tell:
The fellow-feeling in the saint's beholders
    Seems to have acted on them like a spell,
And so this very foolish head heaven solders
    Back on its trunk: it may be very well,
And seems the custom here to overthrow
Whatever has been wisely done below.'

XXII

The angel answer'd, 'Peter! do not pout:
    The king who comes has head and all entire,
And never knew much what it was about—

He did as doth the puppet—by its wire,
And will be judged like all the rest, no doubt:
    My business and your own is not to inquire
Into such matters, but to mind our cue—
Which is to act as we are bid to do.'

XXIII

While thus they spake, the angelic caravan,
    Arriving like a rush of mighty wind,
Cleaving the fields of space, as doth the swan
    Some silver stream (say Ganges, Nile, or Inde,
Or Thames, or Tweed), and 'midst them an old man
    With an old soul, and both extremely blind,
Halted before the gate, and in his shroud
Seated their fellow traveller on a cloud.

XXIV

But bringing up the rear of this bright host
    A Spirit of a different aspect waved
His wings, like thunder-clouds above some coast
    Whose barren beach with frequent wrecks is paved;
His brow was like the deep when tempest-toss'd;
    Fierce and unfathomable thoughts engraved
Eternal wrath on his immortal face,
And *where* he gazed a gloom pervaded space.

XXV

As he drew near, he gazed upon the gate
    Ne'er to be enter'd more by him or Sin,
With such a glance of supernatural hate,
    As made Saint Peter wish himself within;
He potter'd with his keys at a great rate,
    And sweated through his apostolic skin:
Of course his perspiration was but ichor,
Or some such other spiritual liquor.

XXVI

The very cherubs huddled all together,
    Like birds when soars the falcon; and they felt
A tingling to the tip of every feather,
    And form'd a circle like Orion's belt
Around their poor old charge; who scarce knew whither
    His guards had led him, though they gently dealt
With royal manes (for by many stories,
And true, we learn the angels all the Tories).

XXVII

As things were in this posture, the gate flew
  Asunder, and the flashing of its hinges
Flung over space an universal hue
  Of many-colour'd flame, until it tinges
Reach'd even our speck of earth, and made a new
  Aurora borealis spread its fringes
O'er the North Pole; the same seen, when ice-bound,
By Captain Parry's crew, in 'Melville's Sound.'

XXVIII

And from the gate thrown open issued beaming
  A beautiful and mighty Thing of Light,
Radiant with glory, like a banner streaming
  Victorious from some world-o'erthrowing fight:
My poor comparisons must needs be teeming
  With earthly likenesses, for here the night
Of clay obscures our best conceptions, saving
Johanna Southcote, or Bob Southey raving.

XXIX

'Twas the archangel Michael; all men know
  The make of angels and archangels, since
There's scarce a scribbler has not one to show,
  From the fiends' leader to the angels' prince;
There also are some altar-pieces, though
  I really can't say that they much evince
One's inner notions of immortal spirits;
But let the connoisseurs explain *their* merits.

XXX

Michael flew forth in glory and in good;
  A goodly work of him from whom all glory
And good arise; the portal past—he stood;
  Before him the young cherubs and saints hoary—
(I say *young*, begging to be understood
  By looks, not years; and should be very sorry
To state, they were not older than St. Peter,
But merely that they seem'd a little sweeter.)

XXXI

The cherubs and the saints bow'd down before
  That arch-angelic hierarch, the first
Of essences angelical, who wore

The aspect of a god; but this ne'er nursed
Pride in his heavenly bosom, in whose core
   No thought, save for his Master's service, durst
Intrude, however glorified and high;
He knew him but the viceroy of the sky.

XXXII

He and the sombre, silent Spirit met—
   They knew each other both for good and ill;
Such was their power, that neither could forget
   His former friend and future foe; but still
There was a high, immortal, proud regret
   In either's eye, as if 'twere less their will
Than destiny to make the eternal years
Their date of war, and their 'champ clos' the spheres.

XXXIII

But here they were in neutral space: we know
   From Job, that Satan hath the power to pay
A heavenly visit thrice a year or so;
   And that the 'sons of God', like those of clay,
Must keep him company; and we might show
   From the same book, in how polite a way
The dialogue is held between the Powers
Of Good and Evil—but 'twould take up hours.

XXXIV

And this is not a theologic tract,
   To prove with Hebrew and with Arabic,
If Job be allegory or a fact,
   But a true narrative; and thus I pick
From out the whole but such and such an act
   As sets aside the slightest thought of trick.
'Tis every tittle true, beyond suspicion,
And accurate as any other vision.

XXXV

The spirits were in neutral space, before
   The gate of heaven; like eastern thresholds is
The place where Death's grand cause is argued o'er,
   And souls despatch'd to that world or to this;
And therefore Michael and the other wore
   A civil aspect: though they did not kiss,
Yet still between his Darkness and his Brightness
There pass'd a mutual glance of great politeness.

XXXVI

The Archangel bow'd, not like a modern beau,
  But with a graceful Oriental bend,
Pressing one radiant arm just where below
  The heart in good men is supposed to tend;
He turn'd as to an equal, not too low,
  But kindly; Satan met his ancient friend
With more hauteur, as might an old Castilian
Poor noble meet a mushroom rich civilian.

XXXVII

He merely bent his diabolic brow
  An instant; and then raising it, he stood
In act to assert his right or wrong, and show
  Cause why King George by no means could or should
Make out a case to be exempt from woe
  Eternal, more than other kings, endued
With better sense and hearts, whom history mentions,
Who long have 'paved hell with their good intentions.'

XXXVIII

Michael began: 'What wouldst thou with this man,
  Now dead, and brought before the Lord? What ill
Hath he wrought since his mortal race began,
  That thou canst claim him? Speak! and do thy will,
If it be just: if in this earthly span
  He hath been greatly failing to fulfil
His duties as a king and mortal, say,
And he is thine; if not, let him have way.'

XXXIX

'Michael!' replied the Prince of Air, 'even here,
  Before the Gate of him thou servest, must
I claim my subject: and will make appear
  That as he was my worshipper in dust,
So shall he be in spirit, although dear
  To thee and thine, because nor wine nor lust
Were of his weaknesses; yet on the throne
He reign'd o'er millions to serve me alone.

XL

'Look to *our* earth, or rather *mine*; it was,
  Once, more thy master's: but I triumph not
In this poor planet's conquest; nor, alas!

Need he thou servest envy me my lot:
With all the myriads of bright worlds which pass
    In worship round him, he may have forgot
Yon weak creation of such paltry things:
I think few worth damnation save their kings,—

XLI

'And these but as a kind of quit-rent, to
    Assert my right as lord: and even had
I such an inclination, 'twere (as you
    Well know) superfluous; they are grown so bad,
That hell has nothing better left to do
    Than leave them to themselves: so much more mad
And evil by their own internal curse,
Heaven cannot make them better, nor I worse.

XLII

'Look to the earth, I said, and say again:
    When this old, blind, mad, helpless, weak, poor worm
Began in youth's first bloom and flush to reign,
    The world and he both wore a different form,
And much of earth and all the watery plain
    Of ocean call'd him king: through many a storm
His isles had floated on the abyss of time;
For the rough virtues chose them for their clime.

XLIII

'He came to his sceptre young; he leaves it old:
    Look to the state in which he found his realm,
And left it; and his annals too behold,
    How to a minion first he gave the helm;
How grew upon his heart a thirst for gold,
    The beggar's vice, which can but overwhelm
The meanest hearts; and for the rest, but glance
Thine eye along America and France.

XLIV

''Tis true, he was a tool from first to last
    (I have the workmen safe); but as a tool
So let him be consumed. From out the past
    Of ages, since mankind have known the rule
Of monarchs—from the bloody rolls amass'd
    Of sin and slaughter—from the Cæsar's school,
Take the worst pupil; and produce a reign
More drench'd with gore, more cumber'd with the slain.

XLV

'He ever warr'd with freedom and the free:
    Nations as men, home subjects, foreign foes,
So that they utter'd the word "Liberty!"
    Found George the Third their first opponent. Whose
History was ever stain'd as his will be
    With national and individual woes?
I grant his household abstinence; I grant
His neutral virtues, which most monarchs want;

XLVI

'I know he was a constant consort; own
    He was a decent sire, and middling lord.
All this is much, and most upon a throne;
    As temperance, if at Apicius' board,
Is more than at an anchorite's supper shown.
    I grant him all the kindest can accord;
And this was well for him, but not for those
Millions who found him what oppression chose.

XLVII

'The New World shook him off; the Old yet groans
    Beneath what he and his prepared, if not
Completed: he leaves heirs on many thrones
    To all his vices, without what begot
Compassion for him—his tame virtues; drones
    Who sleep, or despots who have now forgot
A lesson which shall be re-taught them, wake
Upon the thrones of earth; but let them quake!

XLVIII

'Five millions of the primitive, who hold
    The faith which makes ye great on earth, implored
A *part* of that vast *all* they held of old,—
    Freedom to worship—not alone your Lord,
Michael, but you, and you, Saint Peter! Cold
    Must be your souls, if you have not abhorr'd
The foe to Catholic participation
In all the license of a Christian nation.

XLIX

'True! he allow'd them to pray God; but as
    A consequence of prayer, refused the law
Which would have placed them upon the same base

With those who did not hold the saints in awe.'
But here Saint Peter started from his place,
  And cried, 'You may the prisoner withdraw:
Ere heaven shall ope her portals to this Guelph,
While I am guard, may I be damn'd myself!

L

'Sooner will I with Cerberus exchange
  My office (and *his* is no sinecure)
Than see this royal Bedlam bigot range
  The azure fields of heaven, of that be sure!'
'Saint!' replied Satan, 'you do well to avenge
  The wrongs he made your satellites endure;
And if to this exchange you should be given,
I'll try to coax *our* Cerberus up to heaven!'

LI

Here Michael interposed: 'Good saint! and devil!
  Pray, not so fast; you both outrun discretion.
Saint Peter! you were wont to be more civil!
  Satan! excuse this warmth of his expression,
And condescension to the vulgar's level:
  Even saints sometimes forget themselves in session.
Have you got more to say?'—'No.'—If you please,
I'll trouble you to call your witnesses.'

LII

Then Satan turn'd and waved his swarthy hand,
  Which stirr'd with its electric qualities
Clouds farther off than we can understand,
  Although we find him sometimes in our skies;
Infernal thunder shook both sea and land
  In all the planets, and hell's batteries
Let off the artillery, which Milton mentions
As one of Satan's most sublime inventions.

LIII

This was a signal unto such damn'd souls
  As have the privilege of their damnation
Extended far beyond the mere controls
  Of worlds past, present, or to come; no station
Is theirs particularly in the rolls
  Of hell assign'd; but where their inclination
Or business carries them in search of game,
They may range freely—being damn'd the same.

407

LIV

They're proud of this—as very well they may,
   It being a sort of knighthood, or gilt key
Stuck in their loins; or like to an 'entré'
   Up the back stairs, or such freemasonry.
I borrow my comparisons from clay,
   Being clay myself. Let not those spirits be
Offended with such base low likenesses;
We know their posts are nobler far than these.

LV

When the great signal ran from heaven to hell—
   About ten million times the distance reckon'd
From our sun to its earth, as we can tell
   How much time it takes up, even to a second,
For every ray that travels to dispel
   The fogs of London, through which, dimly beacon'd,
The weathercocks are gilt some thrice a year,
If that the *summer* is not too severe:

LVI

I say that I can tell—'twas half a minute;
   I know the solar beams take up more time
Ere, pack'd up for their journey, they begin it;
   But then their telegraph is less sublime,
And if they ran a race, they would not win it
   'Gainst Satan's couriers bound for their own clime.
The sun takes up some years for every ray
To reach its goal—the devil not half a day.

LVII

Upon the verge of space, about the size
   Of half-a-crown, a little speck appear'd
(I've seen a something like it in the skies
   In the Ægean, ere a squall); it near'd,
And, growing bigger, took another guise;
   Like an aërial ship it tack'd, and steer'd,
Or *was* steer'd (I am doubtful of the grammar
Of the last phrase, which makes the stanza stammer;—

LVIII

But take your choice): and then it grew a cloud;
   And so it was—a cloud of witnesses.
But such a cloud! No land e'er saw a crowd

Of locusts numerous as the heavens saw these;
They shadow'd with their myriads space; their loud
   And varied cries were like those of wild geese
(If nations may be liken'd to a goose),
And realised the phrase of 'hell broke loose.'

LIX

Here crash'd a sturdy oath of stout John Bull,
   Who damn'd away his eyes as heretofore:
There Paddy brogued 'By Jasus!'—'What's your wull?'
The temperate Scot exclaim'd: the French ghost swore
In certain terms I shan't translate in full,
   As the first coachman will; and 'midst the roar;
The voice of Jonathan was heard to express,
'*Our* president is going to war, I guess.'

LX

Besides there were the Spaniard, Dutch, and Dane;
   In short, an universal shoal of shades,
From Otaheite's isle to Salisbury Plain,
   Of all climes and professions, years and trades,
Ready to swear against the good king's reign,
   Bitter as clubs in cards are against spades:
All summon'd by this grand 'subpœna,' to
Try if kings mayn't be damn'd like me or you.

LXI

When Michael saw this host, he first grew pale,
   As angels can; next, like Italian twilight,
He turn'd all colours—as a peacock's tail,
   Or sunset streaming through a Gothic skylight
In some old abbey, or a trout not stale,
   Or distant lightning on the horizon *by* night,
Or a fresh rainbow, or a grand review
Of thirty regiments in red, green, and blue.

LXII

Then he address'd himself to Satan: 'Why—
   My good old friend, for such I deem you, though
Our different parties make us fight so shy,
   I ne'er mistake you for a *personal* foe;
Our difference is *political*, and I
   Trust that, whatever may occur below,
You know my great respect for you: and this
Makes me regret whate'er you do amiss—

LXIII

'Why, my dear Lucifer, would you abuse
    My call for witnesses? I did not mean
That you should half of earth and hell produce;
    'Tis even superfluous, since two honest, clean,
True testimonies are enough: we lose
    Our time, nay, our eternity, between
The accusation and defence: if we
Hear both, 'twill stretch our immortality.'

LXIV

Satan replied, 'To me the matter is
    Indifferent, in a personal point of view:
I can have fifty better souls than this
    With far less trouble than we have gone through
Already; and I merely argued his
    Late majesty of Britain's case with you
Upon a point of form: you may dispose
Of him; I've kings enough below, God knows!'

LXV

Thus spoke the Demon (late call'd 'multifaced'
    By multo-scribbling Southey). 'Then we'll call
One or two persons of the myriads placed
    Around our congress, and dispense with all
The rest,' quoth Michael: 'Who may be so graced
    As to speak first? there's choice enough—who shall
It be?' Then Satan answer'd, 'There are many;
But you may choose Jack Wilkes as well as any.'

LXVI

A merry, cock-eyed, curious-looking sprite
    Upon the instant started from the throng,
Dress'd in a fashion now forgotten quite;
    For all the fashions of the flesh stick long
By people in the next world; where unite
    All the costumes since Adam's, right or wrong,
From Eve's fig-leaf down to the petticoat,
Almost as scanty, of days less remote.

LXVII

The spirit look'd around upon the crowds
    Assembled, and exclaim'd, 'My friends of all
The spheres, we shall catch cold amongst these clouds;

So let's to business: why this general call?
If those are freeholders I see in shrouds,
   And 'tis for an election that they bawl,
Behold a candidate with unturn'd coat!
Saint Peter, may I count upon your vote?'

LXVIII

'Sir,' replied Michael, 'you mistake; these things
   Are of a former life, and what we do
Above is more august; to judge of kings
   Is the tribunal met: so now you know.'
'Then I presume those gentlemen with wings,'
   Said Wilkes, 'are cherubs; and that soul below
Looks much like George the Third, but to my mind
A good deal older—Bless me! is he blind?'

LXIX

'He is what you behold him, and his doom
   Depends upon his deeds,' the Angel said;
'If you have aught to arraign in him, the tomb
   Gives licence to the humblest beggar's head
To lift itself against the loftiest.'—'Some,'
   Said Wilkes, 'don't wait to see them laid in lead,
For such a liberty—and I, for one,
Have told them what I thought beneath the sun.'

LXX

'*Above* the sun repeat, then, what thou hast
   To urge against him,' said the Archangel. 'Why,'
Replied the spirit, 'since old scores are past,
   Must I turn evidence? In faith, not I.
Besides, I beat him hollow at the last,
   With all his Lords and Commons: in the sky
I don't like ripping up old stories, since
His conduct was but natural in a prince.

LXXI

'Foolish, no doubt, and wicked, to oppress
   A poor unlucky devil without a shilling;
But then I blame the man himself much less
   Than Bute and Grafton, and shall be unwilling
To see him punish'd here for their excess,
   Since they were both damn'd long ago, and still in
Their place below: for me, I have forgiven,
And vote his "habeas corpus" into heaven.'

LXXII

'Wilkes,' said the Devil, 'I understand all this;
　　You turn'd to half a courtier ere you died,
And seem to think it would not be amiss
　　To grow a whole one on the other side
Of Charon's ferry; you forget that *his*
　　Reign is concluded; whatsoe'er betide,
He won't be sovereign more: you've lost your labour,
For at the best he will but be your neighbour.

LXXIII

'However, I knew what to think of it,
　　When I beheld you in your jesting way,
Flitting and whispering round about the spit
　　Where Belial, upon duty for the day,
With Fox's lard was basting William Pitt,
　　His pupil; I knew what to think, I say:
That fellow even in hell breeds farther ills;
I'll have him *gagg'd*—'twas one of his own bills.

LXXIV

'Call Junius!' From the crowd a shadow stalk'd,
　　And at the name there was a general squeeze,
So that the very ghosts no longer walk'd
　　In comfort, at their own aërial, ease,
But were all ramm'd, and jamm'd (but to be balk'd,
　　As we shall see), and jostled hands and knees,
Like wind compress'd and pent within a bladder,
Or like a human colic, which is sadder.

LXXV

The shadow came—a tall, thin, greyhair'd figure,
　　That look'd as it had been a shade on earth;
Quick in its motions, with an air of vigour,
　　But nought to mark its breeding or its birth;
Now it wax'd little, then again grew bigger,
　　With now an air of gloom, or savage mirth;
But as you gazed upon its features, they
Changed every instant—to *what*, none could say.

LXXVI

The more intently the ghosts gazed, the less
　　Could they distinguish whose the features were;
The Devil himself seem'd puzzled even to guess;

They varied like a dream—now here, now there;
And several people swore from out the press,
   They knew him perfectly; and one could swear
He was his father: upon which another
Was sure he was his mother's cousin's brother:

LXXVII

Another, that he was a duke, or knight,
   An orator, a lawyer, or a priest,
A nabob, a man-midwife; but the wight
   Mysterious changed his countenance at least
As oft as they their minds; though in full sight
   He stood, the puzzle only was increased;
The man was a phantasmagoria in
Himself—he was so volatile and thin.

LXXVIII

The moment that you had pronounced him *one*,
   Presto! his face changed, and he was another;
And when that change was hardly well put on,
   It varied, till I don't think his own mother
(If that he had a mother) would her son
   Have known, he shifted so from one to t'other;
Till guessing from a pleasure grew a task,
At this epistolary 'Iron Mask.'

LXXIX

For sometimes he like Cerberus would seem—
   'Three gentlemen at once' (as sagely says
Good Mrs. Malaprop); then you might deem
   That he was not even *one*; now many rays
Were flashing round him; and now a thick steam
   Hid him from sight—like fogs on London days:
Now Burke, now Tooke, he grew to people's fancies,
And certes often like Sir Philip Francis.

LXXX

I've an hypothesis—'tis quite my own;
   I never let it out till now, for fear
Of doing people harm about the throne,
   And injuring some minister or peer,
On whom the stigma might perhaps be blown;
   It is—my gentle public, lend thine ear!
'Tis, that what Junius we are wont to call
Was *really, truly* nobody at all.

413

LXXXI

I don't see wherefore letters should not be
 Written without hands, since we daily view
Them written without heads; and books, we see,
 Are fill'd as well without the latter too:
And really till we fix on somebody
 For certain sure to claim them as his due,
Their author, like the Niger's mouth, will bother
The world to say if *there* be mouth or author.

LXXXII

'And who and what art thou?' the Archangel said.
 'For *that* you may consult my title-page,'
Replied this mighty shadow of a shade:
 'If I have kept my secret half an age,
I scarce shall tell it now.'—'Canst thou upbraid,'
 Continued Michael, 'George Rex, or allege
Aught further?' Junius answer'd, 'You had better
First ask him for *his* answer to my letter:

LXXXIII

'My charges upon record will outlast
 The brass of both his epitaph and tomb.'
'Repent'st thou not,' said Michael, 'of some past
 Exaggeration? something which may doom
Thyself if false, as him if true? Thou wast
 Too bitter—is it not so?—in thy gloom
Of passion?'—'Passion!' cried the phantom dim,
'I loved my country, and I hated him.

LXXXIV

'What I have written, I have written: let
 The rest be on his head or mine!' So spoke
Old 'Nominis Umbra'; and while speaking yet,
 Away he melted in celestial smoke.
Then Satan said to Michael, 'Don't forget
 To call George Washington, and John Horne Tooke,
And Franklin;'—but at this time there was heard
A cry for room, though not a phantom stirr'd.

LXXXV

At length with jostling, elbowing, and the aid
 Of cherubim appointed to that post,
The devil Asmodeus to the circle made

His way, and look'd as if his journey cost
Some trouble. When his burden down he laid,
   'What's this?' cried Michael; 'why, 'tis not a ghost?'
'I know it,' quoth the incubus; 'but he
Shall be one, if you leave the affair to me.

LXXXVI

'Confound the renegado! I have sprain'd
   My left wing, he's so heavy; one would think
Some of his works about his neck were chain'd.
   But to the point; while hovering o'er the brink
Of Skiddaw (where as usual it still rain'd),
   I saw a taper, far below me, wink,
And stooping, caught this fellow at a libel—
No less on history than the Holy Bible.

LXXXVII

'The former is the devil's scripture, and
   The latter yours, good Michael: so the affair
Belongs to all of us, you understand.
   I snatch'd him up just as you see him there
And brought him off for sentence out of hand:
   I've scarcely been ten minutes in the air—
At least a quarter it can hardly be:
I dare say that his wife is still at tea.'

LXXXVIII

Here Satan said, 'I know this man of old,
   And have expected him for some time here;
A sillier fellow you will scarce behold,
   Or more conceited in his petty sphere:
But surely it was not worth while to fold
   Such trash below your wing, Asmodeus dear:
We had the poor wretch safe (without being bored
With carriage) coming of his own accord.

LXXXIX

'But since he's here, let's see what he has done.'
   'Done!' cried Asmodeus, 'he anticipates
The very business you are now upon,
   And scribbles as if head clerk to the Fates.
Who knows to what his ribaldry may run,
   When such an ass as this, like Balaam's, prates?'
'Let's hear,' quoth Michael, 'what he has to say:
You know we're bound to that in every way.'

XC

Now the bard, glad to get an audience, which
    By no means often was his case below,
Began to cough, and hawk, and hem, and pitch
    His voice into that awful note of woe
To all unhappy hearers within reach
    Of poets when the tide of rhyme's in flow;
But stuck fast with his first hexameter,
Not one of all whose gouty feet would stir.

XCI

But ere the spavin'd dactyls could be spurr'd
    Into recitative, in great dismay
Both cherubim and seraphim were heard
    To murmur loudly through their long array;
And Michael rose ere he could get a word
    Of all his founder'd verses under way,
And cried, 'For God's sake stop, my friend! 'twere best—
Non Di, non homines—you know the rest.'

XCII

A general bustle spread throughout the throng,
    Which seem'd to hold all verse in detestation;
The angels had of course enough of song
    When upon service; and the generation
Of ghosts had heard too much in life, not long
    Before, to profit by a new occasion;
The monarch, mute till then, exclaim'd, 'What! what!
Pye come again? No more—no more of that!'

XCIII

The tumult grew; an universal cough
    Convulsed the skies, as during a debate,
When Castlereagh has been up long enough
    (Before he was first minister of state,
I mean—the *slaves hear now*); some cried 'Off, off!'
    As at a farce; till, grown quite desperate,
The bard Saint Peter pray'd to interpose
(Himself an author) only for his prose.

XCIV

The varlet was not an ill-favour'd knave;
    A good deal like a vulture in the face,
With a hook nose and a hawk's eye, which gave

416

A smart and sharper-looking sort of grace
To his whole aspect, which, though rather grave,
  Was by no means so ugly as his case;
But that, indeed, was hopeless as can be,
Quite a poetic felony '*de se.*'

XCV

Then Michael blew his trump, and still'd the noise
  With one still greater, as is yet the mode
On earth besides; except some grumbling voice,
  Which now and then will make a slight inroad
Upon decorous silence, few will twice
  Lift up their lungs when fairly overcrow'd;
And now the bard could plead his own bad cause,
With all the attitudes of self-applause.

XCVI

He said—(I only give the heads)—he said,
  He meant no harm in scribbling; 'twas his way
Upon all topics; 'twas, besides, his bread,
  Of which he butter'd both sides; 'twould delay
Too long the assembly (he was pleased to dread),
  And take up rather more time than a day,
To name his works—he would but cite a few—
'Wat Tyler'—'Rhymes on Blenheim'—'Waterloo.'

XCVII

He had written praises of a regicide;
  He had written praises of all kings whatever;
He had written for republics far and wide,
  And then against them bitterer than ever;
For pantisocracy he once had cried
  Aloud, a scheme less moral than 'twas clever;
Then grew a hearty anti-jacobin—
Had turn'd his coat—and would have turn'd his skin.

XCVIII

He had sung against all battles, and again
  In their high praise and glory; he had call'd
Reviewing 'the ungentle craft,' and then
  Become as base a critic as e'er crawl'd—
Fed, paid, and pamper'd by the very men
  By whom his muse and morals had been maul'd;
He had written much blank verse, and blanker prose,
And more of both than anybody knows.

XCIX

He had written Wesley's life:—here turning round
    To Satan, 'Sir, I'm ready to write yours,
In two octavo volumes, nicely bound,
    With notes and preface, all that most allures
The pious purchaser; and there's no ground
    For fear, for I can choose my own reviewers:
So let me have the proper documents,
That I may add you to my other saints.'

C

Satan bow'd, and was silent. 'Well, if you,
    With amiable modesty, decline
My offer, what says Michael? There are few
    Whose memoirs could be render'd more divine
Mine is a pen of all work; not so new
    As it was once, but I would make you shine
Like your own trumpet. By the way, my own
Has more of brass in it, and is as well blown.

CI

'But talking about trumpets, here's my Vision!
    Now you shall judge, all people; yes, you shall
Judge with my judgment, and by my decision
    Be guided who shall enter heaven or fall,
I settle all these things by intuition,
    Times present, past, to come, heaven, hell, and all,
Like King Alfonso. When I thus see double,
I save the Deity some worlds of trouble.'

CII

He ceased, and drew forth an MS.; and no
    Persuasion on the part of devils, saints,
Or angels, now could stop the torrent; so
    He read the first three lines of the contents;
But at the fourth, the whole spiritual show
    Had vanish'd, with variety of scents,
Ambrosial and sulphureous, as they sprang,
Like lightning, off from his 'melodious twang.'

CIII

Those grand heroics acted as a spell:
    The angels stopp'd their ears and plied their pinions;
The devils ran howling, deafen'd, down to hell;

The ghosts fled, gibbering, for their own dominions—
(For 'tis not yet decided where they dwell,
    And I leave every man to his opinions);
Michael took refuge in his trump—but, lo!
His teeth were set on edge, he could not blow!

CIV

Saint Peter, who has hitherto been known
    For an impetuous saint, upraised his keys,
And at the fifth line knock'd the poet down;
    Who fell like Phaeton, but more at ease,
Into his lake, for there he did not drown;
    A different web being by the Destinies
Woven for the Laureate's final wreath, whene'er
Reform shall happen either here or there.

CV

He first sank to the bottom—like his works,
    But soon rose to the surface—like himself;
For all corrupted things are buoy'd like corks,
    By their own rottenness, light as an elf,
Or wisp that flits o'er a morass: he lurks,
    It may be, still, like dull books on a shelf,
In his own den, to scrawl some 'Life' or 'Vision,'
As Welborn says—'the devil turn'd precisian.'

CVI

As for the rest, to come to the conclusion
    Of this true dream, the telescope is gone
Which kept my optics free from all delusion,
    And show'd me what I in my turn have shown;
All I saw farther, in the last confusion,
    Was, that King George slipp'd into heaven for one;
And when the tumult dwindled to a calm,
I left him practising the hundredth psalm.

CHARLES WOLFE

1791–1823

The Burial of Sir John Moore at Corunna

NOT a drum was heard, not a funeral note,
  As his corpse to the rampart we hurried;
Not a soldier discharged his farewell shot
  O'er the grave where our Hero we buried.

We buried him darkly at dead of night,
  The sods with our bayonets turning;
By the struggling moonbeam's misty light
  And the lantern dimly burning.

No useless coffin enclosed his breast,
  Not in sheet or in shroud we wound him;
But he lay like a Warrior taking his rest
  With his martial cloak around him.

Few and short were the prayers we said,
  And we spoke not a word of sorrow;
But we steadfastly gazed on the face that was dead,
  And we bitterly thought of the morrow.

We thought, as we hollowed his narrow bed
  And smoothed down his lonely pillow,
That the Foe and the Stranger would tread o'er his head,
  And we far away on the billow!

Lightly they'll talk of the Spirit that's gone
  And o'er his cold ashes upbraid him,—
But little he'll reck, if they let him sleep on
  In the grave where a Briton has laid him.

But half of our heavy task was done
  When the clock struck the hour for retiring:
And we heard the distant and random gun
  That the foe was sullenly firing.

Slowly and sadly we laid him down,
  From the field of his fame fresh and gory;
We carved not a line, and we raised not a stone—
But we left him alone with his glory.

Song

Oh say not that my heart is cold
  To aught that once could warm it—
That Nature's form so dear of old
  No more has power to charm it;
Or that th' ungenerous world can chill
  One glow of fond emotion
For those who made it dearer still,
  And shared my wild devotion.

Still oft those solemn scenes I view
  In rapt and dreamy sadness;
Oft look on those who loved them too
  With Fancy's idle gladness;
Again I longed to view the light
  In Nature's features glowing;
Again to tread the mountain's height,
  And taste the soul's o'erflowing.

Stern Duty rose, and frowning flung
  His leaden chain around me;
With iron look and sullen tongue
  He muttered as he bound me—
'The mountain breeze, the boundless heaven,
  Unfit for toil the creature;
These for the free alone were given,—
  But what have slaves with Nature?'

Song: To Mary

If I had thought thou couldst have died,
  I might not weep for thee;
But I forgot, when by thy side,
  That thou couldst mortal be:
It never through my mind had past
  The time would e'er be o'er,
And I on thee should look my last,
And thou shouldst smile no more!

And still upon that face I look,
  And think 'twill smile again;
And still the thought I will not brook,
  That I must look in vain.
But when I speak—thou dost not say
  What thou ne'er left'st unsaid;
And now I fell, as well I may,
  Sweet Mary, thou art dead!

If thou wouldst stay, e'en as thou art,
  All cold and all serene—
I still might press thy silent heart,
  And where thy smiles have been.
While e'en thy chill, bleak corse I have,
  Thou seemest still mine own;
But there—I lay thee in thy grave,
  And I am now alone!

I do not think, where'er thou art,
  Thou hast forgotten me;
And I, perhaps, may soothe this heart
  In thinking too of thee:
Yet there was round thee such a dawn
  Of light ne'er seen before,
As fancy never could have drawn,
  And never can restore!

PERCY BYSSHE SHELLEY

1792–1822

The Mask of Anarchy

*Written on the occasion of the
massacre at Manchester*

I

As I lay asleep in Italy
There came a voice from over the Sea,
And with great power it forth led me
To walk in the visions of Poesy.

II

I met Murder on the way—
He had a mask like Castlereagh—
Very smooth he looked, yet grim;
Seven blood-hounds followed him:

III

All were fat; and well they might
Be in admirable plight,
For one by one, and two by two,
He tossed them human hearts to chew
Which from his wide cloak he drew.

IV

Next came Fraud, and he had on,
Like Eldon, an ermined gown;
His big tears, for he wept well,
Turned to mill-stones as they fell.

V

And the little children, who
Round his feet played to and fro,
Thinking every tear a gem,
Had their brains knocked out by them.

VI

Clothed with the Bible, as with light,
And the shadows of the night,
Like Sidmouth, next, Hypocrisy
On a crocodile rode by.

VII

And many more Destructions played
In this ghastly masquerade,
All disguised, even to the eyes,
Like Bishops, lawyers, peers, or spies.

VIII

Last came Anarchy: he rode
On a white horse, splashed with blood;
He was pale even to the lips,
Like Death in the Apocalypse.

IX

And he wore a kingly crown;
And in his grasp a sceptre shone;
On his brow this mark I saw—
'I AM GOD, AND KING, AND LAW!'

X

With a pace stately and fast,
Over English land he passed,
Trampling to a mire of blood
The adoring multitude.

XI

And a mighty troop around,
With their trampling shook the ground,
Waving each a bloody sword,
For the service of their Lord.

XII

And with glorious triumph, they
Rode through England proud and gay,
Drunk as with intoxication
Of the wine of desolation.

XIII

O'er fields and towns, from sea to sea,
Passed the Pageant swift and free,
Tearing up, and trampling down;
Till they came to London town.

XIV

And each dweller, panic-stricken,
Felt his heart with terror sicken
Hearing the tempestuous cry
Of the triumph of Anarchy.

XV

For with pomp to meet him came,
Clothed in arms like blood and flame,
The hired murderers, who did sing
'Thou art God, and Law, and King.

XVI

'We have waited, weak and lone
For thy coming, Mighty One!
Our purses are empty, our swords are cold,
Give us glory, and blood, and gold.'

XVII

Lawyers and priests, a motley crowd,
To the earth their pale brows bowed;
Like a bad prayer not over loud,
Whispering—'Thou art Law and God.'—

XVIII

Then all cried with one accord,
'Thou art King, and God, and Lord;
Anarchy, to thee we bow,
Be thy name made holy now!'

XIX

And Anarchy, the Skeleton,
Bowed and grinned to every one,
As well as if his education
Had cost ten millions to the nation.

XX

For he knew the Palaces
Of our Kings were rightly his;
His the sceptre, crown, and globe,
And the gold-inwoven robe.

XXI

So he sent his slaves before
To seize upon the Bank and Tower,
And was proceeding with intent
To meet his pensioned Parliament

XXII

When one fled past, a maniac maid,
And her name was Hope, she said:
But she looked more like Despair,
And she cried out in the air:

XXIII

'My father Time is weak and gray
With waiting for a better day;
See how idiot-like he stands,
Fumbling with his palsied hands!

XXIV

'He has had child after child,
And the dust of death is piled
Over every one but me—
Misery, oh, Misery!'

XXV

Then she lay down in the street,
Right before the horses' feet,
Expecting, with a patient eye,
Murder, Fraud, and Anarchy.

XXVI

When between her and her foes
A mist, a light, an image rose,
Small at first, and weak, and frail
Like the vapour of a vale:

XXVII

Till as clouds grow on the blast,
Like tower-crowned giants striding fast,
And glare with lightnings as they fly,
And speak in thunder to the sky,

XXVIII

It grew—a Shape arrayed in mail
Brighter than the viper's scale,
And upborne on wings whose grain
Was as the light of sunny rain.

XXIX

On its helm, seen far away,
A planet, like the Morning's, lay;
And those plumes its light rained through
Like a shower of crimson dew.

XXX

With step as soft as wind it passed
O'er the heads of men—so fast
That they knew the presence there,
And looked,—but all was empty air.

XXXI

As flowers beneath May's footstep waken,
As stars from Night's loose hair are shaken,
As waves arise when loud winds call,
Thoughts sprung where'er that step did fall.

XXXII

And the prostrate multitude
Looked—and ankle-deep in blood,
Hope, that maiden most serene,
Was walking with a quiet mien:

XXXIII

And Anarchy, the ghastly birth,
Lay dead earth upon the earth;
The Horse of Death tameless as wind
Fled, and with his hoofs did grind
To dust the murderers thronged behind.

XXXIV

A rushing light of clouds and splendour,
A sense awakening and yet tender
Was heard and felt—and at its close
These words of joy and fear arose

XXXV

As if their own indignant Earth
Which gave the sons of England birth
Had felt their blood upon her brow,
And shuddering with a mother's throe

XXXVI

Had turnèd every drop of blood
By which her face had been bedewed
To an accent unwithstood,—
As if her heart had cried aloud:

XXXVII

'Men of England, heirs of Glory,
Heroes of unwritten story,
Nurslings of one mighty Mother,
Hopes of her, and one another;

XXXVIII

'Rise like Lions after slumber
In unvanquishable number,
Shake your chains to earth like dew
Which in sleep had fallen on you—
Ye are many—they are few.

XXXIX

'What is Freedom?—ye can tell
That which slavery is, too well—
For its very name has grown
To an echo of your own.

XL

''Tis to work and have such pay
As just keeps life from day to day
In your limbs, as in a cell
For the tyrants' use to dwell,

XLI

'So that ye for them are made
Loom, and plough, and sword, and spade,
With or without your own will bent
To their defence and nourishment.

XLII

''Tis to see your children weak
With their mothers pine and peak,
When the winter winds are bleak,—
They are dying whilst I speak.

XLIII

''Tis to hunger for such diet
As the rich man in his riot
Casts to the fat dogs that lie
Surfeiting beneath his eye;

XLIV

''Tis to let the Ghost of Gold
Take from Toil a thousandfold
More than e'er its substance could
In the tyrannies of old.

XLV

'Paper coin—that forgery
Of the title-deeds, which ye
Hold to something of the worth
Of the inheritance of Earth.

XLVI

''Tis to be a slave in soul
And to hold no strong control
Over your own wills, but be
All that others make of ye.

XLVII

'And at length when ye complain
With a murmur weak and vain
'Tis to see the Tyrant's crew
Ride over your wives and you—
Blood is on the grass like dew.

XLVIII

'Then it is to feel revenge
Fiercely thirsting to exchange
Blood for blood—and wrong for wrong—
Do not thus when ye are strong.

XLIX

'Birds find rest, in narrow nest
When weary of their wingèd quest;
Beasts find fare, in woody lair
When storm and snow are in the air.

L

'Asses, swine, have litter spread
And with fitting food are fed;
All things have a home but one—
Thou, Oh, Englishman, hast none!

429

L I

'This is Slavery—savage men
Or wild beasts within a den
Would endure not as ye do—
But such ills they never knew.

L I I

'What art thou Freedom? O! could slaves
Answer from their living graves
This demand—tyrants would flee
Like a dream's dim imagery:

L I I I

'Thou art not, as impostors say,
A shadow soon to pass away,
A superstition, and a name
Echoing from the cave of Fame.

L I V

'For the labourer thou art bread,
And a comely table spread
From his daily labour come
In a neat and happy home.

L V

'Thou art clothes, and fire, and food
For the trampled multitude—
No—in countries that are free
Such starvation cannot be
As in England now we see.

L V I

'To the rich thou art a check,
When his foot is on the neck
Of his victim, thou dost make
That he treads upon a snake.

L V I I

'Thou art Justice—ne'er for gold
May thy righteous laws be sold
As laws are in England—thou
Shield'st alike the high and low.

LVIII

'Thou art Wisdom—Freemen never
Dream that God will damn for ever
All who think those things untrue
Of which Priests make such ado.

LIX

'Thou art Peace—never by thee
Would blood and treasure wasted be
As tyrants wasted them, when all
Leagued to quench thy flame in Gaul.

LX

'What if English toil and blood
Was poured forth, even as a flood?
It availed, Oh, Liberty,
To dim, but not extinguish thee.

LXI

'Thou art Love—the rich have kissed
Thy feet, and like him following Christ,
Give their substance to the free
And through the rough world follow thee,

LXII

'Or turn their wealth to arms, and make
War for thy belovèd sake
On wealth, and war, and fraud—whence they
Drew the power which is their prey.

LXIII

'Science, Poetry, and Thought
Are thy lamps; they make the lot
Of the dwellers in a cot
So serene, they curse it not.

LXIV

'Spirit, Patience, Gentleness,
All that can adorn and bless
Art thou—let deeds, not words, express
Thine exceeding loveliness.

LXV

'Let a great Assembly be
Of the fearless and the free
On some spot of English ground
Where the plains stretch wide around.

LXVI

'Let the blue sky overhead,
The green earth on which ye tread,
All that must eternal be
Witness the solemnity.

LXVII

'From the corners uttermost
Of the bounds of English coast;
From every hut, village, and town
Where those who live and suffer moan
For others' misery or their own,

LXVIII

'From the workhouse and the prison
Where pale as corpses newly risen,
Women, children, young and old
Groan for pain, and weep for cold—

LXIX

'From the haunts of daily life
Where is waged the daily strife
With common wants and common cares
Which sows the human heart with tares—

LXX

'Lastly from the palaces
Where the murmur of distress
Echoes, like the distant sound
Of a wind alive around

LXXI

'Those prison halls of wealth and fashion,
Where some few feel such compassion
For those who groan, and toil, and wail
As must make their brethren pale—

LXXII

'Ye who suffer woes untold,
Or to feel, or to behold
Your lost country bought and sold
With a price of blood and gold—

LXXIII

'Let a vast assembly be,
And with great solemnity
Declare with measured words that ye
Are, as God has made ye, free—

LXXIV

'Be your strong and simple words
Keen to wound as sharpened swords,
And wide as targes let them be,
With their shade to cover ye.

LXXV

'Let the tyrants pour around
With a quick and startling sound,
Like the loosening of a sea,
Troops of armed emblazonry.

LXXVI

'Let the charged artillery drive
Till the dead air seems alive
With the clash of clanging wheels,
And the tramp of horses' heels.

LXXVII

'Let the fixèd bayonet
Gleam with sharp desire to wet
Its bright point in English blood
Looking keen as one for food.

LXXVIII

'Let the horsemen's scimitars
Wheel and flash, like sphereless stars
Thirsting to eclipse their burning
In a sea of death and mourning.

LXXIX

'Stand ye calm and resolute,
Like a forest close and mute,
With folded arms and looks which are
Weapons of unvanquished war,

LXXX

'And let Panic, who outspeeds
The career of armèd steeds
Pass, a disregarded shade
Through your phalanx undismayed.

LXXXI

'Let the laws of your own land,
Good or ill, between ye stand
Hand to hand, and foot to foot,
Arbiters of the dispute,

LXXXII

'The old laws of England—they
Whose reverend heads with age are gray,
Children of a wiser day;
And whose solemn voice must be
Thine own echo—Liberty!

LXXXIII

'On those who first should violate
Such sacred heralds in their state
Rest the blood that must ensue,
And it will not rest on you.

LXXXIV

'And if then the tyrants dare
Let them ride among you there,
Slash, and stab, and maim, and hew,—
What they like, that let them do.

LXXXV

'With folded arms and steady eyes,
And little fear, and less surprise,
Look upon them as they slay
Till their rage has died away.

LXXXVI

'Then they will return with shame
To the place from which they came,
And the blood thus shed will speak
In hot blushes on their cheek.

LXXXVII

'Every woman in the land
Will point at them as they stand—
They will hardly dare to greet
Their acquaintance in the street.

LXXXVIII

'And the bold, true warriors
Who have hugged Danger in wars
Will turn to those who would be free,
Ashamed of such base company.

LXXXIX

'And that slaughter to the Nation
Shall steam up like inspiration,
Eloquent, oracular;
A volcano heard afar.

XC

'And these words shall then become
Like Oppression's thundered doom
Ringing through each heart and brain,
Heard again—again—again—

XCI

'Rise like Lions after slumber
In unvanquishable number—
Shake your chains to earth like dew
Which in sleep had fallen on you—
Ye are many—they are few.'

England in 1819

AN old, mad, blind, despised, and dying king,—
Princes, the dregs of their dull race, who flow
Through public scorn,—mud from a muddy spring,—
Rulers who neither see, nor feel, nor know,

But leech-like to their fainting country cling,
Till they drop, blind in blood, without a blow,—
A people starved and stabbed in the untilled field,—
An army, which liberticide and prey
Makes as a two-edged sword to all who wield,—
Golden and sanguine laws which tempt and slay;
Religion Christless, Godless—a book sealed;
A Senate,—Time's worst statute unrepealed,—
Are graves, from which a glorious Phantom may
Burst, to illumine our tempestuous day.

Ozymandias

I MET a traveller from an antique land
Who said: Two vast and trunkless legs of stone
Stand in the desert. Near them, on the sand,
Half sunk, a shattered visage lies, whose frown,
And wrinkled lip, and sneer of cold command,
Tell that its sculptor well those passions read
Which yet survive, stamped on these lifeless things,
The hand that mocked them, and the heart that fed:
And on the pedestal these words appear:
'My name is Ozymandias, king of kings:
Look on my works, ye Mighty, and despair!'
Nothing beside remains. Round the decay
Of that colossal wreck, boundless and bare
The lone and level sands stretch far away.

Ode to the West Wind

I

O WILD West Wind, thou breath of Autumn's being,
Thou, from whose unseen presence the leaves dead
Are driven, like ghosts from an enchanter fleeing,

Yellow, and black, and pale, and hectic red,
Pestilence-stricken multitudes: O thou,
Who chariotest to their dark wintry bed

The wingèd seeds, where they lie cold and low,
Each like a corpse within its grave, until
Thine azure sister of the Spring shall blow

Her clarion o'er the dreaming earth, and fill
(Driving sweet buds like flocks to feed in air)
With living hues and odours plain and hill:

Wild Spirit, which art moving everywhere;
Destroyer and preserver; hear, oh, hear!

II

Thou on whose stream, mid the steep sky's commotion,
Loose clouds like earth's decaying leaves are shed,
Shook from the tangled boughs of Heaven and Ocean,

Angels of rain and lightning: there are spread
On the blue surface of thine airy surge,
Like the bright hair uplifted from the head

Of some fierce Maenad, even from the dim verge
Of the horizon to the zenith's height,
The locks of the approaching storm. Thou dirge

Of the dying year, to which this closing night
Will be the dome of a vast sepulchre,
Vaulted with all thy congregated might

Of vapours, from whose solid atmosphere
Black rain, and fire, and hail will burst: oh, hear!

III

Thou who didst waken from his summer dreams
The blue Mediterranean, where he lay,
Lulled by the coil of his crystàlline streams,

Beside a pumice isle in Baiae's bay,
And saw in sleep old palaces and towers
Quivering within the wave's intenser day,

All overgrown with azure moss and flowers
So sweet, the sense faints picturing them! Thou
For whose path the Atlantic's level powers

437

Cleave themselves into chasms, while far below
The sea-blooms and the oozy woods which wear
The sapless foliage of the ocean, know

Thy voice, and suddenly grow grey with fear,
And tremble and despoil themselves: oh, hear!

IV

If I were a dead leaf thou mightest bear;
If I were a swift cloud to fly with thee;
A wave to pant beneath thy power, and share

The impulse of thy strength, only less free
Than thou, O uncontrollable! If even
I were as in my boyhood, and could be

The comrade of thy wanderings over Heaven,
As then, when to outstrip thy skiey speed
Scarce seemed a vision; I would ne'er have striven

As thus with thee in prayer in my sore need.
Oh, lift me as a wave, a leaf, a cloud!
I fall upon the thorns of life! I bleed!

A heavy weight of hours has chained and bowed
One too like thee: tameless, and swift, and proud.

V

Make me thy lyre, even as the forest is:
What if my leaves are falling like its own!
The tumult of thy mighty harmonies

Will take from both a deep, autumnal tone,
Sweet though in sadness. Be thou, Spirit fierce,
My spirit! Be thou me, impetuous one!

Drive my dead thoughts over the universe
Like withered leaves to quicken a new birth!
And, by the incantation of this verse,

Scatter, as from an unextinguished hearth
Ashes and sparks, my words among mankind!
Be through my lips to unawakened earth

The trumpet of a prophecy! O, Wind,
If Winter comes, can Spring be far behind?

To a Skylark

Hail to thee, blithe Spirit!
   Bird thou never wert,
That from Heaven, or near it,
   Pourest thy full heart
In profuse strains of unpremeditated art.

Higher still and higher
   From the earth thou springest
Like a cloud of fire;
   The blue deep thou wingest,
And singing still dost soar, and soaring ever singest.

In the golden lightning
   Of the sunken sun,
O'er which clouds are bright'ning,
   Thou dost float and run;
Like an unbodied joy whose race is just begun.

The pale purple even
   Melts around thy flight;
Like a star of Heaven,
   In the broad daylight
Thou art unseen, but yet I hear thy shrill delight,

Keen as are the arrows
   Of that silver sphere,
Whose intense lamp narrows
   In the white dawn clear
Until we hardly see—we feel that it is there.

All the earth and air
   With thy voice is loud,
As, when night is bare,
   From one lonely cloud
The moon rains out her beams, and Heaven is overflowed.

What thou art we know not;
   What is most like thee?
From rainbow clouds there flow not
   Drops so bright to see
As from thy presence showers a rain of melody.

439

Like a Poet hidden
  In the light of thought,
Singing hymns unbidden,
  Till the world is wrought
To sympathy with hopes and fears it heeded not:

Like a high-born maiden
  In a palace-tower,
Soothing her love-laden
  Soul in secret hour
With music sweet as love, which overflows her bower:

Like a glow-worm golden
  In a dell of dew,
Scattering unbeholden
  Its aëreal hue
Among the flowers and grass, which screen it from the view!

Like a rose embowered
  In its own green leaves,
By warm winds deflowered,
  Till the scent it gives
Makes faint with too much sweet these heavy-wingèd thieves:

Sound of vernal showers
  On the twinkling grass,
Rain-awakened flowers,
  All that ever was
Joyous, and clear, and fresh, thy music doth surpass:

Teach us, Sprite or Bird,
  What sweet thoughts are thine:
I have never heard
  Praise of love or wine
That panted forth a flood of rapture so divine.

Chorus Hymeneal,
  Or triumphal chant,
Matched with thine would be all
  But an empty vaunt,
A thing wherein we feel there is some hidden want.

What objects are the fountains
  Of thy happy strain?
What fields, or waves, or mountains?
  What shapes of sky or plain?
What love of thine own kind? what ignorance of pain?

With thy clear keen joyance
    Languor cannot be:
Shadow of annoyance
    Never came near thee:
Thou lovest—but ne'er knew love's sad satiety.

Waking or asleep,
    Thou of death must deem
Things more true and deep
    Than we mortals dream,
Or how could thy notes flow in such a crystal stream?

We look before and after,
    And pine for what is not:
Our sincerest laughter
    With some pain is fraught;
Our sweetest songs are those that tell of saddest thought.

Yet if we could scorn
    Hate, and pride, and fear;
If we were things born
    Not to shed a tear,
I know not how thy joy we ever should come near.

Better than all measures
    Of delightful sound,
Better than all treasures
    That in books are found,
Thy skill to poet were, thou scorner of the ground!

Teach me half the gladness
    That thy brain must know,
Such harmonious madness
    From my lips would flow
The world should listen then—as I am listening now.

To the Moon

ART thou pale for weariness
Of climbing heaven and gazing on the earth,
    Wandering companionless
Among the stars that have a different birth,—
And ever changing, like a joyless eye
That finds no object worth its constancy?

441

Summer and Winter

IT was a bright and cheerful afternoon,
Towards the end of the sunny month of June,
When the north wind congregates in crowds
The floating mountains of the silver clouds
From the horizon—and the stainless sky
Opens beyond them like eternity.
All things rejoiced beneath the sun; the weeds,
The river, and the corn-fields, and the reeds;
The willow leaves that glanced in the light breeze,
And the firm foliage of the larger trees.

It was a winter such as when birds die
In the deep forests; and the fishes lie
Stiffened in the translucent ice, which makes
Even the mud and slime of the warm lakes
A wrinkled clod as hard as brick; and when,
Among their children, comfortable men
Gather about great fires, and yet feel cold:
Alas, then, for the homeless beggar old!

Love's Philosophy

I

THE fountains mingle with the river
   And the rivers with the Ocean,
The winds of Heaven mix for ever
   With a sweet emotion;
Nothing in the world is single;
   All things by a law divine
In one spirit meet and mingle.
   Why not I with mine?—

II

See the mountains kiss high Heaven
   And the waves clasp one another;
No sister-flower would be forgiven
   If it disdained its brother;
And the sunlight clasps the earth
   And the moonbeams kiss the sea:
What are all these kissings worth
   If thou kiss not me?

Adonais

I

I WEEP for Adonais—he is dead!
O, weep for Adonais! though our tears
Thaw not the frost which binds so dear a head!
And thou, sad Hour, selected from all years
To mourn our loss, rouse thy obscure compeers,
And teach them thine own sorrow, say: 'With me
Died Adonais; till the Future dares
Forget the Past, his fate and fame shall be
An echo and a light unto eternity!'

II

Where wert thou, mighty Mother, when he lay,
When thy Son lay, pierced by the shaft which flies
In darkness? where was lorn Urania
When Adonais died? With veilèd eyes,
'Mid listening Echoes, in her Paradise
She sate, while one, with soft enamoured breath
Rekindled all the fading melodies,
With which, like flowers that mock the corse beneath,
He had adorned and hid the coming bulk of Death.

III

Oh, weep for Adonais—he is dead!
Wake, melancholy Mother, wake and weep!
Yet wherefore? Quench within their burning bed
Thy fiery tears, and let thy loud heart keep
Like his, a mute and uncomplaining sleep;
For he is gone, where all things wise and fair
Descend;—oh, dream not that the amorous Deep
Will yet restore him to the vital air;
Death feeds on his mute voice, and laughs at our despair.

IV

Most musical of mourners, weep again!
Lament anew, Urania!—He died,
Who was the Sire of an immortal strain,
Blind, old, and lonely, when his country's pride,
The priest, the slave, and the liberticide,
Trampled and mocked with many a loathèd rite

443

Of lust and blood; he went, unterrified,
Into the gulf of death; but his clear Sprite
Yet reigns o'er earth; the third among the sons of light.

V

Most musical of mourners, weep anew!
Not all to that bright station dared to climb;
And happier they their happiness who knew,
Whose tapers yet burn through that night of time
In which suns perished; others more sublime,
Struck by the envious wrath of man or god,
Have sunk, extinct in their refulgent prime;
And some yet live, treading the thorny road,
Which leads, through toil and hate, to Fame's serene abode.

VI

But now, thy youngest, dearest one, has perished—
The nursling of thy widowhood, who grew,
Like a pale flower by some sad maiden cherished,
And fed with true-love tears, instead of dew;
Most musical of mourners, weep anew!
Thy extreme hope, the loveliest and the last,
The bloom, whose petals nipped before they blew
Died on the promise of the fruit, is waste;
The broken lily lies—the storm is overpast.

VII

To that high Capital, where kingly Death
Keeps his pale court in beauty and decay,
He came; and bought, with price of purest breath,
A grave among the eternal.—Come away!
Haste, while the vault of blue Italian day
Is yet his fitting charnel-roof! while still
He lies, as if in dewy sleep he lay;
Awake him not! surely he takes his fill
Of deep and liquid rest, forgetful of all ill.

VIII

He will awake no more, oh, never more!—
Within the twilight chamber spreads apace
The shadow of white Death, and at the door
Invisible Corruption waits to trace
His extreme way to her dim dwelling-place;
The eternal Hunger sits, but pity and awe

Soothe her pale rage, nor dares she to deface
So fair a prey, till darkness, and the law
Of change, shall o'er his sleep the mortal curtain draw.

IX

Oh, weep for Adonais!—The quick Dreams,
The passion-wingèd Ministers of thought,
Who were his flocks, whom near the living streams
Of his young spirit he fed, and whom he taught
The love which was its music, wander not,—
Wander no more, from kindling brain to brain,
But droop there, whence they sprung; and mourn their lot
Round the cold heart, where, after their sweet pain,
They ne'er will gather strength, or find a home again.

X

And one with trembling hands clasps his cold head,
And fans him with her moonlight wings, and cries;
'Our love, our hope, our sorrow, is not dead;
See, on the silken fringe of his faint eyes,
Like dew upon a sleeping flower, there lies
A tear some Dream has loosened from his brain.'
Lost Angel of a ruined Paradise!
She knew not 'twas her own; as with no stain
She faded, like a cloud which had outwept its rain.

XI

One from a lucid urn of starry dew
Washed his light limbs as if embalming them;
Another clipped her profuse locks, and threw
The wreath upon him, like an anadem,
Which frozen tears instead of pearls begem;
Another in her wilful grief would break
Her bow and wingèd reeds, as if to stem
A greater loss with one which was more weak;
And dull the barbèd fire against his frozen cheek.

XII

Another Splendour on his mouth alit,
That mouth, whence it was wont to draw the breath
Which gave it strength to pierce the guarded wit,
And pass into the panting heart beneath
With lightning and with music: the damp death
Quenched its caress upon his icy lips;

And, as a dying meteor stains a wreath
Of moonlight vapour, which the cold night clips,
It flushed through his pale limbs, and passed to its eclipse.

XIII

And others came ... Desires and Adorations,
Wingèd Persuasions and veiled Destinies,
Splendours, and Glooms, and glimmering Incarnations
Of hopes and fears, and twilight Phantasies;
And Sorrow, with her family of Sighs,
And Pleasure, blind with tears, led by the gleam
Of her own dying smile instead of eyes,
Came in slow pomp;—the moving pomp might seem
Like pageantry of mist on an autumnal stream.

XIV

All he had loved, and moulded into thought,
From shape, and hue, and odour, and sweet sound,
Lamented Adonais. Morning sought
Her eastern watch-tower, and her hair unbound,
Wet with the tears which should adorn the ground,
Dimmed the aëriel eyes that kindle day;
Afar the melancholy thunder moaned,
Pale Ocean in unquiet slumber lay,
And the wild Winds flew round, sobbing in their dismay.

XV

Lost Echo sits amid the voiceless mountains,
And feeds her grief with his remembered lay,
And will no more reply to winds or fountains,
Or amorous birds perched on the young green spray,
Or herdsman's horn, or bell at closing day;
Since she can mimic not his lips, more dear
Than those for whose disdain she pined away
Into a shadow of all sounds:—a drear
Murmur, between their songs, is all the woodmen hear.

XVI

Grief made the young Spring wild, and she threw down
Her kindling buds, as if she Autumn were,
Or they dead leaves; since her delight is flown,
For whom should she have waked the sullen year?
To Phoebus was not Hyacinth so dear
Nor to himself Narcissus, as to both

Thou, Adonais: wan they stand and sere
Amid the faint companions of their youth,
With dew all turned to tears; odour, to sighing ruth.

XVII

Thy spirit's sister, the lorn nightingale
Mourns not her mate with such melodious pain;
Not so the eagle, who like thee could scale
Heaven, and could nourish in the sun's domain
Her mighty youth with morning, doth complain,
Soaring and screaming round her empty nest,
As Albion wails for thee: the curse of Cain
Light on his head who pierced thy innocent breast,
And scared the angel soul that was its earthly guest!

XVIII

Ah, woe is me! Winter is come and gone,
But grief returns with the revolving year;
The airs and streams renew their joyous tone;
The ants, the bees, the swallows reappear;
Fresh leaves and flowers deck the dead Seasons' bier;
The amorous birds now pair in every brake,
And build their mossy homes in field and brere;
And the green lizard, and the golden snake,
Like unimprisoned flames, out of their trance awake.

XIX

Through wood and stream and field and hill and Ocean
A quickening life from the Earth's heart has burst
As it has ever done, with change and motion,
From the great morning of the world when first
God dawned on Chaos; in its stream immersed,
The lamps of Heaven flash with a softer light;
All baser things pant with life's sacred thirst;
Diffuse themselves; and spend in love's delight,
The beauty and the joy of their renewèd might.

XX

The leprous corpse, touched by this spirit tender,
Exhales itself in flowers of gentle breath;
Like incarnations of the stars, when splendour
Is changed to fragrance, they illumine death
And mock the merry worm that wakes beneath;
Nought we know, dies. Shall that alone which knows

Be as a sword consumed before the sheath
By sightless lightning?—the intense atom glows
A moment, then is quenched in a most cold repose.

XXI

Alas! that all we loved of him should be,
But for our grief, as if it had not been,
And grief itself be mortal! Woe is me!
Whence are we, and why are we? of what scene
The actors or spectators? Great and mean
Meet massed in death, who lends what life must borrow.
As long as skies are blue, and fields are green,
Evening must usher night, night urge the morrow,
Month follow month with woe, and year wake year to sorrow.

XXII

He will awake no more, oh, never more!
'Wake thou,' cried Misery, 'childless Mother, rise
Out of thy sleep, and slake, in thy heart's core,
A wound more fierce than his, with tears and sighs.'
And all the Dreams that watched Urania's eyes,
And all the Echoes whom their sister's song
Had held in holy silence, cried: 'Arise!'
Swift as a Thought by the snake Memory stung,
From her ambrosial rest the fading Splendour sprung.

XXIII

She rose like an autumnal Night, that springs
Out of the East, and follows wild and drear
The golden Day, which, on eternal wings,
Even as a ghost abandoning a bier,
Had left the Earth a corpse. Sorrow and fear
So struck, so roused, so rapt Urania;
So saddened round her like an atmosphere
Of stormy mist; so swept her on her way
Even to the mournful place where Adonais lay.

XXIV

Out of her secret Paradise she sped,
Through camps and cities rough with stone, and steel,
And human hearts, which to her aery tread
Yielding not, wounded the invisible
Palms of her tender feet where'er they fell:
And barbèd tongues, and thoughts more sharp than they,

Rent the soft Form they never could repel,
Whose sacred blood, like the young tears of May,
Paved with eternal flowers that undeserving way.

XXV

In the death-chamber for a moment Death,
Shamed by the presence of that living Might,
Blushed to annihilation, and the breath
Revisited those lips, and Life's pale light
Flashed through those limbs, so late her dear delight.
'Leave me not wild and drear and comfortless,
As silent lightning leaves the starless night!
Leave me not!' cried Urania: her distress
Roused Death: Death rose and smiled, and met her vain caress.

XXVI

'Stay yet awhile! speak to me once again;
Kiss me, so long but as a kiss may live;
And in my heartless breast and burning brain
That word, that kiss, shall all thoughts else survive,
With food of saddest memory kept alive,
Now thou art dead, as if it were a part
Of thee, my Adonais! I would give
All that I am to be as thou now art!
But I am chained to Time, and cannot thence depart!

XXVII

'O gentle child, beautiful as thou wert,
Why didst thou leave the trodden paths of men
Too soon, and with weak hands though mighty heart
Dare the unpastured dragon in his den?
Defenceless as thou wert, oh, where was then
Wisdom the mirrored shield, or scorn the spear?
Or hadst thou waited the full cycle, when
Thy spirit should have filled its crescent sphere.
The monsters of life's waste had fled from thee like deer.

XXVIII

'The herded wolves, bold only to pursue;
The obscene ravens, clamorous o'er the dead;
The vultures to the conqueror's banner true
Who feed where Desolation first has fed,
And whose wings rain contagion;—how they fled,
When, like Apollo, from his golden bow

The Pythian of the age one arrow sped
    And smiled!—The spoilers tempt no second blow,
They fawn on the proud feet that spurn them lying low.

XXIX

'The sun comes forth, and many reptiles spawn;
    He sets, and each ephemeral insect then
    Is gathered into death without a dawn,
And the immortal stars awake again;
    So is it in the world of living men:
A godlike mind soars forth, in its delight
    Making earth bare and veiling heaven, and when
It sinks, the swarms that dimmed or shared its light
Leave to its kindred lamps the spirit's awful night.'

XXX

Thus ceased she: and the mountain shepherds came,
    Their garlands sere, their magic mantles rent;
    The Pilgrim of Eternity, whose fame
Over his living head like Heaven is bent,
    An early but enduring monument,
Came, veiling all the lightnings of his song
    In sorrow; from her wilds Ierne sent
The sweetest lyrist of her saddest wrong,
And Love taught Grief to fall like music from his tongue.

XXXI

Midst others of less note, came one frail Form,
    A phantom among men; companionless
    As the last cloud of an expiring storm
Whose thunder is its knell; he, as I guess,
    Had gazed on Nature's naked loveliness,
Actaeon-like, and now he fled astray
    With feeble steps o'er the world's wilderness,
And his own thoughts, along that rugged way,
Pursued, like raging hounds, their father and their prey.

XXXII

A pardlike Spirit beautiful and swift—
    A Love in desolation masked;—a Power
    Girt round with weakness;—it can scarce uplift
The weight of the superincumbent hour;
    It is a dying lamp, a falling shower,
A breaking billow;—even whilst we speak

Is it not broken? On the withering flower
The killing sun smiles brightly: on a cheek
The life can burn in blood, even while the heart may break.

XXXIII

His head was bound with pansies overblown,
And faded violets, white, and pied, and blue;
And a light spear topped with a cypress cone,
Round whose rude shaft dark ivy-tresses grew
Yet dripping with the forest's noonday dew,
Vibrated, as the ever-beating heart
Shook the weak hand that grasped it; of that crew
He came the last, neglected and apart;
A herd-abandoned deer struck by the hunter's dart.

XXXIV

All stood aloof, and at his partial moan
Smiled through their tears; well knew that gentle band
Who in another's fate now wept his own,
As in the accents of an unknown land
He sung new sorrow; sad Urania scanned
The Stranger's mien, and murmured: 'Who art thou?'
He answered not, but with a sudden hand
Made bare his branded and ensanguined brow,
Which was like Cain's or Christ's—oh! that it should be so!

XXXV

What softer voice is hushed over the dead?
Athwart what brow is that dark mantle thrown?
What form leans sadly o'er the white death-bed,
In mockery of monumental stone,
The heavy heart heaving without a moan?
If it be He, who, gentlest of the wise,
Taught, soothed, loved, honoured the departed one,
Let me not vex, with inharmonious sighs,
The silence of that heart's accepted sacrifice.

XXXVI

Our Adonais has drunk poison—oh!
What deaf and viperous murderer could crown
Life's early cup with such a draught of woe?
The nameless worm would now itself disown:
It felt, yet could escape, the magic tone
Whose prelude held all envy, hate, and wrong,

But what was howling in one breast alone,
Silent with expectation of the song,
Whose master's hand is cold, whose silver lyre unstrung.

XXXVII

Live thou, whose infamy is not thy fame!
Live! fear no heavier chastisement from me,
Thou noteless blot on a remembered name!
But be thyself, and know thyself to be!
And ever at thy season be thou free
To spill the venom when thy fangs o'erflow:
Remorse and Self-contempt shall cling to thee;
Hot Shame shall burn upon thy secret brow,
And like a beaten hound tremble thou shalt—as now.

XXXVIII

Nor let us weep that our delight is fled
Far from these carrion kites that scream below;
He wakes or sleeps with the enduring dead;
Thou canst nor soar where he is sitting now—
Dust to the dust! but the pure spirit shall flow
Back to the burning fountain whence it came,
A portion of the Eternal, which must glow
Through time and change, unquenchably the same,
Whilst thy cold embers choke the sordid hearth of shame.

XXXIX

Peace, peace! he is not dead, he doth not sleep—
He hath awakened from the dream of life—
'Tis we, who lost in stormy visions, keep
With phantoms an unprofitable strife,
And in mad trance, strike with our spirit's knife
Invulnerable nothings.—*We* decay
Like corpses in a charnel; fear and grief
Convulse us and consume us day by day,
And cold hopes swarm like worms within our living clay.

XL

He has outsoared the shadow of our night;
Envy and calumny and hate and pain,
And that unrest which men miscall delight,
Can touch him not and torture not again;
From the contagion of the world's slow stain
He is secure, and now can never mourn

A heart grown cold, a head grown grey in vain;
Nor, when the spirit's self has ceaseed to burn,
With sparkless ashes load an unlamented urn.

XLI

He lives, he wakes—'tis Death is dead, not he;
Mourn not for Adonais.—Thou young Dawn,
Turn all thy dew to splendour, for from thee
The spirit thou lamentest is not gone;
Ye caverns and ye forests, cease to moan!
Cease, ye faint flowers and fountains, and thou Air,
Which like a mourning veil thy scarf hadst thrown
O'er the abandoned Earth, now leave it bare
Even to the joyous stars which smile on its despair!

XLII

He is made one with Nature: there is heard
His voice in all her music, from the moan
Of thunder, to the song of night's sweet bird;
He is a presence to be felt and known
In darkness and in light, from herb and stone,
Spreading itself where'er that Power may move
Which has withdrawn his being to its own;
Which wields the world with never-wearied love,
Sustains it from beneath, and kindles it above.

XLIII

He is a portion of the loveliness
Which once he made more lovely: he doth bear
His part, while the one Spirit's plastic stress
Sweeps through the dull dense world, compelling there,
All new successions to the forms they wear;
Torturing th' unwilling dross that checks its flight
To its own likeness, as each mass may bear;
And bursting in its beauty and its might
From trees and beasts and men into the Heaven's light.

XLIV

The splendours of the firmament of time
May be eclipsed, but are extinguished not;
Like stars to their appointed height they climb,
And death is a low mist which cannot blot
The brightness it may veil. When lofty thought
Lifts a young heart above its mortal lair,

And love and life contend in it, for what
　Shall be its earthly doom, the dead live there
And move like winds of light on dark and stormy air.

XLV

The inheritors of unfulfilled renown
　Rose from their thrones, built beyond mortal thought,
　Far in the Unapparent. Chatterton
Rose pale,—his solemn agony had not
　Yet faded from him; Sidney, as he fought
And as he fell and as he lived and loved
　Sublimely mild, a Spirit without spot,
　Arose; and Lucan, by his death approved:
Oblivion as they rose shrank like a thing reproved.

XLVI

And many more, whose names on Earth are dark,
　But whose transmitted effluence cannot die
　So long as fire outlives the parent spark,
Rose, robed in dazzling immortality.
　'Thou art become as one of us,' they cry,
'It was for thee yon kingless sphere has long
　Swung blind in unascended majesty,
　Silent alone amid an Heaven of Song.
Assume thy wingèd throne, thou Vesper of our throng!'

XLVII

Who mourns for Adonais? Oh, come forth,
　Fond wretch! and know thyself and him aright
Clasp with thy panting soul the pendulous Earth;
　As from a centre, dart thy spirit's light
　Beyond all worlds, until its spacious might
Satiate the void circumference: then shrink
　Even to a point within our day and night;
　And keep thy heart light lest it make thee sink
When hope has kindled hope, and lured thee to the brink.

XLVIII

Or go to Rome, which is the sepulchre,
　Oh, not of him, but of our joy: 'tis nought
That ages, empires, and religions there
　Lie buried in the ravage they have wrought;
　For such as he can lend,—they borrow not
Glory from those who made the world their prey;

And he is gathered to the kings of thought
Who waged contention with their time's decay,
And of the past are all that cannot pass away.

XLIX

Go thou to Rome,—at once the Paradise,
The grave, the city, and the wilderness;
And where its wrecks like shattered mountains rise,
And flowering weeds, and fragrant copses dress
The bones of Desolation's nakedness
Pass, till the spirit of the spot shall lead
Thy footsteps to a slope of green access
Where, like an infant's smile, over the dead
A light of laughing flowers along the grass is spread;

L

And grey walls moulder round, on which dull Time
Feeds, like slow fire upon a hoary brand:
And one keen pyramid with wedge sublime,
Pavilioning the dust of him who planned
This refuge for his memory, doth stand
Like flame transformed to marble; and beneath,
A field is spread, on which a newer band
Have pitched in Heaven's smile their camp of death,
Welcoming him we lose with scarce extinguished breath.

LI

Here pause: these graves are all too young as yet
To have outgrown the sorrow which consigned
Its charge to each; and if the seal is set,
Here, on one fountain of a mourning mind,
Break it not thou! too surely shalt thou find
Thine own well full, if thou returnest home,
Of tears and gall. From the world's bitter wind
Seek shelter in the shadow of the tomb.
What Adonais is, why fear we to become?

LII

The One remains, the many change and pass;
Heaven's light forever shines, Earth's shadows fly;
Life, like a dome of many-coloured glass,
Stains the white radiance of Eternity,
Until Death tramples it to fragments.—Die,
If thou wouldst be with that which thou dost seek!

Follow where all is fled!—Rome's azure sky,
Flowers, ruins, statues, music, words, are weak
The glory they transfuse with fitting truth to speak.

LIII

Why linger, why turn back, why shrink, my Heart?
Thy hopes are gone before: from all things here
They have departed; thou shouldst now depart!
A light is passed from the revolving year,
And man, and woman; and what still is dear
Attracts to crush, repels to make thee wither.
The soft sky smiles,—the low wind whispers near:
'Tis Adonais calls! oh, hasten thither,
No more let Life divide what Death can join together.

LIV

That Light whose smile kindles the Universe,
That Beauty in which all things work and move,
That Benediction which the eclipsing Curse
Of birth can quench not, that sustaining Love
Which through the web of being blindly wove
By man and beast and earth and air and sea,
Burns bright or dim, as each are mirrors of
The fire for which all thirst; now beams on me,
Consuming the last clouds of cold mortality.

LV

The breath whose might I have invoked in song
Descends on me; my spirit's bark is driven,
Far from the shore, far from the trembling throng
Whose sails were never to the tempest given;
The massy earth and spherèd skies are riven!
I am borne darkly, fearfully, afar;
Whilst, burning through the inmost veil of Heaven,
The soul of Adonais, like a star,
Beacons from the abode where the Eternal are.

One Word is Too Often Profaned

I

ONE word is too often profaned
   For me to profane it,
One feeling too falsely disdained
   For thee to disdain it;
One hope is too like despair
   For prudence to smother,
And pity from thee more dear
   Than that from another.

II

I can give not what men call love,
   But wilt thou accept not
The worship the heart lifts above
   And the Heavens reject not,—
The desire of the moth for the star,
   Of the night for the morrow,
The devotion to something afar
   From the sphere of our sorrow?

Music, When Soft Voices Die

MUSIC, when soft voices die,
Vibrates in the memory—
Odours, when sweet violets sicken,
Live within the sense they quicken.

Rose leaves, when the rose is dead,
Are heaped for the belovèd's bed;
And so thy thoughts, when thou art gone,
Love itself shall slumber on.

JOHN CLARE

1793–1864

Written in Northampton County Asylum

I AM! yet what I am who cares, or knows?
　My friends forsake me like a memory lost.
I am the self-consumer of my woes;
　They rise and vanish, an oblivious host,
Shadows of life, whose very soul is lost.
And yet I am—I live—though I am tossed

Into the nothingness of scorn and noise,
　Into the living sea of waking dream,
Where there is neither sense of life, nor joys,
　But the huge shipwreck of my own esteem
And all that's dear. Even those I loved the best
Are strange—nay, they are stranger than the rest.

I long for scenes where man has never trod—
　For scenes where woman never smiled or wept—
There to abide with my Creator, God,
　And sleep as I in childhood sweetly slept,
Full of high thoughts, unborn. So let me lie,—
The grass below; above, the vaulted sky.

Noon

ALL how silent and how still;
Nothing heard but yonder mill:
While the dazzled eye surveys
All around a liquid blaze;
And amid the scorching gleams,
If we earnest look, it seems
As if crooked bits of glass
Seemed repeatedly to pass.
Oh, for a puffing breeze to blow!
But breezes are all strangers now;
Not a twig is seen to shake,
Nor the smallest bent to quake;
From the river's muddy side

458

Not a curve is seen to glide;
And no longer on the stream
Watching lies the silver bream,
Forcing, from repeated springs,
'Verges in successive rings.'
Bees are faint, and cease to hum;
Birds are overpowered and dumb.
Rural voices all are mute,
Tuneless lie the pipe and flute:
Shepherds, with their panting sheep,
In the swaliest corner creep;
And from the tormenting heat
All are wishing to retreat.
Huddled up in grass and flowers,
Mowers wait for cooler hours;
And the cow-boy seeks the sedge,
Ramping in the woodland hedge,
While his cattle o'er the vales
Scamper, with uplifted tails;

*   *   *

E'en the dew is parchéd up
From the teasel's jointed cup:
O poor birds! where must ye fly,
Now your water-pots are dry?
If ye stay upon the heath,
Ye'll be choked and clammed to death.
Therefore leave the shadeless goss,
Seek the spring-head lined with moss;
There your little feet may stand,
Safely printing on the sand;
While, in full possession, where
Purling eddies ripple clear,
You with ease and plenty blest,
Sip the coolest and the best.
Then away! and wet your throats;
Cheer me with your warbling notes;
'Twill hot noon the more revive;
While I wander to contrive
For myself a place as good,
In the middle of a wood:
There aside some mossy-bank,
Where the grass in bunches rank

swaliest] shadiest

459

Lifts its down on spindles high,
Shall be where I'll choose to lie;
Fearless of the things that creep,
There I'll think, and there I'll sleep;
Caring not to stir at all,
Till the dew begins to fall.

After Reading in a Letter Proposals for Building a Cottage

BESIDE a runnel build my shed,
  With stubbles covered o'er;
Let broad oaks o'er its chimney spread,
  And grass-plats grace the door.

The door may open with a string,
  So that it closes tight;
And locks would be a wanted thing,
  To keep out thieves at night.

A little garden, not too fine,
  Inclose with painted pales;
And woodbines, round the cot to twine,
  Pin to the wall with nails.

Let hazels grow, and spindling sedge,
  Bend bowering over-head;
Dig old man's beard from woodland hedge,
  To twine a summer shade.

Beside the threshold sods provide,
  And build a summer seat;
Plant sweet-briar bushes by its side,
  And flowers that blossom sweet.

I love the sparrow's ways to watch
  Upon the cotter's sheds,
So here and there pull out the thatch,
  That they may hide their heads.

And as the sweeping swallows stop
  Their flights along the green,
Leave holes within the chimney-top
  To paste their nest between.

Stick shelves and cupboards round the hut,
     In all the holes and nooks;
Nor in the corner fail to put
     A cupboard for the books.

Along the floor some sand I'll shift,
     To make it fit to live in;
And then I'll thank ye for the gift,
     As something worth the giving.

Sudden Shower

BLACK grows the sudden sky, betokening rain,
     And humming hive-bees homeward hurry by:
They feel the change; so let us shun the grain,
     And take the broad road while our feet are dry.
Aye there, some drops fell moistening on my face,
     And pattering on my hat—'tis coming nigh!—
Let's look about, and find a sheltering place.
     The little things around us fear the sky,
And hasten through the grass to shun the shower.
     Here stoops an ash-tree—hark! the wind gets high,
But never mind; this ivy, for an hour,
     Rain as it may, will keep us drily here:
That little wren knows well his sheltering bower,
     Nor leaves his covert, though we come so near.

from *The Flitting*

I'VE left my own old home of homes,
     Green fields and every pleasant place;
The summer like a stranger comes,
     I pause and hardly know her face.
I miss the hazel's happy green,
     The bluebell's quiet hanging blooms,
Where envy's sneer was never seen,
     Where staring malice never comes.

I miss the heath, its yellow furze,
     Molehills and rabbit tracks that lead
Through beesom, ling, and teazel burrs
     That spread a wilderness indeed;

The woodland oaks and all below
That their white powdered branches shield,
The mossy paths: the very crow
Croaked music in my native fields.

I sit me in my corner chair
That seems to feel itself at home,
And hear bird music here and there
From hawthorn hedge and orchard come.
I hear, but all is strange and new:
I sat on my old bench in June,
The sailing puddock's shrill 'peelew'
On Royce Wood seemed a sweeter tune.

I walk adown the narrow lane,
The nightingale is singing now,
But like to me she seems at loss
For Royce Wood and its shielding bough.
I lean upon the window sill,
The bees and summer happy seem;
Green, sunny green they shine, but still
My heart goes far away to dream
Of happiness, and thoughts arise
With home-bred pictures many a one,
Green lanes that shut out burning skies
And old crooked stiles to rest upon;
Above them hangs the maple tree,
Below grass swells a velvet hill,
And little footpaths sweet to see
Go seeking sweeter places still.

JOHN KEATS

1795–1821

Sonnets

To ******

HAD I a man's fair form, then might my sighs
   Be echoed swiftly through that ivory shell
   Thine ear, and find thy gentle heart; so well
Would passion arm me for the enterprize:

But ah! I am no knight whose foeman dies;
    No cuirass glistens on my bosom's swell;
    I am no happy shepherd of the dell
Whose lips have trembled with a maiden's eyes.
Yet must I dote upon thee,—call thee sweet,
    Sweeter by far than Hybla's honied roses
        When steep'd in dew rich to intoxication.
Ah! I will taste that dew, for me 'tis meet,
    And when the moon her pallid face discloses,
        I'll gather some by spells, and incantation.

How many bards gild the lapses of time!
    A few of them have ever been the food
    Of my delighted fancy,—I could brood
Over their beauties, earthly, or sublime:
And often, when I sit me down to rhyme,
    These will in throngs before my mind intrude:
    But no confusion, no disturbance rude
Do they occasion; 'tis a pleasing chime.
So the unnumber'd sounds that evening store;
The songs of birds—the whisp'ring of the leaves—
    The voice of waters—the great bell that heaves
With solemn sound,—and thousand others more,
    That distance of recognizance bereaves,
Making pleasing music, and not wild uproar.

On First Looking into Chapman's Homer

MUCH have I travell'd in the realms of gold,
    And many goodly states and kingdoms seen;
    Round many western islands have I been
Which bards in fealty to Apollo hold.
Oft of one wide expanse had I been told
    That deep-brow'd Homer ruled as his demesne;
    Yet did I never breathe its pure serene
Till I heard Chapman speak out loud and bold:
Then felt I like some watcher of the skies
    When a new planet swims into his ken;
Or like stout Cortez when with eagle eyes
    He star'd at the Pacific—and all his men
Look'd at each other with a wild surmise—
    Silent, upon a peak in Darien.

On the Grasshopper and Cricket

THE poetry of earth is never dead:
  When all the birds are faint with the hot sun,
  And hide in cooling trees, a voice will run
From hedge to hedge about the new-mown mead;
That is the Grasshopper's—he takes the lead
  In summer luxury,—he has never done
  With his delights; for when tired out with fun
He rests at ease beneath some pleasant weed.
The poetry of earth is ceasing never:
  On a lone winter evening, when the frost
    Has wrought a silence, from the stove there shrills
The Cricket's song, in warmth increasing ever,
  And seems to one in drowsiness half lost,
    The Grasshopper's among some grassy hills.

HAPPY is England! I could be content
  To see no other verdure than its own;
  To feel no other breezes than are blown
Through its tall woods with high romances blent:
Yet do I sometimes feel a languishment
  For skies Italian, and an inward groan
  To sit upon an Alp as on a throne,
And half forget what world or worldling meant.
Happy is England, sweet her artless daughters;
  Enough their simple loveliness for me,
    Enough their whitest arms in silence clinging:
  Yet do I often warmly burn to see
    Beauties of deeper glance, and hear their singing,
And float with them about the summer waters.

from *Endymion*

A THING of beauty is a joy for ever:
Its loveliness increases; it will never
Pass into nothingness; but still will keep
A bower quiet for us, and a sleep
Full of sweet dreams, and health, and quiet breathing.

Therefore, on every morrow, are we wreathing
A flowery band to bind us to the earth,
Spite of despondence, of the inhuman dearth
Of noble natures, of the gloomy days,
Of all the unhealthy and o'er-darkened ways
Made for our searching: yes, in spite of all,
Some shape of beauty moves away the pall
From our dark spirits. Such the sun, the moon,
Trees old, and young, sprouting a shady boon
For simple sheep; and such are daffodils
With the green world they live in; and clear rills
That for themselves a cooling covert make
'Gainst the hot season; the mid forest brake,
Rich with a sprinkling of fair musk-rose blooms:
And such too is the grandeur of the dooms
We have imagined for the mighty dead;
All lovely tales that we have heard or read:
An endless fountain of immortal drink,
Pouring unto us from the heaven's brink.

Nor do we merely feel these essences
For one short hour; no, even as the trees
That whisper round a temple become soon
Dear as the temple's self, so does the moon,
The passion poesy, glories infinite,
Haunt us till they become a cheering light
Unto our souls, and bound to us so fast,
That, whether there be shine, or gloom o'ercast,
They always must be with us, or we die.

* * *

O did he ever live, that lonely man,
Who lov'd—and music slew not? 'Tis the pest
Of love, that fairest joys give most unrest;
That things of delicate and tenderest worth
Are swallow'd all, and made a seared dearth,
By one consuming flame: it doth immerse
And suffocate true blessings in a curse.
Half-happy, by comparison of bliss,
Is miserable. 'Twas even so with this
Dew-dropping melody, in the Carian's ear;
First heaven, then hell, and then forgotten clear,
Vanish'd in elemental passion.

And down some swart abysm he had gone,
Had not a heavenly guide benignant led
To where thick myrtle branches, 'gainst his head
Brushing, awakened: then the sounds again
Went noiseless as a passing noontide rain
Over a bower, where little space he stood;
For as the sunset peeps into a wood
So saw he panting light, and towards it went
Through winding alleys; and lo, wonderment!
Upon soft verdure saw, one here, one there,
Cupids a slumbering on their pinions fair.

After a thousand mazes overgone,
At last, with sudden step, he came upon
A chamber, myrtle wall'd, embowered high,
Full of light, incense, tender minstrelsy,
And more of beautiful and strange beside:
For on a silken couch of rosy pride,
In midst of all, there lay a sleeping youth
Of fondest beauty; fonder, in fair sooth,
Than sighs could fathom, or contentment reach:
And coverlids gold-tinted like the peach,
Or ripe October's faded marigolds,
Fell sleek about him in a thousand folds—
Not hiding up an Apollonian curve
Of neck and shoulder, nor the tenting swerve
Of knee from knee, nor ankles pointing light;
But rather, giving them to the filled sight
Officiously. Sideway his face repos'd
On one white arm, and tenderly unclos'd,
By tenderest pressure, a faint damask mouth
To slumbery pout; just as the morning south
Disparts a dew-lipp'd rose. Above his head,
Four lilly stalks did their white honours wed
To make a coronal; and round him grew
All tendrils green, of every bloom and hue,
Together intertwin'd and trammel'd fresh:
The vine of glossy sprout; the ivy mesh,
Shading its Ethiop berries; and woodbine,
Of velvet leaves and bugle-blooms divine;
Convolvulus in streaked vases flush;
The creeper, mellowing for an autumn blush;
And virgin's bower, trailing airily;
With others of the sisterhood. Hard by,

Stood serene Cupids watching silently.
One, kneeling to a lyre, touch'd the strings,
Muffling to death the pathos with his wings;
And, ever and anon, uprose to look
At the youth's slumber; while another took
A willow-bough, distilling odorous dew,
And shook it on his hair; another flew
In through the woven roof, and fluttering-wise
Rain'd violets upon his sleeping eyes.

The Eve of St. Agnes

I

St. Agnes' Eve—Ah, bitter chill it was!
The owl, for all his feathers, was a-cold;
The hare limp'd trembling through the frozen grass,
And silent was the flock in woolly fold:
Numb were the Beadsman's fingers, while he told
His rosary, and while his frosted breath,
Like pious incense from a censer old,
Seem'd taking flight for heaven, without a death,
Past the sweet Virgin's picture, while his prayer he saith.

II

His prayer he saith, this patient, holy man;
Then takes his lamp, and riseth from his knees,
And back returneth, meagre, barefoot, wan,
Along the chapel aisle by slow degrees:
The sculptur'd dead, on each side, seem to freeze,
Emprison'd in black, purgatorial rails:
Knights, ladies, praying in dumb orat'ries,
He passeth by; and his weak spirit fails
To think how they may ache in icy hoods and mails.

III

Northward he turneth through a little door,
And scarce three steps, ere Music's golden tongue
Flatter'd to tears this aged man and poor;
But no—already had his deathbell rung:
The joys of all his life were said and sung:
His was harsh penance on St. Agnes' Eve:
Another way he went, and soon among
Rough ashes sat he for his soul's reprieve,
And all night kept awake, for sinners' sake to grieve.

IV

That ancient Beadsman heard the prelude soft;
And so it chanc'd, for many a door was wide,
From hurry to and fro. Soon, up aloft,
The silver, snarling trumpets 'gan to chide:
The level chambers, ready with their pride,
Were glowing to receive a thousand guests:
The carved angels, ever eager-eyed,
Star'd, where upon their heads the cornice rests,
With hair brown black, and wings put cross-wise on their breasts.

V

At length burst in the argent revelry,
With plume, tiara, and all rich array,
Numerous as shadows haunting faerily
The brain, new stuff'd, in youth, with triumphs gay
Of old romance. These let us wish away,
And turn, sole-thoughted, to one Lady there,
Whose heart had brooded, all that wintry day,
On love, and wing'd St. Agnes' saintly care,
As she had heard old dames full many times declare.

VI

They told her how, upon St. Agnes' Eve,
Young virgins might have visions of delight,
And soft adorings from their loves receive
Upon the honey'd middle of the night,
If ceremonies due they did aright;
As, supperless to bed they must retire,
And couch supine their beauties, lilly white;
Nor look behind, nor sideways, but require
Of Heaven with upward eyes for all that they desire.

VII

Full of this whim was thoughtful Madeline:
The music, yearning like a God in pain,
She scarcely heard: her maiden eyes divine,
Fix'd on the floor, saw many a sweeping train
Pass by—she heeded not at all: in vain
Came many a tiptoe, amorous cavalier,
And back retir'd; not cool'd by high disdain,
But she saw not: her heart was otherwhere:
She sigh'd for Agnes' dreams, the sweetest of the year.

VIII

She danc'd along with vague, regardless eyes,
  Anxious her lips, her breathing quick and short:
The hallow'd hour was near at hand: she sighs
  Amid the timbrels, and the throng'd resort
Of whisperers in anger, or in sport;
  'Mid looks of love, defiance, hate, and scorn,
Hoodwink'd with faery fancy; all amort,
  Save to St. Agnes and her lambs unshorn,
And all the bliss to be before to-morrow morn.

IX

So, purposing each moment to retire,
  She linger'd still. Meantime, across the moors,
Had come young Porphyro, with heart on fire
  For Madeline. Beside the portal doors,
Buttress'd from moonlight, stands he, and implores
  All saints to give him sight of Madeline,
But for one moment in the tedious hours,
  That he might gaze and worship all unseen;
Perchance speak, kneel, touch, kiss—in sooth such things have been.

X

He ventures in: let no buzz'd whisper tell:
  All eyes be muffled, or a hundred swords
Will storm his heart, Love's fev'rous citadel:
  For him, those chambers held barbarian hordes,
Hyena foemen, and hot-blooded lords,
  Whose very dogs would execrations howl
Against his lineage: not one breast affords
  Him any mercy, in that mansion foul,
Save one old beldame, weak in body and in soul.

XI

Ah, happy chance! the aged creature came,
  Shuffling along with ivory-headed wand,
To where he stood, hid from the torch's flame,
  Behind a broad hall-pillar, far beyond
The sound of merriment and chorus bland:
  He startled her; but soon she knew his face,
And grasp'd his fingers in her palsied hand,
  Saying, 'Mercy, Porphyro! hie thee from this place!
'They are all here to-night, the whole blood-thirsty race:

XII

'Get hence! get hence! there's dwarfish Hildebrand;
'He had a fever late, and in the fit
'He cursed thee and thine, both house and land:
'Then there's that old Lord Maurice, not a whit
'More tame for his gray hairs—Alas me! flit!
'Flit like a ghost away.'—'Ah, Gossip dear,
'We're safe enough; here in this arm-chair sit,
'And tell me how'—'Good Saints! not here, not here;
'Follow me, child, or else these stones will be thy bier.'

XIII

He follow'd through a lowly arched way,
Brushing the cobwebs with his lofty plume,
And as she mutter'd 'Well-a—well-a-day!'
He found him in a little moonlight room,
Pale, lattic'd, chill, and silent as a tomb.
'Now tell me where is Madeline,' said he,
'O tell me, Angela, by the holy loom
'Which none but secret sisterhood may see,
'When they St. Agnes' wool are weaving piously.'

XIV

'St. Agnes! Ah! it is St. Agnes' Eve—
'Yet men will murder upon holy days:
'Thou must hold water in a witch's sieve,
'And be liege-lord of all the Elves and Fays,
'To venture so: it fills me with amaze
'To see thee, Porphyro!—St. Agnes' Eve!
'God's help! my lady fair the conjuror plays
'This very night: good angels her deceive!
'But let me laugh awhile, I've mickle time to grieve.'

XV

Feebly she laugheth in the languid moon,
While Porphyro upon her face doth look,
Like puzzled urchin on an aged crone,
Who keepeth clos'd a wond'rous riddle-book,
As spectacled she sits in chimney nook.
But soon his eyes grew brilliant, when she told
His lady's purpose; and he scarce could brook
Tears, at the thought of those enchantments cold,
And Madeline asleep in lap of legends old.

XVI

Sudden a thought came like a full-blown rose,
　Flushing his brow, and in his pained heart
　Made purple riot: then doth he propose
　A stratagem, that makes the beldame start:
　'A cruel man and impious thou art:
　'Sweet lady, let her pray, and sleep, and dream
　'Alone with her good angels, far apart
　'From wicked men like thee. Go, go!—I deem
'Thou canst not surely be the same that thou didst seem.'

XVII

　'I will not harm her, by all saints I swear,'
　Quoth Porphyro: 'O may I ne'er find grace
　'When my weak voice shall whisper its last prayer,
　'If one of her soft ringlets I displace,
　'Or look with ruffian passion in her face:
　'Good Angela, believe me by these tears;
　'Or I will, even in a moment's space,
　'Awake, with horrid shout, my foemen's ears,
'And beard them, though they be more fang'd than wolves and bears.'

XVIII

　'Ah! why wilt thou affright a feeble soul?
　'A poor, weak, palsy-stricken, churchyard thing,
　'Whose passing-bell may ere the midnight toll;
　'Whose prayers for thee, each morn and evening,
　'Were never miss'd.'—Thus plaining, doth she bring
　A gentler speech from burning Porphyro;
　So woeful, and of such deep sorrowing,
　That Angela gives promise she will do
Whatever he shall wish, betide her weal or woe.

XIX

Which was, to lead him, in close secrecy,
　Even to Madeline's chamber, and there hide
　Him in a closet, of such privacy
　That he might see her beauty unespied,
　And win perhaps that night a peerless bride,
　While legion'd faeries pac'd the coverlet,
　And pale enchantment held her sleepy-eyed.
　Never on such a night have lovers met,
Since Merlin paid his Demon all the monstrous debt.

XX

'It shall be as thou wishest,' said the Dame:
'All cates and dainties shall be stored there
'Quickly on this feast-night: by the tambour frame
'Her own lute thou wilt see: no time to spare,
'For I am slow and feeble, and scarce dare
'On such a catering trust my dizzy head.
'Wait here, my child, with patience; kneel in prayer
'The while: Ah! thou must needs the lady wed,
'Or may I never leave my grave among the dead.'

XXI

So saying, she hobbled off with busy fear.
The lover's endless minutes slowly pass'd;
The dame return'd, and whisper'd in his ear
To follow her; with aged eyes aghast
From fright of dim espial. Safe at last,
Through many a dusky gallery, they gain
The maiden's chamber, silken, hush'd, and chaste;
Where Porphyro took covert, pleas'd amain.
His poor guide hurried back with agues in her brain.

XXII

Her falt'ring hand upon the balustrade,
Old Angela was feeling for the stair,
When Madeline, St. Agnes' charmed maid,
Rose, like a mission'd spirit, unaware:
With silver taper's light, and pious care,
She turn'd, and down the aged gossip led
To a safe level matting. Now prepare,
Young Porphyro, for gazing on that bed;
She comes, she comes again, like ring-dove fray'd and fled.

XXIII

Out went the taper as she hurried in;
Its little smoke, in pallid moonshine, died:
She clos'd the door, she panted, all akin
To spirits of the air, and visions wide:
No uttered syllable, or, woe betide!
But to her heart, her heart was voluble,
Paining with eloquence her balmy side;
As though a tongueless nightingale should swell
Her throat in vain, and die, heart-stifled, in her dell.

XXIV

A casement high and triple-arch'd there was,
All garlanded with carven imag'ries
Of fruits, and flowers, and bunches of knot-grass,
And diamonded with panes of quaint device,
Innumerable of stains and splendid dyes,
As are the tiger-moth's deep-damask'd wings;
And in the midst, 'mong thousand heraldries,
And twilight saints, and dim emblazonings,
A shielded scutcheon blush'd with blood of queens and kings.

XXV

Full on this casement shone the wintry moon,
And threw warm gules on Madeline's fair breast,
As down she knelt for heaven's grace and boon;
Rose-bloom fell on her hands, together prest,
And on her silver cross soft amethyst,
And on her hair a glory, like a saint:
She seem'd a splendid angel, newly drest,
Save wings, for heaven:—Porphyro grew faint:
She knelt, so pure a thing, so free from mortal taint.

XXVI

Anon his heart revives: her vespers done,
Of all its wreathed pearls her hair she frees;
Unclasps her warmed jewels one by one;
Loosens her fragrant boddice; by degrees
Her rich attire creeps rustling to her knees:
Half-hidden, like a mermaid in sea-weed,
Pensive awhile she dreams awake, and sees,
In fancy, fair St. Agnes in her bed,
But dares not look behind, or all the charm is fled.

XXVII

Soon, trembling in her soft and chilly nest,
In sort of wakeful swoon, perplex'd she lay,
Until the poppied warmth of sleep oppress'd
Her soothed limbs, and soul fatigued away;
Flown, like a thought, until the morrow-day;
Blissfully haven'd both from joy and pain;
Clasp'd like a missal where swart Paynims pray;
Blinded alike from sunshine and from rain,
As though a rose should shut, and be a bud again.

XXVIII

Stol'n to this paradise, and so entranced,
Porphyro gazed upon her empty dress,
And listen'd to her breathing, if it chanced
To wake into a slumberous tenderness;
Which when he heard, that minute did he bless,
And breath'd himself: then from the closet crept,
Noiseless as fear in a wide wilderness,
And over the hush'd carpet, silent, stept,
And 'tween the curtains peep'd, where, lo!—how fast she slept.

XXIX

Then by the bed-side, where the faded moon
Made a dim, silver twilight, soft he set
A table, and, half anguish'd, threw thereon
A cloth of woven crimson, gold, and jet:—
O for some drowsy Morphean amulet!
The boisterous, midnight, festive clarion,
The kettle-drum, and far-heard clarinet,
Affray his ears, though but in dying tone:—
The hall door shuts again, and all the noise is gone.

XXX

And still she slept an azure-lidded sleep,
In blanched linen, smooth, and lavender'd,
While he from forth the closet brought a heap
Of candied apple, quince, and plum, and gourd;
With jellies soother than the creamy curd,
And lucent syrops, tinct with cinnamon;
Manna and dates, in argosy transferr'd
From Fez; and spiced dainties, every one,
From silken Samarcand to cedar'd Lebanon.

XXXI

These delicates he heap'd with glowing hand
On golden dishes and in baskets bright
Of wreathed silver: sumptuous they stand
In the retired quiet of the night,
Filling the chilly room with perfume light.—
'And now, my love, my seraph fair, awake!
'Thou art my heaven, and I thine eremite!
'Open thine eyes, for meek St. Agnes' sake,
'Or I shall drowse beside thee, so my soul doth ache.'

XXXII

Thus whispering, his warm, unnerved arm
Sank in her pillow. Shaded was her dream
By the dusk curtains:—'twas a midnight charm
Impossible to melt as iced stream:
The lustrous salvers in the moonlight gleam;
Broad golden fringe upon the carpet lies:
It seem'd he never, never could redeem
From such a stedfast spell his lady's eyes;
So mus'd awhile, entoil'd in woofed phantasies.

XXXIII

Awakening up, he took her hollow lute,—
Tumultuous,—and, in chords that tenderest be,
He play'd an ancient ditty, long since mute,
In Provence call'd, 'La belle dame sans mercy:'
Close to her ear touching the melody;—
Wherewith disturb'd, she utter'd a soft moan:
He ceased—she panted quick—and suddenly
Her blue affrayed eyes wide open shone:
Upon his knees he sank, pale as smooth-sculptured stone.

XXXIV

Her eyes were open, but she still beheld,
Now wide awake, the vision of her sleep:
There was a painful change, that nigh expell'd
The blisses of her dream so pure and deep
At which fair Madeline began to weep,
And moan forth witless words with many a sigh;
While still her gaze on Porphyro would keep;
Who knelt, with joined hands and piteous eye,
Fearing to move or speak, she look'd so dreamingly.

XXXV

'Ah, Porphyro!' said she, 'but even now
'Thy voice was at sweet tremble in mine ear,
'Made tuneable with every sweetest vow;
'And those sad eyes were spiritual and clear:
'How chang'd thou art! how pallid, chill, and drear!
'Give me that voice again, my Porphyro,
'Those looks immortal, those complainings dear!
'Oh leave me not in this eternal woe,
'For if thou diest, my Love, I know not where to go.'

XXXVI

Beyond a mortal man impassion'd far
At these voluptuous accents, he arose,
Ethereal, flush'd, and like a throbbing star
Seen mid the sapphire heaven's deep repose;
Into her dream he melted, as the rose
Blendeth its odour with the violet,—
Solution sweet: meantime the frost-wind blows
Like Love's alarum pattering the sharp sleet
Against the window-panes; St. Agnes' moon hath set.

XXXVII

'Tis dark: quick pattereth the flaw-blown sleet:
'This is no dream, my bride, my Madeline!'
'Tis dark: the iced gusts still rave and beat:
'No dream, alas! alas! and woe is mine!
'Porphyro will leave me here to fade and pine.—
'Cruel! what traitor could thee hither bring?
'I curse not, for my heart is lost in thine,
'Though thou forsakest a deceived thing;—
'A dove forlorn and lost with sick unpruned wing.'

XXXVIII

'My Madeline! sweet dreamer! lovely bride!
'Say, may I be for aye thy vassal blest?
'Thy beauty's shield, heart-shap'd and vermeil dyed?
'Ah, silver shrine, here will I take my rest
'After so many hours of toil and quest,
'A famish'd pilgrim,—sav'd by miracle.
'Though I have found, I will not rob thy nest
'Saving of thy sweet self; if thou think'st well
'To trust, fair Madeline, to no rude infidel.

XXXIX

'Hark! 'tis an elfin-storm from faery land,
'Of haggard seeming, but a boon indeed:
'Arise—arise! the morning is at hand;—
'The bloated wassaillers will never heed:—
'Let us away, my love, with happy speed;
'There are no ears to hear, or eyes to see,—
'Drown'd all in Rhenish and the sleepy mead:
'Awake! arise! my love, and fearless be,
'For o'er the southern moors I have a home for thee.'

XL

She hurried at his words, beset with fears,
For there were sleeping dragons all around,
At glaring watch, perhaps, with ready spears—
Down the wide stairs a darkling way they found.—
In all the house was heard no human sound.
A chain-droop'd lamp was flickering by each door;
The arras, rich with horseman, hawk, and hound,
Flutter'd in the besieging wind's uproar;
And the long carpets rose along the gusty floor.

XLI

They glide, like phantoms, into the wide hall;
Like phantoms, to the iron porch, they glide;
Where lay the Porter, in uneasy sprawl,
With a huge empty flaggon by his side:
The wakeful bloodhound rose, and shook his hide,
But his sagacious eye an inmate owns:
By one, and one, the bolts full easy slide:—
The chains lie silent on the footworn stones;—
The key turns, and the door upon its hinges groans.

XLII

And they are gone: aye, ages long ago
These lovers fled away into the storm.
That night the Baron dreamt of many a woe,
And all his warrior-guests, with shade and form
Of witch, and demon, and large coffin-worm,
Were long be-nightmar'd. Angela the old
Died palsy-twitch'd, with meagre face deform;
The Beadsman, after thousand aves told,
For aye unsought for slept among his ashes cold.

Ode to a Nightingale

I

My heart aches, and a drowsy numbness pains
    My sense, as though of hemlock I had drunk,
Or emptied some dull opiate to the drains
    One minute past, and Lethe-wards had sunk:
'Tis not through envy of thy happy lot,
    But being too happy in thine happiness,—

That thou, light-winged Dryad of the trees,
    In some melodious plot
Of beechen green, and shadows numberless,
    Singest of summer in full-throated ease.

II

O, for a draught of vintage! that hath been
    Cool'd a long age in the deep-delvèd earth,
Tasting of Flora and the country green,
    Dance, and Provençal song, and sunburnt mirth!
O for a beaker full of the warm South,
    Full of the true, the blushful Hippocrene,
      With beaded bubbles winking at the brim,
        And purple-stained mouth;
    That I might drink, and leave the world unseen,
    And with thee fade away into the forest dim:

III

Fade far away, dissolve, and quite forget
    What thou among the leaves hast never known,
The weariness, the fever, and the fret
    Here, where men sit and hear each other groan;
Where palsy shakes a few, sad, last gray hairs,
    Where youth grows pale, and spectre-thin, and dies;
      Where but to think is to be full of sorrow
        And leaden-eyed despairs,
    Where Beauty cannot keep her lustrous eyes,
      Or new Love pine at them beyond to-morrow.

IV

Away! away! for I will fly to thee,
    Not charioted by Bacchus and his pards,
But on the viewless wings of Poesy,
    Though the dull brain perplexes and retards:
Already with thee! tender is the night,
    And haply the Queen-Moon is on her throne,
      Cluster'd around by all her starry Fays;
        But here there is no light,
    Save what from heaven is with the breezes blown
      Through verdurous glooms and winding mossy ways.

V

I cannot see what flowers are at my feet,
    Nor what soft incense hangs upon the boughs,

But, in embalmed darkness, guess each sweet
  Wherewith the seasonable month endows
The grass, the thicket, and the fruit-tree wild;
    White hawthorn, and the pastoral eglantine;
      Fast fading violets cover'd up in leaves;
        And mid-May's eldest child,
    The coming musk-rose, full of dewy wine,
      The murmurous haunt of flies on summer eves.

VI

Darkling I listen; and, for many a time
  I have been half in love with easeful Death,
Call'd him soft names in many a mused rhyme,
  To take into the air my quiet breath;
Now more than ever seems it rich to die,
  To cease upon the midnight with no pain,
    While thou art pouring forth thy soul abroad
      In such an ecstasy!
  Still wouldst thou sing, and I have ears in vain—
    To thy high requiem become a sod.

VII

Thou wast not born for death, immortal Bird!
  No hungry generations tread thee down;
The voice I hear this passing night was heard
  In ancient days by emperor and clown:
Perhaps the self-same song that found a path
  Through the sad heart of Ruth, when, sick for home,
    She stood in tears amid the alien corn;
      The same that oft-times hath
  Charm'd magic casements, opening on the foam
    Of perilous seas, in faery lands forlorn.

VIII

Forlorn! the very word is like a bell
  To toll me back from thee to my sole self!
Adieu! the fancy cannot cheat so well
  As she is fam'd to do, deceiving elf.
Adieu! adieu! thy plaintive anthem fades
  Past the near meadows, over the still stream,
    Up the hill-side; and now 'tis buried deep
      In the next valley-glades:
  Was it a vision, or a waking dream?
    Fled is that music:—Do I wake or sleep?

Ode on a Grecian Urn

I

Thou still unravish'd bride of quietness,
    Thou foster-child of silence and slow time,
Sylvan historian, who canst thus express
    A flowery tale more sweetly than our rhyme:
What leaf-fring'd legend haunts about thy shape
    Of deities or mortals, or of both,
        In Tempe or the dales of Arcady?
    What men or gods are these? What maidens loth?
What mad pursuit? What struggle to escape?
        What pipes and timbrels? What wild ecstasy?

II

Heard melodies are sweet, but those unheard
    Are sweeter; therefore, ye soft pipes, play on;
Not to the sensual ear, but, more endear'd,
    Pipe to the spirit ditties of no tone:
Fair youth, beneath the trees, thou canst not leave
    Thy song, nor ever can those trees be bare;
        Bold Lover, never, never canst thou kiss,
Though winning near the goal—yet, do not grieve;
    She cannot fade, though thou hast not thy bliss,
        For ever wilt thou love, and she be fair!

III

Ah, happy, happy boughs! that cannot shed
    Your leaves, nor ever bid the Spring adieu;
And, happy melodist, unwearied,
    For ever piping songs for ever new;
More happy love! more happy, happy love!
    For ever warm and still to be enjoy'd,
        For ever panting, and for ever young;
All breathing human passion far above,
    That leaves a heart high-sorrowful and cloy'd,
        A burning forehead, and a parching tongue.

IV

Who are these coming to the sacrifice?
    To what green altar, O mysterious priest,
Lead'st thou that heifer lowing at the skies,

And all her silken flanks with garlands drest?
What little town by river or sea shore,
  Or mountain-built with peaceful citadel,
    Is emptied of this folk, this pious morn?
And, little town, thy streets for evermore
  Will silent be; and not a soul to tell
    Why thou art desolate, can e'er return.

V

O Attic shape! Fair attitude! with brede
  Of marble men and maidens overwrought,
With forest branches and the trodden weed;
  Thou, silent form, dost tease us out of thought
As doth eternity: Cold Pastoral!
  When old age shall this generation waste,
    Thou shalt remain, in midst of other woe
Than ours, a friend to man, to whom thou say'st,
  'Beauty is truth, truth beauty,'—that is all
    Ye know on earth, and all ye need to know.

Ode to Psyche

O GODDESS! hear these tuneless numbers, wrung
  By sweet enforcement and remembrance dear,
And pardon that thy secrets should be sung
  Even into thine own soft-conched ear:
Surely I dreamt to-day, or did I see
  The winged Psyche with awaken'd eyes?
I wander'd in a forest thoughtlessly,
  And, on the sudden, fainting with surprise,
Saw two fair creatures, couched side by side
  In deepest grass, beneath the whisp'ring roof
Of leaves and trembled blossoms, where there ran
      A brooklet, scarce espied:

'Mid hush'd, cool-rooted flowers, fragrant-eyed,
  Blue, silver-white, and budded Tyrian,
They lay calm-breathing on the bedded grass;
  Their arms embraced, and their pinions too;
  Their lips touch'd not, but had not bade adieu,
As if disjoined by soft-handed slumber,
And ready still past kisses to outnumber

At tender eye-dawn of aurorean love:
    The winged boy I knew;
But who wast thou, O happy, happy dove?
    His Psyche true!

O latest born and loveliest vision far
    Of all Olympus' faded hierarchy!
Fairer than Phœbe's sapphire-region'd star,
    Or Vesper, amorous glow-worm of the sky;
Fairer than these, though temple thou hast none,
      Nor altar heap'd with flowers;
Nor virgin-choir to make delicious moan
      Upon the midnight hours;
No voice, no lute, no pipe, no incense sweet
    From chain-swung censer teeming;
No shrine, no grove, no oracle, no heat
    Of pale-mouth'd prophet dreaming.

O brightest! though too late for antique vows,
    Too, too late for the fond believing lyre,
When holy were the haunted forest boughs,
    Holy the air, the water, and the fire;
Yet even in these days so far retir'd
    From happy pieties, thy lucent fans,
    Fluttering among the faint Olympians,
I see, and sing, by my own eyes inspir'd.
So let me be thy choir, and make a moan
      Upon the midnight hours;
Thy voice, thy lute, thy pipe, thy incense sweet
    From swinged censer teeming;
Thy shrine, thy grove, thy oracle, thy heat
    Of pale-mouth'd prophet dreaming.

Yes, I will be thy priest, and build a fane
    In some untrodden region of my mind,
Where branched thoughts, new grown with pleasant pain,
    Instead of pines shall murmur in the wind:
Far, far around shall those dark-cluster'd trees
    Fledge the wild-ridged mountains steep by steep;
And there by zephyrs, streams, and birds, and bees,
    The moss-lain Dryads shall be lull'd to sleep;
And in the midst of this wide quietness
A rosy sanctuary will I dress

With the wreath'd trellis of a working brain,
  With buds, and bells, and stars without a name,
With all the gardener Fancy e'er could feign,
  Who breeding flowers, will never breed the same:
And there shall be for thee all soft delight
  That shadowy thought can win,
A bright torch, and a casement ope at night,
  To let the warm Love in!

Ode

BARDS of Passion and of Mirth,
Ye have left your souls on earth!
Have ye souls in heaven too,
Double lived in regions new?
Yes, and those of heaven commune
With the spheres of sun and moon;
With the noise of fountains wond'rous,
And the parle of voices thund'rous;
With the whisper of heaven's trees
And one another, in soft ease
Seated on Elysian lawns
Brows'd by none but Dian's fawns;
Underneath large blue-bells tented,
Where the daisies are rose-scented,
And the rose herself has got
Perfume which on earth is not;
Where the nightingale doth sing
Not a senseless, tranced thing,
But divine melodious truth;
Philosophic numbers smooth;
Tales and golden histories
Of heaven and its mysteries.

Thus ye live on high, and then
On the earth ye live again;
And the souls ye left behind you
Teach us, here the way to find you,
Where your other souls are joying,
Never slumber'd, never cloying.
Here, your earth-born souls still speak
To mortals, of their little week;
Of their sorrows and delights;

Of their passions and their spites;
Of their glory and their shame;
What doth strengthen and what maim.
Thus ye teach us, every day,
Wisdom, though fled far away.

Bards of Passion and of Mirth,
Ye have left your souls on earth!
Ye have souls in heaven too,
Double-lived in regions new!

To Autumn

I

SEASON of mists and mellow fruitfulness
    Close bosom-friend of the maturing sun;
Conspiring with him how to load and bless
    With fruit the vines that round the thatch-eves run;
To bend with apples the moss'd cottage-trees,
    And fill all fruit with ripeness to the core;
        To swell the gourd, and plump the hazel shells
    With a sweet kernel; to set budding more,
And still more, later flowers for the bees,
Until they think warm days will never cease,
        For Summer has o'er-brimm'd their clammy cells.

II

Who hath not seen thee oft amid thy store?
    Sometimes whoever seeks abroad may find
Thee sitting careless on a granary floor,
    Thy hair soft-lifted by the winnowing wind;
Or on a half-reap'd furrow sound asleep,
    Drows'd with the fume of poppies, while thy hook
        Spares the next swath and all its twined flowers:
And sometimes like a gleaner thou dost keep
    Steady thy laden head across a brook;
    Or by a cyder-press, with patient look,
        Thou watchest the last oozings hours by hours.

III

Where are the songs of Spring? Ay, where are they?
　　Think not of them, thou hast thy music too,—
While barred clouds bloom the soft-dying day,
　　And touch the stubble-plains with rosy hue;
Then in a wailful choir the small gnats mourn
　　Among the river sallows, borne aloft
　　　Or sinking as the light wind lives or dies;
And full-grown lambs loud bleat from hilly bourn;
　　Hedge-crickets sing; and now with treble soft
　　The red-breast whistles from a garden-croft;
　　　And gathering swallows twitter in the skies.

Ode on Melancholy

I

No, no, go not to Lethe, neither twist
　　Wolf's-bane, tight-rooted, for its poisonous wine;
Nor suffer thy pale forehead to be kiss'd
　　By nightshade, ruby grape of Proserpine;
Make not your rosary of yew-berries,
　　Nor let the beetle, nor the death-moth be
　　　Your mournful Psyche, nor the downy owl
A partner in your sorrow's mysteries;
　　For shade to shade will come too drowsily,
　　　And drown the wakeful anguish of the soul.

II

But when the melancholy fit shall fall
　　Sudden from heaven like a weeping cloud,
That fosters the droop-headed flowers all,
　　And hides the green hill in an April shroud;
Then glut thy sorrow on a morning rose,
　　Or on the rainbow of the salt sand-wave,
　　　Or on the wealth of globed peonies;
Or if thy mistress some rich anger shows,
　　Emprison her soft hand, and let her rave,
　　　And feed deep, deep upon her peerless eyes.

III

She dwells with Beauty—Beauty that must die;
  And Joy, whose hand is ever at his lips
Bidding adieu; and aching Pleasure nigh,
  Turning to Poison while the bee-mouth sips:
Ay, in the very temple of delight
    Veil'd Melancholy has her sovran shrine,
      Though seen of none save him whose strenuous tongue
    Can burst Joy's grape against his palate fine;
His soul shall taste the sadness of her might,
    And be among her cloudy trophies hung.

from *Hyperion*

BOOK I

DEEP in the shady sadness of a vale
Far sunken from the healthy breath of morn,
Far from the fiery noon, and eve's one star,
Sat gray-hair'd Saturn, quiet as a stone,
Still as the silence round about his lair;
Forest on forest hung about his head
Like cloud on cloud. No stir of air was there,
Not so much life as on a summer's day
Robs not one light seed from the feather'd grass,
But where the dead leaf fell, there did it rest.
A stream went voiceless by, still deadened more
By reason of his fallen divinity
Spreading a shade: the Naiad 'mid her reeds
Press'd her cold finger closer to her lips.

Along the margin-sand large foot-marks went,
No further than to where his feet had stray'd,
And slept there since. Upon the sodden ground
His old right hand lay nerveless, listless, dead,
Unsceptred; and his realmless eyes were closed;
While his bow'd head seem'd list'ning to the Earth,
His ancient mother, for some comfort yet.

It seem'd no force could wake him from his place;
But there came one, who with a kindred hand
Touch'd his wide shoulders, after bending low

With reverence, though to one who knew it not.
She was a Goddess of the infant world;
By her in stature the tall Amazon
Had stood a pigmy's height: she would have ta'en
Achilles by the hair and bent his neck;
Or with a finger stay'd Ixion's wheel.
Her face was large as that of Memphian sphinx,
Pedestal'd haply in a palace court,
When sages look'd to Egypt for their lore.
But oh! how unlike marble was that face:
How beautiful, if sorrow had not made
Sorrow more beautiful than Beauty's self.
There was a listening fear in her regard,
As if calamity had but begun;
As if the vanward clouds of evil days
Had spent their malice, and the sullen rear
Was with its stored thunder labouring up.
One hand she press'd upon that aching spot
Where beats the human heart, as if just there,
Though an immortal, she felt cruel pain:
The other upon Saturn's bended neck
She laid, and to the level of his ear
Leaning with parted lips, some words she spake
In solemn tenour and deep organ tone:
Some mourning words, which in our feeble tongue
Would come in these like accents; O how frail
To that large utterance of the early Gods!
'Saturn, look up!—though wherefore, poor old King?
'I have no comfort for thee, no not one:
'I cannot say, "O wherefore sleepest thou?"
'For heaven is parted from thee, and the earth
'Knows thee not, thus afflicted, for a God;
'And ocean too, with all its solemn noise,
'Has from thy sceptre pass'd; and all the air
'Is emptied of thine hoary majesty.
'Thy thunder, conscious of the new command,
'Rumbles reluctant o'er our fallen house;
'And thy sharp lightning in unpractis'd hands
'Scorches and burns our once serene domain.
'O aching time! O moments big as years!
'All as ye pass swell out the monstrous truth,
'And press it so upon our weary griefs
'That unbelief has not a space to breathe.
'Saturn, sleep on:—O thoughtless, why did I

'Thus violate thy slumbrous solitude?
'Why should I ope thy melancholy eyes?
'Saturn, sleep on! while at thy feet I weep.'

    As when, upon a tranced summer-night,
Those green-rob'd senators of mighty woods,
Tall oaks, branch-charmed by the earnest stars,
Dream, and so dream all night without a stir,
Save from one gradual solitary gust
Which comes upon the silence, and dies off,
As if the ebbing air had but one wave;
So came these words and went; the while in tears
She touch'd her fair large forehead to the ground,
Just where her falling hair might be outspread
A soft and silken mat for Saturn's feet.
One moon, with alteration slow, had shed
Her silver seasons four upon the night,
And still these two were postured motionless,
Like natural sculpture in cathedral cavern;
The frozen God still couchant on the earth,
And the sad Goddess weeping at his feet:
Until at length old Saturn lifted up
His faded eyes, and saw his kingdom gone,
And all the gloom and sorrow of the place,
And that fair kneeling Goddess; and then spake,
As with a palsied tongue, and while his beard
Shook horrid with such aspen-malady:
'O tender spouse of gold Hyperion,
'Thea, I feel thee ere I see thy face;
'Look up, and let me see our doom in it;
'Look up, and tell me if this feeble shape
'Is Saturn's; tell me, if thou hear'st the voice
'Of Saturn; tell me, if this wrinkling brow,
'Naked and bare of its great diadem,
'Peers like the front of Saturn. Who had power
'To make me desolate? whence came the strength?
'How was it nurtur'd to such bursting forth,
'While Fate seem'd strangled in my nervous grasp?
'But it is so; and I am smother'd up,
'And buried from all godlike exercise
'Of influence benign on planets pale,
'Of admonitions to the winds and seas,
'Of peaceful sway above man's harvesting,
'And all those acts which Deity supreme

'Doth ease its heart of love in.—I am gone
'Away from my own bosom: I have left
'My strong identity, my real self,
'Somewhere between the throne, and where I sit
'Here on this spot of earth. Search, Thea, search!
'Open thine eyes eterne, and sphere them round
'Upon all space: space starr'd, and lorn of light;
'Space region'd with life-air; and barren void;
'Spaces of fire, and all the yawn of hell.—
'Search, Thea, search! and tell me, if thou seest
'A certain shape or shadow, making way
'With wings or chariot fierce to repossess
'A heaven he lost erewhile: it must—it must
'Be of ripe progress—Saturn must be King.
'Yes, there must be a golden victory;
'There must be Gods thrown down, and trumpets blown
'Of triumph calm, and hymns of festival
'Upon the gold clouds metropolitan,
'Voices of soft proclaim, and silver stir
'Of strings in hollow shells; and there shall be
'Beautiful things made new, for the surprise
'Of the sky-children; I will give command:
'Thea! Thea! Thea! where is Saturn?'

   This passion lifted him upon his feet,
And made his hands to struggle in the air,
His Druid locks to shake and ooze with sweat,
His eyes to fever out, his voice to cease.
He stood, and heard not Thea's sobbing deep;
A little time, and then again he snatch'd
Utterance thus.—'But cannot I create?
'Cannot I form? Cannot I fashion forth
'Another world, another universe,
'To overbear and crumble this to naught?
'Where is another chaos? Where?'—That word
Found way unto Olympus, and made quake
The rebel three.—Thea was startled up,
And in her bearing was a sort of hope,
As thus she quick-voic'd spake, yet full of awe.
'This cheers our fallen house: come to our friends,
'O Saturn! come away, and give them heart;
'I know the covert, for thence came I hither.'
Thus brief; then with beseeching eyes she went
With backward footing through the shade a space:

He follow'd, and she turn'd to lead the way
Through aged boughs, that yielded like the mist
Which eagles cleave upmounting from their nest.

Meanwhile in other realms big tears were shed,
More sorrow like to this, and such like woe,
Too huge for mortal tongue or pen of scribe:
The Titans fierce, self-hid, or prison-bound,
Groan'd for the old allegiance once more,
And listen'd in sharp pain for Saturn's voice.
But one of the whole mammoth-brood still kept
His sov'reignty, and rule, and majesty;—
Blazing Hyperion on his orbed fire
Still sat, still snuff'd the incense, teeming up
From man to the sun's God; yet unsecure:
For as among us mortals omens drear
Fright and perplex, so also shuddered he—
Not at dog's howl, or gloom-bird's hated screech,
Or the familiar visiting of one
Upon the first toll of his passing-bell,
Or prophesyings of the midnight lamp;
But horrors, portion'd to a giant nerve,
Oft made Hyperion ache. His palace bright
Bastion'd with pyramids of glowing gold,
And touch'd with shade of bronzed obelisks,
Glar'd a blood-red through all its thousand courts,
Arches, and domes, and fiery galleries;
And all its curtains of Aurorian clouds
Flush'd angerly: while sometimes eagle's wings,
Unseen before by Gods or wondering men,
Darken'd the place; and neighing steeds were heard,
Not heard before by Gods or wondering men.
Also, when he would taste the spicy wreaths
Of incense, breath'd aloft from sacred hills,
Instead of sweets, his ample palate took
Savour of poisonous brass and metal sick:
And so, when harbour'd in the sleepy west,
After the full completion of fair day,—
For rest divine upon exalted couch
And slumber in the arms of melody,
He pac'd away the pleasant hours of ease
With stride colossal, on from hall to hall;
While far within each aisle and deep recess,
His winged minions in close clusters stood,

Amaz'd and full of fear; like anxious men
Who on wide plains gather in panting troops,
When earthquakes jar their battlements and towers.
Even now, while Saturn, rous'd from icy trance,
Went step for step with Thea through the woods,
Hyperion, leaving twilight in the rear,
Came slope upon the threshold of the west;
Then, as was wont, his palace-door flew ope
In smoothest silence, save what solemn tubes,
Blown by the serious Zephyrs, gave of sweet
And wandering sounds, slow-breathed melodies;
And like a rose in vermeil tint and shape,
In fragrance soft, and coolness to the eye,
That inlet to severe magnificence
Stood full blown, for the God to enter in.

He enter'd, but he enter'd full of wrath;
His flaming robes stream'd out beyond his heels,
And gave a roar, as if of earthly fire,
That scar'd away the meek ethereal Hours
And made their dove-wings tremble. On he flared,
From stately nave to nave, from vault to vault,
Through bowers of fragrant and enwreathed light,
And diamond-paved lustrous long arcades,
Until he reach'd the great main cupola;
There standing fierce beneath, he stamped his foot,
And from the basements deep to the high towers
Jarr'd his own golden region; and before
The quavering thunder thereupon had ceas'd,
His voice leapt out, despite of godlike curb,
To this result: 'O dreams of day and night!
'O monstrous forms! O effigies of pain!
'O spectres busy in a cold, cold gloom!
'O lank-ear'd Phantoms of black-weeded pools!
'Why do I know ye? why have I seen ye? why
'Is my eternal essence thus distraught
'To see and to behold these horrors new?
'Saturn is fallen, am I too to fall?
'Am I to leave this haven of my rest,
'This cradle of my glory, this soft clime,
'This calm luxuriance of blissful light,
'These crystalline pavilions, and pure fanes,
'Of all my lucent empire? It is left
'Deserted, void, nor any haunt of mine.

'The blaze, the splendor, and the symmetry,
'I cannot see—but darkness, death and darkness.
'Even here, into my centre of repose,
'The shady visions come to domineer,
'Insult, and blind, and stifle up my pomp.—
'Fall!—No, by Tellus and her briny robes!
'Over the fiery frontier of my realms
'I will advance a terrible right arm
'Shall scare that infant thunderer, rebel Jove,
'And bid old Saturn take his throne again.'—
He spake, and ceas'd, the while a heavier threat
Held struggle with his throat but came not forth;
For as in theatres of crowded men
Hubbub increases more they call out 'Hush!'
So at Hyperion's words the Phantoms pale
Bestirr'd themselves, thrice horrible and cold;
And from the mirror'd level where he stood'
A mist arose, as from a scummy marsh.
At this, through all his bulk an agony
Crept gradual, from the feet unto the crown,
Like a lithe serpent vast and muscular
Making slow way, with head and neck convuls'd
From over-strained might. Releas'd, he fled
To the eastern gates, and full six dewy hours
Before the dawn in season due should blush,
He breath'd fierce breath against the sleepy portals,
Clear'd them of heavy vapours, burst them wide
Suddenly on the ocean's chilly streams.
The planet orb of fire, whereon he rode
Each day from east to west the heavens through,
Spun round in sable curtaining of clouds;
Not therefore veiled quite, blindfold, and hid,
But ever and anon the glancing spheres,
Circles, and arcs, and broad-belting colure,
Glow'd through, and wrought upon the muffling dark
Sweet-shaped lightnings from the nadir deep
Up to the zenith,—hieroglyphics old
Which sages and keen-eyed astrologers
Then living on the earth, with labouring thought
Won from the gaze of many centuries:
Now lost, save what we find on remnants huge
Of stone, or marble swart; their import gone,
Their wisdom long since fled.—Two wings this orb
Possess'd for glory, two fair argent wings,

Ever exalted at the God's approach:
And now, from forth the gloom their plumes immense
Rose, one by one, till all outspreaded were;
While still the dazzling globe maintain'd eclipse,
Awaiting for Hyperion's command.
Fain would he have commanded, fain took throne
And bid the day begin, if but for change.
He might not:—No, though a primeval God:
The sacred seasons might not be disturb'd.
Therefore the operations of the dawn
Stay'd in their birth, even as here 'tis told.
Those silver wings expanded sisterly,
Eager to sail their orb; the porches wide
Open'd upon the dusk demesnes of night;
And the bright Titan, phrenzied with new woes,
Unus'd to bend, by hard compulsion bent
His spirt to the sorrow of the time;
And all along a dismal rack of clouds,
Upon the boundaries of day and night,
He stretch'd himself in grief and radiance faint.
There as he lay, the Heaven with its stars
Look'd down on him with pity, and the voice
Of Cœlus, from the universal space,
Thus whisper'd low and solemn in his ear.
'O brightest of my children dear, earth-born
'And sky-engendered, Son of Mysteries
'All unrevealed even to the powers
'Which met at thy creating; at whose joys
'And palpitations sweet, and pleasures soft,
'I, Cœlus, wonder, how they came and whence;
'And at the fruits thereof what shapes they be,
'Distinct, and visible; symbols divine,
'Manifestations of that beauteous life
'Diffus'd unseen throughout eternal space:
'Of these new-form'd art thou, oh brightest child!
'Of these, thy brethren and the Goddesses!
'There is sad feud among ye, and rebellion
'Of son against his sire. I saw him fall,
'I saw my first-born tumbled from his throne!
'To me his arms were spread, to me his voice
'Found way from forth the thunders round his head!
'Pale wox I, and in vapours hid my face.
'Art thou, too, near such doom? vague fear there is:
'For I have seen my sons most unlike Gods.

493

'Divine ye were created, and divine
'In sad demeanour, solemn, undisturb'd,
'Unruffled, like high Gods, ye liv'd and ruled:
'Now I behold in you fear, hope, and wrath;
'Actions of rage and passion; even as
'I see them, on the mortal world beneath,
'In men who die.—This is the grief, O Son!
'Sad sign of ruin, sudden dismay, and fall!
'Yet do thou strive; as thou art capable,
'As thou canst move about, an evident God;
'And canst oppose to each malignant hour
'Ethereal presence:—I am but a voice;
'My life is but the life of winds and tides,
'No more than winds and tides can I avail:—
'But thou canst.—Be thou therefore in the van
'Of circumstance; yea, seize the arrow's barb
'Before the tense string murmur.—To the earth!
'For there thou wilt find Saturn, and his woes.
'Meantime I will keep watch on thy bright sun,
'And of thy seasons be a careful nurse.'—
Ere half this region-whisper had come down,
Hyperion arose, and on the stars
Lifted his curved lids, and kept them wide
Until it ceas'd; and still he kept them wide:
And still they were the same bright, patient stars.
Then with a slow incline of his broad breast,
Like to a diver in the pearly seas,
Forward he stoop'd over the airy shore,
And plung'd all noiseless into the deep night.

BOOK II

So ended Saturn; and the God of the Sea,
Sophist and sage, from no Athenian grove,
But cogitation in his watery shades,
Arose, with locks not oozy, and began,
In murmurs, which his first-endeavouring tongue
Caught infant-like from the far-foamed sands.
'O ye, whom wrath consumes! who, passion-stung,
'Writhe at defeat, and nurse your agonies!
'Shut up your senses, stifle up your ears,
'My voice is not a bellows unto ire.
'Yet listen, ye who will, whilst I bring proof
'How ye, perforce, must be content to stoop:

'And in the proof much comfort will I give,
'If ye will take that comfort in its truth.
'We fall by course of Nature's law, not force
'Of thunder, or of Jove. Great Saturn, thou
'Hast sifted well the atom-universe;
'But for this reason, that thou art the King,
'And only blind from sheer supremacy,
'One avenue was shaded from thine eyes,
'Through which I wandered to eternal truth.
'And first, as thou wast not the first of powers,
'So art thou not the last; it cannot be:
'Thou art not the beginning nor the end.
'From chaos and parental darkness came
'Light, the first fruits of that intestine broil,
'That sullen ferment, which for wondrous ends
'Was ripening in itself. The ripe hour came,
'And with it light, and light, engendering
'Upon its own producer, forthwith touch'd
'The whole enormous matter into life.
'Upon that very hour, our parentage,
'The Heavens and the Earth, were manifest:
'Then thou first born, and we the giant race,
'Found ourselves ruling new and beauteous realms.
'Now comes the pain of truth, to whom 'tis pain;
'O folly! for to bear all naked truths,
'And to envisage circumstance, all calm,
'That is the top of sovereignty. Mark well!
'As Heaven and Earth are fairer, fairer far
'Than Chaos and blank Darkness, though once chiefs;
'And as we show beyond that Heaven and Earth
'In form and shape compact and beautiful,
'In will, in action free, companionship,
'And thousand other signs of purer life;
'So on our heels a fresh perfection treads,
'A power more strong in beauty, born of us
'And fated to excel us, as we pass
'In glory that old Darkness: nor are we
'Thereby more conquer'd, than by us the rule
'Of shapeless Chaos. Say, doth the dull soil
'Quarrel with the proud forests it hath fed,
'And feedeth still, more comely than itself?
'Can it deny the chiefdom of green groves?
'Or shall the tree be envious of the dove
'Because it cooeth, and hath snowy wings

'To wander wherewithal and find its joys?
'We are such forest-trees, and our fair boughs
'Have bred forth, not pale solitary doves,
'But eagles golden-feather'd, who do tower
'Above us in their beauty, and must reign
'In right thereof; for 'tis the eternal law
'That first in beauty should be first in might:
'Yea, by that law, another race may drive
'Our conquerors to mourn as we do now.
'Have ye beheld the young God of the Seas,
'My dispossessor? Have ye seen his face?
'Have ye beheld his chariot, foam'd along
'By noble winged creatures he hath made?
'I saw him on the calmed waters scud,
'With such a glow of beauty in his eyes,
'That it enforc'd me to bid sad farewell
'To all my empire: farewell sad I took,
'And hither came, to see how dolorous fate
'Had wrought upon ye; and how I might best
'Give consolation in this woe extreme.
'Receive the truth, and let it be your balm.'

BOOK III

THUS in alternate uproar and sad peace,
Amazed were those Titans utterly.
O leave them, Muse! O leave them to their woes;
For thou art weak to sing such tumults dire:
A solitary sorrow best befits
Thy lips, and antheming a lonely grief.
Leave them, O Muse! for thou anon wilt find
Many a fallen old Divinity
Wandering in vain about bewildered shores.
Meantime touch piously the Delphic harp,
And not a wind of heaven but will breathe
In aid soft warble from the Dorian flute;
For lo! 'tis for the Father of all verse.
Flush every thing that hath a vermeil hue,
Let the rose glow intense and warm the air,
And let the clouds of even and of morn
Float in voluptuous fleeces o'er the hills;
Let the red wine within the goblet boil,
Cold as a bubbling well; let faint-lipp'd shells,
On sands, or in great deeps, vermilion turn

Through all their labyrinths; and let the maid
Blush keenly, as with some warm kiss surpris'd.
Chief isle of the embowered Cyclades,
Rejoice, O Delos, with thine olives green,
And poplars, and lawn-shading palms, and beech,
In which the Zephyr breathes the loudest song,
And hazels thick, dark-stemm'd beneath the shade:
Apollo is once more the golden theme!
Where was he, when the Giant of the Sun
Stood bright, amid the sorrow of his peers?
Together had he left his mother fair
And his twin-sister sleeping in their bower,
And in the morning twilight wandered forth
Beside the osiers of a rivulet,
Full ankle-deep in lillies of the vale.
The nightingale had ceas'd, and a few stars
Were lingering in the heavens, while the thrush
Began calm-throated. Throughout all the isle
There was no covert, no retired cave
Unhaunted by the murmurous noise of waves,
Though scarcely heard in many a green recess.
He listen'd, and he wept, and his bright tears
Went trickling down the golden bow he held.
Thus with half-shut suffused eyes he stood,
While from beneath some cumbrous boughs hard by
With solemn step an awful Goddess came,
And there was purport in her looks for him,
Which he with eager guess began to read
Perplex'd, the while melodiously he said:
'How cam'st thou over the unfooted sea?
'Or hath that antique mien and robed form
'Mov'd in these vales invisible till now?
'Sure I have heard those vestments weeping o'er
'The fallen leaves, when I have sat alone
'In cool mid-forest. Surely I have traced
'The rustle of those ample skirts about
'These grassy solitudes, and seen the flowers
'Lift up their heads, as still the whisper pass'd.
'Goddess! I have beheld those eyes before,
'And their eternal calm, and all that face,
'Or I have dream'd.'—'Yes,' said the supreme shape,
'Thou hast dream'd of me; and awaking up
'Didst find a lyre all golden by thy side,
'Whose strings touch'd by thy fingers, all the vast

'Unwearied ear of the whole universe
'Listen'd in pain and pleasure at the birth
'Of such new tuneful wonder. Is't not strange
'That thou shouldst weep, so gifted? Tell me, youth,
'What sorrow thou canst feel; for I am sad
'When thou dost shed a tear: explain thy griefs
'To one who in this lonely isle hath been
'The watcher of thy sleep and hours of life,
'From the young day when first thy infant hand
'Pluck'd witless the weak flowers, till thine arm
'Could bend that bow heroic to all times.
'Show thy heart's secret to an ancient Power
'Who hath forsaken old and sacred thrones
'For prophecies of thee, and for the sake
'Of loveliness new born.'—Apollo then,
With sudden scrutiny and gloomless eyes,
Thus answer'd, while his white melodious throat
Throbb'd with the syllables.—'Mnemosyne!
'Thy name is on my tongue, I know not how;
'Why should I tell thee what thou so well seest?
'Why should I strive to show what from thy lips
'Would come no mystery? For me, dark, dark,
'And painful vile oblivion seals my eyes:
'I strive to search wherefore I am so sad,
'Until a melancholy numbs my limbs;
'And then upon the grass I sit, and moan,
'Like one who once had wings.—O why should I
'Feel curs'd and thwarted, when the liegeless air
'Yields to my step aspirant? why should I
'Spurn the green turf as hateful to my feet?
'Goddess benign, point forth some unknown thing:
'Are there not other regions than this isle?
'What are the stars? There is the sun, the sun!
'And the most patient brilliance of the moon!
'And stars by thousands! Point me out the way
'To any one particular beauteous star,
'And I will flit into it with my lyre,
'And make its silvery splendour pant with bliss.
'I have heard the cloudy thunder: Where is power?
'Whose hand, whose essence, what divinity
'Makes this alarum in the elements,
'While I here idle listen on the shores
'In fearless yet in aching ignorance?
'O tell me, lonely Goddess, by thy harp,

'That waileth every morn and eventide,
'Tell me why thus I rave, about these groves!
'Mute thou remainest—mute! yet I can read
'A wondrous lesson in thy silent face:
'Knowledge enormous makes a God of me.
'Names, deeds, grey legends, dire events, rebellions,
'Majesties, sovran voices, agonies,
'Creations and destroyings, all at once
'Pour into the wide hollows of my brain,
'And deify me, as if some blithe wine
'Or bright elixir peerless I had drunk,
'And so become immortal.'—Thus the God,
While his enkindled eyes, with level glance
Beneath his white soft temples, stedfast kept
Trembling with light upon Mnemosyne.
Soon wild commotions shook him, and made flush
All the immortal fairness of his limbs;
Most like the struggle at the gate of death;
Or liker still to one who should take leave
Of pale immortal death, and with a pang
As hot as death's is chill, with fierce convulse
Die into life: so young Apollo anguish'd:
His very hair, his golden tresses famed
Kept undulation round his eager neck.
During the pain Mnemosyne upheld
Her arms as one who prophesied.—At length
Apollo shriek'd;—and lo! from all his limbs
Celestial * * * * * *
 * * * * * * * *

On Oxford. A Parody

I

THE Gothic looks solemn,
  The plain Doric column
Supports an old Bishop and Crosier;
  The mouldering arch,
   Shaded o'er by a larch
Stands next door to Wilson the Hosier.

II

Vicè—that is, by turns,—
O'er pale faces mourns
The black tassell'd trencher and common hat;
    The Chantry boy sings,
    The Steeple-bell rings,
And as for the Chancellor—*dominat*.

III

There are plenty of trees,
And plenty of ease,
And plenty of fat deer for Parsons;
    And when it is venison,
    Short is the benison,—
Then each on a leg or thigh fastens.

La Belle Dame Sans Merci

I

Ah, what can ail thee, wretched wight,
    Alone and palely loitering;
The sedge is wither'd from the lake,
    And no birds sing.

II

Ah, what can ail thee, wretched wight,
    So haggard and so woe-begone?
The squirrel's granary is full,
    And the harvest's done.

III

I see a lilly on thy brow,
    With anguish moist and fever dew;
And on thy cheek a fading rose
    Fast withereth too.

IV

I met a lady in the meads
    Full beautiful, a faery's child;
Her hair was long, her foot was light,
    And her eyes were wild.

V

I set her on my pacing steed,
  And nothing else saw all day long;
For sideways would she lean, and sing
  A faery's song.

VI

I made a garland for her head,
  And bracelets too, and fragrant zone;
She look'd at me as she did love,
  And made sweet moan.

VII

She found me roots of relish sweet,
  And honey wild, and manna dew;
And sure in language strange she said,
  I love thee true.

VIII

She took me to her elfin grot,
  And there she gaz'd and sighed deep,
And there I shut her wild sad eyes—
  So kiss'd to sleep.

IX

And there we slumber'd on the moss,
  And there I dream'd, ah woe betide,
The latest dream I ever dream'd
  On the cold hill side.

X

I saw pale kings, and princes too,
  Pale warriors, death-pale were they all;
Who cry'd—'La belle Dame sans merci
  Hath thee in thrall!'

XI

I saw their starv'd lips in the gloam
  With horrid warning gaped wide,
And I awoke, and found me here
  On the cold hill side.

XII

And this is why I sojourn here
  Alone and palely loitering,
Though the sedge is wither'd from the lake,
  And no birds sing.

INDEX OF POETS

INDEX OF FIRST LINES